Nomad Capitalist

How to Reclaim Your Freedom with Offshore Companies, Dual Citizenship, Foreign Banks, and Overseas Investments

To Mila, for being the most supportive person I know.

ISBN: 9798461831486

Table of Contents

Taking Action

Shuttles are for Slaves: An Introduction

Dateline: Las Vegas, United States

There was only one reason I had chosen to return to the United States that cold January evening. After a year basking in the warmth of the tropics, it was not so that US Airways could destroy my brand-new luggage (as they had), or so that I could gamble on the Strip (as I had many times before). It was not even for the fluffy cotton candy that graced our dinner table that evening.

No, I was in Las Vegas as a messenger.

My mission? To deliver a wake-up call.

I stood in front of a packed conference room full of guests and declared that there was no reason for them to continue living, banking, doing business, or even being a citizen of a country that no longer served them. They had more options.

I knew this because I had been living abroad discovering and enjoying all those options. Not only had I spent years observing the different ways that things are done around the world but I had also worked to benefit from everything other countries have to offer – from higher interest rates to nicer women. The past year abroad was simply an intensification of those efforts.

Barely a year before the conference, I had sold my last US-based business and went from frequent traveler to full-time nomad. Tired of paying 40% or more of my income in taxes and shopping at the same Trader Joe's, I was ready to totally transform the way I lived and did business.

Now that I was finally free, my mission was to find all the

gaps in the world system and use them to my advantage. I would go beyond Tim Ferriss's version of geoarbitrage – using cheap production and labor in one part of the world and selling to high-paying customers in the West – and delve deeper into the global economy to leverage everything it had to offer. I would visit the world's emerging hotspots, places that few were talking about, and discover the opportunities that still fewer could even imagine. In doing so, I would create the conditions for my ultimate personal freedom and economic prosperity.

And that is exactly what I did. I spent all of 2013 traversing East and Southeast Asia, deliberately planning each stop in countries like Laos, Vietnam, and Cambodia to fully understand where the opportunities existed in those countries – the world's new frontiers in an Asian century. I met with a cabinet member in the Philippines, the CEO of Vietnam's largest western bank in Saigon, a private equity fund manager in Cambodia, and countless startups, expat entrepreneurs, and nomads staking their claims and making their fortunes in the world's final frontiers.

Along the way, I shared my experiences and insights with a growing audience of readers, but I knew I could do more to help them. After a year of non-stop travel and research, I returned to the United States to reveal the opportunities I had discovered abroad in person. It was a simple message about how they could keep more of their money and live a better life, but the crux of the whole conference was for them to form their own game plan for everything offshore, ranging from foreign bank accounts to second passports.

For the hundred or so folks who had paid $2,000 each to attend, it was a chance to learn the "secrets of the universe" as it were; a new way to live and make money that few knew about or imagined could even be legal. For me, it felt like Napoleon's return to Paris; the story of a man exiled yet emboldened to come back one last time.

That was because it would be among my last times in the United States. I had made the conscious decision – one you can make, too, if you so desire – that the grass was greener in the Malaysias, Serbias, and Mexicos of the world than where I grew up. Times had changed and the United States that was once lauded as the "best place to be born" was no longer so.

Bearing the theme "Fight or Flight", the conference was designed to help the audience members - who knew little about these greener pastures - decide exactly what they needed to do to survive and thrive in this changing world. Would they stay where things were familiar but in decay, or go where the grass was indeed greener?

For most people, front page stories of chaos in the rest of the world are cause enough to stay home; but not for my guests, nor for me. We realized that the real world is far different than the sensational headlines designed to incite fear and keep people from bettering their lives.

Despite being more aware of the changing world than most, my guests were naturally still confused about what they should do. Should they move overseas? Open an offshore bank account? Get a second passport? Bury gold inside an ammo can in their backyard and mark the spot with an "X"? They had come to my conference to find out.

Amidst the speeches and breakout sessions designed to broaden guests' mindsets to the world of opportunity just waiting for them, a small group of VIPs and I took to experiencing Las Vegas as "Nomad Capitalists" in a private dining room with a balcony overlooking the city. The menu was a 'what's what' of hipster fare only found in the Land of the Free, culminating with a dessert of cotton candy and Oreos. Only in Sin City would a $150-a-plate joint serve up circus food for dessert.

After dinner, as several of the event speakers and I sat sipping cocktails and conversing about our travels ("I disagree! Rwanda is better in the summer!"), a conference manager came through the restaurant advising everyone that the last shuttle back to our hotel was leaving.

When the manager earnestly advised a libertarian raconteur not to miss the final shuttle, the man looked up from what must have been (conservatively) his sixth or seventh rum and Coke and remarked quite matter-of-factly, "Shuttles are for slaves."

That took a while to sink in...

"Shuttles are for slaves."

What exactly did he mean?

As our conference continued throughout the weekend, however, I realized just how telling my friend's remarks truly were. We had all joined together to learn how to escape the fate of becoming slaves to the system. We were tired of the government telling us what to do and how much to pay. We felt uncomfortable in a country that called itself "the land of the free" but did not do much to qualify for the claim. We were watching others pass us by as their businesses and wealth grew faster.

We were bound and determined to do something to change all that, and yet there we were, waiting for a shuttle to take us from Point A to Point B.

How much of our lives is determined for us because we give in to the simplicity of following the system? The masses take shuttles because they are told that it is the way to get from the restaurant to the hotel. We rarely ever consider alternatives to what "the man" tells us to do. If someone says that there is a shuttle, people take it.

Of course, they could spend ten whole dollars and take a taxi and have the freedom to stay as long as they wish and go wherever they want, but they are too busy following the herd to think about what they prefer.

Do not be a slave.

Do not do what everyone else does.

That is what this book is about.

To thrive in an ever-globalizing world, you must do what others do not do and go where others will not go. The world economy is changing and those who operate at the edges of this new economy will find the greatest success. The focus should not be on surviving but on thriving; on enjoying the best of life.

The week before my conference, it was announced that China would soon overtake the United States in the number of self-made billionaires. Emerging world billionaires were buying up more of the world's assets than ever before. The United States and western countries were not keeping pace.

Today, many in the West wonder if it is even possible to be wealthy and live freely anymore. For the folks stuck in the past, there is a lot to be miserable about. YouTube is littered with documentaries on "forgotten Americans" living on scraps in former boom towns in West Virginia.

But for those of us willing to venture just beyond our original borders, the possibilities are endless. Better investments, greater business opportunities, and heightened freedoms are just a few of the advantages I have discovered by choosing to live an international life.

My time in Las Vegas was focused on helping my guests realize these opportunities and choose to leave the places that were not improving their life – "flight" – rather than to stay and "fight" in the hopes that things would get better at home. Fighting is messy, it is dangerous, and it is not a lot of fun. FARC rebels living in the jungle fight. Feral cats defending their territory fight. Seven- and eight-figure entrepreneurs whose tax bills slow down their company's growth, on the other hand, would be better served by "flight".

There is no reason to stay in your home country and fight for change, not when you can go to greener pastures where the change you are looking for is already in place. That is the key to making the Nomad Capitalist lifestyle work for you. It is not about running from something, it is about running toward something much, much better. "Flight" trumps "fight" simply because there are so many green pastures meant to be explored – greener pastures that can increase your freedom and ensure the success of your businesses and investments.

Why sit home and complain about the high-tax, high-regulation, anti-freedom policies of your country when you can just go elsewhere? You have dozens of options. As a businessman, I do not have time to waste on the systems that do not serve me. Chances are, neither do you. As with anything in business, where you bank, incorporate your company, or choose to live is a simple matter of finding and applying a better solution.

Fighting leads nowhere. The people who protest paying US taxes to fund wars they did not choose, or those who object to the election of a president by fleeing to Canada, will both end up paying just as much in taxes. They focus on the bad rather than moving toward something good.

After Donald Trump was elected President in 2016, traffic to my website surged with people searching for "fast citizenships", thinking that becoming Canadian was as easy as turning up at a border crossing somewhere. Of course, it is not that easy, but then again, becoming Canadian is probably not the best solution. More on that later.

That is why this book is not about the doom and gloom that has become so common within the offshore industry. It is about solutions. Being a Nomad Capitalist encompasses much more than the individual shiny objects like foreign corporations or offshore bank accounts. Rather, being a Nomad Capitalist is a lifestyle. It is about being happy. Sure, it is about being prosperous and successful, but only from the standpoint of achieving a better life. It is about being able to have, be, and do anything you want.

I fully expect that the ideas in this book will be controversial. Upsetting the status quo is never going to win me universal popularity. When I sat down for an interview with the Huffington Post to discuss my core philosophies on life and business, the 6,000-word interview was swiftly deleted and any mention of me banned within two hours. So much for the free press.

But I would encourage you to approach these ideas with an open mind. For example, why is it that only humans submit to the idea of things like taxes and countries? Why is it that so many of us spend our entire lives blindly paying taxes because "That's what you do?" We take the 'shuttle' our particular life circumstances have offered us without thinking once about whether or not that shuttle will even take us where we want to go.

When it gets too cold in the north, many birds fly south for the winter for warmer temperatures and a more abundant food supply. They do not feel a duty to stay where it is cold simply because that is where they were born. Doing so would be fatal to their survival! Instead, they go where they can thrive. That is the natural order. You can do the same, not only to find warmer locales but also to help your business and your investments prosper.

This book will help you adopt the mindset needed to do just that. While we will certainly discuss the many "how-tos" of international living such as banking offshore, getting a second passport, and even running a company in a different country, the main purpose of this book is to open your eyes to the possibilities of such alternatives to deliver a powerful change in your life.

Most of the people I help are young and mid-aged entrepreneurs who have had enough with the current system. For years, maybe even decades, they have paid a fortune in taxes only to see their government treat them with less and less respect. They have been told "you didn't build that" and have had their business accomplishments dismissed by politicians still all too happy to take their money.

The truth is that all these problems are symptoms of living and doing business in a place that does not serve you. There may not be anything wrong with a country like the United States per se, but it is increasingly not a good fit for many people. Whatever your situation, the lessons in this book can help guide your path toward greater freedom and prosperity using my "five magic words" that I will share with you in the first chapter.

This book will open your mind to ideas that you are not even aware of yet, but that could be tweaked to massively increase your happiness, wealth, and freedom. Perhaps you do not know about the 100% legal ways to reduce your personal and business tax bills. Perhaps you do not know that it is legal (for most of us) to obtain a second citizenship so that you always have another place to go. And perhaps you have never imagined that you can invest all the extra profits you will earn by doing this into overseas investments that will put the investments "next door" to shame.

Once you begin going where you are not only respected but cherished, you will no doubt enjoy a snowball effect of newfound success, prosperity, and fulfillment. The taxes that you save by going to a business-friendly country can be reinvested to grow your business faster, which in turn increases your feelings of satisfaction, which in turn makes you more open to meeting new people who share your values.

Nomad Capitalist will widen your understanding of how the changing world we live in means a new way for you to do business; everything from hiring virtual assistants in post-Yugoslav states to paying far lower taxes in post-British Chinese enclaves. And you can learn to do it all no matter your current level of international experience.

While most books will either speak down to you as if you could never become an expert in living, investing, and doing business around the world, or will rely on pithy memes to implore you to sell all but eleven of your possessions and move to a hut in Bali, this book will do neither.

Even if you do not yet have a passport from the country in which you were born, you can take steps to go where you're treated best to keep more of your own money and increase your freedom. As with anything else, someone new to this stuff should probably refrain from selling their entire 401(k) to invest it all in real estate in Bolivia, but that does not mean that you cannot take the first step now. After all, walking in the right direction is more important than arriving at the so-called destination.

This book will show you how to become a Nomad Capitalist by improving your business, your life, and your legacy step by step by step. It is part of a never-ending journey based on a new way of thinking. And it all starts with my five magic words...

Chapter One: Five Magic Words

Go Where You're Treated Best

Dateline: Sandusky, Ohio, United States

It was just another late summer day. My parents, sister, and soon-to-be twelve-year-old self were returning home from a typical day at the Cedar Point amusement park near our home in Ohio when my father laid bare a revelation.

For about a year or so, he had been combing the internet and researching exotic relocation options. He was determined to find a better place for his family to live that would best position us for the future. Most kids marvel at the other kids who move to another school district or whose parents get jobs in another state and leave town. What my father shared with us on that balmy August day was a lot heavier.

"Andrew," he started. "We're considering moving to another country. Whether or not we do, I want you to know that you don't have to stay somewhere just because your parents are from there. The world is changing, and you don't have to live in the same city, the same state, or – come to think of it – even the same country as where you were born. Don't stay here for us. You should go where you're treated best."

I have to admit that, at the time, twelve-year-old Andrew was more concerned with what would happen to my relationship with my middle-school girlfriend than with how amazing it would be to live in New Zealand. Despite my budding entrepreneurial spirit, moving would have been the end of the world from my adolescent perspective.

Ultimately, my parents decided against the move. However, despite my initial reticence, I could never quite get my father's words out of my head:

Go where you're treated best.

Those "five magic words" opened my mind to a world of possibilities. It took years for them to fully sink in, but the simple knowledge that I was free to go anywhere and find what best served me unwittingly changed my life.

The Default Mentality

Most people stay in one place by default. A recent survey of my Facebook friends list shows that a larger percentage of my high school classmates still live in the same town where we grew up. Some made the bold move to a neighboring suburb. When you think about it, though, there is no rule stating that they must stay there; the rule is only in our minds. That is why I left.

Don't get me wrong; you do not necessarily have to pack your bags to "go where you're treated best." Your hometown could very well be the right place for you. But it should be something you choose, rather than something you allow to be chosen for you as "the thing to do". Most people never consider which place actually serves their needs. Instead, they simply accept the default mode set for them.

They impose silly barriers such as "but I would need to buy a plane ticket", and other excuses that could be solved with the princely sum of about $500.

The problem with this method of thinking is that you never realize that there are other options. You could easily have your money go where it is treated best and remain in your hometown. However, the default mentality leads most people to erroneously think that they have already got all the best options laid out for them.

You might be surprised that where you live is ranked #1 in… absolutely nothing. It is not the best place for starting or running a business, it is not the best place to get a job, it is not the best place to invest, it is not the best place to raise a family, it is not the best place for security or education or quality of living or any number of important factors we should all be taking into consideration.

Now, there is no such thing as a perfect place. With so many cities, states, and countries around the globe, the chances of your dot on the map taking the #1 ranking in every category are slim to none. And you may choose to accept some of the flaws of the place where you live because you like it. That is perfectly normal. But have you ever stopped to realize that where you live is #1 in nothing?

The key here is awareness; the ability to realize that the country where you were born was not sprinkled with some magic pixie dust that made it the best for absolutely everything. Most of us – at least in the developed world – grow accustomed to living with whatever is offered to us within our geographical comfort zone. Things are good enough that we do not feel that we need to look elsewhere.

Growing up in the suburbs of Cleveland, Ohio, most of my friends supported the local sports teams. I never cared much for sports, and I never quite understood why everyone in one place would universally choose to support the same teams. Until 2016, no major Cleveland sports team had won a championship in my lifetime. Heck, they had barely won anything in my parents' lifetimes. The Browns recently went 0-16; this was not what Donald Trump meant when he said, 'you'll get so tired of winning'. Why would everyone support sports teams with such a losing track record solely because they played at a stadium down the street?

The idea of rooting for the home team was one I never quite understood. How was the geographic location of my birth tied to rooting for some lousy team that clutched defeat from the jaws of victory every time they were given the chance? It made no sense.

When did we lose the spirit of the greatest American pastime of all: immigration? Millions of people throughout history have packed their bags and moved to a place that treated them better when 'the home team' was failing. As the United States was expanding, this meant pioneers and later settlers moving west for better conditions.

What is particularly noteworthy about this westward expansion was that settlers were not only moving from something they were also moving toward something. Settlers could have sat at home along North America's eastern seaboard and griped about the government, immigrants, or dwindling opportunities. They could have worried themselves over the lack of good jobs and decent land to farm. Instead, they staked their claim somewhere better and came out ahead.

In a competitive society full of new immigrants, moving west was about survival. Settlers were able to make a better living in the new safe havens in the likes of Iowa and later all the way to California. They would write letters to family back east telling of the great success they enjoyed on the new frontier and the incredible opportunities still waiting for them. Sure, the chance of being attacked by a coyote was higher in the Arizona territory than it was outside of Boston, but so were the freedoms and chances to strike it rich. When outside of their element, pioneers thrived.

For them, going where they were treated best did not mean being unpatriotic or abandoning their home. It was the embodiment of everything it meant to "be an American". Nothing has changed about that drive to explore and thrive in the world's final frontiers; and having that drive today is the furthest thing from being unpatriotic.

What it does mean, however, is that you acknowledge some cold, hard truths about the lack of opportunity to find good jobs or create profitable businesses in countries like the United States in the twenty-first century.

The gravitation toward the best opportunities is natural. So, perhaps, is the nostalgic romance of ignoring market realities to defend staying in the place where we were born. We all want to have a place to call home, and it is easier to stick with the one we were given at birth... even if it is not the best for us. However, it is never too late to tap into the natural instinct to look for and create something better.

Imaginary Lines and Psychological Borders

On a seemingly normal level, we make decisions to go where we are treated best all the time. I was born in a part of Cleveland that set annual property tax rates at 2%. A mere fifteen miles to the west was a modern form of pioneer country: Lorain County. Family farms in Lorain County realized that they could sell their land to developers and either move further out or retire.

With modern infrastructure, being such a short distance from the big city was much less of a challenge for residents than it was before. Yet, because the 'pioneer' county's government had less time to run up big expenses and waste taxpayer money, it was able to operate on a 1% tax rate.

Families could live in Lorain County for half the price of their next-door-neighbors with many of the same services they were used to in a higher tax city. So, my parents packed up and moved all of fifty feet across the county line. As it turned out, the home they built sat on land that literally bordered the county we had just left. You could throw a tennis ball out the back door and it would land in a place with twice the taxes, all because of imaginary lines.

The neighbors on the other side of the fence were quite snooty about the fact that they lived in the trendier county and looked down upon the new settlers for wanting to live in a modern-day Wild West, but that did not stop us from enjoying the benefits while they paid the bills.

This was one of my first lessons that doing what is best for you and your wallet will not always be easy. People may snicker and sneer and try to belittle you if you buck the trend. Ask most US citizens if they would live anywhere else and they would laugh. After all, the United States is the best country in the history of the world, right? Seems a little too good to be true.

Uninformed boasts do not make something the best. You can see that manifested in the very Lorain County I lived in, where countless factories and automotive plants have now closed, and jobs have been lost as companies went where they were treated best: Mexico.

In much the same way that my family moved a stone's throw across an imaginary line in the grass to cut our taxes in half, US companies have moved manufacturing and operations to — among other places — cities along the US-Mexico border where labor is cheaper and the treatment is better. There are those imaginary lines again.

For years, factories in the United States have been over-taxed, over-regulated, and generally treated poorly by anti-business politicians. Now, they have options. And they have used them. The CEO of Ford may still be a Detroit Tigers fan, but that will not stop him from making the most pragmatic decision for his company.

In the twenty-first century, the ability to do this is not limited to big companies. We all have parts of our lives and businesses that could be improved by merely walking across some imaginary line called a border. The key ingredient is simply to not put all your eggs in the same basket.

It seems that before every election in the United States these days, some B-list actor gets on television and proclaims that "If so-and-so wins, I'm moving to Canada!" (These guys are always moving to Canada.) What they are really saying is that they are going to take all their eggs from their US basket and move them to a brand-new Canada basket. All of them.

The problem with the proverbial "moving to Canada" solution is twofold: First, I do not know of anyone who has followed through on the threat. Going where you're treated best is a positive mindset designed to seek out the best, not flee from the worst. It requires commitment, not just a desire to complain.

Secondly, moving to Canada merely replaces one set of problems with another. Not only have you failed to spread your eggs to multiple baskets, but you have not managed to upgrade to a better basket. While Canada may not have a president who you disdain, it would still give you the same high taxes, endless regulations, and bad weather that you detest in the United States.

Why walk across an imaginary line just to get more of the same? Going where you're treated best means getting the best of all possible worlds by choosing only the best parts of a place while discarding the less desirable elements. You can cross dozens of imaginary lines to put your eggs in many different baskets, each in the best basket for each individual egg.

In some cases, all it takes to put your eggs in a better basket is to overcome the psychological borders that have been placed there. What really makes Calexico, California in the United States and Mexicali, Baja California in Mexico so different? Both are extremely hot, rather boring cities in the middle of a desert. All that divides them is an arbitrary stripe in the sand. The United States can build a wall as tall as it likes between Calexico and Mexicali, but that will not suddenly make one that much different from the other. The real border is in our minds.

These psychological borders impact much more than geography. I remember traveling to Ireland and England during the beginning of the financial crisis of 2008. Walking down the streets of Dublin and London, I noticed something curious: interest rates offered at banks were roughly triple what banks in the United States were offering. Why, I thought, would I keep money in a US bank where 1% was pushing the limits when these banks seemed to offer 3% for a similar product?

To the average observer, there is not much of a difference between banks in the United States, the United Kingdom, or Ireland. All three are wealthy western, English-speaking countries with decent rule of law. Relatively few people who live in any of them are worried about a banking system collapse, even as most people in each country use said banks merely because they are part of the home team.

To an astute financial observer, there is also little difference. While the countries are all wealthy, they are also all broke. To top it off, all three offer fractional reserve banking systems with low levels of liquidity – that is, most of the money deposited is not sitting around the bank.

If they are all the same, why doesn't everyone in the United States just put all their money into banks in the UK or Ireland where they will get a higher return? Why indeed. Putting your money in a place where it will get a higher return is one of the many ways to go where you're treated best. If you can ignore the psychological borders, it is a simple decision to go where the interest rate is higher. Of course, the world is not a totally free market and many countries (the United Kingdom and Ireland included) impose restrictions on who can open an account.

However, there are plenty of other places that are better than the cash-poor banks of western countries that will allow you to open an account. All you have to do to gain access to these banks and the many services that they offer is to surmount the borders you have created in your mind about where you can go and which places best serve your needs.

The Pepsi Challenge

We are taught to believe that our country is 'the best'. Americans, in particular, are of the belief that theirs is the best country on earth. Heck, even political types who believe that the United States is descending into fascism will tell you, "But it's still the best country in the world."

Statistically speaking, though, it is rather unlikely that your country – or any one country – is the best at everything, let alone one thing. Over my career as an international adventurer, I have learned to ignore those who like to whine about home, yet always return to the "but it's actually not so bad" argument. Going where you're treated best is not about going where "it's actually not so bad," it is about going where you're treated best. However, it takes a lot of objectivity to really understand and see each place for what it is.

Take the banking system in the United States as an example. During the financial crisis years of 2008 to 2012, 365 banks were put into receivership in the United States. Yet, many people still consider the US banking system to be the best option.

However, even in an average year, at least one to two dozen banks will become insolvent in the United States. Meanwhile, the FDIC – the government agency that promises to insure depositor money – has well under 1% of all its insured deposits on hand, and the US government that funds it is trillions of dollars in debt. One big bank failure and your life savings are at the mercy of an act of Congress. You know, the guys that read "Green Eggs and Ham" to filibuster a bill they don't like.

In contrast, Singapore has never had a bank failure in its fifty-plus-year history as a country, banks actually keep cash on hand, and the country itself has no net debt. In fact, many banks in Asia are swimming in so much cash that they do not want to open new accounts because they simply do not know what to do with all the money.

When you objectively evaluate places to park your cash, Singapore comes up at the top of almost every list. The reason not everyone has their money there is a function of habit: we are conditioned to go where we are familiar, not where we are treated best.

It is like the age-old battle between Pepsi and Coca Cola. Back in the 1980s, Pepsi was largely a regional brand popular in the Southeast and Midwest, while Coca Cola was already a nationally recognized brand. In places like Texas, Coca Cola outsold Pepsi nine to one. John Sculley, the CEO of Pepsi at the time, decided to change all that with what became known as the iconic Pepsi Challenge. Pepsi knew that their cola performed well in blind taste tests, but as soon as the brand was part of the equation, Coke always won. So, Pepsi created an advertising campaign built around a blind taste test with regular folks off the street.

Their goal was to capture the expression of loyal Coke fans on camera when – after taste testing the colas in Cup A and Cup B – they would discover that the cola they had chosen was Pepsi.

The advertisement that made Coca Cola go nuts was of a granddaughter who persuaded her grandmother to try the Pepsi Challenge while they were out shopping together. The grandmother admitted that she did not know why she had accepted the challenge – she had never had a Pepsi in her entire life! But she went ahead and tried the two colas and selected her favorite. When they revealed the brands, the granddaughter said in disbelief, "Grandma, you picked Pepsi!" The grandmother replied, "I know! I've never had a Pepsi in my life. It must be better!"

I am not going to weigh in on the Pepsi vs. Coke battle, but there is a lot we can learn from the Pepsi Challenge about the power of conditioning and what it takes to go where you're treated best.

There are very few companies that do branding better than Coca Cola. At its core, branding is nothing more than conditioning. Coke works hard to condition consumers to relate the feelings of happiness and joy associated with the Christmas season (or the Olympics, summer BBQs, etc.) to a bottle of Coke. Just from reading this, you have probably already pulled up the image of Santa taking a sip from his glass of Coca Cola that we all have seared into our memory by the mammoth branding genius that is Coca Cola.

Without knowing it, thousands and thousands of consumers have been conditioned to choose Coca-Cola, not because it necessarily tastes better but because Coke has conditioned consumers by developing their emotional relationship to the brand.

All the Pepsi Challenge did was remove that emotional conditioning and let people choose objectively. In doing so, they were able to discover what they actually prefer. Going where you're treated best is no different. It is simply a matter of putting a blindfold on our emotions and objectively assessing what each place has to offer.

The United States has conditioned us to think that it is the best brand of country out there for everything from banking to investing to living. However, if you remove the branding from the equation, it allows you to objectively assess what each country offers. It is no longer about the brand. It is about the formula.

If you can get past the US brand of banking versus the Singapore brand, it is easy to see that Singapore's banking formula is far superior. Going where you're treated best becomes a cut and dried matter of finding the countries with the right formula to solve whatever issues you may have at hand, and then going there to fix it.

The key is to recognize that no one country will have the right formula to solve every issue. For instance, just because Singapore has a fantastic banking formula does not mean that it has the perfect formula for everything else. While Singapore may have rock solid banks, it may not be a great place for you to live. A halfway decent one-bedroom apartment can easily cost $5,000 a month, chewing gum is not sold for fear of litter, and the mere act of sipping Evian on the subway is punishable by a $400 fine.

The good news is that it is possible to open a bank account in Singapore without living there (although it has gotten harder, and the low-minimum accounts are hard to get now). You do not have to forsake chewing gum or sell a kidney for rent money to avail yourself of one of the best banking countries in the world.

Therein lies the difference between "go where you're treated best" and the proverbial "move to Canada." When you empower yourself to go where you're treated best, you get the good parts from every country without the stuff you do not want because you only utilize the corresponding formula that each country has to offer without buying into their entire brand. (Oh, and you do it rather than just yap about it.)

Your Top Priority

As a Nomad Capitalist, you do not have to give up what is important to you to make improvements in your life. You just need to change the way you look at borders. More importantly, you have to decide that you are your top priority. This advice is, by no means, a license to be selfish. It is, however, an invitation to stop and take a moment to examine why you do what you do.

We are wired to be part of a tribe. There are many good things that come from this instinct, but it is our complacency with the tribes that have been chosen for us that causes us to go (or stay) where we are treated poorly. Even in the worst of cases, our sense of patriotism can cause us to stay where we are unwelcome.

Consider when the African nation of Rhodesia achieved independence a generation ago. The enormous victory was followed by a series of "land reforms" that devolved from a fair process between willing buyers and sellers to outright confiscation of large farms from the white minority. Some of those farmers are still there in modern-day Zimbabwe. They had years of advanced notice, but for some reason they chose to stick around and watch their land get confiscated. And they continue to live under that system, fully knowing that it could all happen again.

Think about that: what would compel farmers living in a country with such a storm brewing to stay and ride it out? It is an honest question that deserves an honest answer. Either they were (and are) blissfully ignorant of the imperfections and challenges around them or they are willing to tolerate a great deal of injustice.

When Barack Obama was elected in 2008, some conservatives proclaimed that the new president would round up dissenters and put them into work camps. If I had thought that my future at home was pounding rocks into smaller rocks and foraging for food under the watchful eye of prison guards, I would not have stuck around and complained about the situation. I would have gotten in line for the next flight out.

Most of us do not think in such extremes, but if you have taken the time to read this of your own volition, chances are there is something you would like to improve in your life or business. You may feel that you are paying too much in taxes and would like to keep more of your hard-earned money. Or perhaps you sense that there are better opportunities for your entrepreneurial endeavors somewhere else. Maybe you just have a nagging uncertainty about your country.

You could have any number of concerns that have made you look beyond your present borders. They may not seem like pressing concerns, but no one is going to get an offshore pang like they get a hunger pang. Yet, there is something driving that concern and it is important to listen to that to avoid becoming complacent because you are your top priority.

Open for Business

The basis of going where you're treated best is diversification. If you rely entirely on one place, that one place can come and take your wealth, freedom, or whatever else they feel entitled to. It is the same reason wealthy Arabs have poured money into Istanbul real estate for years. While they may prefer living in Qatar, they know that they need other options. And of course, they want all those options to be Muslim and be within a reasonable distance by business class.

Now that Turkey has had its fair share of challenges, the Arabs are turning elsewhere to countries like Georgia. And in true capitalist fashion, Turkey is attempting to lure them back with the carrot of Turkish citizenship if they invest. Competition at its finest.

The problem with diversifying internationally is that some governments do not particularly like competition. However, some do. In fact, one of my leading indicators for whether a government seeks to compete for wealth and talent is whether they used to be uncompetitive.

Some of the most business-, wealth-, and talent-friendly countries on earth were communist hellholes in your lifetime. Years ago, I was traveling through Europe and enjoying dinner in a small town. Having the place to myself, I watched as a commercial welcoming investment to the small country of Georgia played over and over again. As a marketing guy and a capitalist to the core, there was something heartwarming about the idea of a country advertising itself to the public as if it were the sovereign equivalent of the Snuggie.

Mikheil Saakashvili, then-President of Georgia, took power after the 2003 Rose Revolution and was determined to turn the country into the next Singapore by ending corruption and taking a sledgehammer to taxes. He ultimately managed to flatten tax rates and reduce the number of taxes from twenty-one to just six.

What better way to get the word out, he figured, than to buy television airtime and broadcast the message that Georgia was open for business. Saakashvili was a visionary who realized that the world is an increasingly competitive marketplace for countries, and his needed to stand out.

Today, there is a stark contrast in the former Yugoslav and USSR republics of Eastern Europe. Some, like Belarus, have retained Soviet-era dysfunction, while those like Georgia, Montenegro, Macedonia, Romania, and Bulgaria have opened their arms to business. While I first realized the power of investing abroad in Western Europe, I soon realized that any country, even those you cannot find on a map, offers potential.

I surmised that because Georgia remembers what life was like under the USSR, they have made a point to not go back. That is why just about anyone can open a bank account in Georgia, no questions asked. You cannot do that in the United Kingdom, where the government is more concerned about making rules than about ensuring its continued prosperity and capital inflows. Prosperity in the United Kingdom is taken as a given, whereas Georgia remembers a time when prosperity was far from guaranteed.

Chances are that that you grew up with the former notion that prosperity was a given, that your money would always be safe in the bank, and that your home was the biggest and best investment you will ever make. Once you had that stuff down, all you had to do was show up for work every day until they handed you a gold watch and you retired on a comfortable Social Security check.

That is, until the whole world fell apart and you began to rethink everything. In a post-financial-crisis era, you see people 'leaving the corporate world' on a regular basis. More and more people are beginning to realize that it is not the way forward. Like Georgia, they remember the old way of doing things and they do not want to go back.

People who think like that need countries that think on the same wavelength. While the West holds onto the rules and regulations of their old corporate economies, the Georgias of the world are forging new paths toward greater market freedom and are rethinking the formulas for prosperity in the twenty-first century.

The Connection

Most people give little if any thought to the biggest opportunities available in the global economy, but the opportunities are wide open. It is merely a matter of making the connection between forward-thinking entrepreneurs and investors and the countries that offer them exactly what they need to succeed.

For instance, the trend of global outsourcing has become both a business trend and a political rally cry in our lifetimes. Companies like HP and Apple have lowered costs for everything from production to tech support by having workers in China and the Philippines do work formerly done in more expensive countries. Whether unpopular or controversial, outsourcing is not a new concept.

At the dawn of the industrial revolution, quickly emerging nations often used outsourcing to cut costs and grow faster. After their revolution in 1868, the Japanese realized that their burgeoning industry required the help of experts to flourish — experts that were not available in Japan. So, they summoned the people who did know to come to Japan and get everything set up properly.

These on-site visits were more common 150 years ago because, you know, that thing called the telephone did not exist yet. Today, outsourcing services can be provided remotely anywhere from call centers in Delhi to factories in Shantou. More importantly, access to the tools of international business is no longer an exclusive advantage of big business, it is available to anyone willing to take their business where it is treated best.

For example, I sat down with Jake a while back to discuss the needs of his business working in affiliate marketing. He had been in the game for almost ten years making a steady $200-$300,000 a year while living in San Diego. About eight years in, he finally decided to outsource a lot of the grunt work of his business overseas. By the time he contacted me two years later, he was making $1 million a year.

But now Jake had a bigger problem: folks who earn more than $1 million a year are like shark bait to the California taxman. The Franchise Tax Board of California is perhaps the world's biggest bully. Jake's new success meant he would be sending a $500,000 check to California the following April. He never wanted to repeat that mistake again. $500,000 re-invested would go a long way in his pocket rather than the pockets of the State of California.

So, we got to work creating a plan to fully internationalize Jake's life and business. He had already learned to outsource his work to increase his revenue, but he needed to take advantage of every offshore tool available to him to achieve all the benefits of going where you're treated best.

Jake told me that he loved the beach, so we found him a great location on the beaches of Southeast Asia where he could live for most of the year. He could spend part of his time visiting friends and attending industry events back in California, but he would spend the rest of the year living on a beach that did not cost him $500,000 a year in taxes.

From there, we got him an easy second residency in a zero-tax country and moved his company from California to two offshore jurisdictions. He had a few one-time costs to move his business overseas, but once he paid that final bill he was done forever. If he keeps things up, Jake will pocket an extra $1 million by the end of the second year, and an extra $7 million after re-investment over the next decade.

All of this was made possible because Jake was willing to pick and choose from each of the places that offered him exactly what he needed to improve each aspect of his life and business: outsourcing to eliminate time-consuming grunt work, moving overseas to decrease his personal income taxes, offshoring his company to reduce business taxes, and so on. Each component went to where it would get the best treatment, all while Jake was soaking up the sun and running his business as usual.

Some will tell you that to be treated best, you must stay and fight. If you want lower taxes, just vote for the candidate who promises to lower them. This democracy-focused model misses the point that we are all individuals and want different things. What is good for your country might not be good for your wallet. That does not mean that you hate your country but rather that you want what is best for you.

If your internet business could grow three times as fast because it paid a lot less in taxes – or even none at all – waiting around for the next election is not only a pipe dream; it will cost you a lot of money. I often walk business owners through exactly how much they are paying in tax for every single day they wait, and the amount is often shocking to them. Besides, why wait for others to determine your business success when you have the power to change it for the better right now?

This is what I do, and it is what I help the people I work with every month to do as well. I help entrepreneurs like Jake who started a business doing coaching, or e-commerce, or whatever else in their home country and who have been successful, but only to a point. They are reinvesting all their profits into their business but end up passing on so many opportunities because they do not have enough to reinvest.

Books like *The Four-Hour Workweek* and my friend Chris Ducker's Virtual Freedom opened many of our eyes to the idea that hiring virtual assistants in developing countries was a great way to keep costs low (or in some cases, cut costs completely), be more productive, and grow our business faster. However, this is just scratching the surface of all the options available to entrepreneurs willing to go global.

Like Jake, entrepreneurs who hire an assistant in the Philippines or Romania or anywhere else are going where they are treated best to reduce the cost of labor for their business needs. In the same way, you can reduce your taxes and increase your returns by seeking international solutions. As Jake experienced, the increase in your profits by making a few simple tweaks to your business and lifestyle could yield millions of extra dollars in your pocket in the next few years.

That is why, when I say that I prefer "flight" over "fight", I simply mean that I make decisions about where I live and do business through the objective lens of good financial management and not through the emotional lens of patriotic frenzy. You can love your country and still go where you're treated best. When it comes down to it, it is all a matter mindset.

The biggest example of the "stay and fight" mindset is the people who stockpile automatic weapons in the hills somewhere. They will tell you that they are preparing for a doomsday scenario when FEMA camps and military force come to fruition. While they may plan to sit on their roof picking off Army Rangers one by one, I am sure the military could just as soon send in a helicopter and pick them off first.

These people live by the notion that being a patriot, loyal to their country and government, is the most noble purpose and must be defended at all costs. They condemn guerrilla warriors in other countries yet await the day when they can do the same in their country... all while there are places where their values are already en vogue.

I live by a different motto: fight for yourself, vote with your feet, and go where you're treated best. You come first. You deserve the best. If things have come to the point that you are stocking guns and dehydrated food, chances are that the place where you live is not treating you best. As an Eagle Scout who is risk-averse and a believer in diversification, I can respect the desire to be prepared. However, at a certain point, you have to be honest with yourself. Are you in the right place for you?

Similarly, if you have to call your accountant and dream up crazy loopholes to get your tax bill anywhere close to reasonable, you might also be fighting too hard and should consider a different way. Every once in a while, I hear from some hotshot business owner who is proud of himself for finding some brilliant plan to reduce his taxes, only to come to me and realize that his plan is not even legal.

Why stay and fight the system the wrong way when you can go somewhere else, get all the legal tax benefits of living abroad, and then sit back, relax, and enjoy without the stress? Especially when those all-too brilliant plans often save you a few percentage points; a drop in the bucket compared to the ocean of savings offshore.

In the 1973 Bruce Lee movie Enter the Dragon, Bruce Lee is asked what his style of fighting is. "My style," he explains, "is the art of fighting without fighting." This perfectly sums up the Nomad Capitalist lifestyle. You may not like the system where you are from. You may feel you pay too much in taxes. You may not feel like you belong there and wish to live somewhere else. Whatever you feel, choosing to go where you're treated best is the art of fighting without fighting. Rather than wasting physical and mental energy trying to change the system, you can move on to greener pastures and keep more of your money, feel more at home, and enjoy life more than ever before, and all with more wealth than ever before.

Planting Flags

Now that we know what we are trying to accomplish, let's get specific. When you open a foreign bank account or take some other action that diversifies your assets, business, or lifestyle to a more favorable place, that is called "planting a flag". Back in the 1960s, a man named Harry Schultz created the concept of the "Three Flag Theory," which suggested that those seeking sovereign freedom do three things:

1. Have citizenship somewhere that does not tax income earned outside the country. This was the personal safe haven.

2. Have businesses and investments in stable, low- or no-tax countries. These are called the business havens.

3. Live as a tourist in countries that support your values, rather than society's. These countries are the lifestyle havens, or "playgrounds."

The idea of flag theory, as it became known, was to live life out from under the thumb of the taxman and the bureaucrats that make life no fun. Those who practiced the theory could become "PTs" – known as "perpetual travelers" or even "prior taxpayers" – who would then jet set from one locale to the next going where they were treated best.

While Nomad Capitalists who adhere to flag theory can certainly choose to travel perpetually, it is also possible to achieve the benefits of this lifestyle by obtaining two or three home bases around the world and alternating between them. You can even live in one place if you want, confident that your bank account is somewhere else just as safe. The point is to take advantage of the best treatment possible.

For instance, the third flag is to live as a tourist because countries often reserve their best treatment for the folks who enter their borders as tourists. Unlike a resident or citizen, tourists do not usually get heckled by the police for stupid stuff like jaywalking. They do not have to pay local income tax, either. There are nice offices dedicated to helping tourists find stuff and, in many countries, they can even get their sales tax or VAT refunded when they leave.

While most tourists head back to the reality of a cubicle, snow in the driveway, and tax season when they return from their vacation, Nomad Capitalists leverage this treatment into an ongoing lifestyle.

As a Nomad Capitalist, you may choose to visit the same places over and over again; one couple I know has three homes in three different countries that they visit each year, never exceeding their tourist visa status. They are not residents or citizens of any of those countries; being so would make them subject to the kinds of rules that residents and citizens are subject to. Instead, they are happy to fly under the radar as tourists. They know which cities are best for shopping, which are best for eating and drinking, and they leverage the best of each one.

Other Nomad Capitalists who utilize flag theory choose to stay on the move. I used to prefer this method. I realized at one point in my life that many cities started to bore me after ten days, so I devised a plan to spend one year composed of 36 ten-day trips. It was a fantastic year. Now, however, I tend to prefer slower travel and being able to settle in for a few months at a time in homes that I own as both investments and lifestyle properties. Living the Nomad Capitalist life means you choose the terms.

It was not always that way, though. In the early days of flag theory, a much smaller and wealthier group pioneered a way of living that can now be done with far less money. In the mid-twentieth century, being a perpetual traveler meant summering in Monaco, wintering in the French Alps, and stashing money in Swiss banks accounts. The idea of jetting from place to place in an effort to stay one step ahead of the taxman – sometimes legally, and others not – was a notion of whimsy for Joe Citizen.

It was also much more frowned upon. Tax rates in the United States peaked at 91% before John F. Kennedy took office. Back then, patriotic US persons seemed substantially happier to pay than they would be in today's more global world. They also believed that they were getting something for their tax money back then.

Today, tax rates are lower, as are the stigma and barrier to entry of living a jet set lifestyle. In fact, it is so easy to jet set around the world these days that plenty of modern perpetual travelers choose to spend their winters in Thailand and their summers in Amsterdam. However, most of these folks are not fully availing themselves of the host of financial benefits that come with the Nomad Capitalist lifestyle.

Unlike their jet setting predecessors, many of today's perpetual travelers did not escape the grind because they wanted to lower their taxes – they just wanted to travel. There is nothing wrong with that, but even if you did not set out to reduce your taxes, why not enjoy all the benefits that come with the lifestyle?

I once helped a US citizen and entrepreneur who had been living nomadically in Europe for almost two years. Eric knew the basic tax laws for US persons living abroad and filed a tax return accordingly each year and elected the Foreign Earned Income Exclusion. Yet, despite working with a US accountant, by the time Eric came to me for help, he was still paying $81,000 in taxes every year.

Eric and I got under the hood of his business and discovered that his US company had been set up improperly from the start. We restructured his business to include both a new US company and an additional offshore structure in Asia that enabled him to legally avoid taxation on most of his income and pay about one-third of his previous rate on the rest.

By planting just a few more "flags" around the world, Eric will be able to save approximately $600,000 over the next five years without changing anything about his nomadic lifestyle. The ability to save all that money had been there all along, all he needed to do was to start thinking like a Nomad Capitalist and not just a nomad. These options are available to anyone willing to learn and then take the necessary steps toward greater freedom.

How Is This Legal?

In the fifty years since the concept of planting flags was introduced, numerous revisions have helped expand the theory into more aspects of our lives. In the 80s and 90s, W.G. Hill modified the original three flags and added two more (residence and assets) to create Five Flag Theory. And at Nomad Capitalist, we have added even more flags and adapted the old ones to ensure 100% legality in the age of transparency. Going where you're treated best is all about modernizing flag theory to fit life in the twenty-first century – a time when we really can live, work, and play anywhere we want.

Part of that process is to bring the philosophies of flag theory into the light, examine them up close for all to see, and then fit them into a perfectly legal blueprint. Fifty years ago, the type of person likely to plant flags was more inclined to live in their home country than to travel. As glamorous as the jet set life seemed to be, most people preferred the comforts of life in Boston, Seattle or Dallas knowing that their untaxed cash was safely tucked away in Zurich. Travel was a perk, but not their way of life.

This was also the time when Swiss bankers were more than willing to cater to those very desires. It was common practice for these bankers to arrange to covertly retrieve stacks of cash from your house, fly them back to Europe on their private jet, and deposit them into your anonymous numbered bank account. What was the problem with this activity? Simply put, it was illegal. Not exactly a minor detail. It would still be illegal if you tried to do the same thing today. However, flag theory in and of itself is not illegal. It can all be done in the light of day, 100% by the book.

I was recently having dinner with a business consultant in Ukraine. As we dipped into another bit of Georgian khachapuri, she asked incredulously: "How is what you do legal?! It's OFFSHORE!"

Decades of media portrayals of illegal offshore activity have made the public think that merely having an offshore bank account is illegal. But not every offshore transaction is made with stacks of cash, private jets, and numbered bank accounts. When I explained to my dinner guest that, were she to move to London, she would open a British bank account and stop paying Ukrainian taxes, she seemed to understand.

Offshore is not so dark and complicated. If it were, you would not see me splashing my face all over the world's most-visited website on the topic. I like my freedom, thank you very much.

There is no doubt that a lot of people used to seek a false sense of freedom by breaking the law and bypassing the system. But that was not real freedom. Who could enjoy true freedom while in constant hiding? Real freedom comes from adhering to laws, even those that we do not agree with. I much prefer to find loopholes and exceptions within the law and create options for myself to ensure my continued success.

Besides, western governments have tightened the screws on offshore practices to the point that it has become nearly impossible to get away with illegal offshore activity to begin with. The rules of the offshore world you may have heard about on some spy show on TV have changed. Offshore banking, for instance, is not as easy as just dropping a briefcase of dirty money onto an island bankers' lap.

Going where you're treated best has nothing to do with illegal activity; and the people who follow those five magic words do not concern themselves with the offshore world of the past or in the movies. After all, why pursue illegal routes to protecting your wealth when there are perfectly legal ways to achieve your end goals?

The EKG Formula

When you plant flags, you are internationalizing your assets, businesses, and social life, giving yourself access to the best the world has to offer. Over the years, I have developed a simple three-part formula to help the folks I work with determine which parts of their life and business they wish to internationalize. I call it my E-K-G formula to Enhance, Keep, and Grow your personal and financial freedom.

This approach makes up the heart of the Nomad Capitalist lifestyle and applies the following principles:

E - Enhance Your Personal Freedom

K - Keep More of Your Money

G - Grow Your Money

Each person's approach to planting flags is different; there is no perfect order in which you must complete the steps because the exact steps that make up your strategy are different from anyone else. For most of the entrepreneurs I work with, keeping more of their money is important. However, if you have sold your business or had some other windfall, growing your money may be a more important part of the formula for you.

For all of us, enhancing our personal freedom, building options, and creating redundancies are important steps. What good is a 0% tax rate if you are stuck living in Syria? Remember, the goal is happiness and freedom.

Each part of the EKG system works together as a puzzle, and each part contains a number of potential strategies that you can choose from to create your desired Nomad Capitalist lifestyle:

E - Enhance Your Personal Freedom

- Living Overseas - Whether in one place, a few places, or as a perpetual traveler.
- Second Passports and Residencies - Obtain a residence permit or citizenship in another country for better travel, better treatment, and more options.
- Digital Privacy - Host your website overseas or use secure offshore email.
- Socializing Overseas - Make friends, dates, or a lifelong partner in another country.
- Personal Happiness - Find the place where you feel totally at home.

K - Keep More of Your Money

- Tax Reduction - Legally reduce or eliminate your personal taxes by relocating your business the right way.
- Offshore Banking - Protect your money in quality banks and earn higher returns.
- Offshore Companies - Legally choose the tax rate for your business.

G - Grow Your Money

- Frontier Market Entrepreneurship - Start a business in a less developed market.
- Foreign Real Estate - Buy, rent, sell, or hold property in fast-growing markets.
- Foreign Currencies - Earn high rates of return just by holding another currency.

These are just a few of the ways you can take advantage of what the rest of the world has to offer and go where you're treated best. Reexamine that list and ask yourself if the country where you currently live offers you the best in all those categories. Any objective observer would have to say no, but most of us struggle with objectivity. Still, being objective is essential to achieving results in anything. To be a successful Nomad Capitalist, you must break free from your preconceived understandings and look at the world with fresh, unbiased eyes.

If you want to enhance your personal freedom to travel without restriction, Japan actually takes the top spot as the world's best passport. That is not to say that having a second-place passport from Singapore is a total waste, of course. In fact, Singapore's passport comes with almost all the same travel privileges as Japan's but without the high tax requirements.

If you are looking to enhance your personal happiness, the Danes often claim to be the happiest nation in the world. If you can get past the $24 beers in Denmark, then working about twelve hours a week might make just about anyone happy. (As a native-born American, slurring short European work weeks never gets old.) Yet

Danes suffer the worst privacy protections among their privacy-conscious neighbors, pay triple the price for a car than other places in Europe, and they do not have any banks on that "best of" list. Some dude even wrote a book specifically telling men not to date Danish women. The horror.

If your focus is on keeping more of your money, unless you live in Germany, your local bank is not the safest in the world. According to Global Finance, that title goes to KfW Bank. Of the fifty safest banks, only twenty-one countries are represented, and even that number is a bit skewed. While the United States is represented by four banks (the highest ranking at #33), three are agricultural credit banks; not the type with drive-up windows in the suburbs.

Other countries on the list include China, Chile, Qatar, and the United Arab Emirates; countries that, not too long ago, were ruled by camels or were sleeping under a photo of Mao. The four German speaking countries have always been go-to places for handling money, but Abu Dhabi? Times change.

And if you are looking to grow your money, it may come as no surprise that the growth in countries such as China, India, and many African nations far outpaces the economic growth in any western nation. As you can see, there is no 'best' place on earth. Not even supposedly perfect places are perfect.

In Frank Capra's fantasy Lost Horizon, diplomat Robert Conway rescues ninety of his fellow Brits in a last-minute escape from revolutionary China, only for their plane home to crash in the Himalayas. As it turns out, the crash was no accident, but was planned by a several-hundred-year-old ruler who sought out Conway and his expertise to lead a mystical paradise called Shangri-La.

The movie opens with a question that still applies to all of us eighty years later: "In these days of wars and rumors of wars, haven't you ever dreamed of a place where there was peace and security, where living was not a struggle but a lasting delight? Of course, you have. So has every man since Time began."

We all want to live our best life possible. That has not changed. What has changed in the last eighty years are the means by which we can achieve that goal. You may not be able to find that perfect paradise with all the "best" in one place, but you can build that life for yourself by going beyond your borders in search of the best that each location has to offer. In today's connected world, the best place is numerous places. Some of those places are behind the scenes while others are out front.

The first step is to simply recognize that where you live may not be the mystical paradise you seek. All you have to do is look around at the turmoil in the western world to see that it is not the bastion of freedom and security it once was. Factory closings have given way to "Make America Great Again" signs dotting the lawns of those longing for a bygone era. Stagnant wages and poor job opportunities for many have led to a growing call for socialism and wealth redistribution from the rich.

Meanwhile, seemingly endless terrorist attacks on the West have given rise to a new security state. I have old friends whose neighborhoods in Chicago, London, and New Orleans have become meccas for crime, and others who have bounced from one part-time job to the next in this Uber economy, searching for the type of stable job their parents had.

Yet, despite having little to lose, when I tell these old friends to consider moving to one of my new safe havens, they get scared. Of what, I am not sure. I live part-time in the Republic of Georgia, which was ranked the sixth safest country in the world. When I accidentally left $1,000 sitting on a restaurant table in the capital city of Tbilisi, the staff diligently walked the cash to my lawyer's office, hours after our lunch. Crime in Georgia is lower than most western cities and there are no typhoons, or flesh-eating viruses to speak of. Yet, for some reason, guys living in Chicago with bullets whizzing by think to themselves, "If I can't visualize it, it must not be safe".

I also own a home in Kuala Lumpur, Malaysia, a place that certain friends refuse to visit me in out of fear that Malaysia is a Muslim country. They somehow imagine that all visitors are required to dodge an ISIS firing squad to pass through baggage claim. The media bubble has convinced many that places like Tbilisi and Kuala Lumpur are off limits and dangerous for us. Heck, remember the time when the US State Department issued a travel warning against ALL travel… everywhere in the world? Do not go to Calgary, kids; you might step on a landmine and die.

If you want to go where you're treated best, you will not get much help from governments that are better served by keeping you locked into the system. Just as the Olive Garden would prefer that you masticate on their inedible breadsticks nightly rather than experiencing two Michelin star fare elsewhere, national governments love it when you hitch your entire wagon to their cart. It makes their life so much easier.

They want all your bank accounts. Every dollar, euro, and shekel you own. They want your real estate investment to be within their borders. The want all your personal assets – from cars, boats, and airplanes to gold and silver bars – to be stored on their turf. To them, this makes sense. It is like the cult leader who asks adherents to sign over all their belongings. Life is easier as the cult leader when no one has the resources to leave the compound.

And, in 99% of the cases, the country making these demands of you is not the best place for you to be. It might feel like the best if you have never experienced anything else, but numbers do not lie. Just because Kim Jong-un says North Korea is the best, does not mean that it is.

Different types of countries tend to treat you better. If you want your money under lock and key, the stereotypical best bets are those near Germany or Singapore. If you want a place that does not tax, look to the Caribbean (although that is changing). If you want a place that barely taxes, look to Eastern Europe or Asia.

Nordic countries have the edge on privacy and freedom of speech. If you want to pirate movies and music, Spain is your best bet; with everyone out of work, I guess they figured, "Why not?" And then there is the United States and Canada with free refills and clean tap water. Unless you live in Michigan, that is.

This may all sound a bit tricky, but it is not once you get the hang of it. Planting a flag can be as simple as moving your server from the United States (with all its crazy laws for website owners) to Iceland where privacy is sacrosanct. You can do that in an hour. Other strategies might take a bit longer, but with the right plan, you can go where you're treated best in every way possible.

Your How-To Action Plan

Immediate Action Steps: Make a list of all the different components of your life. Where do you bank, invest, do business, pay taxes, live, vacation, study, work, socialize, have citizenship, have residence, feel at home, host your website, hire, get healthcare, raise (or want to raise) your family, etc.? Consider making a spreadsheet to

---

track each component, where you have planted each flag, the pros and cons of the current locations, and potential new locations where you could move each flag and their pros and cons. You may not know what new locations to consider yet. You will get new ideas that you can add to your spreadsheet as you continue reading.

Travel Action Steps: Consider traveling to the different locations on your spreadsheet. Plan a vacation to destinations of interest to scope out the area for living or investing or make a note to stop at a local bank on your next business trip.

Holistic Planning: You may quickly find that there will be many moving parts to optimizing your life and going where you're treated best. You will want to read the rest of the book for more insights into what is involved, but also consider getting professional help to make each piece of the puzzle fit into the whole and ensure that you are crossing all your T's and dotting all your I's as you go.

Chapter Two: How to Go Where You're Treated Best

"Do I Have to Become a Goat Herder?"

Dateline: Cape Town, South Africa

I had not seen Bryan in thirteen years since he was a missionary for the Church of Jesus Christ of Latter-day Saints knocking on my door during the single year that I spent at Arizona State University. In all honesty, I mostly slept and read books while I was in college. As a neurotic, business-minded youngster, I was out of my league among the throngs of Daisy Duke-clad revelers that surrounded me on the rare times I decided to show up for class. As a result, Bryan and I became friends.

Thirteen years later and I was landing at Bryan's hometown airport in Cape Town, South Africa. He was patiently waiting, sign with my name on it in hand. I was in South Africa to take in the sights and explore business opportunities while Bryan was eager to hear about my location independent lifestyle and a philosophy that had yet to hit South Africa in a big way.

"I want to do what you do," Bryan said as he piloted a late-model SUV along the M18 highway into town. "But do I have to become a goat herder or something like that?" It became apparent that an introductory course to the location independent world was needed. Still, Bryan's question hit squarely at what most people want to know about the Nomad Capitalist lifestyle. For years, he had seen me post Facebook updates en route from El Salvador to Albania or celebrating the opening of a business bank account in Singapore over gin and tonics at The Cufflink Club.

Why was I in so many crazy places? What purpose did a Singapore bank account serve? And who the hell would want to go to Albania? All good questions. To the uninitiated, going where you're treated best seems like an impossible fantasy. While I imagine that Bryan's question was loaded with just a hint of sarcasm, it was not out of the ordinary. As a 35-year-old married father of three kids, Bryan was not exactly sure how to go where he was treated best. But he did have a dream to be free.

That is how the process of becoming a Nomad Capitalist starts for most people: a dream. The challenge is manifesting that dream into a reality with a step-by-step process for gaining not only location independence, but also personal and financial freedom. This book is all about helping you create a personal plan of action to create freedom and prosperity through geographical diversification. There are many potential paths for you to take to get there. As with any process, the 'how' is not the only important part; you must also understand 'what' you need to do and, most importantly, 'why' you are doing it.

If you are reading this book, chances are that you have spent at least part of your life like Bryan. You have lived, worked, paid taxes, and kept all your stuff in one place. Perhaps you have dreamed of traveling the world or living on a beach, or perhaps you just want a change.

About ten years ago, I was in a very similar situation. At least 40% of every dollar I made was set aside for taxes, down a few percentage points from the seven months I spent living in California where politicians have busy careers sucking blood from stones with a straw. Meanwhile, the sum of my wealth was locked up at Chase Bank and an internet savings account. Monthly interest between the two was barely sufficient to pay for a family bucket at KFC. While I deployed some of my savings into other business ventures that performed well, I was afraid to invest in real estate where I lived because I believed it was in a bubble.

In short, my options were far more limited than they are today, and I had far less money to work with. That was right where Bryan was when I spoke to him. The biggest things holding Bryan back were uncertainty and fear. He knew he wanted to be free to live where he wanted and raise his children how he wanted. However, Bryan's mindset was a bit off course. Rather than running toward what he wanted, Bryan spent his time rationalizing how to go where he would be treated best by using spreadsheets.

Over lunch our first day, Bryan told me that if he could earn $50,000 per year, he and his wife could afford to cut the cord and live wherever they pleased. The first thing I asked Bryan was whether that included taxes. He replied that it did, to which I reminded him that he would not need to pay taxes if he left South Africa. Like most people who have lived in one country their entire life, paying that 20-60% tax rate had become almost second nature. However, if Bryan and his family left South Africa, they could choose to live in places that did not tax them on their income, giving him an extra $10,000 to play with. That, or lowering his annual nut by the same $10,000.

The second thing I told Bryan was that nothing was stopping him from living the Nomad Capitalist lifestyle right then. His employees may have been based in South Africa, but his IT business was already global in scope. I explained how he could easily use a foreign company and foreign bank accounts to make doing business easier, bypass South Africa's growing capital controls, and keep his money in dollars rather than the unstable South African rand. He did not need to leave South Africa to accomplish any of that.

The third thing I told Bryan was that his business could be location independent if he wanted it to be. Like many of us, he was afraid to leave his team in charge of the operation. I asked what the point was of having sixteen employees if not even one of them could be left to manage the others while he lived the lifestyle he wanted. The three challenges Bryan outlined are the same ones I hear over and over:

1. He was attempting to work backwards to generate enough income to 'be free' rather than working with what he already had.

2. He was overlooking steps he could take now while preparing to leave, such as setting up foreign bank accounts and companies.

3. He believed himself to be tied to one location for many of the usual reasons – employees who must be managed, parents that want to see their grandchildren, etc. – when that was not really the case. Like a horse that believes it cannot

run away because it is tied to a cheap plastic chair, he falsely believed that he was shackled to Cape Town.

The reality is that anyone can go where they are treated best if they choose to take action to make it happen. My parents are now at retirement age and have realized after twenty years of flirting with moving overseas that life in the United States is best for them. That does not stop them from using tools like foreign trusts to protect themselves from frivolous lawsuits, foreign bank accounts to diversify into other currencies, or foreign brokerage accounts to trade on the Mongolian stock exchange.

For those of us a bit younger – Bryan included – the options are much wider. If you already have a successful business selling stuff online or doing consulting, you have likely already realized that you can do that from anywhere. However, you might not be ready to make that leap because you tell yourself stories about something keeping you where you are. Or you might be confused about how to handle your taxes if you leave. You might not even realize that you will not necessarily have to pay taxes (at least in most situations) if you move out of your country.

Or you might suffer from the "all or nothing" syndrome where you figure that if you cannot run around with three passports, a dozen foreign bank accounts, and a company in a Caribbean tax haven, you may as well be living in California and forking over sixty cents of your every dollar to the taxman.

This book will not teach you how to create a location independent income; there are plenty of other books for that. But this book will encourage you to step outside of your comfort zone and, like Bryan, realize that you are not as tethered as you think. More importantly, it will help you reap the benefits that come with that realization.

Take Jay, for example. Jay runs a successful business manufacturing and selling unique perfumes in the United States. Jay has ten employees working at his production plant and thought he could never leave. When he came to me, Jay and I created a way for him to install a manager to oversee the operation so that he could live somewhere else in the world. And because Jay himself will be managing the business from outside of the United States, he can qualify for a lower overall tax rate.

What this book will teach you is how to use your existing location independence to manifest this freedom and prosperity on a massive scale. Chances are, even if you have started going where you're treated best, there is still a lot more that you can do.

I have spoken with a lot of internet business owners who moved from San Diego to Las Vegas or Phoenix for tax reasons. They did so because the tax savings on an income of $500,000 could easily add up into the mid five-figures. If you were not living extravagantly, you could easily live on the tax savings alone, and then some.

While some may like the arid desert weather in tax-free Nevada, a heck of a lot more people prefer the beaches, the weather, and the popsicle-melting, sun-kissed California girls in San Diego. The good news is that there are places like San Diego all over the world. You can even find places where the girls have less snark. You do not have to choose. It is not an either-or situation. You really can have it all.

Like Bryan, most people fail to realize the full potential of going where they are treated best. A US citizen who moves from California to Nevada may shave 10% or 15% of their tax bill away, but a US citizen who moves from California to Panama City, or Phuket, or even Puerto Rico can potentially shave off 100% of that tax bill – all without removing beaches from their life.

Think about that for a moment: you can get more of what you want in terms of both lifestyle and finances by looking offshore. No longer do you need to make small changes like moving from California to Nevada to get only half of what you want. As a Nomad Capitalist, you can get more of everything you want.

Overcoming Irrelevant Fear

Chances are that the only thing standing in your way is you. If you already have a location independent income, it is easy to make these changes. One of the best ways to get over any mindset issue and maximize the benefits available to you is to use an ancient technique that I shared with Bryan.

In the third century BC, Zeno of Citium devised the concept of stoicism, which espoused the idea that to have a good life, you must overcome irrelevant fear. Zeno's disciples, called the Stoics, recommended that you take time to imagine the worst-case scenario

– everything from your house burning down to losing a loved one – to better appreciate what you have. This technique has become referred to as 'negative visualization,' in which you imagine the worst-case scenario before taking a particular action.

For instance, if there were no insurance, you would be much less likely to buy a home for fear that your villa would go up in smoke and you would be out a lot of money. In the western world, most people buy homes with high-LTV mortgages and probably figure they could walk away from a little equity if the fire damaged their home… which is exactly why banks require insurance policies.

We can evaluate the merits of opening an offshore bank account on a similar scale. What is the worst thing that will happen if you move part of your personal cash from a bank in New York to a bank in Singapore? Both institutions function like the banks you are used to; they have branches, take deposits, and make loans. Both countries provide government insurance that insures the value of your deposits to a certain limit in case the bank goes belly up. Both countries also have agencies tasked with making sure that banks are well run by stable operators and not a guy using some watercolor paintings as security assets.

For all intents and purposes, banks in Singapore run just the same as banks in the United States, with the difference being that all three of Singapore's major retail banks are listed among the fifteen safest banks on planet earth – a title no bank in the United States holds. So, what is it that holds us back from internationalizing our money or any other part of our life?

Let's use negative visualization to determine a reasonable response. Applying Stoic standards to banking offshore, the worst thing that could happen would be that you move your money to Singapore where it is promptly lost. That would be an unacceptable loss, but if you follow the advice in this book, you would not have transferred all your money to Singapore – or even much at all to start – so chances are you would still be in business. Still, the idea of losing all your money certainly sucks.

Now, let's take things one step beyond the standard negative visualization. What would happen if you did not move your money to Singapore? Imagine that you left your money in that bank in the United States. The worst-case scenario would be that another major recession hits one year later. In the last global recession, hundreds of US banks went under, yet not one bank in Singapore did. Where would you want your money under those conditions? In both cases, the worst-case scenario is the same. But if you had a bank in Singapore, you could split your money between the two and suffer only half a loss.

Going where you're treated best means first realizing that where you are is not the best and accepting that. You can still gorge on hot dogs and watch fireworks on the Fourth of July without having to declare that the US banking system is the most stable or solvent. To truly realize why a Nomad Capitalist lifestyle is necessary, you must turn the process of negative visualization onto your current actions and find the holes in what you are already doing.

For those of us who grew up expecting to live every aspect of our personal and financial lives in one country, that is a lot of potential cleanup. If you have already considered smaller moves – such as the aforementioned move to Las Vegas – you just need to expand your thinking a little further. If you can move to Vegas, you can move to Panama. One good deed begets another.

When you think about this stuff, you should quickly realize that the worst-case scenarios involved with moving money overseas, getting a second passport, or investing in a foreign country are rather unlikely to occur. The risks are far greater doing what you are doing now. The risks are less than your current situation and lessened further by diversifying internationally because you are reducing those risks dramatically across several different countries.

A Swiss bank account is little more than a bank account in Switzerland. Think about that for a moment. Millions of Swiss citizens bank in Swiss banks every day, and you would be hard pressed to find any who have had a small problem, let alone had all their money vanish. In fact, they may look at the idea of banking in your country as an unacceptably dangerous risk.

Doing this form of reverse negative visualization does not give you license to be an idiot; moving your money into a Sudanese bank or stockpiling Iraqi dinars is not a smart idea. Nor is getting a North Korean passport (or trying, since Pyongyang is not much of an epicenter for immigration). However, making prudent decisions about your freedom and your finances is an important part of breaking free from a system where you are not treated best.

If you live in a western country, the money you pay in taxes was likely paid not because you wanted to pay it (unless you are Warren Buffett) but because not paying means you will end up in a cage next to Wesley Snipes. The idea that refusing to follow the system of the country where we were born will lead to punishment is something that most of us accept blindly. And yet, the money we pay in taxes pays the salaries of people we do not respect, for violations of human rights with which we do not agree, and for wars we do not want.

The money you are paying now – or have paid in the past – would be much better spent, invested, or given away by you rather than by anyone else. You have total freedom to claim your legal right to go where you're treated best. Doing so can enable you to control exactly how your money is used and to choose the moral causes that you support with your money.

The End Goal

Again, the key is to run toward something, not from something. Run to the freedom to do with your money as your conscience sees fit, not away from a government that takes it away from you. Focus on the end goal.

One of the mistakes many people make when starting this journey is that they get angry, criticize the government, and look for scammy ways to accomplish their goals. There has long been a cottage industry of shadowy figures using pen names and hiding behind stock photos that foment this anger to get business for whatever miracle cure they sell you. Decades ago, this was Swiss bankers. Today, it is guys on the internet selling "anonymous Vanuatu companies with bearer shares."

Going where you're treated best is NOT about hiding money or breaking any laws or doing anything shady or immoral. Quite the opposite. Rather than the old guard of trying to run and hide, Nomad Capitalists are running toward what they want. It is much more productive to find the country that treats your business well and taxes it lightly than to complain about how bad things are in the United States.

Once you find those new safe havens, do not look back. Being a Nomad Capitalist is about moving your life in a positive direction, not encouraging you to get upset. The money you paid in taxes last year is gone forever; there is no sense in worrying about it. There is, however, empowerment in deciding that you can change your life to get more of what you deserve going forward.

The past is in the past, so focus on the present moment. I am a big believer in the view that today is all we have; that is why, as the cliche goes, they call it 'the present'. Look at the strategies for saving on taxes, moving your money to foreign banks, or having a second citizenship and examine how they benefit you today. More money in your pocket means the ability to reinvest in and grow your business, upgrade to a larger suite, or give more money to your favorite causes.

You can also look beyond the present to the long-term implications of these strategies. I do not have children yet, but if you do, you have no doubt thought about what kind of life you will leave your children. Using the strategies in this book, you can grant them such benefits as dual citizenship or a larger nest egg with which they can start their own careers.

Today's tax savings are tomorrow's real estate empire or generational wealth. Money saved today will have a snowball effect over time. So too will being geographically diversified when the countries where you have invested hit their stride.

Warren Buffett became famous as one of the most savvy and prolific investors of our time. When you think about what he has done, it really is not that much. Now, I do not say that to be dismissive; he is, after all, one of the wealthiest guys on Earth. What I mean is what Warren Buffett freely admits: the success of Berkshire Hathaway has largely been based on a few big hits. His mantra is that "You only have to do a very few things right in your life so long as you don't do too many things wrong."

As such, Berkshire Hathaway focuses on long-term investing. They do not buy quick hits, and they certainly do not day trade. Instead, Warren Buffett has focused his entire life on value investing. Using this approach, Buffett and his team review a company's balance sheets before even looking at the stock price. The aim is to determine the true value of the company as if they themselves were running it. Only once a true valuation is determined, Buffett will look at the actual current market valuation on that company.

If a company Buffett pegs at $1 billion has a stock market valuation of merely $200 million, he and his team figure it is a safe bet to snatch up the stock and wait for the market to realize the true value he sees. He once famously advised investors to, "Stop trying to predict the direction of the stock market, the economy or elections."

The Forty-Year Plan

Part of this philosophy is the idea of a forty-year plan. My client Mark's offshore journey perfectly illustrates how this applies to the Nomad Capitalist lifestyle. He told me his story over drinks at a bar in a little-known country that was formerly part of the Soviet Union. Mark was in his late thirties, had two kids, and was running a multi-million-dollar business. He had little fear that his businesses would stop giving him an income, or that he would ever run out of money.

As much as he was focused on growing his business, he was also focused on creating his own version of a forty-year plan. He was working with me to obtain second residency and identify investments in the country's capital. He had come to me because he knew that his plans involved a second citizenship in the country and that he would need my help to get there.

"Imagine this place becomes the next Singapore," he said, echoing my oft-repeated sentiments about finding the next Singapore among the world's emerging markets. "If I can become a citizen here, then not only will I have all of those opportunities, but so will my children."

His forty-year plan involved a unique form of investment in the potential of the country itself. While few people know about Mark's country of choice, even fewer think of Singapore as some dumpy breakaway state. However, a mere half-century ago, that is basically what it was. After race riots in the middle of Kuala Lumpur, the Chinese-run Singapore decided to end its short-lived participation in the Malaysian Federation to become a tiny city-state at the tip of Southeast Asia. With little in the way of development, no natural resources to speak of and a mere 277 square miles of territory, most casual observers would have written Singapore off.

That old school thinking completely ignored the way the world works in the modern era when people can go where they are treated best. Despite the odds, Singapore established itself as a country of law and order, economic development, and free markets. Eventually, people started to come. Today, they are beating off foreigners with a stick. They have too many of them.

Just as Cambodia is said to resemble Thailand in the 1980s and Colombia has many of the growth indicators of Panama, today's emerging markets could be a few decades removed from the success of Singapore.

But why look to emerging markets when Singapore is already on the map? There is one big difference: Singapore has become so successful that it is now largely closed off to business, especially at a small level. Sure, there are one or two decent banks that will open an account for you if you do not live there. The country's private vaults are among the best in the world, but the ability to personally participate in Singapore's success has largely passed.

The window of easy immigration to Singapore for most entrepreneurs and investors essentially closed for good in 2013. Even those entrepreneurs who are already living in Singapore are now having trouble becoming permanent residents or citizens because the country has too many expats. Politicians are under pressure by the natives to stop what they see as an overflow of immigrants and keep them from obtaining precious Singaporean citizenship.

Rather than fight to get accepted in the Singapore of today, Mark decided to focus on identifying countries on the way up and to participate in their ascent. He is smart to do so. Going where you're wanted is a crucial part of going where you're treated best. Emerging markets want investors today, whereas Singapore does not necessarily need them anymore.

Unlike a typical investor, a Nomad Capitalist like Mark wants to participate in more than just an ordinary investment market. Sure, the real estate market may be a good investment in Mark's country of choice, but the real investment for a guy like Mark is the opportunity to obtain a second citizenship in the next Singapore.

In this way, these emerging markets are the sovereign equivalent of Tim Ferriss' concept of geoarbitrage, where companies hire workers in emerging countries, sell their work or product back home in the developed world, and pocket the spread. Mark's goal is to obtain citizenship in several emerging countries in the belief that at least one is likely to hit it big. He realizes the adage of getting in on the ground floor and is seeking to get in early on countries that have a lot of potential.

The best part is that Mark can do this without making a lot of adjustments to his lifestyle. As an investor, he does not have to live in these countries full-time, even though chances are that one of them will catch his eye and he will decide to spend at least part of his time there.

This is his version of a forty-year plan. Unlike long-term investing plans, it does not require him to tie up his money for forty years, merely to take a call option on the future of a country. While going where you're treated best means creating the best life for you now, it also means ensuring that life continues to be great in the future, both for you, your loved ones, and for any future generations.

The Principle of Nomadism

Contrary to how many interpret the meaning of the word 'nomad,' concepts like the forty-year plan show that being a Nomad Capitalist is not about always moving around. In fact, you can lead a Nomad Capitalist lifestyle by living in the United States if that is what you want. Likewise, you can be a Nomad Capitalist without having to travel to dozens of countries as I have done, or by visiting every country on earth as author Chris Guillebeau did. Of course, if that is what you want, then being a Nomad Capitalist can enable that lifestyle, too. It is all about having the freedom to choose.

The core driver of going where you're treated best is the ability to find the three principles we talk about: enhancing your personal freedom, keeping more of your money, and growing that money – the E-K-G formula we laid out in the previous chapter. While finding all that freedom may involve leaving the nest, it is not required. Remember, it is not an all-or-nothing proposition.

Instead, think of the 'nomad' part as being like the attitude taken by nomads on the steppes of Mongolia. These nomads spend their time hunting and gathering. They are not moving around haphazardly; instead, they hunt until there is nothing left to hunt, or allow their herd to graze until the pasture needs to recover. Then, they move on to the next place.

By applying the principles of nomadism, you could choose to camp out somewhere for the rest of your life and pass all you have to your dual citizen children, or you could choose to spend a short amount of time somewhere before moving on to the next location. In the era when being a Nomad Capitalist is possible, you no longer have to make decisions based on where you will be in twenty years; rather, flexibility rules.

You can create a lifestyle that is as fast-paced or as sedentary as you like. Giving yourself opportunities for both current and future growth is more important than the physical location you occupy. The place that you and your dollars occupy today might not pay off right away but investing with a long-term mindset should pay off down the road.

I witnessed an unintentional example of this a few years ago while taxiing into Dublin from the airport. The taxi driver, in true Irish fashion, was brimming with excitement. He was an older gentleman who had come out of retirement to drive a cab in his early 70s after the global financial crisis hit.

He took it all in stride, though, recalling how Ireland was 'a third world nation' when he was growing up. He recalled stories of walking to school in bare feet some days, while not having any breakfast to eat on others. He spoke fondly of his grandchildren and their ability to live in a developed Ireland that was now a member of the European Union and had welcomed so many companies to its shores – from Facebook to LinkedIn to Google – creating great tech jobs.

He became more emotional as he told me that, "For the first time ever, I look at my grandchildren and think," his voice cracked, "they have a real future."

Historically, many Irish citizens left the struggling country to find work elsewhere. This continued into the 1990s until the Irish Tiger of the early 2000s brought great hope to Ireland. While the country was whacked by the global recession along with everyone else, modern Ireland is light years ahead of the country where my cab driver grew up. And now his grandchildren are reaping the benefits.

Had he escaped the country at an early age, his children and grandchildren would have been born elsewhere and would have missed the long-term payoffs that Ireland is now experiencing. His choice to weather the poverty of his youth means that, today, his family can take part in the economic prosperity of modern Ireland.

You do not have to tolerate abject poverty to get the same payoff. As recently as fifteen years ago, it was possible to purchase Irish citizenship outright. Just as Singapore welcomed businessmen and investors with open arms several decades ago, you could have waltzed into Ireland 40 years ago and been treated royally. However, now that my cab driver, his grandchildren, and the rest of Ireland are enjoying the benefits of the country's development, you cannot get the same treatment. It is too late.

The entrepreneur residency program is closed to all but the next Merck or Instagram. Put simply, it pays to get in a bit early.

Which means that if you do not take today's best options, you will be kicking yourself tomorrow. While you certainly want to diversify across several countries, it is worth it to take call options on emerging markets. It is possible to become a citizen of and an investor in countries whose history resembles that of Ireland's, but without having to change your lifestyle or hop on a boat for greener pastures.

This type of diversification is what makes being a Nomad Capitalist incomparable to practically anyone in history. Five hundred years ago, even the wealthiest king could not diversify his empire in the way that you and I can today with our smartphone and a plane ticket. Imagine what it was like for those who became Irish or American before it was the place to be. Countries most people have never heard of will use low-tax, business-friendly, people-friendly policies to vault themselves to the same level in our lifetime, and you can be part of it.

Diversify, Diversify, Diversify

One of the benefits of diversification is that you can soften the blows of any failure while still enjoying the benefits of success. Like the old saying about a problem shared being a problem halved, diversifying your assets can minimize the pain of any problems that may happen.

Take the example of my friend Matt whose family business took on a wealthy partner not long before the economic meltdown in 2008. Their business had been a moderate success for years but had never reached the level of expansion they envisioned because of the capital-intensive nature of their industry. Now, they had a partner who not only had a lot of money at his disposal but other businesses to help support theirs. This guy owned banks, aircraft leasing companies, and many other ventures.

Then the Global Financial Crisis happened. The partner's banks all went bust and were taken over by the FDIC. The aircraft leasing company failed as companies turned in Gulfstreams rather than leasing new ones (I imagine the new President's condemnation of executive jet travel did not help, either). Some of the partner's other businesses continued to stay afloat, but it did not matter because he would soon have to file bankruptcy and have his creditors take over any productive assets to pay for the bad apples.

Here was a guy who had spent a fifty-year business career not only building a great business but a sterling reputation. Just as he was planning to retire and hand the whole thing over to his children, it fell apart. Years later, he is still in bankruptcy court wrapping up his affairs. I can only imagine how painful the whole experience must be.

Had this partner been diversified internationally, the blow would have been far less severe. A financial crisis in the United States would no doubt still have taken an ample bite out of any businesses based there, but this partner had the means to operate businesses on a more global level, including in markets whose economies do not correlate to the recession-prone bubble economies of the West.

He failed to educate himself about the global possibilities – like the fact that Asian companies were buying and leasing more planes than ever – depriving himself of the choice to go elsewhere. Having everything in one country did this captain of industry in, taking down others with him. If your company had money in one of his banks, you would have been reimbursed by the FDIC, the agency that insures bank deposits in the US. However, if your business had more than $250,000 in the checking account, any excess sums could, quite possibly, have been gone forever.

That is why I was always a bit astonished when institutional clients I worked with in my broadcasting business would deal with only one bank. One client in the precious metals business had a single checking account at a major bank through which literally tens of millions of dollars passed in any given month. What would happen if something serious occurred and there was a run on that bank that ultimately led to their failure? Perhaps the US government would try to stop it and bail the bank out, but they likely would not be too concerned with businesses that had $10 million sitting around. They would be concerned about the little guy.

If I have $10 million in cash, I am surely going to diversify it across multiple banks and, with the Nomad Capitalist mindset, I am going to diversify it across multiple countries too. Economic events in one country can spread, but they are less likely to spread to other unrelated countries as they are to spread to other banks in the same country.

In the same regard, plenty of businesses that were banking in Cyprus saw much of their money 'frozen' – and then taken – because they kept more than the EU deposit insurance limit of €100,000. When Cyprus ran into financial trouble, the European Union decided that, rather than provide bail-out funds, they would 'bail in' the banks by confiscating any depositor funds over that limit.

Doing so was far more politically palatable to wealthy Germans fatigued by recessions all over Southern Europe than having to dip into their pockets to pay for the mistakes of an island country in the Eastern Mediterranean. In doing so, the European Union screwed everyone with more than €100,000 to their name, essentially taking their funds to pay for the woes of the Cypriot government.

The hard truth is that what happened in Cyprus can happen anywhere. We will talk about specifics in the chapter on offshore banking but suffice it to say that having only 10% of your money in Cyprus would hurt a heck of a lot less than having all of it there. On the other hand, a diversified portfolio of citizenships and investments can only benefit you.

When I convinced my father to buy Yahoo! Stock at $25 in 1996, he did not complain after selling it at $50 and watching it go to the moon. Combined with his risk profile, he used the information he had at the time to make the best decision for him. Similarly, if you were to allocate 10% of your portfolio to a project in a new country that delivers an excellent return, you may wish that you had allocated everything to that 20X return.

However, hindsight will clearly explain why that never would have been a reasonable approach. Venture capitalists who invest in successful companies do not wish they had put their every dime into Facebook, but rather that they could find more companies like Facebook into which they could deploy their capital.

Opportunity Knocks

Fortunately, the world is brimming with opportunity these days. In fact, there is far more opportunity today than in any other period in our lifetimes. While the United States may be slow to respond to the changing global landscape, other countries have adopted the mindset of attracting people, rather than trying to fence them in (or out).

The former Soviet state of Estonia has become an excellent example of innovation in both the private sector and government. In 2016, US presidential candidate Jeb Bush suggested that his country should adopt a tax system as simple as that of Estonia. Thirty years earlier, Estonia was part of a failed state minutes away from dissolution. In one generation, Estonians went from boiling stones for dinner to inventing Skype and creating one of the most transparent governments on earth.

The reality is that none of us knows what will happen next. Like bankruptcy, countries tend to become irrelevant very slowly... and then all at once. Betting the house on the future of one country is risky, but fortunately you can diversify and take the best parts of each place.

Second passports may have been the domain of the world's yacht and jet set elite only a few years ago, but the process is becoming more accessible. Now, you and I can become dual citizens as well, without the hassles of the Ellis Island-style immigration that our great-grandparents had to deal with. The same way Uber has allowed anyone to be a taxi driver, the offshore world is opening so that anyone with even a modest income can not only travel the world but become a citizen of the world.

While the idea of a Swiss banker driving to your front door in a Mercedes to pick up a bag of cash seems sexy, it is no longer the reality. For most of us, that is a good thing; banking offshore has become available to the mass market so that anyone with as little as $100 may benefit.

Even as recently as the turn of this century, few would have predicted the rise of digital nomads who live and work anywhere in the world, using their laptop to get business done from the beach. Back then, you slaved away in an office for fifty weeks a year only to look forward to a few summer weekends and two weeks' vacation to Aruba or Cancun – or whatever place the travel agency was pitching on the back page of the local newspaper.

Today, location independent business has exploded and will continue to do so. However, I predict that the next wave will be what I call Digital Nomad 2.0: businesses that are not only location independent but government independent as well. These businesses will not rely on any one country, nor be burdened or rendered uncompetitive by one country's rules or tax policies.

There are some who believe in moving their entire net worth into digital cryptocurrencies and storing survival food in their basement to become government independent. However, we still have borders, and borders still matter. Planting flags as we will discuss in the chapters to come is, in my opinion, the best way to be free.

Those of us who live by principles of self-reliance, entrepreneurship, and global diversification will not only prosper but prosper on a far more consistent basis than those who have tied themselves to one economy. While investing in a foreign stock or mutual fund was enough in the 1990s, the new level of savvy diversification is going where you're treated best.

Your How-To Action Plan

Immediate Action Steps: Look at the list you made from Chapter One and perform negative visualization for each one and record what you find. What is the worst thing that could happen if you try to open a bank account in Georgia? What is the worst-case scenario if you spend a month in Colombia to see if you like the place? And then reverse it and apply that negative visualization to the life you are currently living. What is the worst-case scenario if you keep doing what you are doing? Next, look at all the things you complain about. Consider adding them to your list. Then, find a way to solve that problem offshore, stop complaining about it, and go fix it.

Travel Actions Steps: With each solution on your list, determine whether you can take action from home. If you can, start making those changes. If not, travel to your solution. Get a feel for the place. Once you have put a little money in a new bank account or made an investment, it will not seem so scary as you have already planted the seeds of diversification.

Holistic Planning: If something seems too complicated or you are concerned that you are creating extra reporting burdens or may be getting into legal complications, wait to act on that piece of the puzzle until you can get professional help.

E

ENHANCE YOUR
PERSONAL FREEDOM

Chapter Three: The Location Independent Lifestyle

"Come to Cuenca, where flowers bloom from your toilet water!"

Dateline: Medellin, Colombia

A full day had gone by with the members of my inner circle at a small group mastermind event in Medellin. On day two, we woke up to breakfast at the city's best hotel. Over our arepas and fresh-squeezed juice, we discussed the investment opportunities in Colombia and the fact that the average American thought Pablo Escobar was still running the place.

"They would never believe the truth," James – a younger guy from Michigan who had come to scope out the city – chuckled. "I mean, who would believe that the former drug capital of the world is now a thriving capitalist market?"

"I'm glad it still has a bad reputation," Linda chimed in. "That means it hasn't been totally overrun by the western expats taking over other parts of Central and South America." Linda and her husband Rob were an older couple who had lived overseas for decades after a chance meeting in Liberia in 1970. Over the years, they had watched as more and more places were overrun by retirees flocking to live out their golden years on increasingly shaky Social Security checks.

"Colombia still has a unique vibe that makes it a great place to stay," Rob agreed. "It is fast becoming a hotspot for investors, but at least it hasn't made it onto the retirement newsletters yet!"

"Retirement newsletters?" James asked.

"Oh, yeah," Rob replied. "Websites and newsletters about retiring abroad basically prop up the latest and greatest places with punchy copywriting. Just imagine," he continued with his best dreamy infomercial voice, "you can walk down white sand beaches, eat coconuts straight from the hands of monkeys, and salsa dance in colonial plazas with your sweetheart. All for a mere $623 per month!"

"It's true," Randy admitted. Randy had been hit by a car and almost paralyzed before he realized that life was too short to stay in a place he did not like. He had gotten a second residency in South America and now spent much of his time traveling throughout the region to figure out where to live and which passport to get next.

"Those international living newsletters have already burned through Costa Rica, Belize, and Panama like yesterday's news," Randy explained. "Now they're moving to places like Ecuador. It's only a matter of time before a promotional email to pre-retirees will be cooing about how the magical waters of Cuenca cause flowers to spring from your toilet!"

We all got a good laugh out of that.

"In some ways," Linda conceded, "the growing number of bargain hunters living in these emerging cities is a good thing. It increases the number of services available to all of us."

Rob countered, "But in other ways, it's frustrating because some of the people who come are changing the authentic fabric of each place."

I explained that this phenomenon is little different than those who move from Boston to New Hampshire for lower taxes, then vote for liberal politicians that promise free programs that cause higher taxes.

"And it's not just retirees," James added. "I think most people give in to the herd mentality. Sure, it's nice to connect with the other nomads flocking to havens like Chiang Mai, Ubud, Barcelona, Berlin, and Bangkok, but I feel like that herd mentality makes so many people believe that their options are fewer than they really are."

James hit the issue directly on the head. Being location independent as a Nomad Capitalist has nothing to do with following the herd. Most folks reading this book are likely part of one of two camps: they are either a successful business owner sitting in their home country thinking that there has to be something more, or they are already living life as a nomad, perhaps even in one of the popular places my mastermind group mentioned during our breakfast discussion.

If you are the location dependent business owner, you are probably looking for something more: more life experiences, more freedom, and more money in your pocket. Conversely, if you are already location independent, you are probably looking for less: less taxes, fewer hassles running your business, and less nonsense from a country that you do not live in anymore.

Both are possible.

Unlike the solutions you will find by following the herd, the Nomad Capitalist lifestyle encompasses all of it, from the financial aspects of reducing or eliminating your taxes to enhancing your personal freedom. The EKG formula begins with the latter. After all, what would be the point of fixing all the other moving parts if it did not lead to a more fulfilling, happier life? And, since the definition of the perfect life will be different for each person, it is essential for you to start there to know what you are trying to achieve.

Most people work backwards, chasing after shiny objects and promises of getting rich while they travel. While it is possible to travel and earn money, too many folks attempt to do so without a full understanding of their options, leading them to miss out on many of the benefits of living an international life. This haphazard approach creates little true freedom and can often cause more problems down the road.

I like to call what I do Digital Nomad 2.0 to differentiate it from people who are just getting started with making money on the internet while they travel. There is nothing wrong with strapping on a backpack and going to live in Cambodia while you build a portfolio of muse businesses. However, you are not likely worrying much about taxes when your goal is to make $1,000 a month just to keep the noodles on the table, nor are you likely choosing your destinations based on gaining another citizenship.

Other people have simply ignored the benefits of travel altogether and have chosen to stay where they were born and build as best they can. Fortunately for them, Digital Nomad 2.0 can also help those who chose to grow their business the old-fashioned way and have since realized that they need a better approach. These folks can plug into instant tax savings, lifestyle benefits, and capital growth while enjoying the comforts of a Four Seasons hotel – no toiling in a hammock required.

Like many of the people I help today, I ran a location independent business for years, acknowledging that I could work from anywhere but failing to act on that knowledge in any sort of meaningful way. After slinking away from a party school at age 19, I entered the lucrative world of AM radio, connecting people who wanted to create infomercials with other people all too desperate to sell them.

My business involved waking up at 11AM, calling people running infomercials somewhere else and telling them I had many other AM radio stations dying to air their show for a low price. As with any new business, it was intense at first, but over time I graduated to working with billion-dollar companies and even a Fortune 50 company that let me do my own thing much more than the "dollar-a-holler" clients.

Either way, the business was entirely location independent. Whether it was placing cold calls from a VOIP phone (remember Vonage?) or managing a few emails a day as conditions got plusher, none of it had to be done in Phoenix, Arizona. At 21 years of age, I remember thinking, I could do this from anywhere... but it never entirely sunk in. While I took an increasing amount of time to travel while running that business, and even debated moving to China, I never took the leap.

The whole process all seemed so foreign. Despite priding myself on being a citizen of the world and wanting to go where I was treated best, I was holding myself back based on the fear of the unknown. Perhaps you know the feeling; while traveling is one thing, letting go of your identity as a resident of Los Angeles or Montreal or Canberra can be hard. You do not have to do it all at once, but you do need to start somewhere.

I still remember talking to Steve and Anne, an American couple living in Missouri who desperately wanted to leave the United States and save, in their case, about $40,000 per year in taxes. They did not want to travel non-stop, though. They saw the life of nonstop travel I lived at the time and thought that it was the only solution available to them if they were going to live overseas and save on taxes.

Fortunately for them, there is more than one way to live as an expat, and many of those ways do not require that you be a perpetual traveler. There is no 'right way' to live as a Nomad Capitalist. Just as you do not have to follow the herd to any one city, you do not have to live by someone else's definition of what it means to be a Nomad or adhere to any stereotypes. You do not have to stay in Airbnbs, work out of coworking spaces, or flock to the latest co-living space where entrepreneurs live together. You can, but you do not have to. Adopting the Nomad Capitalist lifestyle does not mean you have to live the way others do, it means not caring what anyone else thinks and doing what works best for you.

No matter how much, how little, how often, or how active your desire for travel is, you can fit right in and make it work for you. Having a location independent business and lifestyle is all about personal choice. When it comes to designing your lifestyle, it is nice to have a point of reference to know what options are available. I have identified the four main strategies for living abroad throughout my travels that are conducive to the life of a Nomad Capitalist. While there are no hard and fast rules, let's look at them one by one.

The Expat Strategy

When I first started my Nomad Capitalist journey, I generally visited 30-plus countries each year, but that is not the only way to be a Nomad Capitalist. Some people I work with decide to follow the least aggressive strategy for living abroad: being an expat. The Expat Strategy is straightforward: settle down in one city in a country different than where you are from. That is it.

There is nothing about being an expat that dictates that you can never leave your new city. The same way you can travel from the city where you currently live, you can be a settled expat and travel, too. While being a full-time expat may sound like the option most suitable to families, I am also seeing more and more single people who want to have a full-time home and only travel from there when they feel like it. Sometimes, it is best to "go as far as you can see, and then see further" and, for many people, that means one permanent home and an open mind for growth.

A lot of the multi-million-dollar earners and high-net-worth individuals I have worked with say that routine is one of the most important elements in their ability to focus and achieve success. They do not want to move around the world because they feel it would be too distracting from their other goals. The good news is that countries like Panama will generally allow you to live there full-time and only require you to pay tax on your local income. If you find the right country and create the right plan, you can still live tax-free without playing the perpetual traveler game.

Think of being an expat as doing what you do now, just in another place. And in this case, you get to keep a lot more of your money and actually choose where you live. If you like the idea of exploring, you can still travel on summer vacation or take weekend trips whenever you please, traveling to another country or exploring your new home. The difference in your travels compared to a perpetual traveler's is that you will take Point A – Point B – Point A trips that return you home rather than embarking on never-ending journeys.

Some people like the traditional expat lifestyle because it makes managing finances and life a lot easier. I can understand the need. From time to time, I will pass up otherwise great opportunities that I cannot handle when traveling so quickly. The process of purchasing my home in Malaysia, for example, would have been so much easier had I been able to spend one or two months in the same place.

Spending more time in one place may also help you qualify for a second citizenship. While some countries allow you to spend minimal time there and still become naturalized, some of the best passports require you to live in the country to qualify. Want an Irish passport? Be ready to live there for at least five full years within a nine-year period.

The biggest challenge with the expat style of living is tax concerns; living in Ireland may get you a passport, but it will also get you a "Tax Return Due" notice from Revenue Ireland. If you want to stay in one place, make sure your plan includes a way to ensure that you are not taxed, or at least pay very little.

The Trifecta Strategy

The more time I spend away from my home country, the more I crave a base. I have done the full-on perpetual traveler routine, but my penchant for decorating and the fact that I own a lot of suits and carry-on luggage means that I prefer to have a base these days.

My first base was Kuala Lumpur, Malaysia. It is a great base, especially because it gives you access to two airlines that fly everywhere very affordably, plus quick access to Singapore for even more options. KL is also a great base because you can bank and store your assets in neighboring Singapore while living in the more interesting and cost-effective Malaysia.

However, having one foreign base can start to look a lot like being a traditional expat if you do not travel much. That is where the idea of multiple bases comes into play to create the Trifecta Strategy. The "tri" comes from the ideal of setting up at least three bases so that you can split your time between each one, never spending enough time in any one location to be treated as anything but a tourist, free of tax obligations.

Having multiple base cities simply means that you have homes in different cities, usually relatively far apart so that you can travel to nearby places from each base. Selecting your bases is a matter of personal preference. Perhaps you never want to deal with winter and choose bases where you can always enjoy the sun. Or maybe you love to ski and want bases that will give you year-round access to winter slopes. If you prefer all four seasons, perhaps you create a strategy that allows you to visit Europe in the fall. Or maybe you are like me and just cannot sit still. When I am in Asia, I start wondering about what is going on in Europe, or vice versa.

Base cities can also give you access to more regional travel. For example, I have had bases in Malaysia, Georgia, Serbia, Colombia, and Montenegro. From there, I have easily been able to get anywhere I want without hassles. While one of my current bases in Tbilisi, Georgia is not the best-connected city, it is close enough to get around Eastern Europe, including emerging markets like Ukraine and Azerbaijan, as well as interesting places like Turkey and the 'stan' countries.

Conversely, a place like northern Belgium — a base I considered but passed on — is small enough that it is easy to get to the Brussels, Amsterdam, or Paris airports from anywhere by train and, from there, to anywhere in the world. In KL, as mentioned, it is easy to travel to anywhere in Asia, Australia, or Europe.

This is my current personal strategy. I like the flexibility of having several homes in different regions of the world set up the way I want. While I loved staying at five-star hotels for the first few years of traveling, the allure eventually wore off. And I never enjoyed having to stay at the often-dreadfully decorated short-term rentals in the countries that I visited. I much prefer the option of feeling at home and having that home set up exactly how I want it.

The Trifecta Strategy also allows you to enjoy a lifestyle buffet: the big city, the small town, the beach, and whatever else it is you are after. And if you choose your countries carefully, you can get second residence permits and eventually passports in return for buying property. Just make sure that you follow the tax rules in each country so you do not accidentally get sucked into a tax net.

For example, I own a home in Montenegro but do not spend that much time there, just every other weekend in the summer. I can 'live in Montenegro' but not pay tax there because I do not really work there. I just live, soak up the summer rays, and then head back to my base elsewhere in Europe for the rest of the summer before jetting to Asia or Mexico for the winter.

If you want to achieve something similar, there are several important questions you should take into account when setting up your Trifecta Strategy. First, how many bases do you want or need? And what will you use them for? Do you simply want the comfort of having a home? Or are you setting up shop in Malaysia to have an affordable place to live near your assets and bank accounts in more expensive locations like Singapore and Hong Kong?

Next, how much time will you spend at each base? While you may have a business base in Asia, you might have a leisure base set up somewhere else in a more exotic location that can serve various purposes. For example, when I am not using my beach home in Montenegro, I rent it out and receive passive rental income from the property.

The home is also an investment based on the likelihood that Montenegro will join the European Union someday and property values will rise. I doubt the home will go down in value and I can make a few percent off it every year through occasional rentals – which is more than I would make in the bank. So, my Montenegro base functions as both a beach home and a place to park my cash... with the bonus of being a place where I can satisfy my penchant for decorating.

For me, I am seeing more and more the value of using the Trifecta Strategy. Over the years, I have bought and renovated a total of six properties in different locations. With each one, I not only have a property where things are set up and decorated the way I like but I can enjoy greater productivity and a sense of home. I may overpay a little bit, but the added productivity that comes from having a place to call home is well worth the investment.

The Base City + Travel Strategy

One of the best parts of living as a Nomad Capitalist is the lower level of commitment to any one place. We are taught that commitment is a good thing: historically speaking, settling down and committing have been ways to describe marriage that suggest that devotion to one person, place, or thing is the best way to create happiness in life.

Here is the secret: being 'uncommitted' geographically does not mean you cannot commit to other things you care about. If you already have a family – or simply like the stability of a place to call your own but want plenty of flexibility to roam – then consider merging the best parts of expat life with the perpetual traveler life. I call this the "Base City + Travel Strategy" because it gives you a base to call home, plus plenty of other opportunities to roam.

This approach makes sense for a lot of reasons; for one, most of the younger people I work with want to travel, even if they do not want to do it all the time. Another reason is that spending less than half your year 'at home' can often get you out of the tax net in your home country. Spend a few months per year in the Netherlands and chances are they will not tax you; spend nine months there and they will come looking for a check.

This strategy is similar to the Trifecta, but instead of a few base cities, it involves one base and a number of focus cities. If you are not familiar with the term, airlines refer to focus cities as the cities they serve with great frequency, but that are not full-fledged hubs. For a Nomad Capitalist, focus cities function in a similar manner; while you have not set up a permanent base in your focus city, you frequent the area often enough that you feel at home there.

In any given focus city, you know how to get around, know where the best restaurants are, know where to get your dry cleaning done, and know how to get back to the airport without wasting time. You feel at home without having a home there. Then, you simply determine how long you want to spend in each focus city, or group of focus cities, before returning to base. You will never have to deal with the feeling of newness while in your focus city.

The benefit of having focus cities is that you can develop habits there. For example, I have been to Singapore enough times that I know exactly where I want to stay, where to eat, and how to get around. And most importantly, not only do I know people that I can call and meet there but I have a list of other people and businesses that I would like to get to know.

A focus city can also be a city where you hold assets, have bank accounts, or have other flags planted. After dozens of trips to Hong Kong and Singapore, I feel extremely comfortable in both; partially because I have made the mental connection of having part of my assets there.

Hong Kong is one of my favorite cities in the world. There is something charming about Hong Kong in an almost boorish way. Whether it is fighting pedestrian traffic on Des Voeux Road in Central, watching the old school ferries and junk boats crossing at the Star Ferry Pier, or navigating the tiny hutongs of Tsim Sha Tsui to get a custom suit at Sam's Tailor, the city is one of a kind.

That said, I could never live there full-time. Most people could not do it. Going to Hong Kong is like driving to Vegas and getting excited when you see the lights of the Strip coming over the last hill. By the time Sunday afternoon rolls around, however, you have had one too many Alaskan crab legs and you just barked at a cocktail waitress after losing three grand. The Middle Eastern girls from the buffet who are spending two whole weeks in this blistering heat now seem totally crazy.

For me, Hong Kong is a place to do business and visit on occasion, making it the perfect focus city. I love Hong Kong and I love to spend time there, but I would never live their long term. Following the Base City + Travel Strategy, I can get exactly what I want from a visit to Hong Kong and then move on to another focus city or return to my base.

Building your personal list of focus cities takes time, so this is a strategy that is best used by recovering perpetual travelers, or people who are willing to visit a rotation of cities frequently enough to get used to them. It has taken me almost a decade to develop my list of focus city candidates: Dublin, Warsaw, Brussels, Riga, Tbilisi, Istanbul, Panama City, Kuala Lumpur, Hong Kong, Singapore, and Phnom Penh. Maybe I am missing a few... but you get the idea. As you discover the world and grow into a Nomad Capitalist yourself, your list may be different. It is your world to discover.

The Perpetual Traveler Strategy

Many digital nomads choose to follow the Perpetual Traveler Strategy. It is how I lived once I left the US on a permanent basis and started spending my entire life on the road. The perpetual traveler has no permanent address and no permanent home, choosing instead to live life out of a suitcase.

The ultimate draw of the Perpetual Traveler Strategy is that you go at your own pace. For example, I spent the second half of 2013 traversing most of Southeast Asia, making connections and investigating deals in each country. To successfully do that, I gave myself one month in most countries, which I eventually shortened to two or three weeks. I started in Vietnam and continued to Cambodia, Thailand, Laos, Malaysia, Indonesia, and finally the Philippines. Then, the first half of 2014 was spent in Eastern Europe, beginning in the Baltics and working my way down to the Balkans at a slightly faster pace.

To increase the flexibility of your travel plans, you can reserve your hotel or Airbnb one week at a time and then choose to extend it or not. In most places, there is never a shortage of hotels, which means you can choose how long you stay in each place based on your needs or interests. That is why, for me, being a perpetual traveler is the ultimate freedom.

There is no set approach to being a perpetual traveler and there are many variations to this strategy. The system I used a few years back could work as well with shorter trips, or with more extended trips. Some PTs and digital nomads bounce from place to place at lightning speed; I believe my record was 30 countries in one year. Others choose to go at a slower pace, spending months or even years in a location before moving on.

In the beginning, I thrived on going somewhere new on a regular basis because I wanted to see how different places work, investigate the culture, and figure out how efficiently things run. I could do all of that with a short-term trip. Now that I use the Trifecta Strategy, these shorter trips are more spread out, but I still make time for them. And when I do not have time, I send my team members to locations all around the world to do the research for me. The information we gather is key to our line of work.

For someone who is not writing a blog on the investment opportunities in different countries or studying the nature of economies, slower travel may work better within the Perpetual Traveler lifestyle. Even if you would prefer more stability in the long term, being a perpetual traveler is a great way to try on different cities before committing to a more permanent strategy. You can experience more and work each new country into your global investment strategy.

No matter what pace you prefer, perpetual travel can work for a number of different people and their various needs. A real estate investor, for example, could spend ten days in a city of interest before moving on to the next. This would allow them the opportunity to scope out the local real estate market before moving on to the next city and the next after that. In the Balkans, for instance, they could move from Belgrade to Kotor to Tirana to Skopje to Ohrid to Pristina to Sarajevo. Once they have covered the region, they could then reset to another part of the world and start over again.

One drawback of the perpetual traveler strategy is that it can be prone to loneliness. It is often hard to maintain relationships in places where you are only around for a short period of time. However, it is also possible to develop a massive network of friends throughout the world with this way, especially in this digital age when you can stay connected long-term through social media with people you meet once. You will meet fellow Nomad Capitalists with whom you can form deeper connections than you ever could with someone who does not share your passions and world views.

Another drawback is that it can also be difficult to open a bank account, start a company or even get a second passport without a permanent address. You may, however, be able to get around this by setting up a virtual mailbox that serves as both a permanent address and a mailing service that will scan all communications you receive via mail and send them to your email.

However, non-US citizens may not be able to solve all their perpetual traveler problems with a virtual mailbox. It is becoming increasingly difficult for citizens of countries with residence-based taxation to establish a tax residence outside of their home country without putting down roots somewhere else. To say the least, it is challenging to optimize your taxes when living the perpetual traveler lifestyle if you are from countries like Australia, the UK (most of Western Europe, really), and Canada that require you to establish a center of life outside of your home country before you can qualify as a tax non-resident.

Even so, a perpetual traveler lifestyle – while perhaps not permanent nor tax-optimized for everyone – allows you to go out and see what fits you. The small challenges can be dealt with along the way. The bigger challenges can be worked into a holistic plan as you go as well. The bottom line is to recognize that there are different ways to live as a perpetual traveler and you can tweak the strategy any way that you want to make it work for you.

The Piecemeal Strategy

There are a number of doubts I hear people wrestling with when they are deciding to become location independent and reap the benefits that come with it:

1. What if I hate living somewhere else?
2. What if I do not know where I want to live?
3. How will I make friends and spend time with my family?
4. How will I get my daily green juice, or find a vegan dry cleaner, or be able to listen to live acid jazz on Saturday nights?

Some of these challenges are not that hard to solve and expat groups online can help you clear up many of your doubts. If you are choosing to live in a frontier market to take advantage of low-hanging-fruit business opportunities, then it is only normal that you may have to forego daily kale juice. After all, countries like Cambodia and Paraguay have so many opportunities precisely because they do not have stuff that is common in many other countries. The benefit of living there is that you can be the first guy to sell green juice and have first mover advantage.

For those of us who prefer 24-hour convenience stores, Uber, and great shopping, the reality is that all the things you enjoy at home will likely be available wherever you choose to move. When in my home in Malaysia, I make small adaptations to my lifestyle, such as eating more tropical fruit in place of fresh berries that are rather expensive there. Nothing big.

One strategy that I recommend if you are moving out of your home country for the first time is what I call piecemealing. The idea is that you take a shorter trip as a way to convince yourself that you have the option to return at any time, which you do. It is also a way to test the water before diving in headfirst. Most people who try piecemealing end up staying out of their home country and enjoying the tax relief and other benefits that come with it for years, or even permanently. Some will also discover that the Nomad Capitalist lifestyle is not for them and that is fine too. This way of living is not for everyone.

Piecemealing works by promising yourself a short trip – say, six months – that could easily lead to a longer trip. For instance, when I set off to spend six months in Southeast Asia, I was not only interested in brushing up on business opportunities but also in finding a long-term Asian base where I could hang my hat.

To do this, I created a rough itinerary that included approximately one month in each of the countries of interest, as well as short trips to countries that were purely of business interest. The idea behind this was that I would spend enough time in any one place to be able to make a proper judgment about living and investing there.

Doing this also protected my downside in several ways. For one, if I hated the place, I only had to be there for a month. Additionally, I was setting my mind up to believe that I could return to the old normal after the six months was up. I had no intention of returning to the old normal, but the option to do so was reassuring. I had traveled extensively in Asia before and was sure that I could find a place that suited me, but leaving myself that flexibility meant that, at the end of the six months, I could also say that I would rather live in 'fill-in-the-blank' instead.

Your piecemeal strategy may look very different or take place in an entirely different region of the world. A good starting-point, however, is to spend six or twelve months doing something new. Any shorter and you will be hard pressed to get the full picture; any longer and you will not get the full effect of making a decision. One year seems doable. Try more than that and you might not do it.

Let's say you are working online from your home in Los Angeles and you are reluctant to leave the beaches behind. The good news is that the rest of the world has plenty of beaches, too, so you plan a twelve-month piecemeal trip to twelve beach countries. Your itinerary might include places like Nicaragua, Costa Rica and Panama in the fall, Southern Hemisphere beaches like Chile, Argentina, and

Brazil in the winter, Asian beaches in Indonesia, Thailand, and Cambodia in the spring, and the European beaches of Montenegro, Croatia, and (heaven forbid you would ever actually decide to live there and pay taxes) Greece.

Over the course of a year, you would see a lot of different options for potential bases. You might buy a beach home in Montenegro for summers, another beach condo in Thailand for winter, and spend the rest of the year traveling around. Or maybe you would just find one home, or decide to merely rinse and repeat the whole country-a-month routine again next year.

The other benefit of piecemealing is that it allows you to gauge your preferred pace. If moving every month is too stressful, perhaps you would prefer a life with one or two bases and infrequent travel from there. If moving every month seems too slow, perhaps a life of perpetual travel suits you more.

The benefit of this approach is that you can start taking advantage of the benefits immediately. If you are a US citizen, that year away would qualify you for tax benefits. I like to think of this as being paid by your government to travel. As I will outline in the chapter on tax savings, it is easy to legally avoid most if not all taxes by being outside of your home country for the greater part of a year. While you are investigating the world's best beaches as possible places to spend part of your life, you will also be saving a lot of money.

The "Jet" Set Lifestyle

Finally, no lifestyle design is fully complete until you know how to enhance the travel experience itself: flying. I am not a travel hacker, nor do I churn credit cards to squeeze out more frequent flyer miles. In fact, on a recent interview, my answer to "How do you fly so often on the cheap?" was "I don't". My new travel hack is to save enough on taxes to pay for whatever I want. Nevertheless, air travel is a common component of the Nomad Capitalist lifestyle and I have learned a few things along the way.

For one, I rarely travel first class. The amenities and services in business class are nearly as luxurious as they are in first class, and they come with a lower price point. I fly business class over economy because I prefer the comfort and productivity that I gain by doing so. Flying first class, on the other hand, is more for show – you get the same level of productivity and comfort, so what else could motivate folks to pay four times as much for a flight that will get them to the same exact destination as everyone else on the plane?

There is a fine line between traveling in comfort to increase productivity and blowing your $100,000 of yearly tax savings on overpriced flights with lackluster Thai Airways flight attendants. Why not save that money to spend on champagne and a private bungalow next to a breathtaking beach? Or even better, invest it in real estate that will increase your lifestyle options or passive income. I would far rather invest the $30,000 or more each year that I save 'cheaping out' in business class into procuring a better view or location when upgrading one of my residences.

This, of course, is my personal preference that I have distilled over many years of travel. Your preferences may be different. My personal goal is to avoid the creation of friction and pay what it takes to get what I need instead of settling for something less and dealing with the frustration. I am not going to pay more if it does not serve those end goals.

For others, economy class (and maybe even first class) could be the right fit. I flew economy class for many years before I decided that the productivity of business class was worth the price tag. The trick to successfully surviving economy class is the emergency exit row. It used to be easy to get an exit row seat. If you are flying on a US airline, it still is, you simply pay. As grotesque as I find US airlines, it is worth the extra $150 for more legroom and an increased chance at an empty middle seat.

In most cases, international airlines restrict the exit row seats until you check in. Go to the airport and request one at the check-in desk and you will be told 'no' a few times, but if you insist that the agent call someone to check what can be done, on many occasions that 'no' will quickly turn into 'Window or aisle?' And, even if you can get a seat on the exit row, do not forget to check for cheap upgrades. An increasing number of airlines offer to upgrade to first class for a mere $100.

Being a Nomad Capitalist means going against the herd; if you want to fly first class, be my guest. If, however, you are like me and can turn the money saved each year into another rental property, do not feel compelled to blow all those tax savings on flights just to keep up with the Joneses. In the same way that you are free to follow any of the strategies discussed in this chapter or create one that is wholly your own, there is no need for you to rush to buy first class seats to show off all the money that you have saved.

Oftentimes, the richest people are the ones who flaunt their money the least while they do things that make them happy internally. The location independent nature that comes with the Nomad Capitalist lifestyle brings with it a host of new decisions about what you are going to do with your time, money, and travel. Do not let that overwhelm you. More importantly, do not let the herd decide what that lifestyle looks like. The point is to discover the lifestyle that you want and enjoy.

Do not escape the rat race just to follow another herd. Be authentic. Be honest with yourself about what you want and it will be easier to recognize the opportunities that will help you achieve those end goals. It may take some experimenting to discover exactly what those goals are but take the time to appreciate the fact that the kind of life you have created for yourself allows you to do just that.

Your How-To Action Plan

Immediate Action Steps: Research your piecemeal strategy. What countries do you want to see, test out, research, etc.? What do you want in your ideal location? Climate, community, permanence, adventure, shopping, cuisine? Plan the trip! Book the flights. Figure out how you will run your business while traveling.

Travel Action Steps: Travel! Test out the different strategies we have discussed and decide which one best fits your desired pace and lifestyle.

Holistic Planning: How will your travels impact your taxes, investments, citizenship planning, residencies, etc.? Keep these questions in mind in the coming chapters.

Chapter Four: Second Passports

I Welcome You as the Newest Citizen Of...

Dateline: Dubai, United Arab Emirates

"Put your finger here," Laurent said in a heavy French accent. I had flown to Dubai on 24-hours' notice to be holed up in a junior suite at the Four Seasons with a guy who came to meet me who was carrying nothing more than an aluminum briefcase that looked like it could protect against stray gunfire.

Perhaps I had found myself in the wrong place at the wrong time. My guest's salt and pepper coiffure feigned the look of a US Senator. But I was not there to discuss politics, at least not in that way; the man sitting across from me was taking fingerprints for my soon-to-be-issued passport.

"You can hold this," he said, casually handing me a green passport with the words 'Union des Comores' scrawled across the top. I had never held a green passport before, probably because most green passports are issued by African or Muslim countries, and only one of them – Macao – has any kind of decent travel. But I was a kid in a candy store. The Frenchman could have spent all day punching in numbers and scanning my birth certificate for all I know; I was happy just to flip through this empty passport and dream of how it could be mine.

It was quite the act of salesmanship, to be honest. Give a guy a blank passport to flip through and let the rest happen on its own.

Normally, this works best when a pet shop owner tells a family to take the puppy dog home… just for the weekend. The return rate on that deal must be all of zero. Just as I was thinking how brilliant Laurent's subtle sales pitch was, he stood up.

"Congratulations," he said, his hand outstretched for mine. "I'm proud to welcome you as the newest citizen of the Comoros Islands." He smiled as he handed me my new citizenship identification and passport numbers.

Here I was in a hotel room in Dubai, about to become a citizen of a country I had never been to, with a passport cover written in two languages I do not read, and all it took was sending a few documents, promising I was not a terrorist, and flying to meet a guy in air-conditioned comfort. The hotel even threw in a free fruit basket. Laurent, however, refused not only a fresh mango but also my offer to buy him tea in the lobby – no doubt afraid of the type of public threats that prompted the bulletproof briefcase.

"Now, all you need to do is send the money," he quipped on his way out, harkening back memories of the Swiss banker in Casino Royale that advised James Bond that his poker winnings "Vould be vired to any bank account you designate in the vorld."

Alas, the process of obtaining another nationality is rarely as simple as showing up to claim some far-flung citizenship in a modern-day nod to homesteading, but with passports instead of dirt. This was entirely a business deal. In exchange for $45,000, the Comoros Islands – a deeply poor African nation of three (or, according to them, four) islands off the coast of Madagascar – would grant me citizenship and all the rights that come with it, including that green Comorian passport.

With it, I would now be able to travel visa-free to a grand total of 47 countries, most of them other unheard-of places in Africa, but also to Hong Kong, the Philippines, Malaysia, Indonesia, and the casino mecca of Macau. At least I could gamble with it. Such travel privileges, of course, pale in comparison to that of a US passport, but that was not the point. My aim was to enhance my freedom.

Few people could find the Comoros Islands on a map, but that was exactly what I was betting on. My birth citizenship in the United States was from a country everyone can find on the map (okay, everyone except a few Americans). Having an entirely different type of passport was an interesting form of diversification.

Having a second citizenship and the travel document that comes with it is an excellent way to diversify yourself so that you are never subject to only one government. It is possible to get a second passport for a lot less – or a lot more – than $45,000, and there are different ways to do it. There are also different reasons to get a second passport. For some, it is the first step to dramatically lowering their tax bill. For others, it is an insurance policy. For others still, it is a way to connect with long-lost ancestors. And for a select few of us, at some point it is just fun.

When the personal shopper at Dubai Mall's Zegna store asked what I was in town for, I told him I was completing a citizenship procedure. Knowing that it was practically impossible to become a citizen of the United Arab Emirates, he looked confused. Telling him the citizenship in question was the Comoros did not help the confusion, either.

The truth is that most people do not know about, let alone understand the reasons why someone would need a second passport, or even a second residence for that matter. Beyond the regular immigration requirements for travel visas and temporary residence permits, most people will never even think about such things. They do not need them for the kind of life they are living.

But not Nomad Capitalists.

Nomad Capitalists understand that there are multiple benefits that come with obtaining a second residence or citizenship and that these benefits are well worth the investments of time, money, travel, and work needed to plant flags in other countries as either a resident or citizen. So, let's dive into the finer details of second residencies and citizenships, examine the benefits of planting immigration flags around the world, and discuss how to get a second citizenship and build a passport portfolio to take you to the next level of international diversification.

The Why and What of Second Residencies and Passports

Passports used to be a simple tool of convenience. Rulers would give their subjects a set of papers to show to another ruler requesting their safe passage through their kingdom. One of the earliest passports was mentioned in Nehemiah in the Old Testament. Nehemiah was essentially a diplomat for King Artaxerxes on his way to rebuild the walls of Jerusalem. Upon his request to leave the kingdom, Artaxerxes gave Nehemiah a letter requesting safe passage from other rulers on his way to Judea.

In those days, passports were of a different nature. Rather than functioning as a document that determined whether a person could leave their country, they were requests from one king to the next soliciting safe passage for the individual in question through the foreign territory. Nehemiah received papers from his king requesting "governors of the province beyond the river" to grant him safe passage.

This letter, which came to be known as Safe Conduct, was the beginning of a tradition extending across centuries. The earliest true passport was authorized by the British Parliament, starting with the Safe Conduct Act under Henry V, and becoming more common in the 16th century. Back then, wandering around random lands as a foreigner could pose a great liability – you know, savages and all – so the Brits issued their citizens documents to prove their nationality should they decide to head farther afield.

Not all kingdoms were so open-minded. The Holy Roman Empire used the Diet of Augsburg to exile citizens who left the empire without proper travel documents. Medieval Europe issued scraps of paper to residents that listed the names of other towns that they were allowed to pass through, however this only applied to entering the city walls. Traders could enter via sea, as ports were considered trading hubs and business travel was encouraged.

Today, business travel is promoted only among certain countries, which is one reason to obtain a second passport. Nonetheless, very few circumstances used to exist by which overseas travelers were required to prove their identity or nationality when they arrived. While you might have been subject to whatever risks existed in a foreign land, it was not as if you had to show proper identification when you landed at LAX. Back in those days, you just showed up.

Now, passports are just another form of government identification – albeit a powerful one that dictates your freedom of movement. But passports are not the only factor at play when it comes to where you can go, how long you can stay in any one place, where you can invest and do business, and any number of other activities typical of a global citizen such as a Nomad Capitalist.

In the 21st century, the movement of people all around the world is regulated by everything from tourist visas to work permits to temporary and permanent residencies to citizenships and the passports that comes with them. Each immigration status grants varying degrees of privileges within the country in question. For instance, while a tourist visa will allow you to visit a country for a set number of days, you will likely need some form of residence and a work permit to perform any kind of work in that same country.

The highest level of rights (and responsibilities) is reserved for those who can claim a country's citizenship. And only those citizens who apply for and receive a passport will have the travel privileges that come with that document.

Nomad Capitalists can use this wide array of immigration options in countries all around the world to build an offshore strategy that will ensure that they have access to everything they need to live, invest, bank, and do business in the places where they will be treated best. In some cases, a second residence will provide all the benefits you need, while in others, citizenship and a second passport are the ultimate goal.

But before discussing the benefits of a second passport, it is important to understand how your first passport works. And if you do not have your home country's passport yet, make that your first action step as soon as you put down this book. In fact, put this book down right now and go schedule an appointment to get your passport. There is no use talking about becoming a Nomad Capitalist and getting a second residence or passport if you do not even have your first.

First, second, third, and even tenth passports all perform essentially the same function, even if some allow more privileges than others. The passport itself grants you travel privileges, while the underlying citizenship grants you the right to live, invest, work, own property, vote, and do business within the country.

But as important as your citizenship and passport are, their quality is often determined by a genetic lottery. You did not choose your first passport. You did not choose the social contract into which you were born. Whether it was the soil under your mother's feet at the time of your birth or the blood running through your veins, your first citizenship was decided by forces beyond your control.

With a second passport, you can choose your social contract. You can choose the kind of country and community you want to belong to, the tax system that dictates the government's claim to your money, the travel privileges that you will have as a passport holder, and so much more. In many cases, you can get these same benefits with the smaller commitment of a second residence instead of citizenship. And if it aids your long-term plan, that second residence can be your first step toward a second passport.

But I am getting ahead of myself. We will discuss the different ways you can get a second passport in just a moment. Right now, let's take a deeper look at the benefits of getting a second residency or citizenship and how each can play into a holistic offshore plan.

Your Plan B Citizenship Insurance

Obtaining another citizenship is all about diversification. It is an insurance policy against any number of adverse situations. For instance, if you only have one passport and your government takes it away, your right to travel will be removed entirely. But if you have a second passport, you can literally have a Plan B stored in your back pocket that will allow you to travel regardless of the limitations placed on you by your home country's government.

And there is more than one reason you might need a Plan B. Things could go downhill quickly in your home country, wealth taxes and other laws unfavorable to your asset protection could become a reality, worldwide taxation laws and foreign bank reporting regulations could make it almost impossible for you to live a life of freedom overseas, your government could limit your investment opportunities in cryptocurrencies or foreign markets, or they could start confiscating the property you own at home.

I am not a doom and gloom kind of guy, but I am a realist, and the fact of the matter is that all the things that I have mentioned have already happened in multiple western countries. A second passport allows you an escape hatch for when things at home get 'bad enough' – whatever that means to you. For some, things are already bad enough and they are looking for a way to renounce their home country citizenship as soon as possible and, therefore, need a Plan A. For others, they just want the Plan B in place as a form of citizenship insurance to give them peace of mind knowing that they have a way out if they want or need to take it. Whatever your position, a second passport gives you options.

You may think that if having one passport could hold you back, having two or more must mean you are really screwed. But it does not work that way. I liken having more than one passport to the trick most young children use to get what they want. When an eight-year-old wants something, he will ask the parent he thinks is more likely to approve the request. If mommy says no, he will ask daddy in hopes that he will say yes. If you have two passports, you can play the sovereign country equivalent of the mommy-daddy game within limits.

With only one passport, that one country is in charge. They can decide to take your assets or throw you in jail. They can do this because you technically have nowhere else to go; no other country has to let you in or provide you with assistance. With two passports, you not only have somewhere else to go but also an entire alternate legal system to fall back on to protect you, your money, and your assets.

This happened during the Arab Spring when well-prepared citizens had second residency and citizenship in another country, allowing them to leave Egypt or Syria and head for greener pastures where they were welcomed as legal residents and citizens. Those who did not have another passport were essentially sitting ducks at a time when no developed country was eager to take in fleeing Egyptians, even as tourists.

While you may think that madness of that nature is confined to the Middle East, I look at the problems that unfolded in the Arab Spring as possible anywhere. They say that bankruptcy happens slowly and then all at once; sticky situations like the Arab Spring happen the same way. Most people are not aware of what is bubbling beneath the surface until it is too late. If 2020 did not demonstrate to you how close these challenges are to home, it will likely be too late once you do realize the risk you are subjecting yourself to by not having a Plan B.

It is comfortable to think, "Oh, that would never happen here," but I suppose that even most people in secular Egypt felt that way… until they did not. And most people in the US had never faced travel restrictions until their powerful US passport was reduced to almost nothing for an extended period in 2020. I never thought I would see the day when a Serbian passport would allow for greater travel freedom than a US passport, but that day came. It just goes to show that nothing is off the table in the world we live in today.

When it comes to smart diversification, I often look to Chinese culture. I have met so many smart, pragmatic people during my times in China; their outlook on diversification mirrors that of Nomad Capitalists. One of my favorite stories was from a young man's grandfather who told him to, "Always have a second set of papers and some gold coins in a fast junk in the harbor."

Although I cannot remember how to tie a knot, pitch a tent, or shoot a bow and arrow, I do remember one thing as an Eagle Scout: be prepared. That is why I call a second passport 'citizenship insurance;' you may hope you never need it, but you will be prepared if you do. Remember, with only one citizenship, your life is completely in the hands of one group of (often unelected) government workers. They have carte blanche to tax you, help themselves to your assets, and restrict your freedom of movement around the world.

Having a second passport puts the power back in your hands by dividing that control between different governments and giving you the option to get rid of the one that serves you least if the need were ever to arise. In many cases, you do not even have to move anywhere to get one, and it can serve as a Plan B if nothing else. Having a second passport is the ultimate escape hatch no matter what happens, but it also allows you to live, work, and go to school in another country and gives you the ability to travel and increase your personal freedom.

Having more than one passport means that you always have a place to go. If you are a US citizen and think that things might get bad, being able to live in Panama whenever you want, without fear of being turned away, is a good thing to have.

I am not one to insist that UN tanks are coming to lock you away in a FEMA camp, but there may come a time when you simply do not feel safe in your home country. Sadly, the mass shootings, terrorist attacks, and civil unrest in the US and parts of Europe could make the case that these countries are already unsafe. For many, government response to the worldwide pandemic was enough to set off alarm bells that all is not well at home.

Buying an insurance policy is never fun; who wants to talk about a head-on collision? But protecting yourself from one, both personally and financially, is important if you drive a car. The same goes for citizenship insurance.

Your Door to the Best Real Estate

A second passport can give you more than just a Plan B – it can also increase your investment options. Citizenship often grants exclusive rights within a country. In many Asian countries, this means the ability to invest. In fact, outside of the Americas and Western Europe, most countries restrict foreign ownership of certain businesses, land, and even first floor apartments. If you have a passport, you can invest in the best, most profitable areas in a country.

For example, when I was in Laos, I met a young real estate broker named Alika who had started buying up land near the edge of the city center when she was 22 years old. Her family had a moderately successful business and had ascended to the middle class. Now, she wanted to take things to the next level.

Alika showed me several deals she had done where her real estate investments turned out to be highly profitable speculation thanks to developers who swooped in to buy her land as little as a few months after she bought it. A $5,000 piece of land was sold for $12,000 less than a year later, while larger parcels saw similar gains. Alika was making tens of thousands of dollars through little more than throwing a dart at the wall. Of course, dart throwing is not much of an investment strategy. Alika's winning strategy was in her genes: she was Laotian.

At the time, foreigners were not able to own land in Laos, which is still one of the five remaining officially communist countries in the world. Like China, Laos had opened to free market forces, but you were not welcome to invest unless you carried a Laos passport. Even if you prefer free markets, it is hard to argue with the built-in advantage of being able to buy up the best lands at a discount because wealthy foreigners are kept at bay.

However, in 2020, Laos eased foreign ownership restrictions to attract investment. There are still restrictions on what foreigners can by and Laos citizens are still at a dramatic advantage. But one thing is for sure, Alika is now making a killing on whatever land inventory she owns.

At first glance, it is hard to believe that holding a Laotian passport would add much value; visa-free travel on one gets you into a mere 50 countries. Outside of Southeast Asia's ASEAN economic area, your best travel options include Ecuador, Iran, and Tanzania.

However, a Laos passport is especially useful as a way to cash in on the country's development.

If Laos feels a bit premature – no doubt, the bad Wi-Fi there alone indicates it has a way to go – consider Cambodia next door. Like the expat-friendly Philippines, Cambodia allows foreigners to invest in apartments, but not ground floor apartments or homes. My friend, Reid Kirchenbauer, runs a boutique investment fund in Phnom Penh and does very, very well, but I imagine he could do even better if he could own commercial property or land as a citizen.

In fact, a while back, there was talk of a quasi-legitimate Cambodian passport whereby foreigners could donate $60,000 to the government in exchange for citizenship. They are now asking for a donation of $250,000 or an investment of at least $312,500. But at the cheaper price, some US citizens I know told me that this would be their citizenship insurance policy; I told them they were crazy. Traveling on a Cambodian passport would elicit plenty of unnecessary scrutiny. Cambodian citizenship is not insurance. What the government was really selling, I told them, was a ticket to invest in otherwise inaccessible property.

The only advantage Cambodian, Filipino, or Laotian citizens hold that stops foreigners from scooping up all their land is a travel document. If the government made that available to foreigners, there would be ample opportunity to make a profit.

Your Key to Business and Investment

A second passport also grants access to other business and investment opportunities that are unavailable to foreigners. It is not uncommon for Israeli citizens to obtain second citizenships to do business in Muslim majority countries. There is plenty of money to be made in Malaysia or Indonesia where Israelis are banned from entering, motivating many to get a second passport that will allow them in the country.

There is also a lot of money to be made in countries like the United Arab Emirates where Israelis are allowed entry but may be uncomfortable as Jews. Having another passport gives them an opportunity to sell their goods without intermediaries such as Cyprus getting involved.

In other situations, you cannot have access to certain opportunities unless you at least have a second residency in the country. Peer-to-peer lending services in the United States do alright, but for my money, Twino in the European Union is much more attractive. Twino offers yields starting at 12% for buying consumer paper, and in most cases, guarantees repayment. It is easy for them to do when some of these short-term loans are billed out at 40%; then again, they are doing all the work. The downside is that you cannot use Twino unless you are a resident of certain European Union countries. Similar crowd equity and crowd debt services require you to be a citizen of those countries as well.

Then there is the issue of restrictions based on the citizenship that you do have, not the one that you are lacking. The United States has made a big deal out of 'protecting' its investors by shutting off access to the majority of the world's mutual funds. There are ways to get access to these funds through offshore banks and brokerages, but to get full access to some of the best stock, real estate, cryptocurrencies, and private equity deals, you cannot be a US citizen.

Another disadvantage for American businesspeople is that it can affect your relationships (or potential for relationships) with foreign business partners. Thanks to laws like FATCA, just being American increases your chance of being rejected by banks or being refused a loan. Certain companies may not want to work with you altogether, meaning that any foreign business partner you may have will be taking on a built-in risk to their business by working with you. This can decrease your chances of finding and working with the best business partners. This is an issue that you can fix with a second passport.

Having a second passport can also ensure that you always have access to countries of interest. I had already planned a trip to Turkey when the United States and Turkey mutually denied visa services. Thankfully, I had a second passport with me and was able to enter Turkey as a citizen of another country. I was able to spend a lovely day in the country avoiding any problems that would have presented themselves to an American traveler.

Imagine if you needed access to a country for business purposes and your plans were derailed because your visa privileges were waived due to an international disagreement. Having visa-free access to Turkey taken away is a big deal for many businesspeople with connections in Istanbul. Having a second passport bypasses these issues and allows you to change your identity so that you can be the type of citizen that best serves your purposes.

Your Ticket to Tax Benefits

And then there are the taxes. Ever since there was citizenship, rulers used it to assess taxes from the beneficiaries of such citizenship. In the medieval Islamic Caliphate, passports were issued as a receipt for taxes paid. If you failed to pay the zakat, you were not allowed to travel.

We will cover all the ways to legally reduce or eliminate your tax bill with things like second passports and tax residencies later, but when it comes to citizenship, two countries' flocks are at a significant disadvantage. One of these countries is a former war-torn breakaway state on the Horn of Africa. The other is the United States.

Nestled in between the romantic vacation spots of Sudan and Djibouti, and a stone's throw from Somalia, the Eastern African republic of Eritrea broke away from Ethiopia in 1961 but spent thirty years fighting a bloody war for independence, then spent more years fighting in the late 1990s. Some borders are still a source of conflict, and small battles are still being waged.

With a GDP per capita of about $600, it is easy to imagine that Eritrea was not exactly flush with cash to pay its war tab that exceeded hundreds of millions of dollars. To pay the bill, the Eritrean government had a brilliant idea: impose a 2% tax on the Eritreans who had long gotten the hell out.

Many of the taxi drivers in San Diego, California are Eritrean citizens. In a rare sense of camaraderie, they can talk about the so-called 'diaspora tax' that they are subjected to with citizens from the only other country on earth that demands payment even if you do not live there: the United States.

By virtue only of their citizenship, US citizens are required to pay tax on their worldwide income no matter where they live or where their income is sourced. If you are a US citizen, you must pay taxes on that income to the United States. This concept, known as citizenship-based taxation, was more widely practiced in the past by primarily (then-) communist countries like the Soviet Union, Romania, and Vietnam. Nowadays, only two countries have the gall to make such a demand of their citizens: the US and Eritrea.

For some odd reason, though, a lot more people are afraid of Washington than they are of Eritrea. The Eritrean taxi drivers I have met did not seem too concerned about paying the 2% tax. Even if they do, well, it is 2%. Who cares, right? US citizens, on the other hand, are liable to pay tax on everything, at full market rates.

Let's say you are an employee living and working for a company in Dubai, earning a salary of $250,000. Dubai does not impose an income tax, so if you were anything but American, you would be off scot-free because no other country taxes you once you move out. As a US citizen, after certain exemptions that we will discuss later in the tax section of this book, it is possible you would still pay as much as $60,000 in various taxes on your salary, even if you never set foot back in the United States.

That is $60,000 this year, next year, and the year after that. After ten years, you would have paid $600,000, not to mention the opportunity cost of not being able to reinvest that money. The same goes for investors. Passive income, such as that from real estate investments, is only exempted if you pay tax overseas, meaning your entire rental portfolio or stock trading activity could be taxed from the first dollar.

So, how can a second citizenship help? This is the news that you may not want to hear: the only way to get around all these restrictions – the taxes, the bank account reporting, the FCPA, FATCA, OFAC, etc. – is to renounce your US citizenship. For US citizens, a second passport helps your tax situation only to the extent that you use it to renounce your first citizenship. You can be a citizen of the United States and 99 other countries, but so long as you are a US citizen, you will be subject to their laws. Think of it like the Spanish language rule that states that a group of one dude and 99 women will be referred to with the masculine tense – only, in this case, if you have 99 other passports and one US passport, you lose money and freedom.

One of the top reasons for having a second passport today is as an escape hatch from current or future tax burdens. It may not be 'patriotic' according to politicians, but it is your money, no matter how much they insist on taking it just because you carry their passport. If you are not benefiting from the roads, the schools, or the beloved airport security of the United States, why pay?

We will discuss the pros and cons and ins and outs of renouncing US citizenship in the next chapter, but the takeaway here is that if you have a second passport, you give yourself the option to renounce if you ever wanted to take that route. Without a second passport, that option is not on the table.

There are, however, legal ways to reduce your taxes without renouncing your US citizenship. You will not be able to eliminate them completely or relieve yourself of the US reporting burden, but you can use various international strategies involving everything from travel to offshore companies, and from second residencies to tax residencies and other tax incentives offered in places like Puerto Rico.

The interrelated nature of second residencies and passports with legal tax reduction is one reason I have long advocated for holistic offshore strategies. Everything must work together to achieve the results you want. You would be better off without the wrong citizenship or residency – despite the other benefits that they may provide – if they ultimately create complications and new tax obligations for you. So, stay tuned for the strategies we will cover in Section II to ensure that your second passport strategy works hand in hand with your tax strategy.

How to Obtain a Second Passport

Now that we have covered the benefits of having a second passport, the question remains: how do you get one? Outside of marrying a local, there are four ways to become a citizen of another country. Let's take a quick look at all of them and then dive into each one individually. The four methods are:

- **The "Lucky Sperm Club" Method:** One of my friends is a Swiss and German dual national by birth. She has the best of both worlds; the best EU passport with all the benefits of EU citizenship, and one of the best non-EU passports from a country whose motto is 'Don't piss anyone off.' Not everyone is so lucky. However, even if you were not born with a 'silver passport' in your mouth, there are other ways to take advantage of your family tree to obtain a second passport via your ancestors. This method is also known as citizenship by descent.

- **The "Sit Back and Relax" Method:** This is the method you are probably most familiar with. Whenever you see a group lined up like followers at a Sun Myung Moon service to become naturalized US citizens, that is the Sit Back and Relax method. Those folks started off as temporary residents of the United States, then became permanent residents and – after biding enough time – became eligible for naturalization upon meeting certain conditions. You can become a naturalized citizen of another country as well. The good news is that many countries do not require that you live on their soil full-time to qualify for naturalization. That, and the lower cost of this approach, make it the most popular method for many passport seekers.

- **The "Pay your Way In" Method:** If sitting back and waiting is not your thing, you can speed up the process for a fee. While countries like the United States or Norway are not so gauche and uncivilized to just hand over a passport in exchange for a bag of cash, other countries are not repulsed by the idea. It is possible to gain citizenship in as little as two to three months by making a donation or large investment in a country that allows it. This method is also known as citizenship by investment or economic citizenship.

- **The "Fonzie" Method:** Are you cool enough to have the president of a small country recognize your skills? If you are a star athlete, artist, or even an investor, there are countries where the president or congress can waive naturalization requirements just for you. This method is also known as exceptional citizenship.

Now, let's take a closer look at how each of these four methods work and how each one could factor into a holistic offshore plan.

The "Lucky Sperm Club" Method:
Citizenship by Descent

If you are fortunate enough to have relatives from certain countries, your days of passport seeking may be relatively short. As mentioned, the formal name for this process is 'citizenship by descent' and involves obtaining citizenship through your family tree. The idea is that if a family member had citizenship but you do not, you have been deprived of your rights to citizenship and should be able to reclaim them.

Sadly, the process is not always easy, and byzantine rules often make it hard to even find out if you qualify. As opposed to the other methods of obtaining citizenship – where qualifying is hard, but the process is easy – qualifying for an ancestral passport is quite easy once you have waded through a swamp of bureaucracy that can often take years.

As obvious as it sounds, the easiest place to look to see if you qualify is to your parents, as most countries automatically grant citizenship to children, including adopted ones. I have known some US citizens who had one Canadian parent and had never applied for Canadian citizenship. Ditto with jolly 'ole England. If one of your parents has a different citizenship, you can probably get it as well, unless that country (or your existing one) forbids dual nationality.

If your parents do not yield any assistance, the next step is to check your grandparents and great-grandparents. Most countries allow you to go back two generations and occasionally three. Others allow you to go back to a certain event, such as the founding of Lithuania as a country in its current form. If you have an ancestor who left Lithuania after 1940 and never gave up their Lithuanian citizenship, you qualify to be Lithuanian. The same goes for Italy after 1918.

As of 2021, Armenia, Austria, Belgium, Cyprus, Denmark, Estonia, Finland, France, Germany, Iceland, Liechtenstein, Netherlands, Sweden, and Switzerland all grant citizenship by descent back one generation. Bosnia, Croatia, Czech Republic, Greece, Malta, Portugal, Romania, Slovenia, and Spain, all allow individuals with grandparents to apply for citizenship on the strict basis of being within two generations of one of their citizens. And Bulgaria, Hungary, Ireland, Italy, Latvia, Lithuania, Luxembourg, Poland (legislation pending), and Serbia will allow you to go back three full generations, some of them even farther. These programs do not always last forever, though, meaning that this list will likely change.

Most citizenship by descent programs are in European countries, perhaps because all European countries award citizenship 'of the blood' rather than 'of the soil.' As part of the Old World, they believe that your family should be the source of your citizenship; that is why children born in Europe to foreigners do not become European citizens the way children born in the US or Canada become citizens based on their birthplace, hence 'of the soil.'

However, if your ancestry is of New World stock, there is one option: Spain allows natural-born citizens of Hispanic countries to apply for Spanish citizenship if they live there for two years. If you are a natural born citizen of a Spanish-speaking Central or South American country, or the Philippines, chances are you qualify to gain residence in Spain and then to apply for a Spanish passport.

While the process is easy, do not bother. Living in Spain might be romantic, but you will be subject to Spanish tax for the two years you are there. To make matters worse, the people I know who have followed this route have lived there for two years, then needed another two years just to get an appointment, then almost another two years for the citizenship to be approved. In those six years, you could have obtained another European citizenship – or many others – in a more advantageous place and avoided the Spanish taxes.

Therein lies the challenge of citizenship by descent: money versus time. If you have all the time in the world and obtaining Italian citizenship will help you feel closer to Uncle Giuseppe, by all means, do it. I feel closest to my Norwegian and Lithuanian heritage and would be proud to have these passports, so I get the hobby aspect of it. But if you are seeking a second citizenship for economic reasons, you will probably be better served finding an alternative method. Even if you hire a local on the ground in that country to help you, you will still be doing a lot of the work in most cases – and all the waiting.

That is, unless your grandfather's name started with "O'" or "Mc". Ireland has a very open policy of granting citizenship to those whose family tree includes ancestors from the country. In fact, there are 10 million non-resident Irish passport holders taking advantage of dual citizenship from the Emerald Isle. The process is the most efficient citizenship by descent program on the market. You simply need to find your ancestors' records in the Birth Register and fill out some forms.

Which brings us to a more practical question: what exactly do you need to do to get citizenship by descent? No, you will not need a DNA kit. And even if you have one, that is not the kind of evidence that these countries are looking for. They want documentation – a paper trail that starts with you and leads all the way back to the ancestor who will qualify you for citizenship.

Each country will have different paperwork requirements and rules about how far back you can go. Some will require that the citizenship lineage be uninterrupted. For instance, if Grandma Helen had Polish citizenship and moved to the US where she gave birth to your father who never became a Polish citizen, you would not qualify. In some countries, you may be able to work around this rule by convincing your father to get his citizenship by descent first so that you could then lay claim to yours, but not every country allows for that kind of maneuvering.

Once you understand the rules of the country in question, you can quickly determine whether you have a fighting chance at qualifying. You can start by sitting down with Uncle Joe and Aunt Martha, talking to your parents, and calling up your grandma to explore the potential within your family tree. If you believe your lineage will work in your favor, the next step is to hammer out the story and start building the paper trail that will establish your connection to your ancestors.

If Aunt Martha has the documents that will prove your case stored in an old filing box in the attic, you are already one step closer to your second passport. If not, you can search through old church records, government documents, and even graveyards from the comfort of your home using online family history databases.

Every country's program is different, but most will require your birth certificate and passport, the birth certificates of your ancestors, and any related marriage, divorce, naturalization, and death certificates. Each document will need to be authenticated and written in the country's language or translated. When everything is in order, you can pay the very reasonable fee (anywhere from $5 to $400 depending on the country) and submit your application with all the supporting documentation.

And then you wait. How long? It could be weeks, months, or even years before you get an answer. Some countries have a straightforward system that will produce an answer within 6-12 months. Others have a web of bureaucracy that means your citizenship by descent – or your rejection letter – could be coming down the pipeline in two years' time. During this time, the officials may also reach out for more documentation. But if you are prepared for some back and forth and can deal with the mess of bureaucracy, you can eventually get that second passport.

We have helped many clients get citizenship in over two dozen different countries and I personally helped my wife through the process of becoming an Armenian citizen by descent. It is a time-intensive process that requires a lot of paperwork and patience, but it is an incredible feeling at the end when you hand over a few dollars and get a passport in return.

But should you get every passport you are eligible for just because you qualify? If you are a US citizen and your father is Canadian and your great grandmother was Irish, should you pursue both Canadian and Irish citizenship? In most cases, the answer is yes. Just be sure you weigh up the risks. What system of taxation does each country use? What laws have they considered introducing? Would you have any travel restrictions with this passport? Most ancestral passports do not come with a lot of risks but take a minute to consider them.

You will also need to determine whether your new country of citizenship will allow for dual citizenship and – if the need were to arise – the right to renounce. Countries like Argentina do not allow renunciation. As a Nomad, you should want a way out if circumstances were to change and a citizenship no longer worked for you. With any citizenship you acquire, you need to be aware of the terms and ensure that you can maintain control over your freedom and wealth.

The "Sit Back and Relax" Method: Naturalization

For many people, the most cost-efficient and straightforward way to obtain a second citizenship is by first obtaining residency in another country. Getting a second residence is – hands down – the most popular service that we offer our clients, largely because it is one of the easiest and quickest steps you can take to legally lower your taxes, diversify and plant flags, access new investment markets, give yourself a place to call home overseas, and plant the seeds of citizenship.

In and of itself, a second residence is merely the legal right to live in a country on a long-term basis. How long depends on whether your residence permit is temporary or permanent. In most cases, temporary residence is the first step toward permanent residence, which is a steppingstone to naturalization, if that is what you want.

Most of us are used to the old school way of naturalization: get a residence permit and move to a new country, put all your eggs in that basket, pay taxes, learn the language, and wait. There is nothing wrong with this approach, and a lot of people are still doing it. Back in the 1990's, my parents planned to do just that by selling our house, cars, and furniture, leaving a few bucks in US banks, and moving everything else to New Zealand.

But you do not have to do this to get a second citizenship with the Sit Back and Relax method. There are many countries that allow you to turn an ordinary residence permit into citizenship after a period through naturalization, all while spending as little as one day a year there, exempting you from the tax obligations that would apply if you were to move your whole life to the new country.

In 2012, Panama unveiled its Friendly Nations Visa program, through which it allowed citizens of fifty countries to become an instant permanent resident by tossing $5,000 into a Panamanian bank account and paying lip service to doing business or investing there. While the program has since been discontinued, the residence permit required only one or two days in the country each year to remain active. If you met the requirement, you would be eligible to apply for citizenship after five years. This meant that you could ostensibly become a citizen of a country in which you had spent the equivalent of an extended weekend vacation.

If you do not mind roughing it a bit more, the South American nation of Paraguay allows you to become a citizen after three years, with a requirement to spend just one day per year in the country. You will need to learn some Spanish and have knowledge of Paraguayan culture, but that is about it. They may scrutinize your citizenship application with much more caution these days than in the past, but the country has welcomed immigrants for as long as anyone can remember and is happy to accept westerners with open arms.

Whether you prefer Latin America or Europe (African and Asian countries do not generally naturalize foreigners, at least with any ease), there are a number of countries that will only require you to spend anywhere from one day to a few months a year on their soil to maintain eligibility for citizenship. And outside of the European Union, it is often possible to live in these countries part-time and avoid paying much (if any) tax while still running the clock and eventually qualifying for citizenship.

Why and How to Get a Second Residence

There are many reasons why you may want to get a second residence beyond the possibility of citizenship via naturalization. For one, it is the easiest way for an expat to ensure that they will be able to live in the country. Sure, you can visit as a tourist for a set number of days each year, but if you want guaranteed entrance and no limitations on how long you can stay, you will need a residence permit.

In 2020, many countries closed their borders to everyone except for citizens and residents. So, even if you do not plan to set up your whole life there, a second residence will give you quick, almost-guaranteed access to another country if you ever need to leave your current location. And no matter what is going on in the world at the time, it is nice to know that you can take as many vacations as you want to your country of residence without being asked why you are there.

Like a second passport, a second residence will allow you to diversify both politically and economically. In a country like Colombia, you could tackle three separate aspects of a holistic offshore strategy just by applying for a second residence. Not only will you obtain a residence permit, but you will also invest in one of my favorite real estate markets and set yourself up for a second citizenship. This will allow you to diversify your assets (economic diversification) while also giving you a place to go no matter what is going on in the world (political diversification).

In Armenia, you could invest in bonds or deposit money in a bank account and get residence along with lifestyle and tax benefits. In Asia, while there may not be a path to naturalization, you can get a residence that will grant you access to local investment markets and plenty of lifestyle perks. In other countries, you could get a residence for setting up a business and get tax benefits for your company on top of a path to citizenship for yourself. And with each one of these investments into different countries you will gain currency diversification and asset protection.

It is the ultimate two-for-one: a second residence accompanied by all the benefits of international investments, not to mention the tax planning options that you will create for yourself. And while some residence programs will never lead to citizenship, if you play your cards right, you can get all those benefits while sitting back, relaxing, and qualifying for citizenship via naturalization.

So, how do you go about qualifying for a second residence? As with all things, your options will vary by country. In general, you can get a residence permit in most countries for one of the following reasons:

1. Family Reunification: Governments will grant residence to reunite children, parents, spouses, and legal partners, and in some cases siblings, grandparents, and even nephews and nieces.

2. Marriage: Many countries have a separate residence process for fiancés and spouses of local citizens.

3. Business: Known as an entrepreneur or business visa, you can get residence in many countries simply for starting a business there, hiring staff in the country, or investing in a local company.

4. Investment: Residence by investment programs such as Europe's Golden Visas will qualify you for a residence permit if you make an investment in real estate, bonds, or other pre-approved projects and funds set out by the government.

5. Bank Deposit: In some countries, all you have to do is open a local bank account and transfer a certain amount of money and they will give you a residence permit.

6. Retirement: If you are past a given age and can prove that you have a monthly income or pension, you can get a retirement visa that will allow you to live in the country as a resident.

7. Self-Sufficiency: Other countries remove the age limitation and will give you a residence permit as long as you can prove that you can sustain yourself with outside funds while living in the country.

With each approach, there will be documentation to submit and application forms to fill out. In some cases, you will only be given temporary residence, in others you will be granted immediate permanent residence. The timeline to citizenship and qualifying factors for naturalization will be different for every country, too, and the rules may vary even within one country depending on how you obtained your residence.

But one way or another, you can get a second residence in another country (or multiple countries) and begin working toward naturalization. And in many cases, that work really translates into sitting back and relaxing wherever you please until you have filled the time quota that qualifies you to apply for citizenship.

The Challenges of Naturalization

You will likely confront several challenges when seeking to use the Sit Back and Relax method to obtain citizenship via naturalization. The first of these is the time risk; the risk that some politician will decide to change the laws either in letter or in spirit before you get the chance to apply for citizenship. I know a couple that has lived in Panama for fifteen years (ten years longer than the stated requirement for citizenship), yet their naturalization request remains on the president's desk, unsigned.

The government can change the rules at any time, from lengthening the number of years before you can apply, to requiring you to learn the language, to practically whatever they want. Then there are the de facto rejections such as my friends' experience in Panama, where nothing in the law changed, but bureaucrats have decided to sit on their hands rather than issue formal denials. That is why, as with any other aspect of a Nomad Capitalist strategy, it is important to find a trustworthy country to which you can hitch your citizenship wagon.

My experience with lawyers in Latin America has been rather underwhelming. I do work with several good lawyers there, but if you try to find one without a lot of trial and error, you will probably do poorly. I flew to El Salvador to meet with a lawyer I had known for a while, and he could barely be bothered to show up to get started. Then, he literally could not handle the trouble of taking my money.

On another occasion, I learned that the first lesson of doing business in Latin countries is to never pay more than asked. While that sounds obvious, many lawyers will ask you to pay half upfront and half when the work is done. Quite frankly, I find this to be a deterrent to the client because they are less invested in the process; the lawyer cannot finish the work without the client's cooperation.

Not wanting to send two wire transfers, I paid a Nicaraguan lawyer in full upfront, only to hear nothing but blustering and accusations when I asked what was happening. It was the one time I gave up on a process and cut my losses. My Nicaraguan friends told me that the lawyer would have been motivated had the carrot of more greenbacks been dangling over his head.

You can see why, as a guy who does this stuff, I decided to hang out a shingle and help a few people figure out which passport program is best for them, and how to do it. Dealing with lawyers on the other side of the world can be confusing.

And then there is the issue of scams. The term 'second passport' is a bit of a misnomer because, while having the actual travel document itself is important, it is the underlying citizenship that matters most. And there are all too many people who are willing to take illegal measures just to become a citizen of another country.

Walk outside of the immigration offices in Chisinau, Moldova, and you are sure to find 'fixers' willing to dummy up some papers that make you look Romanian for about $1,500. This practice started when Romania joined the European Union and offered citizenship to Moldovans with Romanian ancestors. Considering that Moldova was a part of Romania until the mid-20th century, almost all Moldovans qualify. And, since Moldova is the poorest country in Europe, the number of people interested in the privileges of EU citizenship via Romania is also almost all Moldovans.

Now, Moldova may be known for many inexpensive things – including fantastic $15 bottles of wine – but considering the price tag for even the cheapest economic passports, $1,500 is too cheap to be legitimate. Add to that the fact that Moldova is not known for stringent regulations and the probability of a scam goes up.

You would think that a country where almost anything goes would not be the unhappiest country in the world, but somehow it is. And that means that the same person who will help an ethnic Romanian find his grandfather's birth certificate might also help a blond-haired, blue-eyed, never-believable-as-a-Romanian guy like me fake some papers. Do not be tempted, though. This is clearly a bad idea. These types of scams never end up well and could subject you to fraud charges and potentially time in jail.

Even if you are not planning on trolling outside of Moldovan government buildings in the hopes of obtaining fake birth certificates, the risk of scams is still real. If getting Panamanian citizenship in five years is a deal worth going for, then getting it in five weeks must be amazing... right? No deal. The internet is littered with illegitimate organizations offering to speed up the citizenship process, not only in countries that do offer programs but also in places where citizenship is not even possible.

One website proclaims that "If it's really urgent, your Panama passport can be rushed within six weeks." How do you think the same government that takes a year to issue a permit to replace a toilet can give someone a citizenship so quickly? With someone on the inside, of course. An entire cottage industry exists where dudes in aviator sunglasses (do scammy dudes wear anything else?) work with corrupt bureaucrats to get blank passports left on the remainder tray that they can then snatch up and slap on anyone's photo.

Good luck trying to use this to do any real travel anywhere, and heaven forbid you renounce your US citizenship confident in that Venezuelan passport you got without even going there – unless the idea of a Caracas prison sounds good to you. So, what do you do if you want a fast second passport but do not want to bribe a prison guard for a fresh arepa? You pay up.

The "Pay Your Way In" Method:
Citizenship by Investment

In a small but growing number of largely tax-friendly, leave-you-alone type of countries, there is a legal market for citizenship that you can buy and obtain in as little as two months. Economic citizenship – also knowns as citizenship by investment – is the practice whereby wealthy foreigners exchange cash for passports.

The modern-day version of economic citizenship began in 1984 when the two-island Caribbean nation of St. Kitts and Nevis decided to offer a fast track to citizenship to those willing to make an investment in the country. For years, they were one of the only games in town, but more recently, a whole new crop of countries has started offering citizenship in wake of the financial crisis.

Interestingly, even as supply has increased as more countries begin to offer economic citizenship, the prices have gone up. There are so many wealthy people in emerging markets tired of waiting in visa lines to go to Europe that supply cannot keep up with demand.

Conversely, some countries have shut their programs down under pressure from big western governments that resent such programs. The English-speaking Central American nation of Belize, whose banks and government have long been a punching bag for the US government, used to offer Belizean citizenship for a mere $40,000 until the early 2000s. After 9/11, the US government applied pressure on them to stop the practice.

While $40,000 was a relatively normal price at the time, by today's standards, it was downright cheap; the right to live full-time on various Caribbean islands tax-free, and to spend up to 180 days per year in London, was an enviable proposition at that price. An even sweeter deal was in Peru. A 1993 article in the New York Times spoke of the South American country's hush hush practice of offering Peruvian nationality for a mere $25,000. Again, the deal might have been more attractive as a lark back then, but by today's standards, it would have been a solid growth investment. In 2015, Peruvians were granted visa-free access to the European Union, and the growing Mercosur Union in South America makes citizenship there even more attractive now.

Today, more people than ever are looking at having a second passport, but the conditions for approval are getting tighter and the price tag is getting higher. At the time I received my Comoros passport, it was far and away the cheapest offer at a mere $45,000. But even if the program were still running, I would not recommend Comorian citizenship to most people. My purposes in obtaining a passport from the Comoros Islands were unique. I do not suggest that anyone renounce their US citizenship having the Comorian passport as their only other travel document, no matter how much tax they were paying.

The Comoros Islands does, however, offer excellent visa-free access to parts of Asia that some other mediocre passports do not, and I suspect that the African Union will expand the privilege of visiting all 54 African countries from just diplomats to ordinary passport holders within the next few years. Since first obtaining the passport, my visa-free access has gone from 47 countries to 53. It is not a big increase, but there is an upward trajectory. If you are like me and want to visit every country on earth Jim Rogers style, having an African passport will save you a lot of time otherwise spent in visa offices.

If being the citizen of an Arabic country with rather poor travel opportunities does not sound like the kind of diversification you are looking for, then Dominica and St. Lucia in the Caribbean are the next cheapest programs at $100,000 each. I initially applied for Dominica's citizenship by investment program but being outside of my country of birth made the process more challenging. I learned from that experience that it is often better to start and complete the economic passport process before you leave your home country. I eventually went through the process to become a citizen of St. Lucia, instead, and have been very happy with that decision. I even added my wife as a dependent a year after receiving my own St. Lucian passport.

The decision you must make when considering the more stable economic citizenship programs is whether you want to merely donate money to a government fund that helps sugar farmers or other development projects, or whether you want to invest that money and potentially see it again someday. In many cases, the investments offered are pretty weak and it is better to make the donation. That means that anyone seriously looking at economic citizenship as a true second passport should be ready to shell out at least $100,000 plus legal fees.

Due to devastating hurricane damage, increased competition, and a worldwide pandemic, all five Caribbean countries offering citizenship by investment are now quite competitively priced, with no donation requirement exceeding $200,000.

You can spend or invest even more – around $1 million in Malta, for instance – to get European Union citizenship in as little as one year. However, just as everything else about the EU is more bureaucratic, so is their citizenship by investment process. It is worth considering if your current passport is of poor quality, but even then, there might be better ways to go about it. Unless, that is, you are a Chinese citizen and merely trying to impress your friends back on the mainland.

But as far as citizenship by investment is concerned, you can pay as little as $100,000 to buy a get out of jail free card from one of two things: paying taxes in your home country by giving up your current citizenship or living in your home country whose passport gives you limited travel options.

There is nothing illegal or even immoral about doing this; Tina Turner rescinded her US citizenship when she was granted Swiss citizenship. The big media event, though, was Eduardo Saverin, who was born in Brazil and naturalized as a US citizen at a young age. Saverin gave up his US citizenship after paying a boat load in taxes, but before paying an even bigger boat load in taxes.

Of course, typical politicians like Chuck Schumer did not like Saverin's choice and branded him a 'traitor,' but hey, the guy was not even born in the United States. And why pay hundreds of millions of dollars in capital gains taxes to a country you do not live in when all you want to do is make investments and pick up Asian girls at exclusive clubs in Singapore?

Eduardo Saverin already had Brazilian citizenship to fall back on, but if you do not, a passport from Dominica followed by renouncing your country's citizenship could absolve you of future taxes earned from your business, your job, or your investments. I know guys working far from home, making $1 million a year who still have to pay $400,000 of those earnings to the United States. If that sounds like you, the ROI on an economic citizenship could be excellent.

The "Fonzie" Method:
Exceptional Citizenship

But what if you do not have a lucky family tree, do not want to wait, and do not have at least $100K burning a hole in your pocket?

Just ask Sergiu Toma.

While Toma has a law degree, his true passion is judo. In fact, he has appeared at three Olympic games, including the 2016 Summer Games in Rio de Janeiro where he proudly represented the United Arab Emirates. He ultimately won the bronze medal in the 81-kilogram judo contest, earning the Emirates their second Olympic medal in history.

If Sergiu does not sound like an Arab name, that is because it is not. Sergiu Toma is Moldovan by birth (and, from what I can tell, does not have a Romanian passport.) His first two Olympic appearances were on behalf of his native Moldova. However, seeking to raise its profile on the global stage, the United Arab Emirates handed out passports to Olympians who the country felt could bring home some medals and Sergiu Toma gladly accepted to compete for the UAE in exchange for citizenship.

Such is the concept of 'exceptional citizenship,' whereby governments issue citizenship to individuals based on promised contributions to the country, or contributions already made. It happens more than you might expect. Small countries like the UAE, Qatar, Singapore, and others that want to be players in the world sport and creative culture are willing to dole out passports to those who can get them their desired result.

Even if your athletic skills have you relegated to rookie ball in the United States, those skills might be exactly what some dusty country in the Middle East needs. The same goes for artists. Singapore is not exactly known as an artsy place these days, mainly because of its many skyscrapers filled with boring bankers. When I told a couple of female Russian bankers who I met sipping mojitos on Marina Bay that I always envied the idea of a banker's office looking out from up high, they laughed and said they kept their window shade closed. They dreamed of living the Nomad Capitalist lifestyle because, despite the alleged glamour of working in a skyscraper surrounded by luxury, they preferred flying to Cambodia, staying at The Plantation, and doing real banking in comparison to the jobs they had filling out forms.

Singapore is well aware of its stereotype as a city full of boring professionals and – already filthy rich – is doing what other wealthy individuals do: class their joint up. Just as the guys who celebrated selling YouTube to Google at TGI Friday's might decide to go on an art-buying spree to join adulthood, countries like Singapore already have enough money and want to diversify into stuff that gets them press in the cultural world. Particularly in Singapore, famous artists, sportsmen, and performers may be eligible to receive residency or even citizenship if their skills are internationally recognized.

While Singapore and Dubai are cosmopolitan cities that half the world would be happy to live in, they are not necessarily looking for more businesspeople and investors to populate their tiny empires. But that does not mean that other countries are not looking for individuals who are ready to do business. Many governments are eager to offer exceptional citizenship to folks with skills in business and investment. These countries turn the tables so that, rather than Moldovans getting UAE citizenship to compete in the Olympics, UAE citizens become Moldovan in exchange for building up the Moldovan economy.

This is the way that we boring business types – unable to pole vault or compose a concerto – can obtain exceptional citizenship for contributing to another country. Instead of adding to the art and sports scene of Singapore, we can help create the next Singapores of the world. While the UAE and Singapore concern themselves with fielding world-class Olympic teams funded by the oil and bank money pouring into their debt-free countries, places like Moldova and Georgia focus on building their economies. To do that, they do not need Olympic athletes or famous artists, they need you. And you can use that need to work your way towards a second citizenship.

Countries like Montenegro, for example, have issues with unemployment and need savvy investors to come help build their economy. As we will discuss in more detail later, Montenegro is one of a number of formerly troubled countries that has opened its doors to investors with low tax rates and a winning smile. But not many people know about the country, and it has not found a way to achieve the reputation some western countries have as being an ideal place to invest, even if it is.

That is where offering citizenship comes in. Right now, a group of foreign investors is building a brand-new Westin hotel in Montenegro's north county. While it does not take much to attract investment along the gorgeous Adriatic coast, the North has been overlooked despite its excellent ski resorts (after all, Montenegro's local name is 'Crna Gora,' meaning 'black mountain').

The company arranging that hotel is in the business of working with Chinese, Russians, and Arabs to grant citizenship to investors, and I am confident that the guys building the hotel are about to be handed shiny Montenegrin passports, complete with the ability to spend just as much time visiting Europe visa-free as Americans, Canadians, and Australians.

Invest money, provide jobs, get a passport. It is a simple concept, and one not every country offers. Austria, which is often touted as 'selling citizenship,' has made a tiny number of exceptions for people who are not only willing to invest to the tune of €10 million or above but who also look 'Austrian enough' so as not to offend anyone's sensibilities.

Unlike citizenship by investment that has a streamlined application process that anyone can use, these exceptional citizenship programs are a series of negotiations with the country. I am aware of about a dozen countries that formally give power to waive naturalization requirements to a high-ranking body such as the president or the congress. These are the best countries to work with because there is no doubt of the legality of the citizenship that comes from the authorized party. In the same way the President of the United States can pardon anyone he wants without the ability to undo his decision later, certain countries allow for the government to make you a citizen for life for any reason they want.

Exceptional citizenship is a particularly effective way to get a second passport if you already plan to invest in an emerging market. If your investing comfort zone ends at New Jersey, you are probably out of luck; countries like the United States, or those in the European Union, do not need to dole out passports. Everyone from mom and pop to crooked foreign dictators are already lining up to invest in property in those places. If you want an exceptional citizenship and you are not the next Da Vinci, you will need to look to countries that need what you offer, which are often the countries that supply 'Tier B' passports.

How to Create a Passport Portfolio

There is this notion that being the citizen of a wealthy western country means that the red carpet is rolled out for you anywhere you go. Indeed, US citizens can visit 185 countries and territories without the need for a visa, whether by obtaining a visa upon arrival (often for a fee) or by obtaining an e-visa online (usually an easy process designed to get $50 out of you). By those standards, the US passport is one of the best in the world; it shares the top ten list with a bunch of Western European countries, wealthy Asian and Oceanic countries, and even Malaysia.

However, numbers on a fancy table do not always tell the whole story. Just because you are entitled to visit a country on paper does not mean it always happens in practice. I have experienced several delays, albeit no outright refusals, even when traveling on a US passport. Perhaps the most daunting was on a visit to London.

"What did you say you're here for again?" the immigration officer asked me as he balanced a scowl with a sense of hubris. (As if there is any other sort of immigration officer.)

"Tourism," I replied. Always a good answer.

Undeterred, the officer asked me to be more specific. When I explained that I was meeting my friend and girlfriend and had originally made plans to see the new James Bond movie before its launch date changed, he interrupted that those were not the details he was looking for.

In the forty-five minutes I spent waiting at his desk, the guy did everything nasty short of throw a handful of mushy peas at me, from commandeering my phone to asking me to rattle off the phone numbers of everyone I knew 'back home.'

Just as I was about to tell him that the War of 1812 was not my fault and I could find another cold, damp country to visit, he stamped my passport and allowed me entry. Either this guy was having a bad day, or the last US citizen he dealt with tried to light the explosives in her bra on fire in the customs hall.

It goes to show that a little diversification cannot hurt.

But how much diversification do you need? Is a second passport enough? Or should you aim to have three or four? I know one guy who has eight passports, and I have often joked about how you could set your kid up to have 14 passports by the age of 30 if you planned their life out just right, starting with where you give birth.

Beyond any other benefit I have already mentioned, getting a second passport also happens to be pretty cool, which is why I caution people to remember why they want one (for some people, 'it's cool' is reason enough). But you do not need to be a passport collector, live the life of a James Bond or Jason Bourne, or even geek out about second citizenships the way I do to benefit from building a portfolio of passports.

Just as a regular investor would create a diversified portfolio of investments ranging from stocks to real estate to gold, a Nomad Capitalist will not only invest in various asset classes around the world but also in different types of passports to build a robust and diversified passport portfolio.

If getting a second passport is all about diversifying away from your first citizenship, then getting a third passport should be about diversifying away from both the first and second passport. Each new passport you add to your portfolio will add another layer of diversification and benefits. You can diversify in different ways, from filling travel gaps to establishing geopolitical balance and government diversity, and from securing access to natural resources to ensuring your safety and even collecting different citizenship types.

For instance, you could replace US passport-level travel with a combination of passports that have visa-free access to different countries. Any economic citizenship from the Caribbean will give you access to Europe's Schengen Area and most of Latin America. Then, you could fill in the travel gaps left from that passport with an Armenian passport that may not have access to a lot of countries but – thanks to proximity – will give you access to all the countries in its surrounding region such as Georgia, Ukraine, Iran, Russia, and all the 'stan' countries.

Having passports from different parts of the world can fill travel gaps thanks to the proximity game. It may also help you establish geopolitical balance. Getting two economic citizenships from the Caribbean is not going to give you much diversification when it comes to travel benefits, geography, geopolitics, or government power. But getting one passport from the Caribbean with a more western facing government along with one from a country that is more pro-Russia, pro-China, or neutral will give you greater geopolitical diversification.

As a diversification play, being British and getting Belgian citizenship is a lateral move – few new benefits, but all the same problems. On the other hand, being American and becoming Paraguayan is real diversification; you get visa-free travel to most of the same countries, plus some new ones, no tax obligations, and the anonymity of being from a place few people could spell, let alone find on a map.

As a safe haven, the countries in the world like Paraguay are perfect for western citizens who want a second passport as insurance from high taxes, tough regulations, and general government craziness. For Chinese citizens who cannot go anywhere with their passport, paying some tax to live in London is not much of a price to pay to escape tainted beef and sucking down the equivalent of a coal factory into the old lungs every day. The right second passport depends greatly on the citizenship you already hold.

On the same note, consider adding passports to your portfolio that come from countries of different sizes, levels of development, and government. Look at the stability of the different governments that back up your passports. Consider whether they will largely leave you alone and allow you the privacy you are seeking or if they pose the risk of canceling your passport or creating tax complications for you in the future. If you already have a passport from a big country, get a second passport from a smaller country. And if you come from a small country, go for a bigger country or something in between.

I also like to look at the different natural resources available in each country. Is there access to fresh water? Oil? Grazing lands and livestock? Factoring natural resources into your passport portfolio will give you better access to valuable commodities for personal use and business or investment opportunities down the line.

You may also want to include countries in the southern hemisphere with stable governments that are far away from everything else. In a time of crisis, you do not want to be competing with hordes of people trying to get into a country. If you have guaranteed access to an isolated country, you will likely avoid the worst of the diseases, civil unrest, crime, and panicked masses looking to escape disaster.

And last of all, look to build a portfolio of passports acquired in as many ways as possible: descent, investment, marriage, birth, exceptional citizenship, naturalization, and more. Each process has its own timeline to citizenship, so you can start the clock ticking toward naturalization in one country while waiting to hear back about your citizenship by descent and then buy an instant passport from a country offering citizenship by investment. One of these passports might not work out in the end, but there is a good chance that at least one of them will.

Secure Your Right to Dual Citizenship

As you are building your passport portfolio, you will need to ensure that each country you add to your collection will not restrict your ability to keep the passports you already have or limit the number of new passports you can add in the future. It is crucial that you understand that not all countries allow dual citizenship.

Most people do not worry themselves with understanding the many ways that they can obtain a second passport. Many have never even asked if it is possible to hold dual or multiple citizenship. And for those who have asked, they have likely encountered a lot of misinformation on the topic. Many US citizens have errantly told me that they will lose their citizenship if they get another passport.

In many cases, the answer to the question of whether dual nationality is possible is, "Yes." However, depending on your current citizenship and how you obtained it, there may be some complications. The general trend in the world is toward dual citizenship. Since the turn of the century, a number of countries have amended their laws to allow their citizens to hold other nationalities as well. This is good news, and even a bit surprising, as many of the countries loosening their nationality laws are bankrupt and may need people to pay the bills later.

Only a handful of well-known countries outright forbid dual citizenship these days. Among those, some are well-known for looking the other way or simply not having the resources to police their citizens who obtain other passports. I met several people in Malaysia who had a family member – usually a child who had studied and worked abroad – that held Malaysian and British citizenship. Since the British government, like most others, is not in the habit of broadcasting its citizen rolls, no one in Malaysia knew the wiser. The only case where someone got dressed down was when he mistakenly entered Malaysia on his British passport.

As of 2021, there are over 50 countries that explicitly forbid dual nationality. Many are in Africa and Asia, but some that may be of interest to Nomad Capitalists include Austria, Andorra, Monaco, San Marino, Slovakia, Ukraine, Lithuania, Estonia, Netherlands, Luxembourg, Norway, and Montenegro in Europe, the United Arab Emirates, Saudi Arabia and many other countries in the Middle East, as well as Vietnam, China, India, Japan, Thailand, Indonesia, Malaysia, and Singapore in the East.

Even among this list of the strictest governments, there are many documented examples of dual nationals. There are many Chinese and Estonians who hold other passports, for example; Estonians mostly Russian passports, and Chinese all over the world. In fact, Hong Kong citizens can have dual citizenship while citizens of the Chinese mainland and Macau cannot (but often still do).

When people suggest that they are not allowed to maintain dual citizenship, they are usually referring to some law by which their country exclusively recognizes them as their citizens when they are on that country's soil. The United States, for example, allows dual and even multiple citizenship, but when you are on their soil, you are only American to them. This is a common practice by which a country will allow you to have other citizenships without really considering you to be anything but theirs. The policy feels a bit clingy but does not really affect much. The only real restrictions are that you must enter and depart a country on its passport and that you may not seek consular protection from any other nationalities while in the country.

That means that if you are a dual US and UK national, you must only use your US passport when entering and leaving the United States. To them, you are not British, and to the UK, you are not a US person. Also, you cannot seek protection from the UK embassy while in the US, and vice versa.

This does bring up one issue worth considering if your desired second passport is some third-world hellhole; if you ever plan to go to that country, you will likely be required to enter on their passport, and as their citizen, they may detain or arrest you, or prohibit you from leaving. If that happens, you will have no one else to turn to, as you are their citizen. This has happened in countries in the Middle East where a western dual citizen is detained and not allowed to leave the country because they are believed to be only Iranian.

In our more enlightened age, dual citizenship is becoming more recognized – by western governments in particular – in response to international marriages, multiple birth citizenships, and other factors. The reality is that these days, you may be more likely to lose your citizenship to some government crackdown for something as simple as not paying your taxes than for dual citizenship. But as you build your passport portfolio, be aware of the possible restrictions that will come with your new citizenship that could jeopardize the rest of your portfolio.

The Perks of "Tier B" Citizenship

A discussion of second citizenships and passport portfolios would be incomplete without talking about the three different tiers of passports. We created the three-tier system years ago as a quick way to reference the general value offered by any given passport. While our Nomad Passport Index ranks every country in the world from first to last, the tier system breaks all passports into one of three tiers: Tier A, Tier B, or (you guessed it) Tier C.

While the formula we use for the index reflects the individualized and holistic approach we take to all offshore planning, the tier system is focused solely on travel privileges and is much more general in its application. Nevertheless, it is a useful way to understand what kind of passport will add the most value to your personal passport portfolio.

Tier A passports are from countries that will grant you visa-free access to the United States. Currently, there are roughly 40 countries in the world that qualify for the United States' visa waiver program. That is the threshold, although many of these same passports will also get you into other hard-to-access English-speaking countries like Canada, the UK, New Zealand, and Australia. Tier A passports include those same English-speaking countries, most EU countries, as well as Japan, Singapore, Brunei, and Chile.

Tier A passports are had to come by unless you are willing to spend a lot of money. You will either need to get a residence and then pay a lot of tax while you wait for naturalization, or you can pay it all upfront for citizenship by investment in Malta. The only way you may be able to save on a Tier A passport is by finding a connection in your family tree.

Tier B passports are much easier to get. While they will not give you access to the United States, they will give you access to Europe's Schengen Area. If the passport also gets you into the UK and Ireland, that would be a B+ passport, as both are much harder to get into. If a passport has access to Europe, it is likely that it will give you access to plenty of other countries around the world as well. Many countries offer Tier B passports, including passports from the Caribbean, Eastern Europe, Central and Southeast Asia, and much of Central and South America.

Tier C passports come from most African countries (with the exception of the islands of Seychelles and Mauritius) as well as many Asian countries and a few in Central and South America. These passports do not have access to either the US or Europe. There are a few decent Tier C passports such as Turkey and Russia that – largely due to politics – will give you visa-free access to everywhere but the US and Europe. I call these C+ passports and regularly recommend Turkey's citizenship by investment program despite its somewhat lackluster travel privileges. But there are some Tier C passports that are truly limited, getting you into less than 40 other countries.

While it would be easy to look at these three tiers and automatically assume that you should create a portfolio full of Tier A passports, that could not be farther from the truth. Going where you're treated best does not necessarily mean having the best as the world defines it. While the Nomad Passport Index ranks Luxembourg's passport as the best in the world, you do not need that passport to go where you're treated best. And let me warn you against the notion of seeking citizenship or even residency in the United States, Canada, Australia, or New Zealand. The requirements to get in are strict, the taxpaying demands are high, and the marginal benefit you get in return over even a Tier B passport is surprisingly small.

Instead, I would urge you to consider the Tier B passports from countries that you may have never heard of before. The fact that you have never heard of these countries is one reason to pursue the passports they provide because it means that they are under the radar. The United States is constantly in the news for spying on its citizens and doing all sorts of other crazy stuff. Tier B passport countries create less fuss. Walk into a bank and tell them you are Georgian and they will not give it a second thought. Tell them you are a US citizen, and they may well shoo you out the door. Citizenship in a relatively anonymous country can come in handy for all the reasons you are seeking a second citizenship in the first place. Tier B passports are far easier to get and will cost a heck of a lot less, too. If you can be flexible, it is often the best way to go. There are countries where the Fonzie method can be applied to obtain a Tier B passport as well. You cannot match the reasonable cost (i.e., not $100,000+) with the quality. I have seen people get citizenship in less than one year with a low-figure investment in a Tier B passport country.

For most Nomad Capitalists, Tier B passports are an excellent fit. They fall right in the middle of the passport scale. The Tier A countries come with a lot of responsibilities, but excellent travel privileges. The Tier C countries do not offer much travel, even if you are willing to wait in visa lines, but you probably do not have to worry about the Cambodian government reading your emails after you skip town.

The happy middle ground is the Tier B passport. You would not know it listening to Fox News, but Mexico has one of the best passports on earth. Mexican citizens can go everywhere in Europe, Central and South America, both developed and emerging Asia, and even Australia and New Zealand visa-free. The only substantial difference between a Mexican passport and a US passport is the ability to visit the US and Canada without a visa. As a second passport, Mexico is practically the gold standard: developed world visa-free travel with minimal nonsense (Mexico is not demanding that foreign banks spy on its citizens, for instance). For my money, I would much rather be Mexican than American, given the trade-offs.

Even El Salvador, currently the poorest country in the Americas, gets visa-free travel to everywhere in Europe except the UK and Ireland. The passport of a country that restaurant owners in Mexico look to for dishwashers is 80% as good as that of your first world passport. For those who want to use the Sit Back and Relax method, the trick is finding a country like this that you either want to live in part- or full-time, or one that does not require you to live there much at all.

If you could spend a month or two a year in a Tier B country like Montenegro or Georgia or Mexico to work toward citizenship, why not? These countries have beautiful beaches and stunning mountains that attract tourists from around the region. They would be great places to live for part of the year, although most will not require that you spend much time there to qualify for naturalization.

If you want a European Union passport, the stakes will be higher. I generally only recommend that a western citizen immigrate to an EU country for one of two reasons: one being to eventually obtain an equally good passport if they plan to renounce US citizenship, the other being for the ability to live and work in Europe's borderless Schengen Area.

A European Union passport is quite the perk because you are not tethered to the country that issues it. If you can get a Spanish passport, you can leave Spain, stop paying tax there, and move to any other EU country without the limitations of a tourist visa. For those of us from the New World who are thrilled by the idea of whisking our way through the Swiss Alps, the romantic streets of Paris, and the not so romantic streets of Bratislava, being able to live in Europe for more than 90 days at a time would be a dream come true.

However, most of tourist-friendly Europe is flat broke and they are not about to let a bunch of people move in and become citizens of their country without making them cough up some tax payments along the way. While it is possible to obtain second citizenship in European countries like Belgium or Ireland, you will find it far easier and less costly to start the process in places like Serbia, Georgia, Colombia, or Armenia. You might scoff at these countries as being subpar, but it is countries of this second tier that are often the best hope for an entrepreneur or investor looking to keep costs and obligations to a minimum.

Know What You Need

The best advice I can give to anyone looking for a second citizenship is to understand why you need one. That is why we began this chapter with a discussion of the benefits of second passports before we even touched on how to get one. Now that you know both the why and the how, it is up to you to decide your personal reasons for pursuing a second passport and your specific path toward obtaining one.

Perhaps you want better visa-free travel. I may be the only guy on earth who thought about investing in a citizenship just to avoid waiting at the Russian Embassy for a visa, but if you are missing out on travel opportunities because of your passport, a second passport could be worth it. Or perhaps you are more focused on paying less in tax or gaining more privacy. Knowing your reasons is important.

So, too, is focusing on those reasons and not chasing the latest shiny object. My team gets a thousand or more messages and emails each year, primarily from Indians and Pakistanis, specifically seeking a Paraguayan passport. They do not want just any second passport, they want a Paraguayan passport. But they do not consider their other options or really know how Paraguay compares. They just know that it is fast and cheap. Paraguay itself means nothing to them. Frankly, this approach is totally off track.

The actual passport you obtain is just one tool in your tool chest. Each person needs a different tool. The US citizen who needs a second passport to escape tax has different needs than the Chinese millionaire who is tired of applying for visas and is worried that his children are eating soup with lead in it.

I am not saying that you should not get emotional about your new country if you want to, but I highly doubt any of the guys writing me from Mumbai are eager to start wearing a Paraguay lapel pin on their suit jacket. They want what a Paraguay passport has to offer: relative stability, freedom from taxes, freedom from intrusive government, and excellent visa-free travel. It is a great deal, but it is not Paraguay that they care about, rather what Paraguay has to offer. Somewhere, someone told these guys that Paraguay was the fastest and the cheapest and the 'fast and cheap' button in their brains went off. But cheap is not always good. And fast is not always best.

The important thing is to avoid being reactionary. After Brexit, my website saw a huge spike in traffic that nearly quadrupled the number of visitors we usually get. Almost all the new traffic was from people in the United Kingdom seeking information like, "The fastest way to get a second passport" or, "How to get an EU passport." They were shocked by their country's vote to leave the European Union and suddenly started to realize that they would lose the ability to hang out in Ibiza for six months every summer, or to study in Paris without a visa, or to use the express immigration lane when they go to urinate in fountains in Riga.

Within a matter of days, though, the extra traffic died down as the emotional frenzy settled. The Brits that came searching did not really need another passport; they were just looking for a shiny object to satisfy their emotions. Some people spend their entire lives going from one emotional 'high' to the next, but it is not a solid way to diversify.

First of all, a British citizen does not need a second passport to live in Spain. He or she already gets 180 days as a tourist in continental Europe every year; for a nomad who has several home bases, that could well be enough. Alternatively, the British citizen who wants to live full-time in Spain (which would be a tax nightmare, I might add) could easily get a residence permit in any European country, allowing them the freedom of travel that they want.

If you are the Chinese millionaire with terrible visa-free travel, then getting a passport with good visa-free travel is probably top on your list. However, the US or UK citizen seeking a second passport should consider a passport that complements what they already have, rather than offering more of the same. If you are a British citizen, adding US citizenship to the mix does not decrease your obligation to pay high taxes. Becoming a citizen of Panama, on the other hand, does offer that; along with the benefits of a country too small to care what you are doing or what your income is when you are living an ocean away.

The secret ingredient in second citizenship is not 'fast,' but 'diversity.' For most Nomad Capitalists who already have a decent passport for travel, a second passport offers the chance to be tied to a country that does not read your emails or tax you into oblivion. The Indians who come to my site have different priorities and may be happy to live in Europe full-time for five years and pay tax the entire time. After all, a better place to live is their goal. For those of us who do not fear for our wellbeing in our home country, the objectives are totally different.

Like anything else in your Nomad Capitalist lifestyle, do not be dogmatic about what constitutes a good or bad passport. Rather than getting stuck on one option,
focus on your desired outcome and work backwards to find the best passport to meet that need. Even as I have added more passports to my collection and continue to work toward at least three others, I recognize that being a Nomad Capitalist is so much more than having a half a dozen travel documents stashed in my bag. Second passports are a small representation of the Nomad Capitalist philosophy, a lifestyle that grants you greater freedom in as many ways possible.

Your How-To Action Plan

Immediate Action Steps: If you do not have it yet, go get your first passport from your home country. From there, figure out if there are any passports or residence programs that you qualify for right away – descent, marriage, birth, family, etc. – and then start doing the work to get those passports.

Travel Action Steps: Are there countries you have wanted to visit for lifestyle, business, or investment purposes? Do they offer programs that would allow you to invest or do business and get a residence or citizenship in return? Go check them out.

Holistic Planning: Second residencies and passports often overlap with other flags for both good and bad. Some immigration programs will facilitate (or be facilitated by) other goals such as foreign real estate investment, currency diversification, offshore banking, offshore companies, and more. Others will bring new complications such as negative tax ramifications and dual citizenship restrictions. Ensure that each passport you add to your portfolio supports your end goals and does not create new dilemmas.

Chapter Five: Renouncing US Citizenship

Are You Sure You Want to Do This?

Dateline: New York City, New York, United States

December 2017, I found myself in JFK Airport in New York City. For the last four years, I had avoided flying through the United States at all costs, but this was a special moment that I knew I would look back on. I wanted to be in the US one last time, if anything, just to say goodbye.

For years, I had been talking about my mantra to go where you're treated best, and I had been living that life. I had been going where I was treated best and was actively building my life outside of the United States. But as I did, I watched from the outside as the US government made changes that made life increasingly more difficult for people like me who choose to live, invest, and do business overseas.

The events of 2017 had been the perfect storm of political changes and emotional resolution within myself that all culminated in my last-minute decision to book an appointment with the US Embassy in Tbilisi, Georgia to renounce my US citizenship before the year was up.

Just that day, I had been with a great group of Nomad Capitalists in Cancun. Now, I was getting drinks with a small group of friends at JFK on a connecting flight to Istanbul before arriving at my ultimate destination in Tbilisi. We did not have the time to go into the city or waltz around Central Park, only a few moments to tap into the sentimentality of the moment, knowing that I may never come back – knowing that it was the last time I would ever be in the United States as a citizen of the country.

After growing up in Ohio, living in Arizona, starting multiple businesses, and having friends and family in the US, it was strange to think that this one moment in JFK may be the very last one.

Earlier that year, I had decided to spend a few days in the United States to take care of some business and to simply see what it felt like to be there after three and half years away. I felt like a tourist. That trip and that feeling got me thinking about what was going on in the United States and where I was going with my own life. That was the moment when I really decided that the United States was once a part of my life, but it was no longer a part of who I was.

I did not feel angry or sad, it was simply time to move on. As I had emotionally distanced myself in a good way from the United States, I gave up the anger that drove me in my early years, gained a greater love and respect for the people who choose to live in the US, and was able to fully embrace my life as a global citizen.

I chose to add this chapter to the new edition of this book because I want to put a name and a face to what it is like to renounce your US citizenship. I am happy to be the guy who says, "Here is what I have done!" I am sure it will not be a popular topic with some folks, but I want to put a human face on what is often regarded as a purely financial decision. My hope is to give you an opportunity to identify with my experience and understand the background and the feelings that preceded my decision to renounce, regardless of whether it is the right decision for you.

This is a chapter for the people who are curious about US citizenship renunciation and who may be considering renouncing themselves. I am not here to tell anyone that they should renounce. In fact, I often try to talk certain clients out of the decision. It is not the right decision for everyone. But if you are a high earner or have a high-net-worth, this chapter is not one to be missed.

What Is US Citizenship Renunciation?

Before we dive into all the reasons why people renounce, how to renounce, what it is like to do so, and what happens once you have done it, it is important to cover the basic terms involved and address the most common questions and misconceptions surrounding citizenship renunciation. As someone who has been through the process, I know what is fact and what is fiction.

We will start with the most basic element of renouncing citizenship: the citizenship itself. What is citizenship? At its core, it is the embodiment of the social contract that Rousseau so famously described and the inclusion in the political community that results from that contract. One of the great challenges of humanity is learning how to live with each other while allowing for the greatest level of freedom for each individual. Without taking you too far back to your high school history class or your college philosophy lecture, the bottom line is that we create communities that protect certain rights by ensuring that all participating members of the community fulfill corresponding responsibilities.

Every country offers its own version of this social contract with varying rights and responsibilities. Some offer too few rights or too many excessive responsibilities. While most people are born into one social contract and never question it or consider the other options available to them, Nomad Capitalists understand that they have the right to choose the contract that will treat them best – the contract that will give them the perfect balance of rights and responsibilities. And in most countries, renouncing your membership in the political community by giving up your citizenship is one of your rights.

Renunciation is the other half of the equation. Put simply, renunciation is the voluntary act of giving up your citizenship. And it must be voluntary. Many folks have asked me questions over the years that all boil down to this one question: can you lose your citizenship involuntarily? No! You are never going to renounce your citizenship by accident or without knowing that you have done so. It is something you must do on purpose.

No one can renounce your citizenship on your behalf or force you to do it. In fact, minors are the one segment of the population that do not have the right to renounce their citizenship due to this very issue. The government wants the assurance that you are making the decision of your own free will and choice. There are cases where someone who has committed naturalization fraud could be turned in and have their citizenship revoked, and some governments have policies that allow them to strip the citizenship of known terrorists, but for the average natural-born citizen, there is no way that you could lose your citizenship involuntarily.

Where many people get confused is when they start adding other political contracts to the mix, including both second residencies and citizenships. A lot of folks worry that if they get a second residence, they will lose their citizenship. This is not the case. Just as moving overseas will not invalidate your citizenship no matter how long you are gone, obtaining a residence permit in another country will not cause you to lose your citizenship.

In fact, in most cases, even getting a second citizenship will not invalidate your first citizenship. As we discussed in the last chapter, some countries do not allow dual citizenship, so you may be forced to give up your citizenship(s) to obtain another, but it will never be done without your knowledge or consent.

What you do have less control over is your passport. Many folks conflate citizenship and passports, but they are two separate things. Again, citizenship is the overall contract, the passport is merely one of the rights granted within that contract that allows you to travel and leave the country's borders. You cannot have your citizenship taken away, but in certain cases, the government may take your passport. Usually, you lose this right because you have not fulfilled certain responsibilities of your social contract... or the government thinks you have not.

If you are a US citizen, the FAST Act allows the taxman to revoke or deny your passport (not your citizenship) for failing to pay a tax debt. Just as medieval Islam conditioned travel privileges on payment of tax, so too does the United States. In fact, if you owe $50,000 or more to Uncle Sam, he can pull your passport whether you are in the United States or overseas.

While $50,000 may seem like a large tax debt to incur, high-priced consultants and small business owners with high seven- or eight-figure incomes could take the wrong deduction and rack up a debt nearly that large. Even worse, the government could wrongly apply your payment and believe you never paid when in fact you did. This happened to me several years ago when a company I ran conducted business in California for one year. We filed a California tax return, paid their ridiculous fees, and marked the tax return as final to indicate that we would rightfully not be paying them again.

Yet, when the next year came, the California taxman came asking for more money, not only for the current year but also for the previous year that had already been paid. We reminded them that we had pressed on and sent a copy of the check. Apparently, they did not properly update our account because I woke up one morning to find a couple thousand bucks levied from my bank account. The reason? Unpaid tax that was either long ago paid, or never due.

According to my lawyer, levying a foreign state bank account was not even legal, but if you were a large bank, would you rather side with a 23-year-old kid, or the State of California? Sadly, the banks will side with the more powerful, even when the powerful are wrong. Now, imagine you are not a nascent business, but a serious operation. Multiply my numbers by ten and you could easily get to $50,000 when you add in penalties and interest, enough to put your travel plans on ice if you do not have a backup plan.

If you are a US person living overseas and did not know until now that you had to file tax returns, it is best to clear things up immediately. The taxman can and will file tax returns on your behalf if you do not, and he will not take nearly as many deductions as you would, if he takes any at all. That means that even an average earner could accumulate a large enough tax debt with enough years of non-filing.

But that is not the only way you could have your passport revoked. I do not imagine that many readers of this book are absconding from basic child support obligations, but just in case, almost any past due child support obligation can get your passport suspended or canceled, as well. Think more in the $2,000 neighborhood. Of course, I am not suggesting that you get a second passport just to thumb your nose at legitimate tax or child support debts, but the trend is clear: if you do not do exactly as your government tells you, they will use any means at their disposal to punish you, including taking your passport.

Now, you have a pretty good chance that the IRS will not misplace your payment and revoke your passport. However, a good Nomad Capitalist strategy involves understanding trends and looking to the future. Governments are increasingly clear: they will take away your travel privileges and potentially even your naturalized citizenship if you do not do as they wish. If anything, many laws create a slippery slope that could be exploited if the government were to extend its reach, which is not too hard to imagine.

But here is why you should be most concerned about having your US passport revoked if you are considering renunciation: if you do not have a passport, you cannot leave the country, and if you cannot leave the country, you cannot renounce. You must be outside of the United States to renounce your citizenship. Otherwise, how would they get rid of you? You must go to a US Embassy or Consulate in a foreign country and that, of course, requires a passport.

That is just one more reason why having a second passport is so important. You do not want to leave your ability to get out of the United States and renounce your citizenship in the hands of the very government that you are trying to abandon. If your US passport is revoked but you have another passport, you will still be able to leave the country and renounce your citizenship. That is why it is the ultimate escape hatch.

But this brings up another question: do you have to have a second passport to renounce? Technically, you do not need another passport to renounce your US citizenship. You can become stateless. You can choose not to engage in any social contracts. This will, however, extremely limit your rights. Your travel will be limited, and if you do not have a residence permit in the country where you renounce, there is a chance that you will be deported. And who knows where they will deport you since you do not belong to anyone. Wherever you end up, you will likely be stuck there.

There are certain travel documents that you can get as a stateless person and there is a nationality code for "no citizenship", but it is a lot more headache and adds more complication to your life than it is worth. Generally speaking, you want to have a second passport if you are going to renounce your citizenship. Perhaps your first experience with the social contract was not a positive one, but there are countries in the world where the rights and responsibilities of citizenship can work in your favor.

If you are dead set on becoming stateless, though, your success will largely depend on where you go to renounce. Some embassies process more renunciations and have different timelines and rules about what they will and will not allow you to do. Most should allow it, even if they frown on it. I have heard some stories of embassies refusing to process a renunciation because the person would become stateless, but you have a lot of embassies to pick from and can usually avoid the worst of problems by going to a smaller embassy like in the Bahamas (where they practically advertise the service) or in Georgia where I renounced.

But this is not to say that there is more than one way to renounce your US citizenship. The only way to renounce is through a

US Embassy or Consulate. I have seen the YouTube videos of the folks who still live in the US who claim that they pulled some trick or know some quick easy loophole that allows you to avoid paying taxes in some weird way by not pledging allegiance to the United States or somehow maintaining your citizenship but not your nationality. This is silliness.

People have been selling these alleged tricks for decades, claiming that you can be smarter than everyone else and not pay taxes. But these are smokescreens. Either you are a US citizen, or you are not. If you want to live in the United States, you need to live by the rules of the United States. People always want to know how they can live in the US – get all the rights and benefits of US citizenship – without paying tax. That is not how it works. The rights and the responsibilities go hand in hand. If you give up the responsibilities, you give up the rights.

And because the United States imposes citizenship-based taxation, you will be required to file and pay taxes there no matter where you live. Apparently, they think that the benefits are so great that the tax responsibilities of US citizenship extend beyond the borders of the country, even when you are no longer partaking of the majority of the benefits available to US citizens, like good roads, clean tap water, and whatever else makes America so great. The only way out is to renounce.

If you have a business that you want to internationalize or you want to go overseas yourself, there are ways to reduce your tax burden and save some tax. I paid zero or almost zero during the years I lived overseas and remained a US citizen. But the idea that you are going to escape the IRS entirely is simply wrong. If you are a US citizen, you will have to deal with the IRS. I am not saying I agree with the IRS, I am saying that there is no great loophole where you can invoke some constitutional clause to give up your nationality. It is ridiculous to assume such things.

If you are a high earner or have a high net worth, you do not want to be running around trying to pull some trick like this. You have a lot to lose. You want to play by the rules. You can choose to go somewhere else and live under a different set of rules, but you have to play by the rules to get there. Renouncing your US citizenship through the process set out by the US government is the only way to do that. There is no snapping of your fingers or waving a magic wand. These games that people say you can play could cause you a big fine or penalty or even land you in jail. You need to be careful to avoid being associated with anything related to these beliefs. You do not want the knock on the door years down the road.

Nomad Capitalist and what I do is all about recognizing what the rules are, following the rules, and then legally choosing the rules that will serve you best. I can tell you personally that having a legitimate detachment from the United States has given me a great sense of relief. I know I did it the right way. So, make sure that whatever you do, it is based on facts and law, because that is what will apply to you in real life.

The Reasons People Renounce US Citizenship

The only reason anyone would ever renounce their US citizenship is because they are a greedy tax evader, right? Wrong. For years, the media has capitalized on the "name and shame" list that the US government publishes every quarter with the names of the individuals who qualified as covered expatriates when they renounced their US citizenship – the folks who had a considerable amount of money when they renounced and were required to pay an exit tax.

The truth about this list is that not everyone who is a covered expatriate is on the list, and not everyone who is not, is not. The list is notoriously inaccurate and there is no way to know the exact number of people who have renounced their US citizenship over the years. As someone who has gone through the process of renunciation, it is frustrating to see just how much of the process – including the motivations behind renunciation – that the media gets wrong.

But what the list can show you is a pattern. Patterns matter. And when it comes to US citizenship renunciation, a clear pattern has emerged in the past decade that should not be ignored. Prior to 2009, renunciation levels had stayed well under roughly 750 people per year. In 2006, all of 268 people renounced their US citizenship. In 2008, that number dropped to 231. The numbers climbed back to the higher end of the spectrum in 2009, with a total of 741 renunciants... and then 2010 hit and the numbers began to grow almost exponentially. These are the numbers of renunciations from what the government has published in the past decade or so:

- 2008 = 231
- 2009 = 742
- 2010 = 1534
- 2011 = 1781
- 2012 = 933
- 2013 = 3000
- 2014 = 3415
- 2015 = 4279
- 2016 = 5411
- 2017 = 5133
- 2018 = 3983
- 2019 = 2577
- 2020 = 6705

Can you see the pattern? A few expats handing back their US passports and saying goodbye to the US every year is one thing, but when more and more people give up their citizenship every year, you begin to wonder what is pushing them to make what is often a very difficult and even emotional decision. And for many of you, you may be trying to put a finger on the reasons you feel a growing desire to renounce your citizenship as well.

From my experience, I have found that there are two types of people who may want to renounce their US citizenship: those who are motivated by philosophical reasons and those whose reasons are financial. Many people, like myself, are motivated by a hybrid of both reasons. But whatever your reasons may be, they likely fall into one of these two categories.

Philosophical Reasons to Renounce US Citizenship

There are many different philosophical reasons someone may want to give up their US citizenship. For example, there are people who, going back many decades, have not agreed with the wars that the United States has waged across the globe. Beginning primarily with the Vietnam War, some protestors burned their passports to make an example of their opposition to the war and the fact that their tax dollars were funding something they disagreed with on such a fundamental level.

Even today, I have people come to me who do not want a penny of their money going to fund a multi-trillion-dollar war. They do not want to be paying taxes to a country where their money and their identity is going to support killing people. As someone who has spent a lot of time living outside of the United States, I sympathize. I never identified with the things that most people do not like about Americans. I may never get rid of my protestant work ethic, and I may always have my American accent, but these more negative parts of the American identity were never part of who I was or what I believed.

Other people do not like the idea of their tax dollars going to support an ever-growing and ever more socialist and inefficient government. One person I spoke to told me that his decision to renounce was not about who was president at the time but more specifically about the role and practices of the government, which her referred to as "the psycho girlfriend." He never knew what they were going to do next. If someone punches you in the face, chances are you do not want to wait around to see if they are going to apologize and make everything right... or stab you in the back. He preferred to get out before the US government had a chance to do the latter.

Around the time I first left the United States to spend a year traveling the world, I shared an evening with friends, including a close business partner. Much of my conversation that night revealed how upset I was about the US government and all the many rules they had. You can see much of that same anger in my very first podcasts and articles on the Nomad Capitalist blog. I was angry and would often speak in sweeping generalizations that I would never use today. I often considered renouncing during this time of my life, but I did not want to throw away a powerful passport just because I was angry. I am grateful I made that choice.

When I finally decided to renounce my citizenship, I spoke once again with my good business friend who had remained in the US. He noticed the change that had occurred within me since those first days of frustration and anger. He told me, "You used to talk about the process of renouncing, and you were angry and all over the map, but now you seem to be at peace. You have thought it out, it is a reasonable decision, and you have a whole plan figured out." And he was right.

The reason I was grateful that I waited to renounce and the reason I often try to talk people out of renouncing for philosophical reasons is that renunciation is a very sobering and permanent decision. If you are acting out of anger or frustration – I have been there, I know what it is like – it is not the place you want to be mentally when you are making important decisions, whether it is renunciation or any other decision in life.

More importantly, I have found that most anger and frustration come from not having options. I have helped people who have said, "I am going to renounce now. I hate this place. It is the worst!" But I tell them to hold on a minute and get a strategy in place first. I help them get a second passport, and then they start traveling on that second passport, and only then can they really take a step back and look at the other options of how they can go where they are treated best. Some move forward with the decision to renounce while others realize that, ultimately, they are fine with remaining a US citizen.

That said, philosophical reasons can still be a valid reason to renounce your citizenship. Even after I calmed down and took a step back to look at things, a major part of my decision to renounce was still based on one particularly important philosophical point: my cultural identity.

I did not start my Nomad Capitalist journey with the intent to save on taxes. I simply never felt American. I was fascinated by other cultures and countries and just did not feel like I fit in with the culture of the United States. I remember walking around my neighborhood in the US during my angry years and telling my father over the phone, "I just want to get some passport and renounce. I do not like it here. I don't want the identity." When you do not feel like you belong, it is difficult to accept the rights, responsibilities, and identity of your home country.

For many people, getting rid of their US passport and perhaps losing some of their travel privileges is worth it for them to feel better about their identity. These people are often the ones who, like me, have found other places in the world where they feel comfortable, where people share their values, and where they feel best in terms of their identity. As I discovered when I returned to the US after so many years away and felt like a tourist, I knew it was no longer my home.

Financial Reasons to Renounce US Citizenship

For other people, their decision to renounce is based on much more practical reasons – mainly, financial. For these people, they realize that there is no other way for them to legally avoid tax. They do not want to live in the United States, and they want to do what every other citizen of every other country in the world can do, which is to go live somewhere else and choose to be taxed by the rules of where they live rather than have their home country continue to tax them. But they know that, as an American, they cannot do this.

As you know by now, the United States is the only country in the world besides Eritrea that requires its citizens (and residents and anyone who spends too much time there) to file and pay taxes on their worldwide income no matter where they live. In most countries, if you live in the country, you pay tax – oftentimes on your worldwide income – but if you leave, then you can opt to become a tax non-resident. For example, if you are Irish and you live in Ireland, you will pay tax in Ireland. But if you leave, you do not have to pay. But if you are a US citizen and you leave the United States and choose to live in Ireland instead, the United States still has jurisdiction over your income, whether it is from Ireland, Cambodia, the US, or anywhere else. It is not about where you live but about where you are a citizen.

While many other countries have worldwide taxation for residents of that country, you can get out of the system by leaving. Some countries are making it more difficult, and you will likely see more countries following the United States' example, but for now, the US is the only country implementing such a demanding and inescapable system of taxation. You can never get out of the US system. The only way out is to renounce.

The good news is that renouncing instantly detaches you from the IRS. You no longer have to report or pay taxes on any of your foreign businesses, and you can earn income subject to only paying where you live. So, if you live in Dubai or as a perpetual traveler or any number of ways, you could pay as little as zero in tax.

But as I have mentioned, there are ways to reduce your taxes (in some cases, even to zero) while remaining a US citizen. There are exclusions like the Foreign Earned Income Exclusion (FEIE), foreign housing credits, and foreign tax credits and treaties that can significantly reduce your tax burden in many cases. There are also several strategies that we will dive into in other chapters of this book that you can use if you own a business to not only reduce your federal income tax but also eliminate Medicare, Social Security, and other taxes. And depending on what state you come from, you may also be able to avoid your state income tax as well. Proper planning is required, but the bottom line is that there are ways to earn some money tax-free by living overseas without renouncing.

But not everyone can save on taxes this way. Employees, consultants, and investors are all in a particularly difficult situation when it comes to saving on taxes as a US expat living overseas. A friend of mine works as a private banker in a tax haven that does not tax his income, but because he is an employee (and a US citizen), his entire salary of $1 million is taxed every single year, even though he has not lived in the US for over a decade. He can exempt the first roughly $110,000 of income through the FEIE, but then everything else is subject to tax, leaving him with a federal tax bill of over $330,000 every year. He had the good sense to move out of California before leaving the US and owes zero state taxes as a resident of Florida, otherwise, he would owe almost $100,000 more in taxes to California.

My friend began to seriously consider renouncing his citizenship knowing that he will never be able to stop paying taxes to a country where he has not lived in years (and does not derive any income) unless he renounces. Even purchasing a Caribbean passport for $100,000 would give him a quick return on investment as the cost of the second passport is less than a third of what he sends to the IRS every year.

Consultants are in a similarly difficult situation because, technically, they do not run a business as they are the only one providing services and cannot use most of the strategies available to offshore companies to pay themself a salary and at least reduce Social Security and Medicare taxes. Most consultants only use a corporation for limited liability benefits and not for tax deferral, so, while they can claim the FEIE, that is the extent of their legal tax reduction strategies outside of renunciation.

And then there are the investors. Unlike consultants, business owners, and employees, investors cannot claim even the small amount of relief offered by the Foreign Earned Income Exclusion. The FEIE only covers earned income, not the passive income that comes from investment. If you are a stock trader, crypto investor, Forex trader, real estate investor, or have any capital gains from selling a business or otherwise, you have never had an effective way as a US citizen to live overseas and escape tax. And for some investors, their US citizenship also restricts them from making certain investments overseas.

As we will discuss in the new chapter on cryptocurrencies, many US crypto investors are expressly denied participation in certain ICOs because those running the fundraising operation do not want anyone with US indicia, be that a US address, residence permit, or citizenship. Some investors will try to circumvent the rules in one way or another, but as institutions like the SEC and others have become more involved in the crypto space, regulation only grows. I have had clients come seeking my help to renounce because they are literally losing millions of dollars in crypto investment opportunities because these ICOs refuse to work with US citizens who pose too much risk when it comes to tax compliance and other US policies and regulations.

Other US expats were thrown under the bus thanks to the Tax Cuts and Jobs Act of 2017 (and in more ways than one). One policy, however, prompted many Americans to renounce their citizenship rather than stick around and pay. The new tax reform introduced a 'transition tax' that acted retroactively to tax all retained earnings from the prior 30 years at a rate of 15%. Whether they had distributed the money or kept it in a company, if the US had not previously taxed it, that income was now taxable.

Many of these folks were not living in some tax haven enjoying 0% tax rates for those 30 years, they were paying taxes in high-tax jurisdictions like the UK. But because of the transition tax, they would be required to either declare and pay taxes on all that money or renounce before the tax reform came into full effect. Many of these people ended up renouncing rather than paying 30 years' worth of taxes all in one blow.

Another reason many people renounce their US citizenship is that they discover that they are 'accidental Americans'. As is the case in most New World countries that were largely populated by immigrants, any child born on US soil is considered a citizen of the United States. While many parents purposefully go to the US to give birth to their children to give them US citizenship, thanks to citizenship-based taxation, this does not always end up being such a great gift. I have known many people over the years who were born in the United States decades ago but never grew up there and are only recently discovering that they are US citizens. This always causes extreme confusion when they go to clean up the mess and they usually end up renouncing their US citizenship than deal with the reporting and tax obligations that come with it. Every US citizen must pay, even if they do not know that they are a citizen.

Every US citizen – accidental or not – must also report, and they must report everything. In one example of the rule of (possibly) unintended consequences, the US government created a law called FATCA which requires all foreign banks and brokerages to report accounts held by US citizens to the US Treasury Department. Ostensibly, the law was designed to stop tax evasion by hiding money overseas. The result was that foreign banks found the paperwork and procedures so laborious that many just threw their hands up in the air and said, "Screw it!"

Rather than deal with the nonsense, banks just stopped accepting US citizens, greatly limiting their financial options. These days, so many banks have shut their doors to US persons that not being able to open a decent offshore bank account is a constant worry of many Americans. And if they do manage to open an account, they must then report those foreign bank accounts as well as foreign brokerage accounts, and accounts with other foreign financial institutions (FFIs). The United States has essentially extended its filing burden onto anyone who works with US citizens, not just the citizens themselves, which has pushed many businesses, banks, and individuals to refuse to work with US citizens at all.

One article I read told the story of an accidental American who discovered her US citizenship when her bank requested her US tax identification and other information. She would need to get in compliance and quick or risk losing her loan. The other option was to renounce, but because of the worldwide pandemic, she could not get an appointment at the US Embassy. The article told of another individual who was faced with losing their home mortgage because they were an accidental US citizen that the bank no longer wanted to work with. Stories like these make it easier to understand how US citizenship can become a liability for anyone living overseas.

Being a US expat is complicated. No one wants to voluntarily expose themselves to the bureaucratic vortex of filing reports, calculating dividends, filling out paperwork, and paying taxes. As a former US citizen, there are still some banks that do not want to do business with me because they say, "Once an American, always an American." For them, even former US citizenship is still a risk. Many who are still in the system are looking for a way out. One person who came to us for help discovered that it would cost him $70,000 to $80,000 a year just to do his taxes. Not to pay them, just to file them. When he saw just how much work and money it would cost him just to be compliant under the new tax reform, he chose to renounce instead.

Paying a large tax bill is one thing, but when your life is consumed by endless piles of forms, tax compliance can become a detriment to your business and your wellbeing. If you have a bank account overseas, you will need to file an FBAR, Form 8938. If you have interest in a foreign corporation, you will need to report that. If you are using an offshore company that has business interests in the United States, you may need to file a different form. If you have a foreign brokerage account, you will need to report that. Basically, whatever you are doing overseas, you must report it.

As far as reporting is concerned, the only two exceptions are privately owned foreign real estate (as long as you do not generate any income from it) and precious metals that are vaulted outside of the banking system. Except for those two caveats, the United States wants to know about everything you are doing, which means you will be filing form after form.

US citizens are also forbidden to do business with a laundry list of foreign countries, citizens, companies, and charities that their government considers to be up to no good. An agency called OFAC keeps a byzantine list of these organizations that totals 2MB just in text format. That means that US citizens are shut out from certain business deals because of OFAC. Add to that the Foreign Corrupt Practices Act that dictates how you can do business in other countries, and it is easy to see how all these restrictions lead to fewer economic opportunities for those who are unfortunate enough to be born with US citizenship.

Fair does not enter this equation. When I first went overseas and saw how difficult things are for US citizens abroad – especially as someone who wants to be compliant with the law because it is the right thing to do – constantly worrying about whether I could talk to the person from Iran or do business with a certain company or wondering if I had missed a certain report or filed something incorrectly was enough to keep me up at night. The sense of dread that I might make a mistake was a burden for someone like me who wants to do everything 100% legal.

I have never agreed with the people out there telling you to hide all your cryptos offline and bury all your wealth in the backyard and simply not follow the rules or report anything. There is freedom in following the law. It is always best to follow the law, even when you do not agree with the laws or find them overbearing. But as a Nomad Capitalist, you also have the ability to choose the laws that apply to you. If this is too much for you as it was for me, you do have the option to expatriate from the United States and get all of this out of your life.

Other Considerations to Make Before Renouncing

Whether you have philosophical, financial, or other more practical reasons for renouncing, you will also need to weigh the pros of renouncing against the cons of such a decision.

Let me be clear: renouncing US citizenship is not the right solution for everyone. Not everyone who comes to Nomad Capitalist wants to renounce, and some folks who come to us wanting to renounce ultimately realize that they do not want to go through with the decision. I am not here to talk you into doing anything. If any of the strategies I discuss in this book do not serve what you are trying to accomplish, I am not here to convince you to go through with them.

I do not recommend renunciation to most people. For most folks, it is worth it for them to put up with everything I already mentioned – paying some tax, filling out a bunch of forms, dealing with the restrictions on US citizens overseas, etc. – in exchange for the benefits of US citizenship. While your reasons in favor of renunciation may be valid and strong, do not jump at the decision to renounce without fully understanding what you may be giving up. This is a decision that must be made not only with a level head but also with a near clinical-level approach that allows you to weigh all the factors.

One of the main benefits of US citizenship is that it allows you to live in the United States. If you are living abroad, it allows you to go back without any issues. It gives you a guaranteed entrance into the country to see family, live in the country, and to work there. If your job is in the US, ask yourself if you will be able to find a similar job in another country. If not, do you have enough saved up to retire or start a business to support you when you renounce? The job market outside of the United States is vastly different. If you do decide to renounce, it will be difficult for you to turn back to the US job market. If you are new to business, have not saved up much, or you rely solely on volatile investments like cryptocurrency, renouncing will completely remove any cushion you currently have to fall back on if things go south.

You will also give up your US passport and its accompanying travel privileges. This also means that you will lose any consular protections you may have had while traveling abroad before. The US government will no longer emergency evacuate you from a war zone. I do not know too many people for whom this will be an issue, but it is a right you will be giving up. You will also lose the right to vote in US elections and the right to bestow US citizenship on any children born to you overseas.

For many people, the biggest factor that keeps them tied to the United States is family. Because US citizenship grants you the unrestricted right to live and travel in and out of the United State, that means unrestricted access to your family, too. Are you prepared to get a visa to attend your grandmother's funeral? Will you be able to get a visa for your brother's wedding? These are real considerations you need to take into account.

Once you renounce, while there are ways to get back in, there is no guarantee that you will be allowed entrance into the United States. Unless you have a Canadian passport, it will be more difficult and will come with several restrictions. I am not saying that it is impossible or that there is a campaign against letting people who have renounced back into the country, but unless you have a Tier A passport, be prepared to do quite a bit of work to get a visa to enter the US once you have given up your citizenship.

Beyond the rights that you will relinquish, you also need to consider whether you are prepared for how your life will change after renouncing. Get down to the root reason you want to leave and examine how your life will be different in both positive and negative ways because you have renounced.

Calculate the cost and the potential return on investment of a second passport. What are you currently paying in taxes? How much would it cost you to get a second passport? How much will it cost you to go through the process of renunciation? Will you be subject to the exit tax (more on that in a minute)? If so, are there ways to reduce or eliminate that obligation before renouncing? What are the legal fees? What are the future tax benefits? What will your tax situation be like after you renounce? Be sure you are not jumping from the fire back into the frying pan. You do not want to renounce and then end up paying more in taxes to another country.

Once you can no longer claim the United States as you tax residence, is there another country that will claim you? Where will you be spending your time and how can you be sure that they are not going to tax you? Where is your company based and how does that work into your new status? There are many considerations to ensure that you as an individual person as well as your company will be taxed the way you desire. So, what is your residence and citizenship strategy? How are you going to travel? How much will you want to travel? Where will you bank? Where will you keep your assets? How will they be affected by your decision? There are some situations where renouncing may put you in a worse tax situation, especially if all your money is being made from US-source investments like US stocks and properties.

You will also want to consider what will change in the future. Perhaps the travel privileges on your second passport will improve as the years go by as mine have. But you may also face the risk that your second country of citizenship will introduce more restrictions and regulations that will put it on par with the United States when it comes to taxation policies and reporting burdens.

Consider whether you will lose certain residencies that you obtained with your US citizenship as well. In some countries, it is possible to make the switch and maintain your residence under another citizenship. You will need to do some footwork and follow the proper order, but it is doable. We have helped clients do this in the past. But there are other countries – often in Latin America – where it simply is not possible to maintain your residence once you have renounced the citizenship with which you obtained it.

In other cases, it is just too much headache to even try. For example, I had a residence permit in Mexico that I obtained with my US citizenship. While it was possible to make the switch, it was a very involved process that demanded more of my time in the country. Ultimately, it was simpler to apply for a new residence permit with my new citizenship.

If all these questions and cons have you reconsidering your commitment to renunciation, know that there are alternatives. As we will discuss in other chapters of this book, there are plenty of strategies that you can use to enhance your life, keep more of your money, and grow your wealth offshore without having to renounce your US citizenship. For some, Puerto Rico's tax incentives are an acceptable solution. Others will get by just fine with a little tax planning, a new place to call home, and an offshore company. This book is meant to shine a light on all the options available to you – not just renunciation.

Renouncing is best for those who no longer rely on the United States for money or lifestyle. If you are not investing there, living there, working or doing business there, and do not plan to do so in the future, it is worth considering. But if you derive much of your life and livelihood from the country, renouncing your US citizenship may not be the right decision for you.

For me, I knew I did not want to go back. Renouncing was a spring cleaning of sorts. Just as you would take that sweater that no longer fits you and donate it to Goodwill, I was ready to give up that which no longer served me and renounce my US citizenship. It was a very cleansing feeling to recognize that, for me, the pros of renouncing outweighed the cons. I had already created a life outside of the United States, now I was ready to give up the forms and the fear of different regulations and laws that were always changing and always complicated and just go live my life overseas.

I realized that I could do this. I had put in years of hard work to figure out my plan and it was finally time to put it into action. This was my last step. It was no longer about anger. I was at peace understanding that the US government could do what they wanted and that I could do what I wanted. I could choose to be proactive and take responsibility for myself and the kind of life I wanted to live. They may impose new laws and requirements in the future that I believed to be unfair, but I had the freedom to simply not be a part of that system anymore and to live my life where I could enjoy greater freedom and be at peace with my identity as a global citizen.

Once I recognized that it was the right time for me to renounce, I became incredibly comfortable with the decision. I knew that even if the circumstances that led to my decision were different, I would still renounce. I knew that the time had come. I was ready to let go. I was able to let go of a part of my identity that no longer served me in order to open up so much more beauty on the other side.

Again, my personal reasons for renouncing do not have to dictate yours. They are likely quite different, but that is not what matters. The key is to think the decision through from every angle so that you can be at peace with it, not just now but into the future as well. This is not a decision to take lightly.

How to Renounce US Citizenship

Making the decision to renounce is one thing, but once the decision is made, you still need to go through with the process. And believe it or not, most folks do not know the first thing about how to renounce US citizenship. If you figured you could just notify the government of your decision on some internet portal and then throw your passport out, you would be disappointed to learn that the legal process to renounce involves not only your physical presence but also paperwork, interviews, and money.

In general, the process can be broken down into eight basic parts, with some parts of the process overlapping with others (for instance, you will pay the renunciation fee at your second interview and the exit tax with your final reports):

1. Choose Your Renunciation Location
2. Fill Out the Paperwork
3. Attend Two Separate Interviews
4. Pay the Renunciation Fee
5. Pay the Exit Tax
6. Fulfill All Final Reporting Obligations
7. Await Authorization
8. Receive the Certificate of Loss of Nationality (CLN)

1. Choose Your Renunciation Location

Once I had made the decision to renounce, my first step was to spend some time with family members, friends, colleagues, and close associates to inform them of my decision and explain the process that followed. I was ready to begin 2018 with a clean slate and a new outlook on life. With those important discussions handled, I arranged an appointment at the US Embassy in Tbilisi, Georgia, one of the many places I had come to call home.

To officially renounce your citizenship, you must appear before a diplomatic or consular officer at a US Embassy or Consulate located outside of the United States. In my case, the officials in Tbilisi were very accommodating and even told me that if I wanted to come in the next day, they could help me with the process. I was in Mexico at the time, so I did not take them up on the offer, but I made my appointment and adjusted my travel plans so that I could renounce before the final weeks of 2017 slipped away.

Not all diplomatic locations will be so accommodating. While the legal process is the same regardless of location, the level of bureaucracy you will encounter and the timeline to renunciation will vary based on the volume of renunciations each location receives. The US Embassy in Canada, for example, is saturated with renunciations from dual Canadian-US citizens who have tired of filing forms, are happy in Canada, and want out of the US system. While they could go anywhere to renounce in a matter of weeks, most choose the convenient option of renouncing in Canada, which can take as long as six months.

Most renunciations occur in a small percentage of diplomatic posts, including London, Dublin, Bern, Amsterdam, Seoul, Hong Kong, Canada, Australia, and New Zealand. If you want someone to hold your hand and walk you through the entire process, you will get that at these locations, along with increased bureaucracy and a long wait time before you can even schedule an appointment. On top of that, you may not even have the chance to schedule in these locations as many of them require that you be a local resident to get a renunciation appointment.

If time is of the essence, you can speed up your renunciation timeline by doing what Nomad Capitalists do best – thinking nomadically – to choose a much less obvious diplomatic post where the entire process is less formal and there are fewer obstacles overall. These locations will have shorter wait times, some even allowing you to complete the entire two-interview renunciation process in one day. As with all things, it pays to go where you're treated best.

When you have decided on a location, you will need to set two separate interview appointments. In most cases, you can schedule these appointments online. However, not all US diplomatic posts have appointment software that will allow you to specify the purpose of your appointment. So, once you have set the appointment time, you will need to call to confirm that you intend to renounce your US citizenship. This allows the officials to prepare everything prior to your arrival.

2. Fill Out the Paperwork

Before you attend your first appointment, you will need to fill out the DS-4079 questionnaire – the Request for Determination of Possible Loss of United States Nationality. The form outlines the other documents you will need to collect and attach to the questionnaire, such as your US birth certificate, passport, proof of other citizenships, and more. The questions cover everything from your basic personal information to when you first learned that you were a US national, and from your other residencies and citizenships to your foreign military and government service and remaining ties to the United States.

While you will fill this form out prior to your first appointment, you should not sign it until you are before a diplomatic or consular officer. You will fill out and sign several other documents during your appointments as well, which you can review beforehand to know what to expect and prepare. These forms include the DS-4080, 4081, 4082, and 4083 and contain your oath of renunciation, a statement of understanding, and the witnesses' attestation of renunciation. Unlike the DS-4079, they are simple to fill out with just a few checked boxes, dates, and signatures.

You will also want to get your finances in order prior to your first appointment to prepare for (or, if possible, avoid) the exit tax – but more on that in a minute.

3. Attend Two Separate Interviews

No matter where you go, you will need to attend two separate interviews to fully complete the process of US citizenship renunciation. The main difference you will find in the various diplomatic locations is the amount of time you must wait between the two appointments. Some locations allow you to complete both interviews on the same day while most require at least a few days between appointments. If you are required to wait more than two weeks for your second interview, you are likely going to the wrong embassy.

The purpose of the first interview is to ensure that you are fully aware of the consequences of your decision and that you are making your choice voluntarily and not under duress. The time between appointments is meant as a cooling off period that will give you time to reflect on those consequences. The second interview is the final nail in the coffin when you will raise your right hand and read the oath stating your desire to renounce US citizenship. Once you take the oath and sign the final forms, your side of the renunciation process is complete.

But what can you expect from the experience? For me, I was quietly surprised at the dignified nature of the entire process and the professionalism of everyone involved. Of course, I had to go through the typical security measures at the embassy entrance, removing my coat, emptying my pockets, leaving my phone and keys with security, and so on. I could only take the paperwork and the renunciation fee with me into the appointment. Honestly, knowing that I was about to give up my US citizenship made this all seem much less intrusive than before.

I was directed back to a private office for the interview. Most people who go into an Embassy must complete everything in public by talking through a window and passing papers under the glass. The renunciation process, on the other hand, is all done in a private office where you can have a dignified conversation with the official assigned to your case.

During the interview, the official did quite a bit of explaining and I had to acknowledge everything that I would lose or no longer be able to access once I renounced. It could have come across as a last-ditch effort to talk me out of the decision to give up my citizenship, but I knew that they were simply assessing whether I was making the decision of my own free will and choice.

The official also asked me several questions. While they may not ask the same questions in every interview, I was asked to give my reasons for renouncing. I answered honestly that I simply no longer felt like an American. When they asked if my renunciation was about taxes, I asked for clarification and the official explained that if I did owe money, the tax debt would not disappear once I renounced. My issue had never been about paying taxes – I was in full compliance and still paid little tax – my main issues with taxation were the paperwork burden and endless regulations. So, with the clarification made, I confirmed that my decision was not about taxes. I was not trying to escape any existing tax debts.

The truth was that, after spending years away from the United States, I was a different person. My friends were different, my family was different, and the country itself was different. The United States of 1984 when I was born no longer existed. I could sit around and wish for it to come back, or I could go where I was treated best and enjoy greater freedoms and a better lifestyle elsewhere. I did not explain all that to the official, but that was at the heart of my decision. What I did say was that I was comfortable with the idea of never being able to return to the United States. My personal identity was no longer associated with the country – not out of hatred – I simply felt like it was not my home anymore.

The official listened intently to my answers, and we talked some more. He walked me through some scenarios, and I confirmed that I understood each one. Finally, he asked, "You know that once you do this, it cannot be undone?" I confirmed that I understood and then we set the appointment for my second interview.

After the first interview, I left the Embassy and took the cooling off period seriously. I gave the decision a lot of thought. I did some journaling and even made some videos to document how I felt. Ultimately, I came to my original conclusion that it was the right choice. While my second appointment was a couple of days later, I have friends who have completed both interviews in the same day, with the first interview in the morning and the second after lunch.

When I returned for the second interview, I once again took my seat in the waiting area before being directed by a friendly official to the window where I could pay the renunciation fee. I paid in cash at the register and was then given a receipt. I returned to my seat before being called back to my interview.

In the second interview, we went over many of the same questions as the first time around, then I signed off on two forms – the DS-4080 and 4081 – and then I raised my right hand and swore the oath of renunciation. Despite my certainty in the decision, it was still an emotional moment. I felt like I was breaking up with someone. I understood the gravity of what I was saying. But the moment it was done, I felt the relief. It was over.

I thanked the officials for being so accommodating and then I went to the front gate to collect my things and walked out of the embassy a free man. As I took my first breath of fresh air as a non-

US citizen, it almost felt like I was walking out of a prison yard. It was a beautiful ending to the process and a liberating beginning of the next chapter of my life.

During my angry years, I imagined my renunciation going down very differently. I anticipated an encounter with a bunch of angry lifetime government officials who I could confront head on and give them a piece of my mind. But not only was I a vastly different person by the time I decided to renounce but I also encountered an amazing staff at the Embassy who were nothing but kind, accommodating, and professional.

Sure, much of the media and the general public are angry at the 1% and will label just about anyone as a traitor, but there is no reason to project that attitude onto the government. Diplomatic officials are professionals doing their job and they understand that you have the right to renounce. I got the sense that they would never make the same decision, but they respected mine.

4. Pay the Renunciation Fee

Now, I already mentioned the renunciation fee. You pay this in person just before your second interview. But it is worth discussing as a step of its own just to highlight the absurdity of the fee and to prepare you for the various costs you will face if you choose to renounce. Yes, I encountered kind and professional individuals throughout the renunciation process, but the US State Department will charge you for such a privilege.

Prior to 2010, the United States did not charge a fee to claim your right to renounce. But with the introduction of FATCA and the subsequent surge in renunciations, the US State Department claimed that the increased paperwork and operational costs justified the introduction of a $450 renunciation fee – five times the average of other western countries that also charge a fee. But only four years later, they determined that even that was not enough and raised the fee to $2,350, an increase of a whopping 422% – 20 times higher than any other country in the world.

When I first heard of the higher fee, I thought, "Wow, they are making it really hard to escape!" But I do not blame them for milking the cow up until the very end. US citizens are a great source of revenue. While I did not enjoy paying the fee, I am a pragmatist. If paying an absurd fee is what it takes to ensure my freedom, I will pay it. And I am certain that I am not the only one who feels this way. The US government could double the fee to renounce US citizenship and people would still pay.

But the renunciation fee is not the only cost attached to renunciation. Many must also pay an exit tax when they renounce.

5. Pay the Exit Tax

The night before my second interview, I sat in my living room in Tbilisi, Georgia, running calculations while talking to my CFO, ensuring my financial affairs were in order on my final day as a US citizen. While I had gone to great lengths to organize my finances long before the eve of my renunciation, the US government literally taxes you until your very last moments as their citizen.

Your final tax bill is calculated based on the value of your assets the day before you take the oath of renunciation, as if you died that day and now must pay a death tax to the IRS before you can start your new life sans US citizenship. For those with enough wealth, the real renunciation fee is not the $2,350 you pay at the Embassy window but the mark-to-market exit tax on all your assets. This was the tax that had me working late into the night on the eve of my expatriation. Not everyone has to pay it, though. Only those individuals who meet at least one of three conditions will be deemed a covered expatriate, triggering the exit tax. The three tests are:

1. A net worth of at least $2 million
2. An average federal tax liability (liability, not income) over a specified amount in the five years prior to renouncing.
3. An inability to certify tax compliance (tax evaders and accidental Americans alike)

If you do not meet any of these tests, you will not have to pay the exit tax, but you will still need to do the paperwork to prove your case. It is vital to know whether you will qualify as a covered expatriate long before you renounce, not only to prepare for this paperwork but also to take measures to remediate the situation and potentially save tens of thousands of dollars from being sent to the IRS on your way out the door.

The first test is the one that causes the most concern for my clients. The good news is that the calculation includes not only the value of your assets but also your liabilities – your total net worth. Depending on your specific situation, you may have some wiggle room even if your assets add up to more than the $2 million threshold.

Some of the components of your net worth are more complicated to estimate than others. For instance, you will need to calculate the value of any companies you own as if you sold them the day that you renounced. This requires an intricate process to determine the worth of your business and how it counts toward your assets. If your business is worth a considerable amount, it may cost you more to leave and pay the exit tax than to continue paying taxes every year as a US citizen. So, if your company is nearing the $2 million threshold, it may be worth it for you to buy a second passport by investment and renounce before your business triggers the exit tax.

Real estate is another asset that can often prove challenging to estimate. Properties in the developed world are usually much easier to calculate than in the emerging and developing economies that I recommend for foreign investment. But even in the US, you may find yourself jumping through hoops to prove to the IRS that your home is not worth as much as they say it is.

And remember, the exit tax applies to all your assets as if you had sold them, which means that even if you do not sell your property (or your business or your stocks or your cryptocurrencies, etc.) before you leave, the IRS will treat you as if you already have the money from the sale in your pocket. You do receive an exemption for your personal residence, but all other investment properties are fair game when it comes to the exit tax.

Other assets such as cash, cryptocurrencies, gold, stocks, and bonds are much easier to calculate. Just be prepared to put a price tag on the worth of basically anything you own. One way or another, you will need professional help well before your renunciation date as well as right at the very end. This is not a tax you want catching you by surprise.

The second test is much less common and involves having a high average tax liability. The specified amount is adjusted for inflation every year. In 2020, the average liability threshold was set at $171,000. You would need to make a significant amount of money to pay an average of $171,000 in taxes each year, especially if you are an entrepreneur living overseas with control over your salary. On the other hand, if you are an employee with a high salary, this test could be problematic for you. My friend earning $1 million a year working in the Middle East would certainly trigger the exit tax with this test.

Whatever your situation, if in the last five years you have paid an average of $171,000 in taxes per year or $855,000 or more combined over the entire period, you will be considered a covered expatriate. With that kind of tax burden, the exit tax may be worth paying. Just be sure you give living overseas a try before you jump ship. You may be able to use other offshore strategies discussed in this book to help you legally reduce or even eliminate your tax burden without needing to renounce. If those solutions do not work, you can at least make the decision after traveling and gaining the knowledge that you do enjoy the lifestyle available to you outside of the United States.

The third and final test deals entirely with tax compliance. If you have been evading taxes, you will certainly be in a world of hurt if you attempt renunciation. But most people who trigger the exit tax via this test do so simply because they have never called the US home and were simply unaware that they had to file and pay taxes in a country in which they had barely set foot. Fortunately, these accidental Americans can back file their returns, declare that they meant no harm, and then renounce.

If you are a regular US citizen who moved overseas and simply assumed that you did not need to file or pay taxes once you were gone, you can use the streamlined filing compliance procedures to file any missing tax returns and avoid triggering the exit tax as well. However, if you simply cannot prove tax compliance for the past five years and choose to renounce before getting in compliance, you will be subject to the exit tax. You will not get away with anything less than compliance. If you do not file everything you need to file, it will come back to bite you one way or another. The only way to legally escape US taxation is to face the taxes you already owe to become tax compliant and then renounce.

While some situations are much easier to fix than others, it is possible to avoid being a covered expatriate at the time of your renunciation whether by becoming tax compliant, gifting money to family or giving it away to a charity, or even purchasing a second passport to lower your total net worth below the $2 million threshold.

But if you cannot avoid the exit tax no matter what you do, here is what to expect: once you calculate your net worth on your final day as a US citizen, you will then need to compute your total capital gains. The exit tax is essentially a final capital gains tax on all your assets, including anything under the $2 million threshold that initially triggered the tax. In 2020, you could exempt your first $737,000 in capital gains – a number that is adjusted annually to account for inflation – so there is some relief and even a chance that you will not owe that much. You can also defer the exit tax on certain assets such as a 401(k) but there are very few exceptions of this type.

The IRS will apply capital gains tax rates to long-term investments and regular income tax rates to short-term capital gains, so you will need to calculate each separately. But even with less than $737,000 in capital gains, you will still face other consequences as a covered expatriate. For instance, if you gift anything to family and friends within a year prior to your expatriation, they will have to pay taxes on the gift. You will also lose your ability to make unlimited tax-free gifts to a spouse who is also a US citizen. If one spouse maintains their US citizenship, they can only exclude roughly $150,000 before their gift becomes subject to the 40% gift tax.

The real challenge is if you have built up assets that you do not actually sell the day before you renounce. If you end up owing a substantial amount but all your money is tied up in your investments, you may not have the cash on hand to pay. Ultimately, if you can avoid becoming a covered expatriate, it will eliminate many complications from your life.

Still, for some folks, it may be worth it to pay the exit tax and just be done. It is estimated that Eduardo Saverin saved as much as $700 million by renouncing before Facebook went public. Paying an exit tax may not be the end of the world for you. But that is up for you to assess, preferably with the help of a professional by your side.

6. Fulfill All Final Reporting Obligations

As nice as it would be to take the oath of renunciation and automatically enjoy total freedom from the IRS and the US government, there are a few final loose ends to tie up – namely, two more reports. If you fail to file these final reports, you have not fully expatriated for tax purposes.

First you must file one final US tax return for the year in which you renounced. This is considered a dual status income tax return because you will be considered a US citizen for the part of the year prior to your renunciation and a non-US citizen for the latter part of the year. Thankfully, you will only be taxed for the part of the year in which you were still a US citizen.

The second report you must file is Form 8854, which is where you will declare all your assets and make any applicable exit tax payments. Your exact date of renunciation will determine which parts of the form you must complete. You must file Form 8854 alongside your income tax return. Until you file this form, you may remain subject to US tax.

Fortunately, since 2017, you no longer need to file tax returns for additional years following your renunciation. There is only the one final return, and then you are done.

7. Await Authorization

Once you file these final two forms, you are done with US citizenship as it relates to tax reporting. But for your renunciation to be officially complete, you will need to receive your Certificate of Loss of Nationality (CLN), and this can take some time following your renunciation interview.

At my interview, they informed me that it would take them a couple of weeks to send the paperwork to the US State Department in Washington D.C., have everything processed, stamped, and sealed, and then receive the certificate in return. A couple of weeks sounded fast, so it was no surprise that it took a couple of months. I have helped clients whose CLN arrived a full five months after they took the oath of renunciation.

Whatever the wait time, once you have taken the oath, the certificate is basically guaranteed. There is always the chance that something was not done correctly on the technical side of your renunciation, but it is rare if not unheard of for a renunciation to be rejected once the oath is taken and your forms have been submitted. That said, there are a few opportunities and challenges that come during this period of limbo.

Even though the day that you take the oath of renunciation is the day that you are officially considered a non-US citizen, you will need to await authorization before you can prove that status to any concerned parties such as banks and immigration programs. Many banks will only allow former US citizens to open an account if the bank officials can physically see the Certificate of Loss of Nationality. They want 100% certainty that you do not carry the liability of US citizenship. (Yes, FATCA really is that bad.)

There are some limited-time opportunities that come during this waiting period, though. The officials in Tbilisi were nice enough to say that if I needed my passport to travel, I could keep it and continue to use it up until my CLN was issued. I have even had clients who have been told by Embassy officials that they could keep their passport and travel back to the United States to tie up any loose ends. I would not count on this happening, especially if you go to a larger diplomatic post to renounce. While the CLN is the final nail in the coffin, it is always better to have your affairs sorted out beforehand.

8. Receive the Certificate of Loss of Nationality (CLN)

I received an email on January 17, 2018, stating that my renunciation had been approved. In all, even with the holidays, the approval went through in about a month. The Embassy contacted me a couple of weeks later to inform me that they had the certificate in their offices.

Because they could not mail it to me and since I had traveled to Malaysia by then and could not pick up the CLN myself, we took a few days to set up a basic power of attorney so that someone could pick it up on my behalf. It took another week for them to approve the power of attorney and confirm that I could send my friend to pick up my certificate. On February 12, she picked it up and sent me pictures. It was over.

That was the moment it felt real to me. I never felt like it was not real or that I had skipped any steps along the way or did not know what I was getting into but having documentary evidence that I was no longer a US citizen made that reality very apparent.

In my core, I tend to be a bit sentimental. At Nomad Capitalist, 2017 was the year that we focused on the concept of home and defining the what and where of its meaning, especially for Nomads. Going through the process of renouncing, I began to understand that even if I did not feel at home in the US, it is still hard to go through a procedure to totally swear off the option of being a citizen of a certain country for the rest of your life and not wonder if that place really is your home.

I have said for years that you do not have an obligation to be patriotic or madly in love with the place where you were born. You do not have to stay there forever. You have a literal world of other options to consider. I still believe that. But that does not mean that you might have to fight off some of those conditioned beliefs when making such a monumental decision. As I felt in the moment of taking the oath of renunciation, it is like breaking up with someone who you know is not right for you. Maybe you wanted the relationship to work, but it still needs to come to an end. Even though you know it is the right decision, it is emotional to say goodbye and realize that it is over.

I felt the gravity of the 'breakup' when I was taking the oath of renunciation but receiving the Certificate of Loss of Nationality convinced me that it really was over. The biggest gut punch though was getting the news that the Embassy had sent my old US passports on to the US State Department in Washington D.C. where they were destroyed. I had asked them to set aside the passports for me and send them back when they had been cancelled. They had said that there were no guarantees, but I was not quite prepared to hear that they had been destroyed. That was a bit gut-wrenching.

Those passports had taken me all over the world for the past 33 years. My nostalgia was not for the US passport itself but for the history it contained. Thankfully, I had taken pictures of the passports. When another government asked me to prove that I had not been in the country during a specific period so that I could file my tax exemption, I was able to prove it to them with pictures of stamps in my US passport. So, regardless of whether you have formed an emotional attachment to your US passport, it is smart to hold onto it or at least get pictures to document the places you have been as a US citizen.

In the end, knowing that the passports were gone was a great way for me to move on with the rest of my life. With the passports destroyed and the CLN in my hand, there was no looking back.

What Happens After You Renounce?

If there is no looking back, what happens next? Knowing what comes after renunciation is important information to incorporate into your decision to renounce in the first place. Renouncing does come at a cost – both financially and otherwise. As we have already discussed, you need to know how this decision will impact you. There are a lot of questions to ask and consequences to consider, both good and bad.

In this final section, we will go over some of the biggest changes that renouncing will create in your life post-renunciation. But know that there will always be an element of the unknown when stepping into a new life. There are things about the renunciation process and its impact that you cannot know, and you would be a little crazy if you did not say, "I don't know how that's going to turn out." I remember wondering whether I would be able to get visas or worrying if my next passport plan would work out. What would I be if I was not American? Even with a solid plan and certainty in my decision, there were still a lot of 'what ifs'.

I once had a coach who taught me that "you have to lean into fear." It is part of the process. Any great thing in life that requires dramatic change – whether it is creating a business empire or doing something beautiful – will involve a level of uncertainty and fear. Shying away from that kind of change is likely an indication that you are too settled in the wrong ways. As I faced the uncertainties of what life as a renunciant would bring, I sought to lean into the fear and embrace it knowing that everything would work out in the end. And it has.

You may never be 100% certain. It is like going out on stage. Performers like Frank Sinatra would say that you are always going to have some butterflies. But despite the butterflies, you can still know that whatever happens, you can deal with it. And that is what I discovered as I stepped into life as a non-US citizen. I realized that I had figured out enough and that it was easier to be ready than I had thought. I had created a life outside of the US, I had my Plan B in place, and I knew enough about what was coming to take it all in stride.

As I have worked with clients through the years who are facing the decision to renounce, I have found that many of the same questions come up repeatedly. From personal experience and from working with these individuals, I have learned the answers to those questions and can speak to the realities of life after renunciation. So, here is what to expect after you renounce:

Do Former US Citizens Still Pay US Taxes?

There are a lot of myths out there about US tax obligations for renunciants. Part of this misunderstanding comes from the different requirements that have been imposed over the years. One of the main myths is that you will have to pay taxes for ten years after you leave. This is an old law. Back in the 90s, there was a high-profile renunciation and people got upset so the IRS implemented some rules that if you renounce, you cannot leave the tax net right away.

That law has since been replaced with the exit tax that we have already discussed. If you trigger the exit tax via one of the three tests, you will have to pay the exit tax with your final dual status tax return after renouncing. But once you have done that, you are done. You can move on with your life. And if you do not qualify as a covered expatriate, then all that is required of you is to file your final dual status tax return. You can make a clean break.

Renouncing allows you to prevent new tax debts and free yourself from most future tax obligations and reporting requirements, however, it does not erase what has already been done. Whatever has already happened prior to your renunciation does not simply disappear when you renounce. You will still need to pay existing tax debts and meet all financial responsibilities such as child support payments. You can also still be charged with crimes and be hauled in by the IRS for past tax violations.

Once you have left, you will be treated as a non-resident alien for tax purposes. This means that you will not be taxed by the United States unless you choose to live, invest, or do business there. There are, essentially, two ways that you can fall back into the US tax net and reacquire filing obligations with the IRS even after renouncing. The first is to become a US person, which covers more than just US citizens. US persons include residents, US partnerships and corporations, US estates and certain trusts, and anyone who spends too much time in the country and qualifies as a tax resident.

The second way that you can fall back into the US tax net even after renouncing is to own US assets that are subject to US tax or filing obligations. This can include investing in US real estate, having ownership in a company that is majority-owned by US persons, having US-sourced stocks and bonds, or generating income within the US by some other means. If you make money in the US, you owe money to the US – plain and simple.

And if you plan on maintaining your investments in the US until your dying day, you may end up paying more taxes by renouncing than by sticking around. How? Estate taxes. At first, it may seem like a good idea to renounce to shield your foreign assets from the up-to-40% federal estate taxes that apply to your worldwide assets at the time of your death. But the estate tax also applies to US property owned by non-US citizens, and only US citizens can shield up to $11.2 million in assets from the estate tax. Non-US citizens can only shield $60,000. That is a stark difference.

If you truly want to escape the death tax, you will need to relinquish your US investments before you die and move to one of the many countries with no estate taxes. This will take high levels of professional planning to successfully execute, but it is possible.

Can I Still Use US Banks?

While it is a good idea to give up your US investments before you get hit by the estate tax, you do not have to close all your US bank accounts and give up your credit cards to stay out of the US tax system. Citizens of countries with residence-based taxation, like Australia and Canada, are not so lucky. If they want to leave their tax system, they must cut all ties to become tax non-resident. But the US government actually encourages non-citizens to bank in the US by offering no interest income tax for non-resident aliens. Once you are gone, you can earn interest in US banks tax-free.

As a renunciant, you can keep your existing accounts and cards and potentially even apply for more. It may be more difficult to be approved for additional credit, but not impossible. Even after renouncing, you will maintain both your Social Security number and your credit score. So, while your options may be more limited in both quantity and quality, there is a good chance that you can get new accounts. And if you keep your existing accounts in good standing and pay your bills on time, it is unlikely you would lose them after your renunciation.

The fact is that there are not that many distinctions between citizens and non-citizens in terms of what you can do within the US besides the ability to live there. Beyond taxation concerns, there is no reason that you cannot keep any homes, raw land, or US companies (excluding S-corps) after you have renounced. There may be tax and reporting requirements in some cases, but you are not barred from participating in the US market simply because you are no longer a US citizen.

On the flip side, you may find that foreign banks will be much more open to working with you once you have renounced your US citizenship. I have seen banks in places as difficult as Switzerland and Hong Kong be more open to non-US citizens. Not only is it easier but also faster to open accounts in other countries once you have relinquished US citizenship – assuming, of course, that you can present your Certificate of Loss of Nationality.

Will I Still Receive Government Benefits as a Renunciant?

One of the main concerns that I hear from clients about renouncing is that they do not want to lose out on government benefits like Social Security once they have renounced. They have spent their whole life paying into the system, so what happens to all that money if they give up their citizenship? The truth is that – in most cases – it is still yours to claim, regardless of your citizenship status.

The three main government benefits of concern are Social Security, Medicare, and military pensions. Of the three, military pensions are the only benefit you will completely lose if you were to renounce. While seven- and eight-figure income earners and high-net-worth individuals may not be concerned about the paltry payouts that they may get from these government benefits compared to their personal investments, it is worth looking at how each benefit is impacted by renunciation.

First, Social Security. Not only can you receive your Social Security benefits while living overseas but you can also receive those benefits even after you renounce. The key is to qualify for the payments in the first place. To do so, you must have worked a minimum of forty calendar quarters in the US, which works out to be roughly ten years of work. That count is cumulative and does not have to be consecutive, so even that job you had the summer after your sophomore year of high school could count. You do, however, need to meet a certain earning limit within each quarter for it to qualify. In 2021, that limit is just under $1500 total.

If you meet the minimum requirement of 40 quarters, your earnings over time will be averaged out to determine how much you will receive in Social Security payments. The longer you work and pay into the US system, the more your payment will build up over time. Because I left the US at such a young age, the last time I got on the Social Security website, my calculated payout was a whopping $1200 a month. Even if I did have to give up that money, it was not enough to keep me tied to the US for the rest of my life.

There are too many questions about the Social Security system, in general, to make it a deciding factor in any decision. Who knows what the age limit will be when I can finally start receiving that money? And who knows if any money will be left in the system when I reach retirement age? There is a chance that Social Security will eventually be means-tested, so people with any kind of net worth may not qualify for Social Security at all by the time their turn rolls around.

But at this point, whatever is left in the system when it is your turn to cash in is yours whether you maintain your citizenship or renounce. Renouncing will not add any more problems to the Social Security equation than those that already exist. What you get is what you paid in. If you have been offshore for a long time using the strategies that I discuss in this book, you probably have not been paying into the pot for some time. But whatever is already there will be yours to claim.

Just like Social Security, Medicare benefits are available for you to claim even after you renounce. The challenge with Medicare is that you need to be in the United States to make use of those benefits. You cannot get Medicare benefits overseas. That means that if you do not have a passport that grants you visa-free access to the US and you cannot secure a visa, you will not be able to return to the US to access those benefits. There is a chance that the program may change in the future to cover overseas medical care, but it is not an option now. In summary, you maintain the right, but access is not guaranteed as a renunciant.

When it comes to military benefits and other municipal and state government pensions, there is almost no doubt that you will lose your right to claim those benefits if you renounce. I have talked with veterans who served ten years in the US but no longer agree with what is going on and want out. But if you are going to get a $50,000 yearly pension from the military sometime soon, you may want to reconsider renunciation. Military pensions are much more secure, especially compared to all the questions surrounding the future of Social Security. If you are younger and can afford to give up whatever benefits that you have, renunciation could still be on the table. Just know that your military benefits will not stick around if you do renounce.

Can I Visit the United States as a non-US Citizen?

Perhaps the biggest question of all on the minds of those considering renunciation is whether they will be able to return to the United States once they have given up their citizenship. The idea that you can never return is largely a myth. It is true that the Reed Amendment was passed in 1996 and stipulates that renunciants can be denied entrance to the United States if they renounced to avoid paying income taxes. However, implementation of this law has been nearly impossible. From 2002 to 2015, only two people were denied entry into the US on the grounds of the Reed Amendment.

While they could come out with a more workable version of the amendment, all efforts to date have been unsuccessful. Growing nationalism in the United States means that it is always a possibility, but the current reality is that a renunciant is the same as any other non-citizen in the eyes of the State Department when it comes to determining admissibility. In other words, after you renounce, the United States will treat you like a citizen of any other country. And for everyone else in the world, there are three different groups with varying levels of tourism access to the United States:

1.   Canadians
2.   Visa-waiver countries
3.   Visa-dependent countries

Due to geographic proximity and the amicable relationship between the United States and Canada, Canadians have greater visa-free travel privileges to the United States than any other nationality in the world. Canadians are the only people on earth besides US citizens who can enter the United States without filling out any forms. They can simply show up at the border or get on a plane and be greeted with open arms upon arrival. US citizens share reciprocal privileges when entering Canada.

If you are a dual US-Canadian citizen and choose to renounce your US citizenship, you can return to the United States almost as if you were still American. Canadians can stay up to 180 days at a time. (And if you do not want to fall back into the US tax net, you do not want to spend more than 180 days per year in the country anyway.) Technically, they can still deny you entry because you are not a US citizen, but even at the height of COVID-19 border closures, Canadians could still enter the United States by plane.

The second level of US access is for individuals from countries that have a visa-waiver to the United States. Currently, there are 39 countries with visa-waiver access to the US, including most countries in Western Europe, Australia, Singapore, Taiwan, South Korea, Japan, New Zealand, and more recently, Chile. To make it into the visa-waiver program, a country needs to have a visa refusal rate of 3% or less over time.

We discussed these countries in the last chapter as the Tier A passports because they are the ones that can get you into the United States. The one difference between Canadians and people from these countries is that they need to fill out ESTA – the electronic system for travel authorization – which is a form that must be filled out online before traveling.

To do so, you register your passport, indicate that you will be traveling to the United States, pay a very small fee, and then they run your information through a database. More than 99% of the time, they approve you, you print out the little form, and you show it at the airport counter if asked. This must be done once every two years. It will give you up to 90 days in the United States at a time and can be used for multiple trips within that two-year period. Without this form, you will not be allowed to enter the United States.

While some people claim that you can renounce with a visa-waiver passport and enter the US the next day, you must apply for ESTA at least 72 hours before you travel, which gives you a three-day window where you will not be able to enter the country. That said, I know one guy who renounced with a visa-waiver passport but had a trip planned to the US for a conference and he was able to keep his US passport during the limbo period and get in with that instead of his ESTA paperwork. I also know someone who renounced with a Swiss passport who found that it was easier to enter the US with ESTA than as a US citizen. In all, I have not heard of many people having problems with the visa waiver program.

The one caveat is if you have visited countries like Iran, Iraq, Sudan, or North Korea. Even if you have a passport from a visa-waiver country, visiting one of these countries will make you ineligible for ESTA. I had a client from the UK once who visited Iran and he had to go to the embassy to get approved for a visa instead of using ESTA. The bottom line is that you cannot just get on a plan and show up in the United States if you are from a visa-waiver country. You must apply in advance and pay a small fee. And that is assuming that you can get a passport from one of the select countries that are part of the program in the first place.

Most people in the world fall into the final category and must obtain a tourist visa prior to traveling to the United States. This requires a trip to a US embassy, a significant paperwork load, and a large fee starting at $160. In comparison to ESTA, you can get a US visa that lasts as much as ten years and is good for 180 days at a time. The trick is getting approved.

With a Tier B or Tier C passport, you will need to go to the US embassy and demonstrate where you live and why you are going to return to your home country. If you are nomadic and cannot prove that you have a real home where you will return after your trip, you may have difficulty getting a visa. You need to show that you have a home, money in the bank, friends, and everything that normal people have who live in one country. Otherwise, it is difficult to disprove immigrant intent.

You should also be prepared to explain why you are traveling to the United States, whether it is to attend a conference, visit your mother, or do XYZ. You will need to tell them what you will be doing and show them your travel plans. If you can demonstrate your return flight, you usually have a greater chance of getting a visa. While it is a lot easier than most people think, the reality is that the United States is not an easy place to get into.

There is usually some luck involved in the process too. There is always someone who is nice and someone who is not that nice working at the embassy on any given day. It can be a bit of a gamble. Do not assume that you can just waltz in and get a visa. You need to have a plan. Most people are not out to reject renunciants, but if you have a passport from a country where 40% of visa applicants get rejected, there is a chance that you might be part of the 40%. In the end, no one except US citizens have a guaranteed right to get back into the United States. They can accept and deny anyone.

Beyond tourist visas, there are other immigrant and non-immigrant programs that will allow you to return to the US, often by starting a business or making investments in the country. If this is your intent, certain passports will give you a leg up in this regard. For instance, among the countries that offer citizenship by investment, only a couple have E-2 access to the US, including Grenada and Turkey. If you plan to get back into the US with an E-2 visa, make sure that you have the right second passport to get the job done before you renounce.

What Will My Visa-Free Travel Be Like Without a US Passport?

But what about the rest of the world? Depending on the passport portfolio you have built, your travel privileges could vary widely once you have renounced. With my current passport portfolio, the list of countries that I cannot visit without a visa includes Angola, Australia, Brunei, Canada, the Central African Republic, Equatorial Guinea, Mexico, Morocco, New Zealand, Papa New Guinea, Paraguay, Saudi Arabia (technically, an e-visa), and the United States.

The CUNA countries – Canada, the United States, New Zealand, and Australia – are going to be difficult for almost everyone. If you do not have a Tier A passport, the question you have to ask is whether you can live without visiting these four countries or deal with the hassle of getting a visa or residence permit for each one. At one point, I had a serious FFOMO (future fear of missing out) of not being able to visit these countries. When I took a step back and looked at things with a level head, though, I realized that I had spent a combined total of 11 days in all four countries in a three-year period. A little more time spent traveling convinced me that I could be happy anywhere. I did not need an English-speaking country with free tap water to make me happy, even if the people there were some of the few in the world that got my dry sense of humor.

Since renouncing, the only country still on my list that I have wanted to visit that I do not have visa-free access to is Mexico, and that is because I decided to not go through with the paperwork to switch the residence that I had obtained there as a US citizen to another citizenship. Other countries that are often difficult include Thailand, Serbia, South Africa, and Costa Rica. But even these difficult countries are not that difficult. When I still needed a visa to go to Thailand, I simply went to the Thai Embassy in Kuala Lumpur, filled out a form saying where I was going and staying, and then printed out a copy of my flight ticket. I left my application and documents at the embassy with my passport and came back the next day to pick up my visa.

Many Americans equate visa requirements to essentially not being able to travel to a country. This simply is not the case. What I have found in the few instances where I have had to apply for a visa is that it is not the end of the world. You can apply for visas with relative ease. Living without a US passport – or even a Tier A passport – has not been as difficult as I had imagined. I have not encountered any big travel issues. There have been some small inconveniences like having to change my travel plans so that I did not fly through Australia between Malaysia and Colombia, but the inconveniences have truly been minimal.

To be honest, most countries do not care where you are from. The CUNA countries may be a bit more inquisitive, but even they are not that bad. There is even a chance that it will be easier to travel without a US passport. With my passport portfolio, I have added half a dozen new countries to my visa-free list that even US passport holders cannot access visa-free.

The truth is that my FFOMO, and probably yours, was based largely on old beliefs about where the good life can be found – the classic name brand trap. I used to think, "What if I want to live in Miami one day?!" But now I know that Mauritius has even better beaches than Miami. And the luxury living that I thought I could only find in the CUNA countries is totally blown out of the water by places like Dubai and Singapore. What is more, these places are open to people from basically anywhere. It is amazing to talk with people from Kenya, the Philippines, Cote d'Ivoire, Mauritius, and Malaysia all in one country. I feel happy, at peace, and understood in these places with these people.

I used to buy into the belief that the only good service was in English-speaking countries. I even thought that I would eventually want to return to an English-speaking country. But the reality is that there is an entire world out there full of nice people who make me feel at home more than I ever thought possible. And it turns out that it is not that hard to explore that world without a US passport.

Could You Renounce on Just a Tier C Passport?

The question remains, could you renounce with just a Tier C passport? People tend to go overboard thinking that they need a Tier

A passport. We talked about that in the last chapter and why Tier B passports are the wave of the future. But could you travel with only a Tier C passport? Potentially, yes. The sweet spot is certainly Tier B because it gives you access to the EU and likely several other countries. Even with just a relatively basic passport portfolio of two passports, you could probably access most countries in the world besides the more difficult countries like CUNA, Thailand, South Africa, etc.

But there is also the chance that you do not want to do much traveling and plan to stay in one place. If that is the case for you, then a Tier C passport could work. When I renounced, I had only publicly spoken about my passport from the Comoros Islands. While I had other passports at the time, imagine that this was my only passport after giving up my US passport.

At the time, Comorians had visa-free access to less than 50 countries. However, I could visit places like Singapore, Hong Kong, Macau, the Philippines, Indonesia, Myanmar, and India. I could also visit Malaysia for 30 days at a time, where I could have applied for the Malaysia My Second Home (MM2H) program by depositing some money in the bank to get a residence permit that was good for ten years. I could use Malaysia as my base and then travel around Southeast Asia visa-free while I worked on other passport options.

The Comoros passport is a true Tier C passport, but I could have made it work. If your goal is to stay in one place or one region, you could make a Tier C passport work as well. There are plenty of countries that offer residence permits to anyone willing to purchase real estate, put money in the bank, or do business. So, even without citizenship, you could find a place to call home by getting a residence permit in a place where you do not mind settling down. Most countries are not that particular about your passport. If you want to invest, you will usually find the door wide open.

A residence permit can also serve to increase your travel options in some cases. For example, getting residence anywhere in the Schengen area in Europe grants you a regional residence permit with opportunities to live and even work throughout the European Union. There are several investment migration programs that will get you EU residence and the chance at a passport in the future.

With a Tier C+ passport like Turkey and an EU residence, you could have almost Tier-B-level travel privileges. At the very least, you will add some of the most popular places to visit in the world to your list.

There are even some countries that will let you in visa-free if you have an EU residence permit, even if your passport does not grant you the same privilege.

While it is a good idea to have a passport portfolio before you renounce – or at least a Tier B passport – you could potentially renounce with only a Tier C passport. The key is to think through the various scenarios, have a plan, and to be happy with the options that will be available to you once you hand in one of the best passports for visa- free travel in the world.

Is it Possible to Reclaim US Citizenship?

When the officials at the US Embassy asked me if I was sure I wanted to renounce, it almost seemed like they felt bad enough for me that if I had called the next day and said, "Just take the paper off your stack, I'm coming in to get my passport back!" they might have done it. I do not know what the bureaucratic procedure is at that point in the process, but I felt like they might have done it because they want to stop you from renouncing, not because they are bad people but because they are very proud of their country and could never imagine doing anything like that themselves.

In some countries, it really is as simple as saying you want your citizenship back. But in the US and Canada, they make it extremely difficult to regain your citizenship once you have renounced. If you do regret your decision to renounce once you have gone through with it, you have two options. The first is to challenge the renunciation through a court or administrative procedure claiming that you never meant to give your citizenship up in the first place. This route is basically impossible.

The second route is to get in line with everybody else. You will need to get a visa that leads to permanent residence and then play the waiting game to become naturalized, being sure to meet the physical presence requirements, pay your taxes, pay the fees, and pass all the language and history tests along the way. You will not be able to claim your parents as a path back to citizenship by descent. You simply get back in line.

There is no quick and easy procedure to reinstate your citizenship. According to the US State Department, the act of renouncing is "irrevocable" and cannot be reversed. Your renunciation is permanent. After you renounce, for better or worse, the United States will treat you like the citizen of any other country. And if you do manage to make it through the naturalization process like all the other folks hoping to become Americans, the difference between being a naturalized citizen versus native-born citizenship is that if you do anything wrong, the government could denaturalize you.

As always, there are no guarantees that they will let you back in. As I have said, renunciation is not a decision to take lightly. Yes, there is a pathway back, but it is long and comes with its own consequences. If you are considering renunciation, be sure that it really is what you want now and in the future.

How Can I Plan for My Future as a Renunciant?

You will face many new challenges after you renounce. We have tackled some of the biggest questions here, including taxes, banking, government benefits, travel to the United States and around the world, and what it takes to regain your US citizenship. But we have only begun to scratch the surface. That is what the rest of this book is for. We have already taken a deep dive into topics like second passports and lifestyle, but there is more to come. You will need to take all these different pieces of the offshore life and work them into a holistic plan to ensure that the future you embrace once you have renounced is one that you desire.

And when I say holistic, I mean holistic. Everything needs to work together as a whole. Take your residence as an example. Once you are no longer a US citizen, you will need to have a new place to call home for more than one reason. Banks and immigration programs will want to know where you live (your physical residence) and where you are taxed (your tax residence), or they may reject you. And if you do not clearly establish both your physical and tax residencies, you may create a more complicated tax situation for yourself than before. Your residence also plays into your travel privileges, as we have already discussed, as well as your lifestyle opportunities.

With just one example, it is easy to see how one piece of the puzzle can play into everything from taxes to banking to immigration to lifestyle to travel. You want to be sure that every piece of the puzzle is working together before you renounce because that is when you will need the plan to operate at 100%. Yes, you can learn and adapt and evolve according to your needs as time goes by, but it is much better to know where you are going before you take the plunge than to simply dive into the deep and renounce without a plan.

If you have never lived outside of the United States and you want to renounce, do yourself a favor and give living abroad a test drive before you renounce. Find the places that you love, the cultures that resonate with you, the foods and the amenities you crave, the people with whom you can connect, and the lifestyle you want. But do not stop there. Think through your financial situation to ensure that you are not stepping out of the frying pan and into the fire when you renounce. Get a second passport. Open an offshore bank account. Invest in a home. Make a plan. Then, whether you renounce or not, you will be ready for anything that comes.

Embrace Your Newfound Freedom

Three days before I renounced, I stood on the Bosphorus in Istanbul while on a long layover from New York to Tbilisi. Five years earlier, I had stood in almost the same place on a trip I took right before I began Nomad Capitalist. There was a lot going on back then. The Cyprus bank debacle was just starting to unravel in late 2012 and I remember walking along the Bosphorus and thinking how much easier life would be if I could be one of the ships on the river carrying a flag of some different country heading toward any number of different places. Life would be so much easier if I did not have the restrictions of being an American.

That was the beginning of trying to determine how I could go where I was treated best. I had talked to the people who said, "Oh, just get an offshore company and don't report it! Get an offshore bank account and don't tell anybody." But I knew that those strategies would not work. Not anymore. More importantly, I knew they were not legal. They would not work. I knew I needed a legal strategy to go where I was treated best to truly have the freedom that these ships had to go where they wanted and do business where they needed under a flag that they chose.

Even then, I had a feeling that if I was not a US citizen, I would be freer. Standing in that same place five years later, I knew I was on the brink of freedom. But that freedom did not come from my impending renunciation alone, it came from everything I had learned and implemented during the last five years. I had learned to be the architect of my own life. Letting go of the United States was the final step in being able to say, "They will do what is best for the United States and I am going to do what is best for me." I knew that the time had come. I felt more comfortable standing on the Bosphorus with the majestic Blue Mosque behind me than I would standing in New York City watching ships go out to the Atlantic.

It had been a roller coaster over the previous weeks watching the laws change in the United States and trying to figure out what I would have to pay if I stayed or if I left. The numbers were constantly changing with every proposal as Congress worked out the new tax bill. That morning in Istanbul, I woke up and realized that it was not about the money at all. I just wanted to be free. I wanted the world to truly be my oyster. I did not want to be caught up in the circus anymore. I wanted all the options available to me, and I could no longer pursue the life I wanted and remain a US citizen.

The mental burden alone of worrying about doing something wrong or filling out a form incorrectly had become too much. I wanted to calm down a bit, relax, and be free. That desire was just as appealing to me that day as it had been the first time I had come to the Bosphorus in Istanbul five years earlier. That was the moment that I realized that the elements surrounding the decision to renounce could come and go, but I was not at peace with the decision. I was ready to be free.

Three days later, I took the oath of renunciation and began a new life, one with bigger and better things ahead. That decision pushed me to be a different kind of me. I opened a priority bank account in Singapore and made it my main account. I moved a lot of my money out of the United States to do it. I accepted my new life as one in which I did not rely on the United States much at all. I was no longer going to use it as a crutch simply because it was what I was used to. I began to embrace my identity as a new global citizen at a new level and in ways I never had before.

In doing so, I gained the peace of mind that I had been seeking. In the past year of chaos, I watched as people became increasingly uneasy in the United States and the western world in general. But I was at peace. As more and more people were presented with fewer options, fewer travel freedoms, fewer places to bank and invest and do business, more rules, more regulations, and more restrictions, all accompanied by fewer profits and less power to control their money and freedom, I breathed a sigh of relief that I had left that system behind.

I still choose to act ethically and run a normal business and make relatively straightforward investments, but I can do so without someone breathing down my neck or worrying about the next rule or regulation. As they say in the Balkans, "It is not my problem" anymore.

The events of 2020 have become a convenient excuse for governments around the world to restrict freedoms on almost every front. In fact, it became virtually impossible to renounce your US citizenship during this time. As time goes on, the strategies in this book – foreign bank accounts, residence programs, setting up companies in other jurisdictions, second passports, even expatriating – are becoming more difficult. You need to have options. And exercising those options sooner rather than later is a good thing.

If you have been considering renunciation and have determined that it is the right move for you, the time to take action is now. Get a second passport whether it is for a Plan A or a Plan B so that you can be ready to go or simply go. The time to get ready is now. There is a great sense of peace to be found in knowing that you are in control of your own destiny. If you have planted the right flags, you can move on to a life of greater freedom and abundance by handing in your US passport and following through on the decision to renounce.

Your How-To Action Plan

Immediate Action Steps: Make a list of your personal reasons for and against renunciation. Assess the following: Can you sufficiently reduce your taxes with other strategies besides renunciation? Calculate the return on investment if you were to renounce. What is your timeline to a second passport based on your current strategies? If you are planning on renouncing, will you have that second passport before you qualify as a covered expatriate? Have you already passed the threshold for the exit tax? Are there ways you can reduce your net worth below the $2 million mark?

Travel Action Steps: If you have never traveled outside of the United States on a long-term basis before and you are considering renunciation, test whether you even like living overseas and work on your lifestyle design before saying goodbye to the US forever.

Holistic Planning: The timing of your renunciation may depend on other factors in your offshore plan, such as when you acquire a second passport, set up your business offshore, or find a new home base. Renunciation should only come after you have created and carried out the other parts of your Plan A or B. It may simplify your offshore planning in many ways if your renounce, but it may also add new challenges. Review the final section of this chapter and plan how you will address each question.

Chapter Six: Love and Family on the Road

Is This Only a Young Man's Game?

Dateline: Hanoi, Vietnam

"Where did your mother go into labor?" a throaty voice greeted me at the other end of the Skype call.

I had just arrived in Hanoi – the 1000-year-old historic capital city of Vietnam – where I was about to embark on a six-month scouting trip throughout Southeast Asia looking for investment opportunities. In preparation, I had arranged calls with several fellow nomads with experience in the area.

On the other end of the call was Pete Sisco, a long-time internet business owner who had perfected a system for getting buff while lifting weights in your spare time. Having lived a nomadic lifestyle with his wife for years, Pete knew a lot about certain boom areas, making him one of the first people on my list.

After his question, there was a substantial pause.

"Um, Cleveland," I replied. For some reason, I had to gather my thoughts before I knew what to answer.

"The US, as I expected," Pete stated with a calm surety.

Pete explained that he asked everyone where their mother went into labor as a sort of libertarian calling card. As a nomad, Pete had long dealt with the challenge of answering the question "Where are you from?" and started asking his question as a cheeky alternate to throw people off guard.

Alas, nomads have different ways to answer the question, "Where are you from?" The author Taiye Selasi tells people to ask instead, "Where are you a local?" implying that where you feel at home is really where you are from. Infamous anarchist commentator Jeff Berwick tells people he is 'from earth' before explaining the whole deal about how we are all just God's creatures on one planet. Pete's quip, however, does raise questions for Nomad Capitalists: Where are you from?

One of the key takeaways of this book is that each of us is a rugged individual, able to go where we want to go and be who we want to be. The judgment of having to fit into someone else's barriers is no longer important. If you want to say, "I'm Canadian," do so. If you are a frequent traveler, that may be enough. If you settle down somewhere, you can say "I'm Canadian, but live in Serbia at the moment." Still easy enough.

But what happens when you obtain multiple second passports, marry someone from another country, have three homes on different continents, and never spend more than three months in any one location? It may sound complicated, but you will figure it out as you come to understand your new identity as a citizen of the world. No need to worry too much. The real conundrum is how so many of us manage to pigeonhole ourselves into one identity based solely on where we were born.

This was the exact riddle Pete wanted to discuss during our call. If our birth location is what has caused us to pay high taxes and deal with crappy banks for all these years, it would be a good idea to identify what makes us paint ourselves into such a corner against our best wishes.

Pete articulated that, of the seven billion or so humans on this planet, we are divided into approximately 200 camps by a thing called 'nationality.' Based on which camp we are in, we get a little book that allows us to travel around. Seeing as we are all humans, you would think that we would have equal travel privileges. However, the way our world is designed, humans are not so equal. Because my mother went into labor in Cleveland, Ohio in a place called 'the United States,' I inherently had more freedom to travel around the world than someone born on the same October 21st in Colombo, Sri Lanka.

Where your mother went into labor can tell a lot about you. For those of us born in North America, it dictates our citizenship. While having a second citizenship is an excellent idea, some of us benefit more than others from our birth citizenship. Yet, whether we asked for it or not, our nationality – our camp – dictates who we are and what rules we are meant to follow. If your mother went into labor in the United States, you will be branded as an American by virtue of your birth and childhood there. As a result, you will need to pay taxes for your entire life, avoid anti-US government protests when you travel, abide by any rules the United States government insists upon, and never associate or do business with people from other camps that the CIA does not like.

You had no choice in the matter, but because your mother went into labor at a certain point on the map, you inherited characteristics, responsibilities, and debts through the age-old 'social contract.' However, you can flip the script on this situation by using many of the strategies in this book to benefit from the system in a sort of government arbitrage by which you take the best parts of each country while tossing out the worst. One way to do this is through birth tourism.

Birth Tourism

As Pete and I discussed the merits of his theory, we examined an entirely different angle of giving birth: birthright citizenship. Certain countries grant citizenship to anyone who is born there, regardless of status. As we reviewed in the chapter on second passports, most of Europe and Asia determine an individual's citizenship by their parents. Two German parents living in Thailand will give birth to a German child. European and Asian countries, with rare exceptions, do not award citizenship based on the location of birth but on blood.

Most countries in the Americas, on the other hand, give citizenship based on birthplace. That is why two Mexican immigrants living in California automatically give birth to a US citizen. I am a native-born US citizen, not only because my parents are both US citizens but also because I was born on US soil. If my parents had been vacationing on the other side of Niagara Falls at the time of my birth, I would have been Canadian by virtue of where I was born and American because my parents would have no doubt registered their new bundle of joy as an American born overseas to US citizens so I could live with them back on the other side of Lake Erie.

This principle of citizenship by birth is a unique twist on the Lucky Sperm Club we talked about in the second passports chapter. While you have no control over where your parents gave birth to you, anyone can take advantage of the Lucky Sperm Club on behalf of their child by simply giving birth overseas. As I write this, 31 countries grant instant citizenship to babies born on their soil, hence the term citizenship of the soil or 'jus soli'.

The United States and Canada have long been targeted by foreign mothers-to-be as a place to give birth to an American or Canadian child. For them, giving their child such an opportunity would set them up for life. Since the people I work with are trying to escape bankrupt, high-tax, anti-privacy countries like the United States and Canada, the other 29 countries are of particular interest to Nomad Capitalists.

You can use birth tourism as a tool to not only give your children more opportunities in life but to plant new flags for yourself. If you are planning on having children, why not take advantage of these countries that will give your child a second passport at birth? Not only can you and your spouse pass your natural-born and naturalized citizenships to your child, but you can also gift them an additional passport by choosing to give birth abroad. And as a cherry on the top, some countries will even put you on a fast track toward citizenship just for giving birth to a new citizen on their soil.

If the thought of giving birth outside of your home country has you worried, consider this: People give birth to children all around the world every day – 385,000 on a daily basis, in fact. Given current birth and death rates, we are net adding one billion people to the planet every thirteen years. Only 4% of those babies are born in the United States, and barely 1% of them are born in England, Canada, and Australia combined. That means that a lot of people are having babies in places other than where you think you 'need' to have them.

There is something to be said about the culture of giving birth in different countries as well. Mrs. H. has met friends around the world who have given birth in countries like Singapore and Malaysia, and they cannot say enough good things about the experience. Her friend who gave birth to her first child in Singapore was thrilled by the support she received from the affordable maid/nanny who was by her side from the start to clean her home and care for her baby. In places as distinct as Malaysia and Colombia, many apartments will have a separate room and bathroom for a live-in maid. Not only is it affordable to hire someone to help and support you in these countries but it is also culturally acceptable and even expected.

Just as people come to the US in hopes of giving their children better opportunities in life, you can give birth or even create a home in places where your values and needs are supported by the culture. Western countries are increasingly less family-oriented and birth rates have dropped dramatically, but there are still places in the world where families are welcomed and supported.

While some politicians, particularly in the US and Canada, frown on the practice of handing out citizenship to the children of foreigners born on their soil, that does not make the practice illegal or even immoral. Going where you're treated best means taking advantage of legal loopholes to create opportunities that others do not see. In this case, better hospitals, lower medical costs, better communities for your family, and of course, dual citizenship for your children and perhaps even yourself. For the same reason that you should have a second passport, your children should have multiple passports. This will save them the time and money that you invested in reading this book as well as set them up for numerous opportunities as they get older.

So, where can you give birth to give your kids a leg up in the second citizenship department? Sadly, not in Europe; Ireland was the last European nation to abolish their law allowing birth tourism some time ago. The countries to investigate are the pro-immigration countries where anyone can fit in. The Americas fit this bill, with Colombia being one of the few exceptions. One of the most interesting loopholes is the island of Dominica, which sells citizenship for $100,000 per person, yet grants citizenship to children at birth for the cost of a few low fees.

A more reasonable suggestion is Mexico. Mexico City and other parts of the country have better healthcare than you might imagine. At Nomad Capitalist Live, we heard from one expat mother who gave birth in Mexico City. She shared how her doctor spent quality time with her at every visit and provided a level of service that she has yet to encounter with doctors in the United States. And because of the low cost of medical care in Mexico, she had access to more and better studies that were able to identify a serious complication in her pregnancy that her doctor dealt with safely and professionally.

She gave birth to a healthy baby boy in a state-of-the-art hospital. And even without insurance, the cost of all her medical care was less than she has since paid toward a deductible in the United States for the birth of her second child. From the level of care to the cost of that care, she benefited on every side. In fact, because she gave birth to a Mexican citizen while living in the country as a permanent resident, she automatically qualified for Mexican citizenship too. As we have seen, Mexico offers one of the best passports in the world. And anyone can be Mexican; all they have to do is be born on Mexican soil.

Another great country to consider for birth tourism is Brazil. There are some truly spectacular hospitals in cities like Sao Paolo and any child born on Brazilian soil is instantly a Brazilian citizen. Plus, anyone can fit in as a Brazilian: blondes, Hispanics, Asians, blacks, and so on. The best part is that you as the parent can put in a little time on the ground and qualify for citizenship for yourself as well. Brazil is a little too bureaucratic for my taste to make this worth your time – the process will likely drag out longer than the promised one year – but, at the very least, you can get residency out of the deal.

Another unique benefit of giving birth in a country like Brazil is that the Brazilian government has a standing policy that they will not extradite native-born Brazilians to other countries. In the past, people came to me to ask if obtaining Brazilian citizenship by naturalization would help them if they were ever on the run from the law (yes, I get a lot of crazy questions). While many blogs will tell you it can, the truth is that only those born on Brazilian soil get the privilege.

While I highly suggest reevaluating your life choices if extradition is a high-priority quality you are seeking in a country, it does highlight the fact that natural-born citizens tend to have more rights. Just as Arnold Schwarzenegger cannot run for President of the United States by virtue of his birth in Austria, the flip side is that any children you have in another country will get special privileges there.

Whatever way you look at it, there are attractive perks to giving birth abroad. From great health care to citizenship parlor tricks, it is worth your consideration. If you and your partner have different or multiple nationalities, your children will be set with opportunities for life. If you are a citizen of a high-tax country, your children can have the advantages of your home country passport as well as the benefits of a more laid-back country that is not on the warpath for cash. They will also be able to travel, live, and work in a wide variety of locales. What better start in life could you possibly give your progeny?

World Schooling

Concepts like birth tourism are part of the remedy to one issue I see again and again in my line of work. The problem is that even those who decide to live overseas to save a boatload on taxes and create a lifestyle of freedom tend to think that they will eventually have to move back home. Several years ago, I began working with Patrick, a young Australian businessman who admitted that he was in this camp.

"I'm saving about $300,000 a year since working with you," Patrick told me, "But after five or six years, Mari and I will be married and we want to start a family in Australia."

To Patrick and others like him, living overseas – whether being constantly on the go or settled in one low-tax place – was a young man's game that ends when the clock turns thirty. But age is just a number. There is nothing that forces you to return to your home country and forego many of the benefits you have gained by living overseas. There are certainly social constructs that act as unwritten rules dictating that digital nomadism belongs to the young and only a rare breed sticks with it forever, but there is nothing forcing you to pack up your bags and call it quits. Increasing your freedom and prosperity through travel does not have an expiration date.

Most people are born in one country, go to school, go to university, get married, work, raise children, and die in the same country. Many of those people do so in the same state or province and, of those, some do so in the same city – except perhaps for the short break they took to 'escape' to university a few towns away. That is how 'normal' society works. But you do not have to be normal.

Before you decide that this lifestyle is only a temporary one for you, realize that doing it at all is already flying in the face of society's rules. Go to your hometown bank and ask them if you can send a wire transfer to Cambodia. Go to your hometown insurance agent and ask how to get medical coverage for a trip to Bolivia. Go to your hometown tax collector and ask how you can pay your property taxes while living and banking in Greece. The result will be a series of stunned looks and blank stares – a sign that while this lifestyle is growing, it is still a long way from the days when everyone will 'get' why you are doing it.

But they do not need to get it. You do. And if you can understand that you can increase your freedom by banking, investing, doing business, and living abroad. All that is missing is to go one step further and ask yourself what is holding you back from living this lifestyle at all stages of life and not just during your carefree youth.

When I asked Patrick what made him think he had to go back to Australia, he was ready with an answer, "Andrew, we want to get married and have kids." The logic seemed so painfully obvious to him. "They'll need to go to school." My friend's voice exposed his impatience with my lack of understanding of something so basic.

"Is Australia the only place they can go to school?" I asked in feigned innocence.

"Well, no," Patrick said in frustration. "But I'm not going to send my kids to some mediocre school in some random country. And how would that even be possible if we're traveling all the time like we do now? Besides, I know Australia has a good school system."

"Is it the best?" I pressed.

"What do you mean?" he asked.

"Is an education in Australia the very best you can offer your children? Will it prepare them for the kind of success and freedom you now enjoy?"

"I don't know…" Patrick sounded perplexed. "What else is there?"

"Great question!" I said cheerfully now that we were getting somewhere. "When you started your business, you never thought once about running it anywhere but Australia. Why?"

Patrick mulled that one over for a minute and then said, "I guess, I didn't know I had options. I had always believed that Australia was good enough, so why look elsewhere."

"But you did, eventually. So, why did you?" I asked.

Patrick laughed. "My tax bill, of course! And as soon as I started reading about what I could do to fix that problem, I realized that there was great potential for my business to expand and my investments to earn higher yields outside of Australia."

"So… could the same be true for your children's education?"

I could see a little light switch on in Patrick's eyes as he grinned back at me. "Possibly," he admitted.

For each of us, going where we are treated best happens in stages. When we first dive in, we do not wonder what it would be like to be squirreled away in Panama City when we are 89. However, with each step we take, we must constantly reevaluate the fact that, yes, it is possible to give birth to children overseas, and to raise them overseas, and even to school them overseas.

Your children do not have to be raised in the same corner of the world where you grew up. If doing that is truly what treats you the best, then do it. I am not suggesting that you abandon your every desire just to save on taxes, but merely that you ask yourself whether the suburbs of Melbourne are really that different from the suburbs of Kuala Lumpur, far apart as they may seem.

The truth is, going where you're treated best can add to your ability to raise your children and provide for their education. A child who can legally live, work, and easily do business in foreign countries thanks to multiple citizenships, who speaks several languages because they grew up living in different countries, and who understands other cultures from making friends around the world will be far better equipped to become a success in any area they choose to focus on. Fancy schools, towering debt, and pieces of paper with Latin characters scribbled on them are not necessary anymore.

The concept of world schooling is one that has been catching on quickly as an increasing number of expats and world travelers discover that traditional schooling no longer suits their needs or those of their children. The editor of Nomad Capitalist spent months researching her book on the topic and met hundreds of people who are educating their children on the road in unconventional ways.

These days, if you want to teach your child entrepreneurship, they will learn a lot more by selling gum on the streets of Nicaragua with the other eight-year-olds than they will waiting until they are 18 to attend a theoretical lecture given by some wonk who quite possibly failed at his own venture. Not only that but they can learn Spanish or any other language in a natural environment and make friends along the way too.

As my friend Taylor Pearson discusses in his book *The End of Jobs*, the days of getting ahead by hanging a sheepskin on your wall are quickly coming to an end. The children you give birth to today will enter a totally different economy than the one for which traditional educational institutions will prepare them. Numbing indoctrination by college degree is no longer the meal ticket it once was.

In the new entrepreneurial economy, countless jobs will be converted from corporate to freelance and self-employment positions. Employers no longer care about credentials; they care about results. What will matter are skills like critical thinking, connecting with others across different situations, and the ability to communicate and spread your message. If we raise our children as if it were 1993, they will be as ill-equipped to compete in the world as a child raised learning inefficient farming practices after the dawn of the industrial revolution.

The key to making this all happen, though, is to get on the same page with your partner. Communicate about how you want to raise and educate a family. There are numerous ways to world school, from homeschooling to placing your children in local schools to hiring a tutor. Each approach comes with its own benefits. Whatever approach you take, raising your children out in the world can provide them with more educational value than anything they would receive inside the four walls of a classroom. Be assured that if you choose to live the Nomad Capitalist lifestyle long-term, your children will benefit from your choice, not suffer.

Just as giving birth abroad will give your children a head start with second passports, raising your children abroad and giving them a non-standard childhood and education could be one of the best things you could possibly do to prepare them for a life of freedom and success in a globalized world.

Dating on the Road

But what if you do not have children yet? Maybe you have not even met 'the one' who has you thinking about settling down. Maybe you are silently wondering if it is even possible to meet someone and develop a long-lasting relationship while you are out traveling the world. You wonder if perhaps you should just stay home until you find the right person to go with you. What is the use of talking about birth tourism and world schooling, you ask, when you are struggling just to find someone to be with?

After all, "First comes love."

To be honest, I debated whether I should include anything about dating and relationships in this book, and some people even told me outright that I should not. It is a delicate topic with as many opinions on how it is all supposed to work as there are people. But it is also a very important topic and one that should not be ignored. We would be lying to ourselves if we did not acknowledge that we want to know how to develop real, lasting relationships – even while living an atypical life.

At the end of the day, the goal is to be happy and to fill your life with love. You would not think that the word 'love' applies to the offshore world, but it has everything to do with it. Everything about being a Nomad Capitalist comes back to loving your life, loving what you are doing, loving the people around you, loving the relationships you are in, and loving where you are. It may not be the first word you think of when you think 'offshore,' but it is the foundational motivation for much of what we do.

Creating meaningful relationships may seem like an entirely different ballgame compared to the ins and outs of, let's say, getting a second passport, but when you boil it down to the basics, the reasons are the same. And as with every other topic we cover in this book, the concept of dating does not have to follow old norms either. Travel has a way of opening your possibilities and freeing you from local notions and expectations where love is involved.

That is not to say that there are not already some preconceived notions about what it means to date as a nomad. Some have the erroneous belief that their relationships must be as nomadic as they are because commitment to a place is somehow a prerequisite for commitment to a person. Others simply want to 'try out' every culture before choosing to be with one person, always putting off a real relationship until they have gone out with someone from every continent.

Then there are the guys who go to a place like the Philippines with the sole goal of sleeping with a new girl every day for a month straight – two a day if they can manage it. I am not going to try to define the kind of relationships that you should have, but that is probably not the best use of your options. The point of nomad dating is not to go out and get a bunch of notches on your bedpost. Setting a goal to sleep with 60 women in a month stinks of the same mentality as the folks who inundate my email asking about the Paraguayan residency and citizenship program. They do not really want to be a citizen of Paraguay, they have simply heard that the program is cheap, easy, and relatively fast. It is a quick answer to a bigger problem that they could solve if they took the time to reflect on what they really want and need.

The travel lifestyle is not meant to be a dating smorgasbord that you use to binge on a million different meaningless relationships. Instead, it should serve as a means of increasing your dating pool so that you can find the right person for you. Some people see all the options that open when they travel and feel that they must pursue a certain kind of relationship lifestyle just because it is available to them. You will naturally meet and date people from various cultures as you travel around the world; you do not have to follow anyone else's script about how those relationships should play out.

The script for many digital nomads is to go out and get drunk on the options. They move to Thailand or somewhere else in Southeast Asia and suddenly the party lifestyle of beer and drugs is cheap and they do not want to miss out. So, they follow the party lifestyle script. Or guys worry that if they do not go out and sleep with every Asian girl who will have them, they are a schmuck who is missing out. So, they follow the script of the loose expat looking to get lucky.

You do not have to follow the script. Being a Nomad Capitalist is not about following the crowd, it is about knowing what you want and then utilizing the entire range of options available to you to find the solution. You do not have to use every option, just the one that works for you. And that is the key – find and do what works for you – because not everyone is looking for the same thing.

The benefit you get from taking your dating life international is that it is much easier to discover what works for you and then to find the people that match that picture. This discovery is made possible because the simple act of going to a new place can give you a new outlook on life and open your mind to new ideas and new people.

September 11, 2008, seems like a long time ago. So long ago that I was just getting started traveling the world, my list of places to visit about ninety countries lighter. On that day, I was adding Norway to my list of visited countries. But Norway was not the highlight of that trip. Along the way, I met someone who would have a bigger impact on my life than I could imagine. She had moved from China to study and work in Ireland and was using her six weeks of time off in Ireland to get out and explore the rest of Europe. The best news of all was that she already had plans to visit the United States later that year. To say the least, it was serendipitous.

Every plan we made from that point forward always entailed one of us getting on a plane. Seeing as we both loved to travel, we made it work. Though the romance eventually ended, this woman inspired me in a way no one back home ever had. She had a view of the world that changed my own perspectives and was what pushed me to start taking more trips and eventually do what I do now.

Even when we first met in Norway, I remember looking at how she had planned out each decision in her life and how each country she had chosen was unique and specifically tailored to her needs. Her philosophies on life mirrored the first lessons my father taught me about going where you're treated best. Being a part of her life further cemented the validity of those principles in my own.

Before meeting her, I had almost become complacent with living in the US as I was consumed by running my businesses in the United States at the time. Meeting her began to change all that and I was reminded that where I was from was not the epicenter of the world. She made it easy to see that people are doing well in other parts of the globe and that opportunity exists elsewhere, as well.

Prior to our relationship, I had been a casual traveler. After (and because of) our relationship, I began to travel with more purpose and intensity. I visited Switzerland to check out the banking culture there, then traveled to Liechtenstein to indulge my fascination with micro-states and how they do things, I then headed to Austria to enjoy the music, and I finally made my first foray into Eastern Europe with a trip to Slovakia to discover the opportunities there beyond the tourist zone in Bratislava. That trip turned into so many others that have formed the backbone of Nomad Capitalist, and I owe much of it to the fact that I met someone during my travels who changed the way I see the world.

That relationship also helped me realize that it is much easier for me to connect with people from other cultures than with the culture that is technically my own. I have discovered since then that I am not the only one for whom this is true. It is a pleasant surprise for many to discover that you can meet people who are better suited for you simply by going overseas.

When I lived in Phoenix, I met a lot of people that I just did not feel comfortable with. I had no trouble meeting people, but nothing ever seemed to work. Even when I left the United States, I would occasionally go on Tinder and meet people from the US and there would always be some disconnect. I did not know what it was, but for the longest time I thought there was something wrong with me. I finally realized that blaming myself was not the answer. The United States was simply not the place for me. It was not a good fit.

And then I met Asians and Europeans and I realized that all the things that people got ticked off about or ghosted me for back in the US seemed to do well with these cultures and the women I would meet there. I have come to learn now to remove the judgment from my life and look at US culture and recognize that the people there are not terrible people because we failed to connect. They were just not a good fit for me.

You will likely find that they are not a good fit for you, either. Some may be and you could content yourself with trying to find them, but by and large, I have found that most people in the United States are not so open or globally minded. If you want to be those things, it is probably not going to work out for you to find someone in the United States. It may not be the right fit for you.

This was the case for David, an incredibly smart guy I met at a client mastermind a couple of years ago. At the time, David spent his days running a family business and his nights making side hustle investments that few others would want to touch. By all outward appearances, David was a success. He was smart, accomplished, and had a good deal of money. What he did not have was a life partner. David came to meet with me and other clients in Colombia, ostensibly to see how I personally invested overseas and to tour real estate for investment. However, we spent much of our three days together talking about how he could find a wife.

For a guy who could not get a date in high school, I was a bit surprised to realize that David was coming to me for advice. He told me that, in his city, most of the people he met were government workers only interested in advancing to the next rung on the ladder, too focused on blindly following orders for his taste. The rest of his social circle worked at the local university and, in his mind, treated him with a bit of contempt for being the evil capitalist exploiting labor for a profit. David had a hard-enough time finding guy friends to hang out with, let alone a woman he could really connect with.

Growing up, he told me, kids in school had made fun of him for being smart. I could relate. While I imagine today's culture of seven-year-olds creating apps and making billions from their bedrooms means that being smart is more socially acceptable now, those of us who grew up before software started eating the world may remember a different cultural norm.

Each place is defined by its culture. In Poland or Ukraine, being 'dumb' gets you beat up on the playground by chess-playing bullies. Everyone I have met from Central and Eastern Europe cannot understand why being a science nerd would not be considered cool. It makes sense; whereas Times Square is adorned with banners of TV characters wailing "OMFG," Warsaw's squares feature memorials to Tesla. Even Christmas displays take on a solar system theme.

Yet, in countries living on gravy, you might be more well-liked for posting butt selfies on Instagram than for checkmating a classmate. The OMFG and butt selfie crowd might be exactly your type, in which case you should either move as close to Times Square as possible or put this book down immediately if you can already see it out your window.

But if those folks are not your type, you may feel extremely out of place in your home country dating scene. Hannah, a German woman I met in Central America, struggled with this very issue. She grew up in a small town and never found a deep connection with someone else in Germany. Having traveled to Australia as a high school student and throughout Asia and the Americas in university, Hannah no longer felt connected to German men.

Over a dinner of gallo pinto, Hannah admitted that she wanted someone to understand her, and she was not getting that in Germany. "German guys are tedious," she asserted, expressing greater command of English synonyms than most Americans. Hannah was not bitter; she merely knew what she wanted and that she was not getting it where she came from. Normally, the 29-year-old me would have scoffed at a 22-year-old saying she knew what she wanted, but I found Hannah – like many Europeans I have met in my travels – to be surprisingly mature. Perhaps she would outgrow her self-styled verboten on German men, but for now, she liked the idea of dates that spoke in more dulcet tones.

The same was true of Alizz, a Colombian girl in Bogota. "All Colombian men cheat," she told me confidently. It reminded me of my business, where employees will often say, "Everyone is really upset," or "All of our clients liked that video," and only upon further investigation is it revealed that all of two people are upset and the employee is acting emotionally. Nevertheless, emotions are real. If I have learned anything from visiting nearly 100 countries, it is to trust your instincts. If you are not happy where you are, it may be time to make a change. You can go where you're treated best.

Fortunately, the same principles of going where you're treated best apply to your relationships just as they do for setting up your offshore bank accounts and companies, making international investments, obtaining second passports, and doing everything else that impacts the life of a Nomad Capitalist. A great place to start is to simply go somewhere else and begin to experience different cultures and meet new people.

The more time you can spend traveling, the easier it will be to start thinking about and naturally creating long-term relationships with people outside of your own country. When I was in Arizona, although I traveled, my trips were only occasional excursions to Europe. If I had been looking for love at the time, I probably would have stuck to Phoenix. And maybe I would have met a girl there whose parents were from Mexico, but even then, there was a good chance that she was culturally American.

If you are in a similar situation, maybe once in a blue moon you will meet someone who has moved from another country, but unless you live in New York, London, or Los Angeles, you are probably not dating that diverse of a population. And even if you are, if you are not content with where you are, your chances of finding someone with a desire to travel as big as yours will be low. You will have a better chance of finding someone who loves the lifestyle you want by simply living that lifestyle.

If a place and the people do not appeal to you, do not linger. In the wake of the Harvey Weinstein ordeal in the US, my assistant and I were reviewing Twitter when we saw that a woman was complaining that Drake was building a thirst dowry because he was buying Birkin bags for his future wife. We were literally rolling on the floor laughing at such a ridiculous claim. This is what people in the United States are worried about? An entire culture has been reduced to arguing about the evils of a celebrity buying expensive bags for his future wife?

Now that I do not have to deal with this cultural mindset all the time, I can just laugh at it and say "Wow!" and then move on. I no longer need to worry about the silly things that occupy the minds of a culture I have left behind because I now know that there are people and cultures that value the same things that I do. I can find people who are on the same wavelength as I am. And you can find someone on the same level as you are, too, to the point that it becomes effortless to be with and date others.

Several years ago, while preparing for a Passport to Freedom conference in Cancun, three of my friends and I met four German girls standing out by the beach bar. Two of us hit it off with the girls and we began to talk. I had been hanging out with a bunch of Americans the week before and so – as we were having this intelligent, deep conversation – I decided to try a silly hand-reading trick that worked on the Americans. The girl just looked at me in a very German way as if to say, Dude, really? And then she simply said, "Just do your thing. Be yourself. That's interesting to me."

I was blown away. There I was with four interesting and smart women and the entire interaction was effortless. In the United States, I had always felt that it was too much effort to make anything happen, like I always needed to be entertaining someone to get their attention. It was the complete opposite in this situation and has been with so many of the women I have met while traveling. Dating has become effortless.

It is possible to find people who make it easy to converse and create a relationship. By traveling to more places, you are expanding your pool and increasing the possibility of finding the kind of people with whom you can effortlessly connect on a deep level. That can be difficult to believe for someone who grew up in a village of 100 people where options are limited and everyone knows who everyone else is dating (and if you date too many people, you will be branded the wrong way). Getting out of the 'village' is a simple way to make the world your new sample, not a village or a town or a hamlet or even a city – the world.

That does not mean that you are going to go date everybody in the sample, it simply means that you have a better pool to choose from. And with that better sample, you can raise your standards and trust that you will find someone with whom you can really connect and who truly shares your worldview and values. Once you expand your pool, all that is left is to determine what you want. Do you genuinely want to go out and hook up with every girl you can? Is that really what you want? Or are you just following a script? Be open-minded and honest with yourself. This is not a self-help book, but I imagine that someone who is doing that has some other issues going on. So, ask yourself, is that sincerely what you want?

What I did in my personal life before finding Mrs. H. was to be upfront with myself about what I was really looking for. I knew I wanted something serious, more so than ever, and that meant that I had to lock in on what I truly wanted and not just what I thought I wanted or should have. For example, I admitted that physical appearance is important to me. In the US, I felt like women could judge based on appearance but if men ever said anything they were considered a jerk because it is not about appearance. But it is part of the equation. You need to be physically attracted to the person. Once I acknowledged that it is okay to feel that way and I had a larger sample to choose from, I could be honest about what I find attractive.

I also wanted to find someone who was intelligent and globally minded. I did not want to date somebody who was happy living in one place their entire life. I imagine that if I lived in Rolla, Missouri, I would have a lot fewer options of people who are globally minded. I do not want someone who knows all about the St. Louis Cardinals or who wants to go to University of Kansas football games and dress up in their school colors. Instead, I prefer someone who knows who Nikolai Tesla is, or someone who knows that NATO bombed Serbia in the 90s.

At some point in my life, I had to accept that the girls I went to high school with were more likely to fit into the former category and not the latter. I was not interested in pursuing someone like that. It may work for other people and that is wonderful, but it never worked for me. I also discovered that I wanted someone who is warm. After ten years of dating cold people, I realized that I wanted warmth. I always knew that I wanted someone smart, but I prioritized smart over warmth and failed to realize that I could have both. The more honest I was with myself about what I wanted, the more I discovered that it was possible to meet people who fit all those standards.

That is one reason I believe that finding who you want to be with is more about your mindset than anything else. The key is to keep an open mind and understand that there is no need to be angry about the people and places that are not a good fit for you because it is possible to find relationships that are effortless. Do not spend your time complaining about what is not working, focus instead on the good and spend your energy going after what you want.

In the case of my client David, he was angry because he did not think he could find girls in the United States who wanted to talk about the things that he wanted to talk about. He was not what they wanted. Whether David was right or wrong about this, I told him that he could not take that mindset with him. If he did, he would end up in the same situation because his mindset would color all his interactions.

The power of your mindset not only applies to finding someone you can connect with but also making that relationship work long-term. Personally, I decided that I would pursue anything that looked like it could work until it did not. I prefer this approach over playing the mediocre game of putting in minimal effort to protect myself from rejection or, even worse, sitting around and waiting for people to come to me. As with business, I would go for what I wanted and be open about it. It was freeing to allow myself the confidence of being overseas and totally being honest about what I wanted without worrying about what society dictated I should do.

When I finally matched with Mrs. H. on Tinder, I was in Kuala Lumpur and she was in Moscow. We started talking and when we realized that there was something there, I traveled 15 hours to meet her in Georgia where she was visiting family. I could drop everything I was doing and fly around the world at a moment's notice and play that relationship out.

Being free from the pulse of local society meant that we could both do what made sense for us. Even though she had never traveled much, I made the bold move and invited her to come to Kuala Lumpur. She said yes. Her willingness to travel far from home for the first time just so we could see where the relationship could go was a strong sign that she was not only serious about the relationship but also the kind of person worth pursuing.

Through my experiences dating overseas, I had gained the freedom to focus on what I wanted and came to the ultimate realization that I would rather drop everything and leave a country that guys go to just to chase after women so that I could try to make things work with one woman I cared about – someone I ultimately chose to be with for the rest of my life. That is the most powerful part of Nomad dating: you have the power to reset your mindset and open yourself to the possibility of something real happening with someone you truly care about who exceeds your wildest expectations.

Building a Committed Relationship as a Nomad

Since first writing this book, Mrs. H. and I tied the knot and have learned numerous lessons about what it takes to build a committed relationship alongside a global lifestyle. While every relationship is different, I know that many readers are looking for advice about how to balance marriage and the Nomad Capitalist life. So, while our experience may be different from yours and I am no relationship expert, Mrs. H. and I decided to share some of the foundational principles that have allowed us to strengthen our marriage while traveling the world.

For simplicity, we have boiled our advice down to the Four C's of Building a Committed Relationship as a Nomad: Communicate, Compromise, Cultivate, and Choose.

The first principle is to communicate. Solid communication is essential for any marriage, not just for Nomads, but if you want to make this nomadic lifestyle work, you need to communicate about it. Communicate openly and frequently. From the very beginning, Mrs. H. and I talked about our plans, goals, and desires for the future. We both came into the relationship and lifestyle with the mindset that this was not an experiment. And we both knew that about the other person because we talked about it.

We have talked about how neither of us likes where we are from. We like to explore and find other places that really warm our souls and make us feel welcome. It is something we have to communicate about to ensure that both partners are happy with the situation and the direction we are taking. The communication required to work together as a team on something as monumental as a global Nomad Capitalist lifestyle has strengthened our marriage in ways that you may not even encounter living a regular 9-to-5 life in the suburbs where your life script is largely written for you. As a Nomad couple, you are building something completely new. It is exciting, but it requires clear communication about what it is you are creating and how you build that life.

It also requires compromise, the second of the Four C's. Many of my clients and readers have asked what they can do if their spouse does not want to travel or leave their home country. This is often a difficult situation for those who are already married. If you are dating someone and they have a different lifestyle than what you want, there is always the option to break up. If you are still in the dating phase and you want to pursue this lifestyle, be sure that the person you are dating wants the same things. But if you are facing this challenge with someone you are committed to already, the way forward is going to be through compromise.

Mrs. H. had never considered perpetual travel before meeting me. She was a dentist practicing in Russia – not the most nomadic profession in the world. She had dedicated years to medical school and there are limited opportunities to practice in other countries, but I encouraged her to give the lifestyle a try. As she did, she found that she not only enjoyed the lifestyle but also discovered new and rewarding professional pursuits. She has become very good with a camera, all self-taught.

But in her own words, the bottom line was that "Sometimes you have to switch and adjust to life and decide what you want more." Now, when she looks back at her old life and talks to friends back in Russia, she has openly expressed how being with me and traveling are ultimately more fulfilling and interesting.

Now, just because she made the compromise to give up her career and try a new lifestyle does not mean that I do not need to make compromises as well. As we have traveled together, we have found that there are countries that I like that she does not and vice versa. I love Serbia, but Mrs. H. has not enjoyed it. My interest in Georgia as a lifestyle destination has waned over the years, but Mrs. H. still loves it. Our compromise has been Malaysia and Colombia. We both like those countries and so we have put our time and energy into building our homes and community in those places.

This is the third of the Four C's, to cultivate an atmosphere where your relationship can flourish. We have done this first by trying out different countries and then by testing different living accommodations. We have often given certain places a second chance and have found that it was not the country that we disliked but the living conditions we had the first time we were there.

Together, we have realized that our accommodations impact our opinion of a place dramatically. If we stay in a hotel room or apartment for too long, it can get depressing. Or if we end up selecting an Airbnb that has exposed wires all over the place, it really affects what we think and feel about the experience.

When we have not been sure about a country, we are sure to stay in a different place the next time we go or even explore a different area and really do our research on the best places to go. One year, we went to Bogota in November during the rainy season where the rain begins in the afternoon and lasts until the evening.

After sitting in the hotel room all day and getting depressed by the weather, we started to think that the country was the problem. We thrive on getting out and exploring and that simply was not possible with all the rain. But we did not give up on Colombia. The next time we visited, we chose to go at a different time of the year and the weather was fantastic. It was an entirely different experience.

More importantly, we had finished renovating our home and were no longer staying in an apartment or hotel. There is something about having your own home that changes the experience of a place. We enjoy the whole atmosphere. We have chosen the furniture, the decorations, and every detail of the place where we now live. It is all ours. We put our time, thought, and heart into it, and we are so happy there now. The country is the same, but it is no longer a place we just visit, it is our home. Cultivating that atmosphere has made all the difference not only in how we feel about the place but also the energy we put into understanding the people and adjusting to the culture.

As a couple you can work together to cultivate the life of your choosing. Cultivating is not just about where you live or what your home looks like, it encompasses the entire Nomad lifestyle. People assume that being a Nomad is a single man's game, but the same freedom you can find by going offshore as a single person is available to married couples and even families. That freedom all comes down to the final of the Four C's: choice.

People will put limitations around just about everything you try to do as a Nomad Capitalist, but in the end, the choice is yours. Many will say that it is impossible to live this life as a married person, that eventually your spouse will get sick of the nomadic lifestyle or children will come along and everything will come tumbling down.

But if I have learned anything in the past 15 years of doing business, it is that you can do what every else says you cannot do. If you want to have a partner or be married, you can find people who appreciate this lifestyle. It may be challenging, but it can be done.

You do not have to choose between being a Nomad Capitalist or being married and having a family. You simply have to choose that you can do both, and then put in the work to make it happen.

Finding Friendship and Community Abroad

Prior to meeting Mrs. H., I had made many new friends around the world; but I have to give credit where credit is due: she has taken our social life to a whole new level. She is an expert at finding and connecting with the larger expat community wherever we go. Since she came along, we have built close friendships, hosted large parties, and even made local friends who have taken us into their homes and shared their worlds with us. Her relentless pursuit of friendship and community has brought a new and beautiful quality to my life.

She has contributed greatly to the update of this chapter, and much of this next section comes directly from her. For those of you who were fortunate enough to meet Mrs. H. at Nomad Capitalist Live, you know her advice is solid. In this section, we will look at how you can leverage technology to connect with community and make new friends, suggest ways that you can create local friendships, and address some of the challenges of adapting to different cultures and the various mentalities you will find as you meet new people throughout your journeys.

The easiest way to make friends while living abroad is among the expats of your own country. They will be the most eager to be friends with you and you will understand each other, making things much easier on both sides. A great place to start is with Facebook groups like Americans in Bogota, Expats in Mexico, or Russians in Malaysia, etc. After you join, you can post something as simple as, "Hello, I'm looking for friends!" and you will be surprised by how many people will comment. You have to advertise yourself a little bit, but someone might comment and offer to meet up for coffee and then you are off to a good start.

You can also use Instagram by searching hashtags like #Bogota and find friends who are looking for connection and adventure. There are plenty of apps that you can use to connect as well. HelloTalk is an app that uses your location to connect you to people who want to learn another language in your area. It is like a dating app for language learning. Once you connect with someone, you can set up a meeting and then you exchange your language skills – you teach them English and then they can teach you Spanish.

Another great app that can be used for both dating and meeting new friends is called InterNations. It is specifically geared toward expats, but if dating is your specific interest, you can also use other dating apps like Tinder, Bumble, and Grindr (for the LGBTQ+ community). If you use the paid version of Tinder, you can change your location and match with people in the place of your choosing. That is how Mrs. H. and I found each other while living worlds apart.

When it comes to meeting locals, it is usually easier to make friends when you are staying in a place for longer. If you are going to be somewhere for three months, you can tell people you just moved to the area. If you are brave, you can simply approach people in public and strike up a conversation. If you do that, though, be ready for the possibility of rejection. Some people might not be interested. Not everybody likes foreigners, but it is possible to meet people on the street and become friends.

Another great way to make friends with locals is to find expats from your country who are friends with locals. You can become friends with their friends, and they will trust you more and be interested in you. If they already have a foreign friend, it shows that they are more open-minded to a friendship with someone different from them.

Making friends with locals is a great achievement because they will show you a whole new perspective of their country. They know much more and can share their culture and things you would never expect to see. It is like seeing the country from the inside out. You can get to know their religion, traditions, history, families, and more.

When dating or making friends with someone from a different country, you are bound to encounter cultural differences and distinct worldviews. This is not a bad thing. If anything, it is a great way to grow as a person and learn new ways of seeing the world. But it can be challenging. One thing that Mrs. H. suggests is to work at understanding the reasons behind those differences. Understand your own psychology and where your beliefs come from, and then do the same for the people who surround you in the places where you travel.

Westerners, for example, come from an individualistic culture while Easterners are raised in a collectivist culture. These differences impact everything from how we think to how we speak to how we act. For example, Americans who visit Eastern Europe often complain about the service. They are accustomed to an individualistic western culture that promotes competition and fosters better quality service. You, the individual, are paying your personal money and you care about what you get. You expect good service and quality food. When you do not get that, you are understandably disappointed.

Easterners see things differently. They are not individualists; they are a community. Each individual is a part of society – everyone is tied to everyone else. If you go out to eat and the food is bad, maybe it is the chef's fault, but maybe it is not. Easterners always find excuses for other people. Everyone is together in the situation. They are not going to get mad at the chef for the bad food because they already assume that it is not his fault. And the chef is not thinking about how he can solve your problem, he is thinking about how he can defend himself to show you it is not his problem but a problem belonging to the community at large.

I am not saying one way is better than the other. Frankly, I am still trying to understand the collectivist mindset. But your experience in these places can improve tremendously if you are willing to see things from others' point of view. When appropriate, talk to locals about their way of seeing the world. If you want a less direct approach, try reading some of the classic literature from that region of the world or watch films from the country. Just showing that you are making an effort to understand instead of simply judging that your way is right and their way is wrong goes a long way.

At the end of the day, you can only control what you think and do. There will be some people who will never accept you fully into their culture. Even if you have a piece of paper stating that you are a citizen of that country, you may always be considered a foreigner to them. You may also face racism and nationalism. Just move on. There are ignorant and rude people everywhere, but there are nice people everywhere as well. You can always choose the places and the people who make you feel the most welcome and go where you're treated best.

But most importantly, do not give up on building the kind of relationships you need within the lifestyle you desire. Quality relationships are worth pursuing. And they are possible to achieve, even as a Nomad Capitalist. Whether you are looking for someone to date, are working to build a strong marriage, or are looking to add children into the balance, understand that none of these life goals are mutually exclusive to the Nomad lifestyle. Your priorities may change over time, but the great thing about a global lifestyle is that you can adapt it to fit your needs.

Your How-To Action Plan

Immediate Action Steps: Sit down and have an honest conversation with yourself about what you really want out of life when it comes to your relationships with other people. Are you looking for a serious relationship with a future life partner? If you are already married, do you want children one day? Are you open to giving birth abroad? How can you maintain your relationships with those you leave behind at home? How do you plan to make new friendships and build community as you travel?

Travel Action Steps: You can enhance your dating pool and find the kind of people you can effortlessly connect with by choosing to date overseas. Once you find someone to create a life with, there is no need to give up the Nomad Capitalist lifestyle. In fact, giving birth to and educating your children on the road will give them a leg up in life and will create more opportunities for you to plant flags.

Holistic Planning: I understand that you are not making decisions about living offshore in a vacuum. Relationships matter and they can be affected by where you choose to live and plant other flags. There are some parts of your offshore planning, though, that are agnostic, Plan B strategies that do not alter your holistic plan or force you to live in a way that may impact your relationships. They are often cheap and can be added as additional options. Agnostic strategies can include setting up an offshore bank account, getting a paper residence, or even purchasing a Caribbean citizenship.

Chapter Seven: Nomad Healthcare

Go Get a Big Mac

Dateline: Bangkok, Thailand

"Go eat at McDonald's. Get a Big Mac."

You might expect to hear that from a lot of people. Your doctor is not likely one of them. Yet, there I sat in Bumrungrad Hospital in Bangkok's Sukhumvit district, one of the most upscale districts in Southeast Asia, being told by a trained medical practitioner that the answer to my recent weight loss was to eat fast food.

Thailand, like many countries in Asia, is hardly a place with a weight problem. In fact, of all of the countries where I suggest planting a flag, practically none of them rank among the highest in the world for obesity. Perhaps there is something in common between the attitudes that go with healthy living and treating wealth more favorably.

I had been in Southeast Asia for almost three months, making my way to Hanoi via Hong Kong, then south through Ho Chi Minh City, Phnom Penh, Siem Reap, and now to Bangkok. The journey was a hodgepodge of healthy living and totally unhealthy living. My preferred mode of transportation – particularly in new cities with poor English skills – is to walk, meaning I would often walk five or even ten miles in a single day. I was drinking plenty of water, and at times would eat healthy local foods. At other times, I was rounding out my twenties spending days munching fatty western foods served at riverside cafes alongside backpackers. Evenings were spent sipping cocktails, even after narrowly escaping death by jumping off a balcony to escape a group of Chinese dudes angry one of their drunk girlfriends was talking to me.

During this time, I managed to lose almost thirty pounds. For those not from the United States or Myanmar, that is fourteen kilograms or – my favorite – a little over two stone. In what I dubbed 'The Southeast Asia Diet,' I was perhaps able to accomplish what infomercial pitchman Kevin Trudeau was sentenced to ten years in prison for: "The fastest, easiest way to lose weight... period." Who knew it was as easy as walking around Phnom Penh, Cambodia in a pair of Zegna loafers, taking meetings with real estate investors? Whether it was the Southeast Asian humidity, the copious amount of water consumed, some sort of higher quality food, or pure exercise, the pounds simply melted off.

As I never had a weight problem to begin with, I had become rather thin to the point that I was starting to feel my ribs when lying in bed. Hence my visit to Bumrungrad. I arrived at the hospital at 10:00 am, prepared for whatever diagnostic tests they would throw at me. By 10:05am, I was introduced to two nurses who, despite sing-songy Thai accents, spoke near-perfect English. They asked me again why I was there and went on to inform me of the battery of tests I would undergo to diagnose what was going on.

Things were already off to a great start. Go to the doctor for a 10:00 am appointment in the United States and you will be lucky to have a clipboard of paperwork in your hand by 10:30. In Thailand, nurses were waiting for you with a cup of tea before getting down to business. Within a few hours, all my tests were done. I would go in and out of various lab rooms, never waiting more than a few minutes before being summoned once again. By the time it was all done, I waited perhaps all of ten minutes before the Thai doctor called me into his office to go over the results. We joked around and he asked why I was in Thailand. I had never seen anything like it.

Then he hit me with the results: a clean bill of health. When I asked what the possible cause could be – after all, I did lose quite a bit of weight in less than three months – he chalked it up to different food than I was used to traveling in Europe or North America. That is when he hit me with the McDonald's line. The weight loss was a non-issue to him, and he was not concerned about it. If I had gone on to die, I might be a little upset about his nonchalant demeanor. However, the weight loss stopped, and my weight remained steady.

Nothing bad happened. Turns out, freaking out about every problem the way doctors in the West do is not normal everywhere.

Ask a doctor in the United States if the hangnail you have sought his counsel for could kill you and you will be told, "Hey man, you never know. There have been some pretty bad cases of acute paronychium osis going around. One lady just dropped dead after a hangnail came free and got stuck in her lung." One time, when I went to the doctor to treat a scratched cornea from trying to get a contact lens out, I was cautioned that we could not rule out blindness as a result of the incident.

For all these circumspect admonishments, far more people in the United States die of medical malpractice every year than from hangnails or scraped up eyeballs. To make matters worse, the cost of this care is absolutely out of control. My bill for having my eye checked out topped $500. "Can't be too careful," they say. If you were to listen to my Thai doctor, maybe you can be. Meanwhile, in many countries with socialized medicine, wait times are so ridiculous that many patients are simply opting to go elsewhere for care, or paying out of pocket for private care.

In an excellent balance between cost and quality of care, Bumrungrad solves the problems westerners experience when seeking care at home. This is a book about capitalism and business, but the ability to receive quality care is important to busy entrepreneurs who do not have time to sit around in doctors' waiting rooms receiving alarmist scares. The concept of medical tourism allows busy people to get excellent care in comfortable surroundings without paying a king's ransom that could otherwise be invested.

Bumrungrad Hospital is no slouch when it comes to quality. It has been accredited by the American Joint Commission International multiple times. The medical chief is an accredited physician in the United Kingdom, and many of its physicians studied overseas. Bumrungrad was one of the original hospitals built for medical tourism in Asia, designed to attract not only the Asian elite and tourists with sprained ankles but also patients from all over the world who purposefully seek care there.

Two months after my visit to Bumrungrad, I had a similar experience in Kuala Lumpur when my gigantic tonsils got infected after a week of getting little sleep. Being from the West, where seeking medical treatment is often a last resort, I sweated it out for two days before my hotel advised me to go to the emergency room.

"The emergency room?! Do you think I'm dying?!" I asked, suddenly fearing that death was again imminent, just as the hangnail doctor had warned. It turns out that in Asia, prompt, quality emergency room care only costs a few bucks. So, I dragged my sickly self to Prince Court Medical Center in the middle of Kuala Lumpur during the evening rush hour. Despite the promises of prompt service that I had received at the hotel, I knew that I had no appointment to save me from waiting, and I was betting that the nurses there would not bring me a cup of mint tea as they had in Bangkok.

It turns out that medical care in Malaysia was even more efficient than in Thailand. Within mere moments of arriving, I was ushered in to have my vital signs checked and my height and weight recorded. The Indian-Malaysian nurse asked what I was there for and quickly put together a treatment plan. This time, there was actually something wrong: tonsillitis. I feared for the worst, preparing for a long wait that would last into the night. As it turned out, I was given some intravenous medications, did some tests, and managed to see the doctor within an hour.

In under two hours, I was treated, feeling wonderful, and sent out the door. My only sense of regret was that I had wasted two days putting off the visit when I could have come to such an efficient hospital, get the cure, and be on my way.

I later learned that Prince Court Medical Center was ranked the #1 medical tourism hospital on planet Earth. The level of efficiency I experienced there bore that out. As in Thailand, the doctor not only spoke excellent English but had studied in London. Unlike doctors in the West, he did not seem rushed and answered all my questions without trying to hastily bounce me out of his office.

Then came the bill, priced of course in Malaysian ringgit. (I have converted based on that day's rates.) It started with a $1.56 hospital administration charge to cover the beautiful facility. The nursing fee that covered an hour of on-and-off care as an IV dripped into me was $4.67. The actual consumables, such as the IV and bandages, were $21.24, plus pharmacy charges of $82.01. And the cost of visiting with the physician was all of $10.90.

All in all, a trip to the ER cost $123, charged to my American Express card. You could not get the receptionist to take a five-minute break from filing her nails for that price in the United States. Costs like this also raise an important point about travel insurance while living and traveling overseas; sure, it is important, but if you are going to the types of places I recommend, the only time you will want to bother with insurance is if you are hit by a bus. For $123, it is just not worth the paperwork.

Going where you're treated best means literally going where the treatment is best. If I get some crazy illness, I pray it is not in a western country. Getting sick in the United States would cost a fortune, which is another reason I avoid the United States. Getting sick in Europe is a coin toss; you might get lucky and merely get a grouchy old doctor who remembers 'the good old days' before microneedles, or you might be unlucky and wind up in a state-run infectious disease hospital.

In this day and age, the idea that the United States or any 'developed' western country is the only safe place to receive medical care is absurd. In fact, you might be doing yourself a disservice, or even put your health in danger. In the United States, medical error is the third highest cause of death. Patients are literally dying by the thousands, and likely hundreds of thousands, due to doctor error.

What is more, life expectancy in the United States recently dropped for the first time since the first Bush administration twenty-some years ago. Asia is where it is at for seeking medical care. From Dubai to Singapore, there are some surprising places to get top quality care. For example, India is well known for excellent cardiologists, all of them costing 90% to 95% less than cardiologists at top US hospitals.

If you are used to only getting care in your home country, venturing offshore can be concerning at first, but I can assure you that the quality of care is better than anything you have seen back home. Quite frankly, there are great hospitals in most countries you will wind up. While I have occasionally thought, "Gee, I hope I don't fall deathly ill while I'm in Timor-Leste," the places where you cannot find a good hospital are few and far between.

During the many years I have been based in Kuala Lumpur, I have frequented Prince Court for all kinds of services. In addition to the occasional painful run-in with a street cat I would attempt to help, the hospital has offered efficient care for just about anything you could need. That mole on your eyebrow that you are sick of? Get rid of it with ease. That knee that is not quite what it used to be? Get it checked out. Experiencing chest pain? Head on over to Prince

Court. They have everything you need with greater efficiency than you have ever experienced.

Wellness Tourism

The biggest advantage of choosing to be treated well when it comes to your health care is that it is easier to stay healthy through preventative care. In the United States and parts of Europe, it seems that medicine is all about stitching you back up after you have fallen ill. In Asia, on the other hand, I was able to take care of my health before it became a problem. In that way, the term medical tourism does not exactly fit.

A medical tourist gets on a plane to save $3,000 on a hip surgery. Conversely, a Nomad Capitalist who is willing to go wherever they need to care for their general health, wellbeing, and beauty can achieve a higher level of healthy living. I call it wellness tourism. Keep your mind and body in good shape and you will have more energy to live the rest of the Nomad Capitalist lifestyle.

The principles of wellness tourism fit perfectly into the mantra to go where you're treated best – quite literally, actually. If you want to be healthy, go where people live healthy lifestyles. If you want to look sexy, go where people strive to be sexy. For example, Venezuela has produced about a gazillion beauty pageant winners thanks to parents applying largely distasteful tactics for beauty. That said, if you are in the market for cosmetic surgery, you might consider the place where people have such a sick obsession with it that a simple tummy tuck is child's play. Who would you trust as the expert in making people look good: doctors in a country with never-ending pageant winners, or doctors advertising on billboards in Manhattan, Kansas?

For now, however, you might not want to go to Venezuela – what with the food shortages and, well, everything. Colombia, Brazil, and South Korea are just as renowned for elective procedures. While I do find some of the operations people in these countries go through sad, remember that going where you're treated best does not always mean changing the world. You will not get Koreans to stop having eyelid surgery, nor do they want to, but you can benefit from the expertise that exists because of it.

We all know someone in the West who dipped into savings or ran up credit card debt to get a nose job or breast implants. When

I inquired with Prince Court as to their average prices and compared them to prices from surgeons in the United States, they were, on average, about 70% cheaper. If doctors were not such sticklers for ethics in marketing, they would call it, "Get paid to get a butt lift... and we'll give you a free beach vacation with palm trees and monkeys and coconuts."

So, where can you travel to get quality care? Thailand and Malaysia are two of the best, but many other countries are getting into the medical tourism game, too. Singapore, for example, is known for excellent quality cancer care. Despite the expensive cost of living, you can save about half on the prices in many western countries. One US-based grocery chain had a policy of sending employees in need of expensive surgeries to Singapore, paying full price for the procedure along with round-trip tickets for two. Even with the high price of hotels in Singapore, the grocery chain saved money by sending their employees to the other side of the world for medical care.

While Brazil is known for cosmetic procedures – they have more plastic surgeons than any other country on earth – they are branching out into general medicine. Hospital Israelita Albert Einstein is the country's first JCI accredited hospital and has a five-star rating for care. If I were having a child, I would strongly consider it (especially since my kid would get a passport, to boot). The cost of childbirth in Brazil is as much as 90% less than in the United States. Even prices for plastic surgery are as much as 60% less.

India is building out a $2-billion-a-year medical industry, supported by two of the top ten hospitals on the planet. The Asian Heart Institute in Mumbai frequently performs among the most complicated cardiology procedures in the world and boasts the lowest heart surgery mortality rate at just 0.26%. As for Malaysia, Prince Court in Kuala Lumpur has one of the world's most advanced burn units and IVF facilities. And for those of us from countries where certain treatments are restricted for moral or other reasons, Asia can provide care that your home country's government does not think you can handle.

Even dental care can be better overseas, proving that routine medical care is possible while living the Nomad Capitalist lifestyle. You do not have to go to your home country every six months to have your teeth cleaned when countries in Eastern Europe have become renowned for excellent care. The most advanced dental clinic I have ever been to was in Bucharest, Romania, and a regular check-up and cleaning cost about $25, complete with advanced images of all of my teeth to check for problem areas. Serbia is also known for affordable dentistry.

When ranked by an independent group, the world's top ten hospitals for medical tourism were in Malaysia, Germany, Lebanon, India, South Korea, Thailand, Turkey, and Singapore. How many of those countries would you have considered before? Yet, they offer world-class care with the added benefit of often extreme efficiency, and – thanks to currency devaluation in some countries – relatively low costs.

Healthy, Quality Food

Wellness tourism is not just about physician care, though; it is about leading a full and healthy life. If you have spent any time in the United States, you have likely heard about 'Mexican Coke.' By the level of ballyhoo, you would think this was a secret miracle liquid, but in reality, it is merely the cross-border version of Coca-Cola. While the US uses widely discredited high-fructose corn syrup to take advantage of American corn subsidies, Mexico and the rest of the world use real sugar. While sugar has now been found to be pretty deadly stuff, many say it is still better than its modified corn syrup version.

Some of the healthiest foods can be found outside of your home country. Many foods in the West are bland, processed, and uninviting. There are fruits and vegetables I found tasteless in North America, but love eating overseas. In many small and emerging countries, most produce is organic and grown locally; the vegetables and meat you are eating were sourced locally, not on some factory farm where chemicals and hormones are used.

Anti-poverty group Oxfam International published a survey called the "Good Enough to Eat" index, which studies food quality in practically every country around the world. Of course, all developed countries ranked well overall, buoyed by categories such as "Plenty to Eat", but the United States fell to 21st place thanks to mediocre food quality and high levels of diabetes and obesity. Apparently, there is something in the food there.

Standouts in terms of food quality were much of Western Europe, but also New Zealand and Argentina. Some of the best countries in the second tier were Ukraine, Macedonia, Albania,

Ecuador, and Estonia; these countries ranked as well as some developed Western European countries.

There is a reason the Chinese, who historically harbor great fears about food quality in their country, covet Australian beef and New Zealand lamb. In the same way we may find better countries that tax us less, we can also look for the best countries for food, where crops and meats are organic and void of harmful substances. India has created more organic farmland than any other country on earth in an attempt to cash in on our desires for healthier eating.

Ironically, some of the healthiest countries for eating do not offer the stereotypical 'healthy eating' options. In Georgia, the juice bar concept is just finally opening up, with several small stores blending fresh juices for healthy consumers. The healthy smoothie concept is almost nowhere to be found. However, produce in Georgia is almost universally organic, locally sourced by farmers – even part-time ones – and high quality.

Looking for a business to start? Let me give you an easy one. Bring the healthy food culture to countries in Eastern Europe and parts of Latin America. Quality foods are abundant in many of these countries, but not their quick serve delivery.

Go To the Source

Living the Nomad Capitalist lifestyle can give you access to the tools you need to live longer. Since you can choose where to live, you have total control over the healthy living habits from which you can benefit. The Japanese are known for their long life expectancy, probably largely thanks to being the world's healthiest nation, with low levels of many forms of cancer. They also have the world's longest 'healthy life expectancy,' which takes into account the amount of time you can expect to be in good health. If you want to learn their secrets, you can go to the source and learn directly from the culture in Japan.

Just being around healthy environments can inspire you in a way that merely being a tourist could not. The Nomad Capitalist lifestyle opens your mind up to a new realm of possibilities. Before spending time in Japan, I would never have eaten seaweed, yet, finding it in so many dishes convinced me it was an excellent source of protein and great at fighting disease.

Likewise, I was never a tea drinker before spending substantial time in Asia. Being in that environment encouraged me to learn more about which teas were best, including the fact that black tea – a fan favorite of the West and the basis for Earl Gray – is the most fermented, most caffeinated, and probably the worst tea for you. White tea is apparently where it is at, with little fermentation or caffeine and plenty of disease-fighting properties that make it better to drink than even green tea. Somehow, I doubt I would have gotten on the white tea bandwagon sitting in Arizona.

Japan has also pioneered the concept of 'forest therapy,' which encourages citizens to take recuperative walks in green spaces and the country's temperate rainforests. You can feel the healthy living culture if you spend enough time in Japan, not only in much of their food, but in the way they live.

Another example is Japan's onsens, or hot spring baths. They are widely known for their healing benefits and the feeling of overall well-being you get from being in them. Iceland, Georgia, and any number of other countries are also known for similar sulfur or hot spring baths which can improve skin quality and general health. Even Vogue took to writing about Georgia's sulfur baths, calling them "the ultimate skin-softening soak."

You may not want to move to Tokyo or Tbilisi, but you can certainly pop in from time to time to enjoy the rejuvenating benefits, without relying on inferior versions wherever you choose to spend most of your time. Unlike the cheap knockoffs of most procedures in your home country, you can get a Thai massage in Thailand, cleanse your body in Istanbul's hammams, and get wellness treatments in Switzerland's famous clinics in the Alps.

No longer do you have to settle for London's overpriced spas importing what they claim is some mystical beauty ingredient from the swamps of Namibia; you can go right to the source for better quality care.

The best news is that you do not have to settle in any given place to get these health benefits. You can devote a few weeks a year for annual check-ups and any necessary procedures, which can include revitalizing treatments not available in your home country. You can experience different foods and add healthier items to your diet, learn from the locals, and take it all with you when you go.

The Nomad Capitalist lifestyle is about far more than just money; without good health and a sense of wellbeing, it might as well be for naught. Fortunately, the lifestyle of going where you're treated best means you can have the best of everything, directly from the source.

Your How-To Action Plan

Immediate Action Steps: If you have any upcoming medical procedures, consider traveling to receive care. Research the best places for your specific needs and compare costs.

Travel Action Steps: If you are in Southeast Asia, stop by Prince Court Medical Center or one of the other incredible hospitals in Malaysia, Thailand, or Singapore just for the experience. You could even get your annual physical done simply to enjoy the low costs and great care. If you are expecting a baby, choose a birth destination based on the quality care and the opportunities to plant new citizenship flags for your child and possibly yourself.

Holistic Planning: If you are already living overseas full-time, incorporate your medical checkups, procedures, dental care, and other treatment and wellness measures based on where you will be traveling and the best hospitals and clinics you want to visit.

K

KEEP MORE OF YOUR MONEY

Chapter Eight: Offshore Banking

In Other Words, Just Being Smart

Dateline: Bucharest, Romania

It was a productive day for me in Bucharest. I had safely moved out of my short-term apartment in the capital city's depressing Unirii Square and into a beautiful hotel room in the much sunnier University Square. The gloominess of living on the ninth floor facing a dreary view had sapped my productivity, but today I was refreshed and ready to do what I came for.

I strolled through the trendy University Square which was practically brimming with life. I decided to make a quick stop before arriving at my destination and entered a quaint restaurant. The waiter moodily shuffled over to my table, practically threw a menu at me, and then waited in silence for my order. I have come to expect poor customer service such as this in many places in Eastern Europe, but I was still caught off guard. Because of the progressive development of the area, I had not expected customer service on par with the dark days of Soviet oppression. I took this as a sign not to expect great service from the bank I was about to visit, either.

I make a habit of inspecting the banks in almost every country I visit. I have opened more unneeded bank accounts than you would imagine, all to understand the banking climate in each country. I have an entire team that helps me research banks and calls them up to determine how they operate, but nothing compares to physically going into a bank and working with them in person.

Romanian banks had been on my radar for some time before this particular visit. Remarkably, Romania has one of the best budget situations in the European Union. They have managed to avoid all the problems of Greece, with a tax rate just a fraction of what France collects from its citizens. My curiosity was piqued, and I knew I had to check out the banks.

My meal finished, I continued my walk through University Square and entered one of the more well-known banks in the area. I approached a stern-faced banker, bracing myself for an unpleasant repeat of the poor service at the restaurant. As she looked up from her desk and surveyed me inquisitively, the sun reflected off the banker's name tag – Teodora, I noted.

"Hello," I began. "I'm here on vacation and would like to open a bank account." While I did not consider my visit an actual vacation, I have learned to speak in a language that people will understand.

Without missing a beat, Teodora responded, "Sure. Have a seat."

Surprised, I explained, "Well, hold on, I just came to see what you need from me and what documents to bring in."

Raising an eyebrow Teodora asked, "You have passport?"

"Sure, I've got my passport."

"Okay, fine. Sit down," she insisted.

"You don't need any other paperwork from me?"

"No, just sit down."

I accepted Teodora's advice and took a seat across from her as she feverishly pecked away at her computer. Less than 25 minutes later, she was handing me the paperwork for my account. She gave me my token for accessing online banking where I could answer any further questions and then she walked me to the ATM where she explained that I could deposit as little as one euro to activate my account.

"That's it?" I asked in wonder.

Teodora nodded, "We'll send card to address on file, but you're all done now."

Amazed, I told her, "Wow, you guys make this easy!"

She threw me a quizzical look and simply asked, "Why would it not be easy?"

She was certainly right; banks should have a large incentive to make working with them a breeze. Why would banks make it hard for us to hand our money over to them? However, her response reflected a level naiveté about the rest of the banking world where banking is increasingly more difficult.

Many people I work with tend to think that they can open a bank account anywhere, but most places offer nothing like my experience in Romania. In some countries, banks will not even open an account for you, in others they require much more paperwork. Thankfully, there are still some countries like Romania left in the world. You may need to know what to do and where to go, but these countries are on the rise and want to make it easy for folks like you and me to do business with their banks.

Unfortunately, these banks are getting harder and harder to find. The banking world has become a madhouse. One study a few years ago suggested that banks in the United States were only the fortieth safest in the world, and the United Kingdom was slightly behind at forty-fourth. Some European countries fared worse. It seems that every time I turn around, some new stress test is uncovering a bunch of insolvent banks putting your money at risk.

If you have not implemented a Nomad Capitalist strategy yet, chances are that your money is held in one country and in one currency. For instance, most people rely on a country like the United States to not only store all their money, but also to maintain the value of their currency. Ask people in Zimbabwe, Turkey, or Argentina how that worked out for them.

Now, being a Nomad Capitalist is not about focusing on doom and gloom. Nomad Capitalists are, first and foremost, businesspeople and investors who focus on finding pragmatic solutions. Sure, we understand that governments and many financial institutions have their problems, but we are not going to dwell on that. Instead, we simply take note and then go where we're treated best. However, 'taking note' does mean realizing that the banks in your home country are probably not the best in the world. You may think that 40th is not such a bad ranking, but go ahead and name 39 countries that you would say have better banks than the US, or 43 countries that have better banks than the UK. When you stop to think about it, that is a lot of countries.

Since October of 2000, over 550 banks have failed in the United States. This is due, in part, to the fact that the US has many banks, but it is also an issue of US banks investing in garbage and overleveraging their assets. But remember not to dwell too long on how terrible the banks are in your home country. Instead, simply recognize that you can have better. While a place like Singapore only has three banks, none of them have ever failed or are likely to ever do so. Why bank in a country where bank failure is a regular occurrence when you can go to a country where it has never happened and probably never will?

This is not to say that all US banks are bad. In some situations, going where you're treated best may mean having a US bank account, especially for business. While it is not necessarily true for US citizens or residents living in the United States, the US is the world's largest tax haven. As we discussed in the renunciation chapter, for US citizens living abroad and non-citizens outside of the country, there are ways to bank in the United States without having to pay tax.

It certainly is not the answer for everyone, but the US may be the answer for some. Is it ideal? No. But if you are looking to run a business, it can be the best from an operational and logistical point of view. The key is to find the good US banks. The person with Bank of America, for example, is probably not researching their bank's financials. Nomad Capitalists, on the other hand, are doing their research because they do not want to rely on politicians to bail their bank out if things head south.

The good US banks are those that understand international business, especially how to wire money overseas. They are those that will take the time to get to know you so they can comfortably keep your account open while being compliant with Know Your Customer (KYC) rules. In all honesty, the fact that most US banks do not know how to handle clients with international lives, investments, and businesses is one of the biggest problems with US banks, especially for Nomad Capitalists. While you can find the rare gem here and there, most US banks do not have a clue about other countries or what is going on in the rest of the world. They have enough 'easy' customers to deal with who fit inside the box that they do not have to deal with 'difficult cases' like us.

And they are even worse when it comes to servicing clients who travel on a regular basis. During another visit to Romania (i.e., in the European Union) I logged in and tried to send a wire to myself with my Chase account and they blocked my online access. Their solution, of course – like most US banks – was for me to show up at a branch in the US with my debit card. It was as if they could not understand that someone on the other side of the world would not find it inconvenient to travel all the way back to the United States just to reboot their online banking or reactivate a debit card.

Many US banks are not international friendly. There are a few, but you will need to do your homework. Just make sure that you are dealing with people who have a clue. And while US banks are not off limits, limiting yourself to just one country is an investment risk that no savvy businessperson should be making.

The key is to diversify.

Most people equate the old saying of 'never keep all your eggs in one basket' to diversifying your assets across numerous asset classes, such as growth stocks, blue chip stocks, bonds, and real estate. And that is certainly part of it. But Nomad Capitalists add one more factor into their diversification strategy: geography.

Many people in the West have never considered diversifying geographically. That does not mean it is a new idea, though. I recently spoke in Shenzhen to a group of entrepreneurs, importers, exporters, and Americans doing business in China. In my presentation, I told the tale of two people: one is a businessman who was born in Long Island, New York. His parents always raised him to be smart and think about business. He reads the WSJ every day and he knows what is happening in Hong Kong, but he never travels. Everything he has is in the United States.

The second individual is the child of immigrants. Because of his parents' experience, he recognizes that you cannot put your trust (or your money) in any one place. His parents chose to go where they believed they would be treated best and instilled that same belief in their child. As such, he realizes that everything needs to be diversified beyond the borders of just one country.

For the first individual, the United States seemingly offers everything they could ever need. They diversify within the 'greatest country on Earth' and never consider diversifying across countries. Perhaps they feel that it is a bit unpatriotic, or even wrong to go out and invest in other countries.

Let's examine that belief. Is there anything wrong with investing in short small cap stocks rather than blue chip stocks? Or is there anything illegal or shady about investing in bonds rather than equities? People in the US already invest in African, Middle Eastern and Asian countries' stocks, equities, and mutual funds. Is that unpatriotic? No! They are diversifying. So why not extend those investments to the best other countries can offer when it comes to banks?

For me, this is just being smart. I have worked with people who run $100 million businesses and, as far as I could tell, everything that they did – all their money – was with a Bank of America account. That just seemed ridiculous. With that much at stake, would you keep all your money in the same bank? No! You would spread it out. Diversifying geographically simply means that you accept that there is an easier and legal way to put your money in other banks in other countries and get the benefits of services that you would not have in your bank account back home.

For many people I work with, opening a foreign bank account is one of the first steps toward internationalization – especially if their life and business practices reflect the mindset and situation of the first individual. It is a fantastic first step to take because it brings with it numerous benefits that can make the rest of your transition into the Nomad Capitalist lifestyle much smoother. Relative to getting a second passport, opening an overseas bank account can be accomplished with minimal time and expense.

The Benefits of Offshore Banking

I am not going to be one of those guys who scaremongers with stories that the US dollar is tomorrow's toilet paper, or that there is some vast conspiracy to steal your money and give it to the Illuminati. Instead, I am going to show you the numerous important benefits to legally banking offshore for any high achiever.

Moving part of your money into another banking system reduces your risk, subjects you to a different set of laws than those from your home country, gives you a Plan B for your money if things do get bad, offers the potential benefit of high returns, gives you access to new opportunities and foreign investments, and allows you to diversify your wealth to new currencies. Having a bank account overseas is the first step to protecting your wealth and your freedom. Let's look at some of the greatest benefits in more detail.

Get Higher Interest Rates

When people think of offshore, they almost always think about numbered bank accounts (more on that in a minute). And, since they do not want a numbered bank account and do not have anything to hide, they wonder, "What would I do that for?" Well, how about 11% interest in a currency that will likely rise against the US dollar over the next five years? How about doubling your money, just in a bank, in five or six years? Going offshore is not about numbered and anonymous bank accounts, it is about diversifying and increasing your options.

Currency diversification through foreign bank accounts is an excellent way to protect your asset base from the destruction of one single fiat currency. It is also a great way to obtain higher interest rates on your money. Many overseas banks offer interest rates that are five, ten, or even 100 times better than what you can get at home. If you are used to relying on interest income, this can be a game changer for you.

New Zealand bank accounts currently pay up to ten times the interest that American banks do. If you are more adventurous, there are emerging market currencies that offer interest rates as high as 18%. The key is to know which ones are good and which ones to avoid. In some cases, you do not even have to sell your US dollars or euros to profit. Several foreign banks pay 5-6% annual yields on US dollar accounts if you do not want to invest in foreign currencies.

Banks in financial centers like Hong Kong, Singapore, and Andorra offer as many as 12-15 currencies, all in one account. You can easily sell your dollars and buy pounds, euros, or renminbi at any time. An offshore bank account is an excellent way to get exposure to emerging currencies and profit from global financial trends.

In some countries, you can even use your bank deposits to qualify for a second residence or passport. In Armenia, you can get a residence permit by investing $20,000 in securities denominated in Dram (which has managed to keep pace with the US dollar over the last five years) and look at earning between 7-10.5% on your investment depending on maturity and marketing.

Usually, the residence permit is good for a one-year period and is then upgraded to a five-year permit upon renewal, followed by a ten-year residence permit. However, it is not uncommon for US citizens to get a five-year residence permit from the get-go. Best of all, Armenia has one of the shortest timelines to citizenship. After becoming a resident, you only need to wait three years before applying for Armenian citizenship.

There are similar programs that will get you a residence permit in exchange for a bank deposit in countries as different as Malaysia and Ecuador. Or, if you are willing to up the investment amount and deposit at least half a million in a Turkish bank, you could automatically qualify for citizenship and get one of the best Tier C passports in the world. With these kinds of programs, you can kill more than two birds with one stone by not only getting higher interest rates but also diversifying your assets and planting residence and citizenship flags around the world.

Avoid Confiscation

Having your bank account under a different legal system from your own can also prevent the government from confiscating your money. As you already know, I have had personal experience with the government bypassing its own laws and bank policies to take my money when, because of an error made by the California Franchise Tax Board, they claimed that I owed them a tax fee for a year that I had not even lived or conducted business in the state. They then illegally confiscated money from my account to pay the fee that I technically did not owe.

Situations like this cause you to wonder why people make fun of all these banana republics when California is not even following its own laws and courts. The fee I was charged had already been ruled unconstitutional by the courts of California, but the tax collectors continued to charge it and the banks put up with it because... well, it is the government. Having my bank account levied was a wake-up call for me as to what could happen. The government could just dig in there and take my money any time.

Having a foreign (also known as offshore) bank account can give you that extra layer of protection between your money and a government that feels entitled to it. The banks in the US did not put up much of a fight when the government asked them to allow them illegal access to my account, but a bank in another country does not have to bend over backwards like this.

Unfortunately, account confiscation can take place for many reasons in many different countries. Chances are that your government is broke. The United States is the largest offender, having run up a tab of national debt and unfunded liabilities over $100 trillion. It is a ticking time bomb. Asset confiscation has already taken place in recent years in Cyprus, Ireland, Hungary, and Poland. Having an offshore bank account can protect your money from fat-fingered government agents and wealth confiscation, as well as aggressive lawyers, creditors, and ex-spouses.

You may not know it, but bureaucrats can freeze your account without having any proof or even charging you with a crime. Imagine what would happen if you could not access your own money for weeks, months, or years. Moving your money elsewhere can protect your wealth and give you peace of mind. It is all about being sovereign over your own wealth.

Satisfy Business Purposes

Opening an offshore company is another 'quick win' in the offshoring game. While some countries have an overwhelming array of forms, other countries make it extremely easy to form a corporation, even online. The trouble for most entrepreneurs comes when they want to use that company. The most important tool needed to use any company, whether offshore or in your home country, is a bank account.

Without a bank account, you cannot do much of anything. Unless you are using your shiny new foreign company to hold and license intellectual property – something US citizens should be wary of – or hold tangible, non-income producing assets, there is little use for a company with no bank account.

Foreign banks are usually much more in tune with internationalization than the United States. They understand that a business based in Hong Kong with a bank in Singapore is going to want to send money to an employee in Mexico, a contractor in Australia, and a law firm in Georgia. Foreign banks oftentimes will not even blink at a situation like this. The bank in your home country, on the other hand, might just freeze your account if you attempted even one of those tasks.

Dodge The Nomad Tax Trap

I frequently tell people who come to me for help that they can continue banking in the United States because that is not a tax problem. However, for Canadians, Australians, and many Europeans who want to leave their home country, become a non-resident, and leave the tax system, having a bank account there is a problem.

For years, I have been talking about the Nomad Tax Trap that applies to citizens of basically every western country except the United States. For these folks, living nomadically has become increasingly problematic because they cannot prove to their home country government that they have left until they have broken all ties to their home country and established new ties in another country.

If you have kept your bank account in Australia, it is hard to tell the Australian government that you have left. Closing your bank accounts in your home country and banking offshore is a good way to become a non-resident and enjoy the full tax benefits of living abroad.

Acquire Better Deposit Insurance

While the US dollar is certainly not tomorrow's toilet paper, it is always nice to have insurance against such a possibility. The FDIC in the United States has well under one percent of deposits in its reserves. If every US bank were to fail at once, depositors would only see $1 for roughly every $300 on deposit returned to them.

The US government has said for years that the FDIC is insolvent, and the FDIC has long operated in the red. Even President Obama said that the FDIC is mired in red ink. So, while I am not going to waste my time worrying about my financial 'house' burning down, I am going to look for a good way to insure it by turning to offshore banks. Many foreign banks and countries offer deposit insurance on their bank accounts. There are even a few places with unlimited deposit insurance. The most important thing to look for is bank stability, not which country the bank is in. Chances are that the next round of 'Too Big to Fail' will make your local bank account a target anyway.

Better deposit insurance is just one piece of the larger benefit of having a better bank in general. Some of the world's safest banks are in Germany, Singapore, and even Australia. Safe banks in the US and much of Europe are fewer and farther between than ever. That is because most of those banks only keep one or two cents per dollar of your money on hand. Compare that to 20, 25, or even 30 cents per dollar in some offshore banks.

Just because a bank is in a wealthy country does not mean it is safer. If you have ever wondered what would happen in a modern-day bank run, just look at Europe: banks there have limited their customers' access to their money. And when banks went under, not even deposit insurance protected them in some cases. If the entire country is bankrupt, the government cannot very well guarantee your money anyway.

Why not go with the best? Why not go with the strongest? Why do you want to deal with a problematic or tiny bank? Do you really want your money in banks that are "Just OK?" Or do you want your money in the safest banks on earth?

Build "Tunnels"

If you open an offshore bank account now – instead of waiting for some hypothetical future date – you will be able to reap another benefit to offshore banking: tunnels. To understand this concept, think back to when you were a little kid and you would go to your friend's birthday party to eat cake and play party games. One game at these parties always got me going: musical chairs. You would run around and around in a circle, waiting for the music to stop, only to hope you could find a place to sit before all the available chairs were taken.

I look at offshore banking today in much the same way. There are many great banks out there, but if you take too long to grab your seat, it may be too late. Yes, it is still possible to bank offshore in Singapore, but you should be aware that even this bastion of economic freedom is starting to wake up to the reality that the bankrupt countries of the world are gunning for it. Not wanting to be isolated from the world financial system, Singapore may take steps that will make it less attractive for people from western countries.

Banks in places like Hong Kong have already started limiting the number of new US customers that they take on and, in some cases, flat out refuse to open accounts. The strict requirements on US persons have led many banks around the world to simply deny service to Americans.

In 2010, the United States passed a law called FATCA – the Foreign Account Tax Compliance Act – which mandates that all foreign financial institutions report the details of every American-owned account to the IRS or face a 30% withholding tax. Because foreign banks need access to US capital markets to conduct business, banks are forced to comply with FATCA. That is why US citizens need to act now if they want to open an offshore account before more banks begin to decline their business.

Oftentimes, those who open accounts before requirements are tightened get grandfathered in. This strategy is also known as building a tunnel. For example, there are banks like those in China circa 2016 that allowed you to bank with them for a minimum deposit as low as $1,000 or even $1 in some banks. In many cases, once you have an account open, the bank will not close it. So, even though these Chinese banks have now stopped accepting new accounts from foreigners, yours will remain intact.

You have built your tunnel.

That is why it can be a great idea to open small accounts now with the understanding that, if you do not, they may be unavailable to you in the future. When I talk about acting now, part of the reason is that flags available for you to plant today will not be available tomorrow. Those who will be affected the most by inaction will be small depositors who do not have a lot of cash. Some banks may continue to open accounts for foreigners, but only for those able to deposit higher and higher sums. The person with smaller amounts to their name will have fewer and fewer options as time goes by.

With greater compliance costs and more and more wealthy people from the emerging world, banks do not have time for foreigners that do not live there to drop $1,000 into their bank. The key is to find banks that will take you now so that when the door closes, you are already inside.

What is Offshore Banking?

Now, for many, knowing the benefits of offshore banking is still not enough to prepare them to open their own account. Ask the average person what they think about offshore banking and they are sure to tell you that it is illegal and out of reach for all but the über wealthy. Both points are false and only further prove that going where you're treated best means doing what others do not. The rest of this chapter takes a closer look at exactly what offshore banking is, what it is not, the requirements you must follow to legally bank in another country, and – most importantly – the best places to legally bank offshore.

When I say, 'offshore banking,' what I really mean is merely banking in another country. If you live in the United States, your offshore account could be just a day's drive away in Vancouver, Canada. Even if connected by land, Canada is just as 'offshore' for Americans as anywhere else. What is a Singapore bank to a Singaporean? A local bank. It is like the old joke that one friend tells another when going to China: "Have some Chinese food while you're there. Or as they call it in China: food." Your offshore bank account in Singapore is someone else's normal course of business. It is not different; it is just you using it as a foreigner.

Feel free to remove the mental barrier in your mind of offshore versus onshore. All offshore means is having a bank in another country. That is it. I mention this to help you see the places that you should avoid, as well. Do not go rushing off to the traditional 'offshore' locations like Belize, BVI and the Seychelles of the world just because they are 'offshore.' You will likely suffer problems.

I use the term 'offshore banking' as a demarcation. Really, it is just choosing to go where you're treated best. In many respects, Singapore's banks are just better. They have better online services, lower fees, and allow customers to hold different currencies. You cannot do any of that in the United States. That is the difference: a different bank in a different country with different laws. And if those laws and services favor you, then going 'offshore' is merely going where you're treated best.

What Offshore Banking is NOT

Since this book is called Nomad Capitalist and not The Art of the Deal or some other artifact of the 1980s, it is important that we bust some myths that were true twenty or thirty years ago, but no longer are today. Banking offshore has an image problem. It has a reputation that, for some reason, is stuck in the 1980s. People picture a bunch of rich tax evaders putting bags of cash together so that some Swiss banker can drive by their house, pick it up, and fly back to Switzerland so everything is undetectable by the authorities.

Of course, this kind of thing still goes on, but it is not my job to moralize over the rights and wrongs of the practice. What I will say is that this is the old-school way to bank offshore. At Nomad Capitalist, we practice transparency in a modern way and in accordance with the law. We are not about hiding money. Unfortunately, a lot of the other videos and resources that you can find on the internet are still telling you reasons to open offshore bank accounts that have illicit or shady overtones.

What is most unfortunate about such advice (besides the fact that individuals actually follow it and land themselves in a load of trouble) is that it is not necessary. You do no need to hide your money or run around making backroom deals to get second passports. You can follow the law and create a life of greater freedom and prosperity for yourself. You just need to know how. So, to clean up the industry's image and to help you avoid the offshore traps and scams that are still out there, here is what offshore banking is not:

Misconception #1: The Media's Offshore Bank

Many of the false beliefs about offshore banking are influenced by movies like James Bond and the profuse number of spy shows on TV that show criminals dropping off wheelbarrows full of cash at the doorstep of some shady banker with overly white teeth and leaving with little more than a numbered receipt.

An offshore banker once told me that he only knew of one bank down in the Caribbean somewhere that was still accepting cash deposits for a 16% fee. He said, "They might as well have put up a sign that says, 'We launder money.'" Nobody wants cash these days. It is pretty much a dead giveaway that you are a money launderer, so most banks stay far away from it.

However, if you go to the Middle East, they still want cash. If you go to Hong Kong, they still like cash. I closed a bank account in Hong Kong once and they said "Hello, Mr. Henderson, here's your $23,000 in cash." I immediately thought, What the hell am I supposed to do with this?! I was fortunate enough that I could go across the street to another bank with which I already had a business relationship and they opened an account for me before I left Hong Kong, but it was a bit unnerving even walking that far with a suitcase full of cash.

There is nothing wrong with cash. Obviously, you must report it, but who is carrying around cash? This idea that people are just carrying around cash and depositing it into some offshore bank account is a myth. The rest of the world's banks work just the same way they do in the United States or wherever you are from: you wire money in, you transfer money around Europe, you withdraw money when you need it, you get an ATM card. Banks are banks.

If you are watching TV for your offshore advice (or news, or pretty much anything else), you are going to land yourself in trouble. If you are getting your offshore news from someone who does not know offshore, you are probably getting incorrect advice. Even if they are a professional, if they do not know offshore, they do not know offshore. And if professionals can get this stuff wrong, you know that the media is way off the mark.

Takeaway: Get your information about offshore banking from someone who knows the offshore world. That includes ignoring the mainstream media's portrayal of offshore banking, as well as seeking out expat-focused accountants, lawyers, and other professionals.

Misconception #2: Offshore Banks Are for Hiding Your Money

One of the big reasons people are advised to bank offshore is to get privacy. We have already discussed the benefit of putting a firewall between yourself and another government or creditor by having an offshore bank. This makes it harder for anyone to just come and grab your money and that is good. What is wrong about the offshore privacy advice is when someone tells you that your government never needs to know.

If you are a citizen (or even a resident) of any number of countries, including the United States, you have a legal obligation to report your foreign bank accounts to your government. That means that offshore banks are not a way to achieve privacy. You are obligated to share that information. What you are achieving is more distance between your funds and your creditors.

Do not get confused by the difference between 'privacy' as a term for confidentiality and 'secrecy' as an act of concealment. Seeking privacy is fine but do know that there are laws that you must follow when it comes to declaring offshore bank accounts. You do not wish to run afoul of those. Besides, if you really are living the Nomad Capitalist lifestyle, why do you need to hide your money? You want to put up an extra layer of protection between you and the government, sure; but freedom means having nothing to hide.

Which brings us to one of the biggest myths about offshore banking: numbered bank accounts. This is the idea that you can open some numbered bank account in Switzerland where nobody will know your name or identity and you can move your funds without being traced. Let me kill this myth now: numbered and anonymous bank accounts no longer exist. And only in a few countries can you even store stacks of paper in a box without providing identification (more on that in the chapter on foreign asset storage).

Two things happened that put an end to numbered bank accounts, the first being 9/11, and the second being the US government going bananas on Swiss banks for allowing US citizens to evade taxes. As a result, opening the fabled numbered Swiss bank account will prove rather difficult these days if you are a US citizen, unless you live overseas and have a ton of cash.

Chances are, many of the people who are reading this book have never even heard of numbered bank accounts. Just like people these days might not know what vinyl records are (or even dial-up internet!) there are individuals coming into the offshore world who have not been poisoned by all this nonsense and illegality that went on in the 70s and 80s. For them, they just look at Singapore and see that their banks are strong and that they actually keep money sitting around and they are easy to deal with and they think, Why wouldn't I go there? Why wouldn't I go where I'm treated best?

This is the mindset that gives me hope for the future of international business and investment. This is a mindset that does not go looking for anonymity and secrecy and numbered bank accounts so you can do whatever you want without anyone knowing. Instead, it allows you to harness the systems that are in place with total transparency to build a life of greater freedom and prosperity for yourself, your posterity, and the many other people you care about.

However, if you are still bound and determined to achieve anonymity, cryptocurrency is about the only way to obtain some anonymity in your financial dealings these days. The US recently issued an edict making Bitcoin unfavorable from a capital gains perspective, but at least you can maintain some anonymity.

If you are looking for anonymous banking, the first step you should consider is renouncing your citizenship. There are benefits to not having citizenship in a populous, bankrupt country when it comes to availing yourself of bank secrecy laws. For example, Austria is still clinging to bank secrecy laws despite pressure from the European Union. And since countries like Singapore do not much care what you do with your money outside their borders, you will have more freedom being from a country that is not a member of groups like the OECD and that is not attacking your right to bank privacy.

Takeaway: If you come across an offshore service provider offering you a numbered bank account, run the other way. There are legal ways to achieve greater privacy, but there is no legal way to outsmart your government. If your government finds that you are keeping money offshore and not declaring it, they will come down on you like a ton of bricks.

Misconception #3: Offshore Banks are for People Who Want to Avoid Taxes

The term 'tax haven' is a troubling one. As with privacy versus secrecy, it is a term that is often misused as a way of appealing to people who are trying to run from their legal tax obligations rather than set things up properly. This is completely unnecessary. There are ways to legally live overseas, operate your business overseas, and bank your money overseas, all without paying tax; but it is not so simple as upping sticks and moving to Panama. You should be concerned by anybody who talks a lot about tax havens and how you should move to a tax haven country.

When we talk about going where you're treated best, that could mean where you pay the lowest taxes, but it could also mean going where you have high-quality banks. And some of the banks that I have seen in a lot of these so-called 'tax havens' are low quality. They end up causing people a lot of other problems, and they certainly do not qualify as going where you're treated best.

It is also important to note that if you live in the United States, you are probably going to pay tax in the United States. If you live in Europe, you are going to pay tax where you live in Europe. If you live in Canada, Australia, or any number of other countries in the world, you will need to pay tax there. Sure, there is a way to legally avoid taxation on what you do, but this idea that all you need to do to get out of paying taxes is open a Panama bank account gets a lot of people into a world of hurt.

People have gone to jail, been fined, and worse, all thanks to the advice they received from these nameless, faceless advisors. They get told they can just open a bank account and invest their money however they wish and not pay tax. It does not work that way.

Takeaway: The marketing that talks about privacy and tax havens and tells you that you will not have to pay any tax because it is 'offshore' and tries to sell you a one-size-fits-all solution at a supposedly low cost is a recipe for disaster. At best, the guy who charges the least is offering a very formulaic process. He does not care what you need and has not taken your specific circumstances into account.

Misconception #4: I Will Automatically Be Audited if I Have an Offshore Bank Account

A lot of people in the offshore industry tend to play on people's fears. Their message is that the big, bad government wants to take your money, so you better go offshore and hide it. In all honesty, I doubt the government cares that much. They care in the sense that they want to keep money in their country, but the individual dude working at the government office is not out to get you.

Yes, maybe the politicians are using shady tactics, but the guy working at the IRS does not care. There is no need to go around imagining that the entire Internal Revenue Service is out to get you. Some people have this irrational fear that they are going to get audited if they have an offshore bank account. I have been in this industry for a long time and I do not know a single person who has been audited my entire life.

I do my taxes cleanly, and I encourage everyone else to do the same and play by the rules. Hire an expat accountant and report bank accounts so that you will not be audited. There is always the random chance that you might be audited, but it will be because you were going to be audited regardless. It will not be because of your offshore bank accounts. Anyone can be audited, regardless of whether you are set up in a high or low tax jurisdiction.

Takeaway: Banking offshore or seeking out low tax locations does not mean that the taxman is going to come after you.

Misconception #5: What If My Bank Goes Under?

This misconception is rooted in the erroneous belief that everything in your own country is automatically safe and the best of its kind. However, as we have seen over and over, this simply is not true. People who worry that their offshore bank is going to go under are probably not the same people worrying about the banks in their home country – even though those are the banks that should be causing them worry.

Imagine your local bank were to go under: who would protect your money? If you answered, 'deposit insurance' or 'the government,' think again. Not only do many banks keep mere pennies on hand to pay depositors, but sovereign insurance funds in the West often have less than 1% of bank deposits on hand. Having a bank account overseas can offer you the peace of mind that at least you have diversification in a worst-case scenario.

The US does have some of the highest deposit insurance in the world (at $250,000), but that is because they need it. People would worry too much about bank failures without it. In some cases, when the FDIC knows that a bank is on the brink, they will find buyers to come in instead of offering insurance. For example, a bank like Capital One that has a lot of money and wants to expand will simply take over and pay you in full, even if you had more than the limit in your account.

If your offshore bank were to go under, the situation is generally resolved in much the same way. Do keep in mind that not all countries have deposit insurance, but even in countries that do not have insurance, many banks are still too big to fail. If a bank in Georgia were to go under, the potential damage to the economy would probably be enough to convince the Georgian government to step in.

However, I have seen one or two instances in other countries where the banks say, "You're a foreigner. Screw you." The worst case is what happened in Cyprus where they just did a bail-in; but Cyprus was not a great place to bank to begin with. Everyone knew what was going on. I was talking about it a year before the bail-in occurred when I first started my blog. Everyone knew that it was the hot money capital for Russians. The lesson, then, is to avoid making a stupid decision going in.

It is easier to avoid stupid decisions than you might think. Sure, some places fall from grace, but most of the time you can see the writing on the wall from a long way out. If you go to the right banks in the right countries, the fear of bank failure should never be an issue.

Takeaway: Find the right bank going in. Look at your bank's numbers. If you do not have the time to do your own research, then you can go to a consultant. Having someone who knows what is going on in the world and who helps you avoid the big issues upfront is important. Whether you do your homework or have someone else do it for you, you are far less likely to have a problem.

Misconception #6: Why Would I Need an Offshore Bank?

There is one final false belief about offshore banking, and that is the belief that it has no potential benefit for you. Because people do not understand the reasons for having a foreign bank account, they fail to see that their bank is not really that great.

Bank of America is leveraged to the hilt. Their service stinks. They do not understand the rest of the world. If I want to buy a property somewhere else in the world, I cannot do it with a Bank of America account. They are going to hassle me. I have had clients who have gone to their bank in the United States and requested to send money to someone overseas and received nothing but trouble. That should not be the case.

For the Nomad Capitalist, offshore banking is part of a diversified international lifestyle. People assume that the only reason to have a foreign bank account is to hide money, but they are mistaken. It is about getting the kind of service you need for the life you live. If you are going to live out your entire life in your home country, then maybe you do not need an offshore bank. But if you plan to expand your horizon, you will likely benefit from having an offshore bank account.

Takeaway: The problem is that people have beaten into our heads that offshore is wrong in and of itself. No! If you follow the laws, there is nothing illegal or immoral about it at all. It is a good diversification strategy, and it is essential for living a freedom-infused international lifestyle.

The Legality and Requirements for Offshore Banking

We all must follow the law. Having an offshore bank account is 100% legal (and, if you follow my advice, there is little reason to keep it a secret), but you must report it! There is only one way to go offshore and that is to be transparent, to report what you must report, and to file what you are supposed file.

I once helped an individual who was a US citizen as well as a citizen of three other top-tier countries. Though he was not an accidental American – he knew he was a US citizen – he had not lived in the United States as an adult and he never even thought about filing. He had almost a million dollars in bank accounts and he could have been penalized half of that if he did not come clean and report it. He was not purposefully hiding it like the guys in Switzerland, he just did not know that he had to.

But that is the penalty for hiding this stuff: half!

Are you willing to risk half your money to go after anonymous bank accounts (that do not even exist anymore)? Half is a lot. I do not care if it is a million dollars or ten thousand dollars. I remember having $10,000 and going to the ATM and seeing my balance and thinking "Woohoo!" Imagine going in the next day and only having $5,000. Not good.

Going offshore requires you to comply with the government's regulations. If you have foreign bank accounts, you need to report them. Banks that are not compliant with the US will give you problems. I know people who have had their accounts frozen for six months just because they got an account with the wrong bank.

Now, I am not a lawyer or an accountant. I am the guy who dropped out of Arizona State to be an entrepreneur. I work with professional accountants and lawyers to handle everything for me so that all is as it should be. I strongly suggest you do the same. But what I can tell you is that US citizens are required to report every bank account they have if they keep $10,000 or more in all those accounts combined at any time during a given year. There is a form called the FBAR expressly for this purpose and it is due on June 15 every year. There are no extensions. The IRS takes this stuff seriously. Other countries have their own rules, so it is important to have someone who can help you figure them out and ensure that you are compliant.

Takeaway: There is nothing illegal or immoral about opening a bank account in another country. Nor is there anything particularly unsafe about the procedure. Just report and make sure that you are in compliance with all the laws in your home country and you will stay on the right side of the law.

Where to Bank Offshore

The idea behind offshore banking is jurisdictional diversification to ensure return of capital in addition to better returns on your deposited capital. That is why the best offshore banks that are accessible to you are either in places like Singapore that cater to foreign wealth and have maintained an open-door policy, or places that actively encourage Americans... again, because they have an open-door policy.

While it is more difficult to open a bank account in many countries today, other countries are moving in the opposite direction. That is the beauty of going where you're treated best: where one door closes, another opens. Yesterday, Switzerland was the en vogue place to bank, today it may be Singapore, and tomorrow it may be Azerbaijan.

But before we discuss the best places to open an offshore bank account, we need to start by crossing several places off our list. Going offshore does not mean throwing a dart at a map and going wherever it lands, it means going where you're treated best. Some offshore banks are truly terrible, others have been harassed, and others simply do not want your business anymore.

For example, all the offshore banks in the tiny Caribbean islands have been harassed to the point that it is no longer worth banking there in many cases. If you were the United States and you wanted to find all your tax cheats, the easy solution would be to simply go down to Belize and tell them that you are coming in lock, stock, and barrel. What is Belize going to do? Even Panama has recently experienced their own little scandal, but it was never on my list of favorites anyway.

Then there are the tax havens like Seychelles where the banks are hanging by a thread. You also have European strongholds like Switzerland, Liechtenstein, and Luxembourg that are part of the old offshore world and, for many individuals and businesses, no longer offer the perfect panacea for offshore banking. And in countries like Cyprus and Ukraine, the banks are either run by the mob or have fallen flat on their face in recent years. As a general rule, do not bother banking in any of these countries.

But who takes the title of "The worst offshore bank?" You might think that a small bank in a rather inaccessible part of the world with early 2000s technology would earn such a title. In my opinion, the truly worst offshore banks are those that appear to be good but fail to fulfill their promises. If that is the case, then the worst offshore bank in the world is HSBC. While it is supposedly the international banking solution, the reality is that banking with HSBC is miserable.

There are many offshore banks that are not worth the hassle and fees. That does not mean that you should not bank offshore; it merely means you should do your homework on which banks are best for you. Everyone deserves a bank that is highly liquid and stable – an increasing rarity in North America these days – as well as one that matches their needs. For me, customer service is a top priority because I conduct a lot of transactions and occasionally have a question or need help. That is why I have crossed HSBC off my list forever.

There are also banks in certain countries that simply do not want your business anymore. Hong Kong, for example, is very conservative and stable and I would trust them more than most with my money. However, they are becoming incredibly difficult to work with, not because of the government but because the banks are getting pickier about who they will work with. Hong Kong banks do not waste money on garbage, and they will only lend on good projects. That is the kind of bank you want, but they no longer want you.

So many rich Chinese are coming in and depositing large sums that they do not need the small people anymore. The banks have so much money that they do not know what to do with it. So, why would they take your money? If you have ten million dollars and you are a wealthy Chinese guy and the bank does not have to comply with US FATCA regulations, then you are probably worth it. If you are the average person, even with $100,000, it is not worth their time. And all of this is because their banks are good.

But Hong Kong is not the only place in the world with good offshore banks. As with my investigation in Romania, I am constantly looking for the next great place so that I can take advantage of the arbitrage opportunities still out there. The key is to find the banks that are good but have not quite realized it yet – the 'next Hong Kong' of the offshore banking world.

I have found that the opportunity is usually in the middle. Places like Hong Kong do not need you anymore, Switzerland cannot take you anymore, and the tiny little islands have been so harassed that they are basically under the thumb of the West. So, look to the middle. Focus on the places that need your cash just as much as Hong Kong or Singapore did twenty years ago. Those are the places where you will be welcomed.

It is also essential to work with the right foreign banks for your specific situation. If you do not, you might end up spending time closing bank accounts you wanted to keep but no longer can, or traveling all over the world just to close accounts that are causing you problems. The best offshore banks for you depend on three factors:

1. Are you willing to travel there?
2. What is your citizenship?
3. How much money do you have?

Knowing which banks will work for you and your situation is a must if you want to avoid spending your precious time chasing your tail. For instance, Cambodia is a country that you may have never thought of, but if you invest around Asia, it could serve a useful purpose. Add to that the recent promotion I saw at a Cambodian bank for 11% on US dollars and Cambodia starts to look even better. However, for someone who operates in Latin America, a Cambodian bank may not have so much utility.

Essentially, every country is a potential option. One limiting factor is each country's central bank. I have not been to all 196 countries yet, but many central banks around the world make things difficult. Some countries do not want foreigners' money. I once asked to open a bank account in Bosnia and, after the banker picked himself up off the floor from laughing at the fact that I wanted a bank account in his country, he explained the process to me. I needed to go 'here' to get this certified and 'there' to get this stamped and then I needed to obtain a bank reference letter and have it translated and this other document apostilled and then get a copy of my passport translated into Bosnian. Basically, I needed to get it kissed by a priest and signed, sealed, delivered Stevie Wonder-style.

Unsurprisingly, all these requirements came from the central bank – not the banks themselves. Apparently, Bosnia wants to stay broke and in terrible shape. In a region that I like, it is not the success story. In Serbia, on the other hand, the central bank allows you to open a bank account, but the banks themselves are just difficult. The nearby country of Montenegro has a different attitude and lets everyone know that the central bank has no restrictions, they are pro-capital, and they want your money.

Restrictions may also be based on the individual person working at the bank. For example, when I tried to use a non-US passport to open my account in Montenegro, they said, "We don't know where this is, do you have another one?" When I went to a different branch of the same bank across the road, it was fine.

Balkan countries like Montenegro are improving by leaps and bounds. I have several employees from the Balkans who have told me stories of hearing NATO planes on bombing raids fly over their homes when they were children. Roughly twenty years later, Montenegro just got approved to join NATO. And that is not the only progress that Montenegro has made. They want to be a great place to invest. They do not want to become Greece. They want to avoid their mistakes and be more open to receiving capital. Because of that, they have built up a great banking infrastructure and they have consistently increased their deposit insurance.

On a macro level, Montenegro has said that they are open to your investments. In Bosnia, I am sure the banks are open to your money, but the central bank has stunted growth because of all their rules. Some banks in Eastern Europe only ask to see your passport to open an account for you. They do not even want proof of address. In Switzerland, they want your proof of address, your ID card, your residence card, your passport, and ten million other things. Some banks in Germany will also open an account for you, but generally only for EU citizens.

Again, just go where you're treated best. If you really want to be in Switzerland or Germany, then realize that you will need to spend much more of your time, money, and peace of mind to do so.

The country that tops my list, however, is Georgia. Georgia is hands down the easiest place in the world to open an offshore bank account today. Because it is somewhere in the middle of the offshore spectrum, a jurisdiction like Georgia has not seen the problems you find at the top and bottom of the offshore world, precisely because it is not a tax haven, nor is it a large offshore financial center. It is not even on the radar of the vast majority of the world.

It is possible to open a bank account in Georgia with as little as $7. The process at my favorite banks takes as little as ten minutes. If you are a US citizen or have US indicia, you will be asked to fill out a few forms for the IRS, but that is about it. You do not need piles of paperwork, you just show up with the cash in your wallet, make a minimal deposit, and get started. Once you are in the door with a bank, opening additional bank accounts is quite easy. Georgian banks do not offer remote account opening, but service once you have opened at least one account is good, and you can handle most account functions from overseas once you are set up.

In fact, online banking for the Georgian banks I deal with is refreshingly simple. Almost stupidly simple. For as much as I love banking in Singapore, banks there sure do give you a lot of codes, PINs, and access numbers to remember. In Georgia, it is simple. You can move money between Georgian lari, US dollars, euros and British pound with a single click. Exchange rate spreads at the bank are extremely small; if you are making a large deposit, you can get one-way spreads of as little as 0.13% on the street.

Banking in Georgia comes with many benefits. The only real challenge is flying to Georgia to appear in person. Once you make the trip and open your account, Georgian banks offer both ATM and debit Visa Electron cards that can be used anywhere in the world where Visa is accepted. It is also a great tool to have for booking travel online in Europe, as Electron cards incur lower transaction fees from cheap airlines.

While bank fees there are rather low, interest rates are quite high. I have even seen 5% interest rates on short-term US dollar term deposits; and if you are willing to bet on the Georgian lari, you can earn even higher yields. If you are willing to get on a plane, I would strongly consider Georgia for its ease of account opening and maintenance. I might even be so bold as to say that it is the best place to go right now if you are looking to deposit a mid-sized sum.

If you are not willing to get on a plane, you may be tempted to consider remote bank account opening. This has long been a staple of the internet's nameless, faceless promoters. If you are a remote worker, then you might think that opening a bank account remotely would be a good idea, too. While Caribbean islands like St. Vincent and the Grenadines – and even European Union islands like Cyprus – have long touted their willingness to open a bank account for someone they will never meet, the practice is becoming dangerous.

As you might imagine, authorities around the world are cracking down on anything that makes opening a bank account too easy. Tiny islands in the West Indies are typically not as well-equipped with all the bells and whistles that western countries would like them to have to stop terrorists and money launderers. This has led groups of western governments to make banking in those countries harder.

These days, if you want to open a quality bank account, be prepared to show up. A client of mine recently contacted me to tell me he wanted an extra bank account for his company. Since having redundancies is a great idea, I was happy to help him... until he asked what he could open without leaving the couch. If you are working with someone like me, you can probably set up a power of attorney to open a good bank account remotely. In my client's case, there were a couple banks that I could have helped him open remotely, but even an experienced guy with people to support him like my client would spend about $500 to open an account this way. For $500, he could have flown to one of these banks and knocked everything out in an hour or so.

For those who do not have a cadre of lawyers and people like me, the trip to a bank is definitely recommended. Traditional offshore banks – those on flyspeck islands that few people live on – are not only very paperwork happy but fee happy, too. Open an account in St. Lucia and you will pay $100 every time you receive a wire transfer, $80 to send a payment, and $40 a month just for the privilege of the online banking equivalent of one of those early mobile phones you would wear around your hip.

In case it is still not clear, I am not a big fan of banks in the Caribbean and other distinctly 'offshore' locales. In all but the rarest of cases, they simply are not worth it. Just as Swiss banks fell out of favor due to their aggressive marketing of shady practices, banks on the tax haven islands can no longer keep up with changing times.

As globalization continues its aggressive march, the trend is for countries to become more compliant with the world system. Since Nomad Capitalists are not worried about hiding their money, this is not a big issue. This is just the new normal. There are plenty of foreign banks that will accept you as a customer. You can still open an offshore bank account and receive all the benefits that come with it. Everyone can open a bank account somewhere. It just depends on where you can do it.

Your How-To Action Plan

Immediate Action Steps: Diversify! If you have all your money in one bank account, change that. If you cannot travel immediately, consider setting up an offshore bank account remotely (but traveling to do it in person is better). If you cannot do that, at least diversify out of the one domestic account you hold by getting a second bank account.

Travel Action Steps: Setting up an offshore bank account is the perfect Nomad baby step. It could easily be your first real step into the offshore world. I have had many people come up to me on the street in Georgia telling me that they are there setting up a Georgian bank account based on my advice. Do this! Travel somewhere like Georgia or Ecuador where setting up an offshore bank account is easy and just put a little money in the bank there. It will automatically make "offshore" seem less intimidating and give you the comfort of knowing that you have begun to diversify.

Holistic Planning: Report, report, report! Banking offshore does not make you a criminal, but hiding your money offshore is illegal and could land you in a world of hurt. Report everything that needs to be reported. I recommend getting the help of an expat accountant or lawyer to ensure you are doing everything correctly. Beyond reporting, find ways to dovetail your offshore banking with other flags such as getting residence or citizenship by depositing money in a foreign bank.

Chapter Nine: Offshore Companies and Tax Savings

Choose Your Tax Rate

Dateline: Monte Carlo, Monaco

The Mediterranean glistened as it always does in Monaco. Nestled in between France and Italy with its grand total of 0.6 square miles, the principality of Monaco is among the world's best known hot spots for the jet set elite. Only here can a four-minute taxi ride from the train station cost €20 and a mediocre hamburger cost €37.

Port Hercule, the heart of Monaco's harbor, is capable of holding up to 700 vessels in its deep waters. On that warm April day, it was full, brimming with vessels from around the world. As I walked up and down the rows of boats, I noticed the mix of super-yachts, regular yachts, and outright dinghies by comparison. And then I noticed something truly interesting: On the back of each vessel was not only its name – often something cheeky like "It's Hers," but less so than usual since this was Monaco – but I also noticed that the boat's country of registration was listed underneath its name. I saw yachts from the Cayman Islands, the Marshall Islands, and Malta, as well as boats registered to Liverpool, or even France.

What intrigued me most was that, consistently, the boats registered to offshore jurisdictions like the Cayman Islands were much larger than those registered in higher-taxed Europe. The French boats were cute, but the Cayman and Malta boats were the real gems.

I realized that in a chicken-and-egg scenario, the wealthiest yacht owners sought out the most favorable, lowest tax countries in which to register their yacht, while those with smaller boats seemed, on the whole, less concerned about choosing the best country. It was unclear whether the offshore guys had more money to begin with because they were accustomed to going where they were treated best, or if their purchase of a larger yacht simply implied more planning.

What was clear was that going where you're treated best meant a bigger yacht. Unsurprisingly, the same principle holds true for your business.

The Cost of Delay

Most of us run businesses in our home country and pay full taxes. If you live in a place like Montenegro, where profits and income tax are both a paltry 9%, it might not be a big deal. However, if you are anything like me when I was running businesses in the United States, your tax rate may well be either approaching 50% or even higher.

The same is true of folks in most western countries, from Canada to Australia to the UK to all over Western Europe. By the time you add up federal income tax, state or provincial income tax, local income tax, Social Security tax, Medicare tax, and every other tax and levy, anyone productive could easily be giving close to half of their income to the government (if not more).

I could argue that taxation by the government bears little difference to an extortion racket by the mob. Both control territories through force and demand protection money. However, as a pragmatist, I could also argue "Who cares?" The government is not going away, nor is it likely to change. What you do have the possibility to change is whether you remain in the system.

Imagine the amount of money you have paid in taxes in your lifetime. Now, imagine what you would do with that money if you had it all back. In my case, my tab was approaching $1 million before I decided that I had to change something. While I was fortunate enough to realize that these options existed in my mid- and late twenties, imagine what I could have done with $1 million in tax savings. If you are like most business owners, even an extra $50,000 would make a huge difference to your growth trajectory. My friends who sell online are always looking to manufacture and launch new products but never seem to have enough money to keep up with all the opportunities and demand.

Tim, a 24-year-old entrepreneur who had recently launched his Amazon FBA, was in this very situation when we met. Tim was living in Southern California at the time making about $9,000 a month. To most people, he was living the life. However, Tim had a problem. He did not have enough money to reinvest in his company. When I spoke to Tim, it was not difficult to identify his two main culprits; one, his cost of living in the beautiful but expensive San Diego, and two, the $43,000 tax bill his accountant had just prepared for his first year in business. Like most entrepreneurs, myself included, Tim started his business without the proper structure or without even giving much of any thought to taxes. He was just thrilled with the idea of making money on his own terms.

The ironic thing is that most people, even many business owners, earn just enough to pay their taxes and the cost of living. It is the ultimate example of water seeking its own level. Housing prices are correlated with local taxes, goods and services are correlated with income and sales taxes, and wages tend to be just enough to get by in many cases. Even the engineer making $200,000 for Google in Venice Beach will not have much discretionary income after taxes and rent on his $7,000-a-month pied-à-terre near headquarters.

As much as we entrepreneurs want to believe that we are different, many of us have fallen for the same challenges that befall salaried employees, barely scraping by no matter how successful we become. The difference is that most entrepreneurs can get out of this trap with much more ease than a salaried employee tied to one location.

In Tim's case, his Amazon business was growing so quickly that every $1 he invested quickly became at least $3 as products launched and created new (almost somewhat passive) income for him. I explained that, based on those numbers, his real tax costs were $129,000 rather than the actual $43,000 he paid. The reasoning was that, had he been able to use that $43,000 to grow his business, it would have been able to grow into something much bigger. He was losing the return on his investment.

The funny thing was that Tim's business was already globally minded in many ways. He had a Filipino virtual assistant that he hired through Upwork and was planning on hiring more people. When asked why he was not hiring American workers, Tim said it just did not make sense for where his business was at. Yet, because Tim himself was running the business from California, he had no choice but to hand over 40% of his income and seek ways to get financing to expand his company, even if that meant paying double digit interest rates for inventory financing.

Many entrepreneurs start out like Tim, setting up corporations in their home country or merely acting as a sole proprietor because they do not know any better. Many others never thought their business would get so large; even I started Nomad Capitalist as a retirement project after selling my last US business and never expected it to be more than a personal brand. The issue with setting up shop this way is that it locks you into paying taxes until you fix it.

I know one business owner in Asia who, despite not even living in California or having any other ties there, uses a California corporation to conduct his business. He is literally missing out on hundreds of thousands of dollars in savings that could fund his lifestyle or be reinvested in his business because he is incorporated in high-tax jurisdiction that he does not need.

Most of us are familiar with the tax loopholes used by companies like Starbucks, Google, and just about every other tech company on planet earth. Starbucks operates over 32,000 stores all over the world and has successfully shifted much of its revenue from those stores to subsidiaries in low-tax or tax-free countries by selling its intellectual property and other assets back to itself. Other restaurant chains and businesses do the same. You may have heard about the recently neutered Double Irish Dutch Sandwich, whereby companies like Facebook would shift money back and forth around Europe before finally parking it in Bermuda or some other speck in the Caribbean where taxes are low or nonexistent. Your business can do the same.

Not only is it possible in many cases to pay zero tax – unlike the 3% paid by companies like Starbucks – but you do not have to set up a network of subsidiaries all over the world and hang an org chart on your wall. In fact, the cost of setting up your company overseas is quite affordable, if you know what to do.

What Companies Can Go Offshore?

Usually, the first step is to move the active control of your company out of your home country. In Tim's case, he either needed to hire a CEO and an entire organization based outside of the United

States (which is rather tricky unless you are approaching Starbucks volume), or to move himself, as the owner and effective CEO, out of the country. Not all companies can do this.

For anyone considering going offshore, understanding who can take advantage of opportunities to incorporate and save on taxes overseas is fundamental. The Arizona swimming pool company I invested in would have never qualified for any kind of huge tax break. Having a bunch of guys running around on the ground in Arizona means that Arizona – and the United States – can make a good argument that you owe them tax. After all, you are driving on their roads and using their services for your direct benefit. Conversely, the consulting companies that I built in the media and financial industries could have easily operated outside of the United States, making them good candidates as potential offshore companies.

To further illustrate, I recently received a call from a lady who provides the perfect case study of the kind of business that will not benefit by going offshore as far as taxes are concerned. She is a bankruptcy attorney in the United States. She works with her clients personally, appears for them in court personally, and does not want to abandon her practice, which is entirely set up and controlled in the US. Not only is this very nice lady physically working in the United States, but she is appearing in US government buildings for clients who also live in the US, to discuss their US financial matters in front of the US government. There is a whole lot of US involved in this setup, which means her income is considered 'US source.'

The source of income determines where it is taxed. A rental property in Barcelona is always going to be taxed in Spain because it is inherently a Spanish source of income. There is no way to argue that the income from that property should be taxed anywhere else. After all, the Barcelona police protect it, the Barcelona fire department keeps it from burning down, and the Spanish government (despite my belief otherwise) believes that its wonderful, high-functioning government is the reason you have a potential tenant at all. Without them, the argument goes, there would be chaos and no one would want to live in your home.

By the same logic, the lawyer who called me is not only doing work in the United States but also using their system. The question to ask yourself before deciding whether your business should go offshore is if you can make a case that you and/or your business operate from the place that you claim. While I could have set up a Hong Kong company for my pool business in Arizona, it would have complicated things without any tax benefit since the work was obviously being done in Arizona.

If you have staff or virtual assistants operating overseas, that may be a good indication of where your company's work is being done. If you are living the true *Four-Hour Workweek* lifestyle and spending minimal time supervising other people doing the real work, that will help your case as well.

If you or your business are location independent, chances are that you can save some serious money. E-commerce store owners, Amazon sellers, Kindle publishers, coaches, consultants and, in many cases, even passive income investors, among others, can take advantage of greatly beneficial tax laws by going offshore.

One way to look at these tax laws is to say that your government will pay you to travel and live overseas in their appreciation for you leaving. Even someone making only a few thousand dollars a month could see enough tax savings to pay his or her entire cost of living in a place like Tbilisi, Belgrade, Cebu, or Phnom Penh. When your business only uses the internet, phone lines, and human beings who can do the work from Lima or Limassol, it becomes easier to structure your business to either completely eliminate or dramatically lower your tax bill.

For the average entrepreneur earning $100,000 per year, these changes could mean savings of $25,000 – not just this year, but every year. If you make $250,000 a year, you might save $75,000. If you are in the seven-figure club and you are currently operating in a developed country, you could easily save $500,000 on profits of $1 million. But before we get into the details of how to make this all possible, we need to cover just a few more fundamentals. Namely, what is an offshore company?

Offshore vs. Onshore

Terms like 'tax haven' and 'offshore' can often get in the way of understanding what it really means to internationalize your life and go where you're treated best. They make a very natural, legal process of moving your company to a jurisdiction where it can grow sound mysterious and forbidden. Capital is fungible and tends to go where it is treated best. That is the bottom line.

In the old days, offshore for many people was about hiding money. That is how phrases like 'offshore company' and 'Swiss bank account' got a bad reputation in the media (politicians pandering to increasingly destitute voters did not help, either). But just as a Swiss bank account is simply a bank account set up under the laws of Switzerland, an offshore company is merely a company incorporated under the laws of another country. In and of themselves, having offshore bank accounts and setting up offshore companies are both completely legal strategies.

The question of legality comes with what you do with these accounts and companies. It is not legal to use them to hide money and I do not recommend that you try. Today, more than 100 countries have started working together to ensure that businesses and individuals are not evading taxes illegally. And even if you did not have 100 countries peering over your shoulder, why waste your time hiding when you could legally be doing business offshore in the light of day ang getting all the same benefits? It is not only illegal to hide your money with offshore companies, but it also does not make any business sense to do so. Why break the law when you can get better results without the risk of ending up in jail?

Moving your business offshore in a transparent way is smart diversification. While mainstream politicians may call you unpatriotic for going to a tax haven, the reality is that you are under no obligation to base your business in their country, or to even live there. Doing business in high-tax countries does not offer as many benefits as you would suppose. It is much more efficient to manage a company from the Republic of Georgia – one of the most efficient governments on earth – than it is a California corporation. While you may think the high taxes you pay there are getting you special benefits, the opposite is probably true.

Your business can benefit both in terms of tax treatment and efficiency by going offshore. You can structure a company to legally pay no tax, or it may make sense for you to pay a little tax and still save 80% of what you used to pay. Either way, you can probably do better than where your company is currently incorporated. The question, then, is not about staying in your high-tax country or leaving, but whether you should go fully offshore or seek out more conservative onshore solutions.

What do I mean by 'offshore' versus 'onshore'? In general, we use the generic version of the term 'offshore company' to mean incorporating your business 'somewhere other than here.' It does not have to mean some tiny island with treasure chests washing up on the beach. By this definition, an offshore company owned by a non-resident, non-US citizen could be in the United States. While there are a lot of common mistakes that screw up the whole structure, when organized properly, Delaware is one of the world's great tax havens – just not for people who live in the United States.

But when we dig a little deeper into the offshore world, there is a difference between 'offshore' and 'onshore' jurisdictions. 'Onshore' refers to traditional mainland countries which will require at least a little tax to be paid and will usually require you to keep records. Onshore jurisdictions are what most of us are used to, except that we will select a country with far lower taxes, more lenient rules, and (particularly if you are coming from the US) greater asset protection.

True offshore countries offer companies to practically anyone and apply very few restrictions to the companies that operate in their jurisdiction. These countries include, among others, Nevis, the Marshall Islands, Seychelles, Belize, and the Gambia. Many require little more than payment of an annual fee and a registered agent in the country the same way a US company would.

For instance, Seychelles, a small archipelago of 115 islands off the coast of East Africa, has little to lose by selling itself as an offshore market. Almost half of the economy is based on tuna fishing and tourism. Guests to the Raffles Seychelles, where standard rooms can run north of $1,000 per night, care little about whether the Seychelles government harbors a million 'international business companies,' as long as there is also room for their boat in that harbor. Nor has anyone ever protested by refusing to eat fish sourced from a tax haven.

So, the Seychelles government sells access to an environment where, for $100 payable to them plus agent and legal fees, you can pay zero tax, file zero accounting records, and keep your name from appearing on any public record for prying eyes to find. The only restriction is that you usually cannot sell to people in the country where your offshore company is registered, but few readers of this book will have many Seychellois clients. There is little harm to the government in doing this, and with a population of just 90,000, those $100 bills every year do not need to be spread out among a lot of beneficiaries.

Why, then, would you even consider going onshore and dealing with pesky taxes – even if they are only 5% – when you can have the red carpet rolled out for you in a place like Seychelles? For one, doing business in a tax haven is not as simple as it sounds. The fact that just about anybody can set up a Seychelles company, do nothing, and move money around with impunity does not sit well with governments, particularly as they step up enforcement against terrorism, drug cartels, and other shadowy activity.

In many cases, it has become harder to open these offshore companies. Island governments have been put under the microscope by the high-tax countries in the OECD that encourage them to crack down on companies. The consequence if they choose not to cooperate is to be cut off from the world economy. As a result, many banks that used to accept offshore companies from these jurisdictions no longer do so.

Even in the last couple of years, the more lenient banks in Europe and Asia have put out the closed for business sign to this type of anything goes company. Foreign banks have little ability to control what happens in the company; and given the reputation among these countries for dirty stuff, banks do not want the hassle. One misstep could put them on the wrong side of powerful governments with an agenda.

Even PayPal caves to the pressures of such governments. The company operates in most countries on earth, but the limits on withdrawing money are far stricter in Panama than they are in the United States. There is something about a big, high-tax, militaristic country that makes banks do what they say.

That means that while a Nevis company is easy to set up and offers benefits like a required $25,000 bond from anyone wishing to sue you, you will be hard-pressed to get a bank account for your Nevis company. While there are some reasons to have a company without a bank account (holding patents, perhaps) it is not going to be very useful for most entrepreneurs. It is possible to set up a second company to be owned by your Nevis company and have that company get a bank account, but that may be too complex for your needs.

A small, but sure-to-be-growing number of countries are even outright blacklisting these offshore companies. On a recent trip to Asia, a real estate agent told me that his country had announced that they would ignore the tax benefits of any Belize company and treat all assets held in Belize companies owned by their citizens as taxable because they could not trust what they believed to be a banana republic to prevent the money from going toward wars and political payoffs.

Another point to consider is whether your customers will like you doing business in Nevis, Seychelles, or the Gambia. If you asked for my help in crafting your perfect tax-reducing strategy and I asked you to send thousands of dollars to the Gambia so I could get started, you might think twice. Again, there are exceptions to this rule. Maybe all your clients know and trust you and you do not need any more of them. If they are happy to deal with the questions their bank will ask them when they send money to the Bank of West Africa and you are happy to live hoping that your bank does not lose its right to send and receive US dollars, then a simple Nevis company with a Belize bank account might be just fine.

For the rest of us, a better solution is required, especially if we do not want just any bank account. Chances are that you will need good bank accounts with reasonable fees, debit cards you can use, and online banking that will make your life easy. That is where onshore companies come into play. Companies incorporated in more reputable countries give you access to the bounty that a 'real country' offers, including all – or possibly far more – of the services you currently enjoy. If you do not want to wait a week and pay $100 every time you receive a wire transfer, these onshore countries will serve you better. The trick is figuring out which one.

Finding The Right Jurisdiction

You may have heard that all the cool kids like Uber have set up shop in the Netherlands thanks to Amsterdam's favorable tax treatment of large multinationals, but unless you, too, have offices in 92 countries, it is probably not worth it. Many European entrepreneurs start their business in the United Kingdom where taxes are moderate at a flat 20%, but for US citizens and some others, the total cost – not to mention the high cost of compliance – is also a deal breaker.

Nomad Capitalists still have plenty of other options. Today, we have the benefit of a truly global economy in which more and more countries are lowering their tax rates to attract businesses. In a recent study that we conducted, my team and I found more than forty countries around the world that had lowered their corporate tax rates within the last five years. Some made small changes, like the Baltic state that decreases its rate by 1% bi-annually, while others made more significant drops.

There are almost too many options to choose from these days. The breakup of places like the Soviet Union and Yugoslavia created nearly a dozen relatively business-friendly, low-tax countries; and the desire for growth among many developing countries adds more and more 'tax havens' to the list each year. Montenegro, Lithuania, Romania, Georgia, Bulgaria, Ireland, and others offer tax rates of 10% or less in many circumstances. If you are willing to go up to the neighborhood of 15%, the list expands extensively, including several European Union countries and other world-class destinations.

The first step in knowing where to set up your company is to answers a few essential questions. To begin, what are you trying to accomplish? How do your customers pay you? Do you accept wire transfers? Do you need PayPal? Or do you need a full merchant account? Who are your customers and what kind of service and experience do they expect? Of those needs, which countries offer the solutions?

Second, what do you expect? If you are planning to run a clean business and move money around easily and frequently, you will want a place that facilitates that with ease; Swiss banks, for example, tend to dislike frequent transactions. Will that create complications for your business?

Third, what is your business about? If you own intellectual property such as patents or trademarks, for instance, you will need a different strategy compared to an e-commerce business because IP is often taxed differently, meaning businesses with intangible assets may have more planning to do.

Getting more specific, will you need support from grants and investors? Most private equity investors want companies in their backyard. Silicon Valley types do not want to fund a Nevis company. That does not mean that those same guys do not use the Cayman Islands as a more advantageous place to raise capital, but they usually want to see it deployed at home. Mark Cuban, the renowned investor of "Shark Tank" fame, heartily implores investors to avoid companies doing anything to avoid tax, arguing that companies should pay their fair share. Meh.

If you want to raise cash for your new tech startup in California, you might be stuck with a California company. There are ways to structure US companies to pay very little tax, but that may not be suitable for investors. Just as I often advise people that I work with to give up on the idea of credit card miles in exchange for huge tax savings, you may have a harder time raising capital. However, the Nomad Capitalist lifestyle means freedom, and I would encourage you to re-examine your need for investors who will prove a serious curtailment to your ability to do as you please.

On a more positive note, it may be possible to set up shop somewhere that offers grant money or other incentives. The United Kingdom has a number of programs to incentivize new technology ventures with cash. One of my friends received a six-figure grant from the UK government, which made the prospect of setting up a UK tax-paying company more palatable.

Going where you're treated best is not code for 'screw the government at all costs.' Nomad Capitalists are not angry; they are pragmatic. If you can get more in business incentives than you will pay in taxes for a while, that may be the better deal for you. Many businesses do not qualify for those grants, but if you do, take advantage of them. You should not look a government gift horse in the mouth. If they are offering, you should consider taking.

Other countries have variations on the old-fashioned grant approach. Chile, for example, has made it easy for entrepreneurs to join its state-run incubator, Start-up Chile. Through this program, entrepreneurs can receive an equity-free grant in exchange for setting up a business in Chile, even if only temporarily. The prospect of a pile of cash with no strings attached has brought many primarily Spanish-speaking entrepreneurs to Chile.

The important thing to understand is that every country has its own rules and priorities and will offer incentives to match those needs. Hong Kong, which offers an interesting hybrid of both offshore and onshore benefits for certain active businesses, gets most of its tax revenue from real estate transactions. Sir Li Ka-shing, the richest man in Hong Kong, made a fortune in property on the island and helped build the economy for real estate and the taxes that those properties pay every time they are transferred.

Because Hong Kong makes a large part of its tax revenue from real estate dealings, almost every other form of tax is low. Corporate taxes are a low 8.25% for income up to HKD 2MM and

16.5% for everything above that – a relatively low rate considering how sophisticated Hong Kong is – but even that low rate can be reduced to 0% with proper planning. And payroll taxes are practically non-existent. Hong Kong does not need your tax dollars because guys like Ka-shing are footing the bill.

The same is true in places like Nevada where the government can apply extremely light taxation to businesses and completely cut out personal income tax thanks to the hundreds of casinos run in the state. Steve Wynn pays the bills so no-one else has to. Similarly, most Gulf states can get away with zero corporate and personal income taxes due to heavy taxation of oil revenues. People were shocked when Dubai went so far as to impose a VAT.

The point is that if you understand why a country offers the incentives (or disincentives) that it does, you will have a better idea of where your company can be treated best. Finding the right jurisdiction for your company is a matter of knowing your business needs and then identifying the country that has provided the matching solution as an incentive for you to bring your business to their shores and bolster their economy. When done right, offshore incorporation should be a win-win for both you and the jurisdiction. There is no right answer that covers every company and every issue, but for most small businesses, zero tax or close to it is possible with a proper offshore business structure.

The Tax-Friendly Quadrant

Up to this point, we have largely focused on the ins and outs of offshore companies – who can go offshore, what it means to go offshore, and how to find the right jurisdiction. Obviously, the biggest appeal of setting up an offshore company comes down to the tax treatment your company will receive balanced with the functionality of operating your business from that jurisdiction.

But saving on taxes involves more than just setting up an offshore company. Business taxes are only half of the tax reduction equation. If you want to save the maximum amount on your taxes, you also need to factor in your personal taxes. To simplify what can often feel like a complicated process, I created the tax-friendly quadrant to illustrate the different elements that must be addressed to ensure that you are legally lowering your taxes on all fronts.

When creating an international tax strategy, you need to consider where you are leaving both as an individual and business as well as where you are arriving, including where you will incorporate your business and where you will personally live and be taxed. As with any holistic strategy, each piece of the puzzle plays into the whole. You must have a strategy to address every part of the quadrant, or you will end up with complications that could lead to tax bills that you did not plan to pay.

The Tax-Friendly Quadrant		
	Personal Tax	**Business Tax**
Leavin	**Quadrant One** You personally need to leave a high-tax country to enjoy tax reduction benefits. Each country determines what counts as "leaving" differently.	**Quadrant Two** You may or may not need to restructure your business to move it offshore. It all depends on the business and its tax obligations.
Arrivin	**Quadrant Three** Tax reductions options include permanent travel, the Trifecta Strategy, foreigner exemptions, residency in a zero or low-tax country, and more.	**Quadrant Four** While countries with 0% corporate tax rates still exist, onshore jurisdictions with better reputations and low tax rates are the 21st-century havens.

Q1: Personally Leaving a High-Tax Jurisdiction

The first quadrant deals with your personal tax in the place you are leaving. If you are personally a tax resident in a high tax country, it does not matter where you incorporate your business, it will be taxed in your home country. All that an offshore company will give you is more paperwork. If you want the tax benefits of an offshore company, you personally need to go offshore as well. You do not need to live in the place where you have incorporated your business, but you cannot remain a tax resident in your high-tax home country.

As stated in the quadrant, each country determines what counts as leaving for someone to no longer be considered a tax resident there. And as we briefly discussed in the last chapter on offshore banking, citizens from most western countries with residence-based taxation cannot simply leave their country and expect to stop paying taxes. Folks from places like Australia, Canada, and much of Western Europe must establish a clear center of life in another country from which they derive their income. They must also dissolve all ties with their home country like bank accounts, income, cars, homes, mailing addresses, etc. Otherwise, they risk falling into the Nomad Tax Trap.

Let's assume that you are a Canadian citizen who wants to leave the Canadian tax system so that the income you take out of your offshore company is untaxed. Even as an employee of your foreign company, you will be subject to income tax in Canada until you check out of the system. That means cutting your ties with Canada. If you are married, it means your spouse should be on board as well; ditto in countries that recognize civil partnerships. You and your entire family, if applicable, need to be on the same page. You all need to leave.

Each country has its own protocol that must be met to officially bow out of their tax system. In most cases, getting an offshore bank account, securing a second residence, purchasing a foreign property, obtaining a second passport, or setting up an offshore company will go a long way to establish the case that you have, indeed, left your home country and established a life elsewhere. But you need to move. Obtaining a second residency is, for many people, the first step on the road to a second passport, but it is also a way of showing that you live in that place now and not Canada, Australia, New Zealand, or any other country that taxes you based on your residence there.

As governments in the West get more desperate for cash, it will be even more important to be able to say, "Here's where I live" rather than, "I'm not in my home country." Your home country wants to tax you unless you can give them a good reason not to. You need to craft a story for your life and select a base of operations where you spend some time, perhaps maintain an apartment, keep a little money in the bank, and call home.

That said, Canadians, Australians, and many Europeans can spend anywhere from 16 to 182 days in their home country, so long as they do so as a tourist. But no matter who you are, if you want to spend all your time in your home country, you will not qualify as a non-resident. You need to follow the protocol to officially leave. If you do, you can enjoy living outside of your country's tax system without giving up your citizenship.

As we saw in the chapter on US citizenship renunciation, US citizens do not have this advantage. The only way to fully exit the US tax system is to renounce US citizenship. However, US citizens can obtain some tax relief without having to adopt such extreme measures. Much of this relief comes in the form of the Foreign Earned Income Exclusion (or FEIE). While US citizens must file tax returns even after they leave the United States, the FEIE allows each US citizen to exclude roughly $110,000 of earned income (adjusted annually for inflation) from federal and, in most cases, state income tax if they spend all but about one month of the year in a foreign country or countries.

In other words, all you must do to "leave" the United States to get this specific form of tax relief is to leave. This means that US citizens have a unique advantage in that they can live as perpetual travelers or embrace any other global lifestyle so long as they are outside of the United States and inside any other country. That could be one country for the entire year, or a new country every day. It does not matter. They can even keep their home, car, bank accounts, etc. in the US if they want. They just need to physically leave the country.

If you qualify, you can simply check a box on your income tax return and you will not have to pay a cent on the excluded amount. Of course, anything earned above that amount is taxable at regular rates. And no passive income can be excluded, so there are limitations to the Foreign Earned Income Exclusion. For some, the FEIE will provide enough tax relief. For others, it will barely begin to protect them. If you are a sole proprietor, for instance, you will still have to pay Social Security and Medicare tax because you are not an employee of a foreign company. However, if you have an offshore company, you are treated as the employee of that foreign company.

And, since employees of non-US companies do not pay US payroll tax, you can avoid that tax, too.

If you want to spend more than one month each year back home in the US, you can still qualify for the FEIE, but the requirements will be harder to meet. As with citizens from countries with residence-based taxation, US citizens will need to set up a 'bona fide residence' overseas. If they do, they can spend approximately 90 days each year in the US and still exclude the $110,000 of earned income from taxation. But that is the extent of tax relief for US citizens. Beyond the FEIE and hiring yourself as an employee of a foreign company to avoid Social Security and Medicare taxes, renunciation is the only other option for gaining greater personal tax relief as a US citizen.

When it comes to taxation in your home country, there is little room for error. You need to work with people who know what they are talking about. When I lived in the United States, I used a well-respected tax firm for businesses, which successfully churned out an annual tax return the size of a small town phonebook. However, when I began traveling overseas long enough to qualify for a tax exemption, my otherwise savvy CPA had no clue that I even qualified for said exemption. No matter how good your home country accountant is, they likely do not know anything about taxes for expats.

My personal US tax attorney who specializes in expats says that he has heard of clients being dissuaded from even the most simple and straightforward offshore strategies because some bean counter did not think that it smelled right. If you plan to live an international life, you will need an international accountant as well as someone to quarterback that accountant with your other service providers. A Canadian CPA will not have any idea about tax laws in Hong Kong, nor will the guy in Hong Kong know about your residency status in Serbia. Make sure you are working with expat service providers who know how to help you leave your country and get the most tax benefit from doing so.

Q2: Moving Your Business from a High-Tax Jurisdiction

Moving on, the second quadrant addresses your business tax in the place you are leaving. We have already discussed how your ability to take your company offshore will rely on what your business does and how it operates. But what is required for your business to leave a high-tax country? As we saw in the first quadrant, much of that depends on whether you are personally a tax resident in the same jurisdiction as your company.

For example, if you are not a tax resident in the US and you have an LLC there, you can simply move it to a new jurisdiction and you will no longer have US tax obligations. But if you are a US tax resident, you will need to contribute your US LLC to a new jurisdiction. With the right professional assistance, if you are a consultant, coach, or run some sort of services business where you and any other employees make (or break) the business, then your transition into a new offshore company should be relatively painless. In many cases, the owner of a business that is just a one-man show could simply quit and then move assets to a foreign country.

However, if you own valuable intellectual property or passive income streams such as patents, royalties, domain names, or even websites, you will have some extra planning to do. If you own intellectual property, the best-case scenario would be to do a tax-free reorganization to a foreign country, but countries like Australia and Canada may force you to sell it and pay tax on the sale. After all, you would not give away that $10,000-a-month AdSense website, so why would your company in the United States simply gift it to your shiny new offshore company? You would not do that, and the tax man knows that.

In a similar vein, if you have an actual business with daily operations, you will need to work with a tax advisor to determine if you are liable to pay tax and how you can minimize the amount owed. In that situation, you may need to sell the business to yourself. And if you have hard assets that you could sell, you will need extra professional advice on how to handle your new company.

You will not always need to undo your entire business structure to move your company offshore, but that can be the case. If you are just getting started in business, it may be worth it to simply start offshore rather than build something in your home country and move it. But whatever you do, it is always better to consult a professional to ensure that you are making the right moves both for legal purposes and to ensure the greatest financial benefit for your company.

Q3: Choosing Your New Personal Tax Rate

There are a few ways you can select your new personal tax rate. The first is to obtain tax residency in a country with zero or low taxes. Like with corporate tax rates, you may sacrifice quality of life for that 0% rate. There are jurisdictions like the United Arab Emirates, the British Virgin Islands, Seychelles, and the Cayman Islands that offer a 0% tax rate, but if you do not want to live in one of these places, you can choose to pay a low rate somewhere else for a better quality of life.

Another option is to move to a territorial tax country where you are only taxed on money earned within the jurisdiction. The key with this option is to set up your offshore company in one country where you earn your money and then establish your personal tax residence in the territorial tax country. This way, you can ensure that you do not have any locally sourced income and you can then pay zero tax in your new residence. While the country may have low or even high tax rates, your tax obligation will be zero.

Territorial tax countries include places like Malaysia, Thailand, Georgia, Singapore, Hong Kong, Panama, Costa Rica, and others. Establishing tax residence in one of these countries will also enable you to demonstrate to the tax authorities back in your high-tax home country that you have a new home base and tax residence, thereby ensuring that no other jurisdiction will try to tax you as an individual.

A third option is to become a tax resident in a country with a lump-sum tax incentive. While the local tax rate in these countries is usually quite high as well, they offer a special flat tax to successful foreign entrepreneurs, investors, and high-net-worth individuals. If you qualify as a tax resident under one of these programs, you will only pay a single lump-sum tax each year with little to no other tax obligations once that payment is made.

The lump-sum amount ranges anywhere from 32,000 pounds per year in Gibraltar to over 400,000 Swiss francs in Switzerland. These programs become much more attractive the more you make. For example, if you are making $10 million USD per year, the $100,000 lump-sum tax in Italy works out to be a 1% tax rate. Greece, Jersey, and Anguilla also offer lump-sum tax programs. Overall, the countries offering this particular tax incentive provide a high quality of life, making the programs even more appealing.

For those who want to live abroad but do not plan to permanently settle down in one location, a fourth option would be to take advantage of certain tax exemptions offered in countries like Uruguay and Portugal. Both offer multi-year exemptions for certain types of income for new residents. I recently applied for Portugal's Golden Visa and look forward to adding this option to my list of possibilities for tax-free living in Europe. You will need to know your way around the tax code (or work with someone who does) to make this work, but you could essentially live in one of these countries completely tax-free during a set period and then move on once the tax exemption expires.

If you do not want to settle down at all, your other option is to live the life of a perpetual traveler, visiting multiple countries every year and never spending enough time in any one location to become a tax resident. If you are from a country with residence-based taxation, this may not work for you as easily due to the issues we have discussed, but there are ways to make it work.

In general, you can avoid triggering tax residency requirements by spending less than six months in any one location. Personally, I have come to prefer my Trifecta Method that we discussed in the chapter on the location independent lifestyle, splitting my time between three bases in Europe, Latin America, and Southeast Asia and occasionally making small trips from each one. But you can travel as much or as little as you want and live tax free, as long as you do not pass the threshold for tax residency in any one country.

That said, most folks will need to establish tax residence somewhere to appease the tax authorities back home. It is vital to understand that there is a difference between a second residence and your tax residence. You can be a resident of a country without having tax residence there. On the positive side, this means that you can obtain residence in a country without automatically shouldering new tax obligations. On the negative side, you will need to put in a little more work to earn your tax residence and prove to your high-tax country that you really do have a new tax home.

Ideally, you want to obtain tax residency in a country that does not tax you if you live there part-time, like the countries that we have just discussed. Once you have found a country that is a good fit for you, the next step is to acquire residence there. If you are already a Nomad and have not established a second residency, I would strongly suggest you do so as soon as possible. With your residence permit in hand, you can then work on fulfilling the requirements for tax residency.

The rules vary by country, but generally, you will want to spend at least 90 days there, rent or purchase a place, get a driver's license, and establish other connections within the country to solidify your tax residence case. You will not need to live there full-time, but you should plan on spending more time there than you do in your high-tax home country. If you spend four months in Australia and two weeks in 16 other countries per year, there is no reason for the ATO to believe that country five out of those 16 is your new tax home.

Q4: Choosing Your Corporate Tax Rate

The final quadrant focuses on much of what we discussed at the beginning of this chapter: where to incorporate your offshore company. We have already spoken about the benefits of an onshore jurisdiction versus a traditional offshore tax haven; we have also covered some of the main questions you should be asking about your business to find the right jurisdiction for your specific needs. But now that we know how an offshore company works together with all the other pieces of an international tax strategy, I want to get even more specific about how to choose your corporate tax rate.

With every choice you make about your tax strategy, the concept of strategically planting flags comes into play. There is a reason every cruise ship you have ever sailed on is registered in a place like Liberia or Panama. In the same way that the yacht owners in Monaco chose where to register their vessel, you can choose where your company is domiciled. You do not need to pay taxes in a country that does not provide the benefits that you or your company need. You have the freedom to choose where you want to base your company and what tax rate you pay. You can literally choose your tax rate.

Where to base your company is the $64,000 question. It can save you tens if not hundreds of thousands of dollars a year or more. But we have already seen that choosing an offshore jurisdiction for your company is not just a numbers game. Given the challenges of traditional offshore jurisdictions and the wide variety of offerings from governments around the world, planting your business flag also comes down to questions of efficiency, perception, functionality, banking, residence, citizenship, and the motives of the countries involved.

Your best option may not be a 0% tax rate. Let me bring this concept a little closer to home: if you are a consultant living in California, you will pay federal and state income taxes. In California, high earners are subjected to the highest state income tax in the United States at just over 12%. Meanwhile, nearby Nevada has no state tax on personal income at all. You could move your home base from Los Angeles to Las Vegas and eliminate that 12% tax, immediately saving those thousands upon thousands of dollars a year at the state (and, in some cases, local) level.

However, if you are recovering from a wild gambling addiction, moving to Las Vegas may not be a good idea for you. Instead, you may choose to move to Arizona, which has substantially lower taxes than California and top tax rates of about 5% accompanied by a more business-friendly attitude. Of course, 5% is not zero. You will still pay some state tax (on top of the federal tax that you cannot control within the US), but there are likely other factors that go into your decision. Perhaps Arizona has better schools than Las Vegas, a lower cost of living, better weather, or other amenities that make it worth paying that 5%. Sure, you would love to pay 0%, but for lifestyle reasons, cutting your state tax bill from 13% to 5% is good enough.

Establishing your company offshore is not so different from this scenario of moving your company to a different state. And if you are willing to move from California to Arizona to save on tax, why stop there? Why not get rid of federal taxes as well? Why not go to the places where countries have rolled out the red carpet to those willing to incorporate their business in their jurisdiction? Zero taxes, low taxes, better services, better business banking, tax treaties... they are yours for the taking. All you have to do is show up.

In general, there are four different corporate tax systems offered around the world that should be of interest to Nomad Capitalists. They are not necessarily the same as the income tax systems we discussed in the last quadrant, but there is some crossover. Each system offers different levels of corporate tax savings as well as other benefits and requirements to qualify. Let me walk you through each one so you can understand how they each work and could potentially benefit your business. This knowledge will give you a better idea of how to choose your tax rate as part of a holistic offshore tax strategy.

The first system is the traditional offshore jurisdiction that we have already discussed that offers zero corporate taxes. If you incorporate in one of these jurisdictions, they will not tax your company. We have already named places like Belize, the British Virgin Islands, Seychelles, the UAE, and others. We have also analyzed the many drawbacks of these traditional offshore locales. Countries like the United Arab Emirates that have some weight in the world and something to offer beyond the 0% tax rate are the only jurisdictions of this type that I would give any serious consideration.

The other three tax systems are all part of the onshore world; most of these governments carry similar or greater weight and offer comparable benefits to a jurisdiction like the UAE. The list of low tax systems, for example, includes countries like Ireland, Bulgaria, Cyprus, and Montenegro in Europe, as well as more tropical locations such as Labuan (Malaysia) and Mauritius. These countries offer low tax rates that range from mere pennies in Mauritius to 12.5% in Ireland. They also offer a number of benefits such as incorporating in certain markets or qualifying for a tax treaty, among others. These countries are the equivalent of moving from California to Arizona. You will significantly lower your tax burden even if you do not eliminate it, plus you get some extra benefits for your company.

The third option is to incorporate in a jurisdiction with a deferred tax system. Deferred tax countries may have low corporate tax rates to begin with – like the 10% rate in Macedonia – but most are in the range of 15-20%, so they are usually only worth your consideration if you can capitalize on the benefits of tax deferral itself. Estonia was the first country to introduce the deferred tax system and it has worked so well for them that both Georgia and Macedonia have adopted similar incentives.

But what is deferred tax? In a nutshell, the government will let your company pay zero tax on all earnings until you take the money out of your company. As long as you keep the money in your business by reinvesting instead of redistributing to shareholders or other companies, you can defer taxes indefinitely. As soon as you distribute the money, though, it is taxable at the regular corporate tax rate.

But who will benefit the most from this particular setup? Let me illustrate the answer by retelling the classic 'penny a day' story that many of us learned in elementary school. The story goes that a penny doubled every day for one month might not seem like much, but it will turn into a large fortune at the end. By merely doubling the previous day's balance, your penny will balloon to $5,368,709 at the end of the month. The power of compounding returns is indeed impressive.

What they do not teach you in elementary school is that high taxes will knock those returns to the ground like having a cat for a Jenga opponent. If you factor in a 30% tax rate on each day's gains – be it short-term capital gains in this case, or a profits tax in a more realistic example – your return changes substantially. Instead of that $0.01 turning into north of $5 million, it turns into... a measly $48,197. The difference between earning the equivalent of an average salary and an average lottery win is simply taxes.

If your company reinvests profits to grow, you can see the difference between reinvesting tax-deferred money compared to post-tax money. That is why growth companies in places like the United States are such great success stories. Imagine what companies working on only a fraction of their capacity could do if they had more fuel in the tank. Anyone running a business – such as an e-commerce business where investing in more SKUs and new launches is the growth model – should consider forming a foreign company to run their business.

If you have a quickly growing business that needs to operate in the EU and you are turning capital quickly, Estonia's tax deferral system may be exactly what you need. While the 20% tax rate will mean that you may pay $1 million in taxes on $5 million in earnings when you do distribute profits, you will still be left with $4 million instead of $48,197. And in the meantime, you will be able to use all that extra time and money to continue growing your business.

But if you are running a cash flow business and want to distribute money from your company on a regular basis, tax deferral systems are not going to make much sense. You will, essentially, be subjecting your business to the Jenga-playing cat every single time you distribute your money, completely eliminating the benefit of a tax deferral system in the first place. The better option is to simply pay a lower tax rate elsewhere.

The final of the four corporate tax systems is found in the countries that offer tax exemptions for qualifying companies. In these jurisdictions, governments basically create a different tax system for companies that operate outside of the country. If you incorporate and operate a business on the ground, you will face regular tax rates. But if all you do is incorporate in the jurisdiction and then carry out all business operations outside of the country – removing direct competition with local companies – you can enjoy rates as low as 0%.

Hong Kong is the perfect example of this system. Corporate tax rates there range from 8.25% to 16.5%, but through the Offshore Profits Exemption Claim system you can potentially pay as little as zero in taxes. Malta offers a similar program, but instead of a 0% rate, if you do not reside in the country, you can reduce Malta's corporate tax rate from 35% to 5% or lower. In both cases, you are not running an international business company (IBC), you are running a legitimate onshore corporation that simply gets extra benefits for not doing business on the ground.

Putting All the Pieces Together

Now that we have examined all the different components of creating a holistic tax strategy, we can put them together. Let's imagine you have done everything needed to move your business out of your high-tax jurisdiction and have set up a company in Hong Kong. Because you have set it up properly as a company doing business outside of Hong Kong, your corporate tax rate will be 0%. You can now check off Quadrants Two and Four – where your business is leaving and arriving – from your tax-friendly quadrant.

With your offshore company incorporated, the next step is to understand the role that you play in your business. For most entrepreneurs, that role is one of an employee. I know, I know; we entrepreneurs hate to be titled as an employee, but from a government perspective, that is what we are. When you establish a Hong Kong company and move your business assets there, you can become an employee of that company. And if properly structured, the employee of a Hong Kong company based outside of Hong Kong should not be subject to Hong Kong salary tax, but rather salary tax in the place they live.

With this strategy, we have only begun to work on Quadrants One and Three. If you are a US citizen, there is an objective way to handle where you live and how much you pay yourself. While you will not be able to leave the US tax net, you can take a salary from your company to the tune of roughly $110,000 and exclude all of it from tax through the Foreign Earned Income Exclusion, reducing your personal income taxes to zero. And as an employee of a foreign company, you can also avoid Social Security and Medicare taxes.

If you take a distribution from your company or pay yourself over the FEIE income threshold, you will be subject to US tax rates on the rest of your income, but besides renouncing, you have done everything you can to reduce your tax burden as a US citizen. Just make sure you are meeting the requirements to qualify for the FEIE and you will have satisfied both Quadrants One and Three.

If you are a citizen of a country with residence-based taxation, your strategy will look a little different. We will assume that you are from the UK and that you have already closed all your bank accounts, sold your home, and cut all other ties with Britain, largely satisfying the requirements for Quadrant One. All that is left is to work on Quadrant Three and choose your new personal tax rate (and tax home).

Wanting to stay close to Europe but also wanting to appease the tax authorities back home, you have obtained a second residence in Portugal and qualified for the non-habitual tax resident regime which simultaneously makes you a tax resident in Portugal and exempts you from Portuguese tax on all non-Portuguese source income. Because your income is derived from a Hong Kong corporation, you will not be taxed in Portugal. And because you do not live in Hong Kong, you will not be taxed there either.

By addressing all four quadrants, you can now enjoy zero corporate taxes for your business and zero personal income tax for you. Simple enough? Perhaps too simple to take this as a personalized tax plan. I have skipped over many of the details to provide a basic example. I am not an accountant or lawyer, and you should not take any of this as personal tax or legal advice. Before you implement any of these strategies, you need to consult with a professional expat accountant and lawyer. But can you begin to see the bigger picture?

By now, you have hopefully started to get the idea that having a location independent business is no longer just about ziplining through jungles and taking selfies with cheetahs. It is about saving a fortune and, with that fortune, both elevating your lifestyle and saving and investing for the future.

Even if you do not need to invest back into your business, you can invest for future passive income. Imagine saving $50,000 a year on taxes and investing that into real estate. In Tbilisi, Georgia, you can get a renovated one-bedroom flat in the tourist center of the city for that amount, and potentially $5,000 a year in rent. After ten years, you will own $500,000 in real estate (plus any appreciation in value during that time) and have annual cash flow of $50,000 — the same amount you were previously paying in taxes.

Or if you prefer, you can up your game from the Ibis to the Ritz-Carlton every day of the year. Or stockpile rare comic books. Or whatever else tickles your fancy. I have increased my charitable giving to causes ranging from the environment to aspiring entrepreneurs in Africa now that I am less subject to forced giving in the form of taxes. There is plenty you can do to multiply the good in your life and the lives of others with more resources at your disposal.

It is a simple matter of choosing to work smarter, not harder. People talk about working smarter all the time, but they say it in reference to increasing conversions on a landing page by 4% by changing the button color from red to green. Why not eliminate 50% of the expenses you have to pay at the end of the day instead? That sounds like working smarter to me. You can double your income by eliminating taxation simply by moving your business to a country that will treat it with respect. That, in a nutshell, is what it means to have an 'offshore company.'

Your How-To Action Plan

Immediate Action Steps: Start working to answer the many questions discussed in this chapter. Can your business benefit from going offshore? Where is the work being done in your business? Can that be moved offshore? Do you already have staff overseas? Clearly establish your company's goals and needs. Identify countries that match those needs with tax and other legislative incentives. Then, review the tax-friendly quadrant and address each of the quadrants.

Travel Action Steps: As you travel, find the places where you personally want to move. If you are from a country with residence-based taxation, start working as soon as possible to establish your center of life in another country and obtain tax residency there.

Holistic Planning: Perhaps more than any other topic we have discussed so far, tax planning requires a thoroughly holistic approach. If you do not address every part of the tax-friendly quadrant, you risk nullifying every other part of your tax reduction plan.

Chapter Ten: Foreign Asset Storage

Super-Spy Vaults or Tinfoil Chapeaus?

Dateline: Singapore

You could have heard a pin drop. Here, where the wealthiest people on earth keep their amassed fortunes, the halls were silent.

They did not exactly make it easy to get in. Just getting through the first gate required an appointment that I spent a full week arranging with my host who now guided me through the cool, steely corridors beneath the balmy pavement of a city that was nothing but swampland a mere 50 years ago.

Looking up, I noticed a zig-zag effect on the housing of the rather dim lights, as if inspired by some caper movie with rotating laser sensors that had to be stepped over in a carefully choreographed pattern. Of course, anyone who could pass by a steel gate, a blast-proof entry door, a metal detector, a backscatter machine, and a series of guards – seen and unseen – would probably deserve to walk off with everything behind the doors along this corridor, no lasers required.

I stood inside the Singapore Freeport. All around me were the trappings of wealth in their ultimate form, hard assets from rare art to classic cars to the hardest asset of them all: gold.

My tour guide was Joshua, an Israeli guy who had quickly worked his way up the corporate ladder at a huge logistics firm to be put in charge of his company's operations here, and he certainly looked the part. I had just started Nomad Capitalist at the time and was introduced to Joshua through a friend of a friend who suggested

I call him and arrange a meeting to discuss Ron Paul, or Venezuelan hyperinflation, or whatever it is that gold bugs discuss.

Ever so kindly, Joshua agreed not only to meet but to show me around the vaults. I was about five minutes late in arriving, having found the only taxi driver on the island who barely spoke English. Joshua politely awaited my arrival before shepherding me through the so-called naked body scanner machine.

I was now deep in the belly of the beast.

"That guy isn't too happy today," I said as I pointed to a crate of five hundred 100-ounce silver bars. The spot prices of precious metals were in free fall that week, and silver was no exception, plunging by some 15% in a matter of days and 25% year-to-date. However, the guy probably did not even notice; those who likely did were the people who stored gold and silver in the private vaults there.

The Freeport – since renamed Le Freeport to amp up the air of sophistication even further – is among the world's most secure private vaults, where the world's wealthy store the stuff that they do not need quick access to. Singapore's push to be a world wealth haven means that almost anyone can store their own stuff here.

When the Swiss government capitulated to the world's high-tax countries and gave up on the idea of banking secrecy, Singapore stepped in with the promise of a discreet place to park cash and assets. With dozens of private banks already established in the city-state, the next reasonable step was a place to park physical assets.

Alain Vandenborre, the man who founded the Freeport, explained, "When you go to a bank and rent a safe, nobody knows what goes in. It's the same thing here." Private vaults like Le Freeport are not only better protected than your average bank safe deposit box but they do not have to disclose who owns what is stored there.

Physical precious metals is one of only two assets that US citizens can own overseas without having to report them to the IRS. If you have ever thought about going offshore as a way to gain privacy, gold is perhaps the best way to go about it without breaking any laws. While you are required to report your bank accounts and balances to the taxman, you are not required to list privately vaulted precious metals. Some guy who worked at the IRS when they wrote the law must have owned a ton of gold bars somewhere in Switzerland. The point is, if you want to store wealth privately, the Freeport and other private vaults like it are the place to do it.

Singapore made it easy for investors to move tangible assets like gold bars into their country by introducing limited customs controls on bullion and ending taxes on its purchase. That means that anyone can ship gold or silver that they already own to Singapore without having to declare anything other than 'gold', and with no one's name in particular on the shipment.

The best part is that average entrepreneurs and small-time investors can take advantage of this vestige of wealth by storing their own gold there. Le Freeport, at its core, is merely another commercial building available for lease. It just so happens that it is among the world's most secure commercial buildings with tenants like Christie's storing what will no doubt be Steve Wynn's thirteenth Renoir and Jay Leno's 117th classic car. However, it also has lesser-known tenants that rent their own private vault within the facility and allow clients to store gold there.

In fact, it is possible to store as little as one silver coin worth about $20 in Le Freeport. It is also possible to start with $20 and gradually build up each month. In the same way that services like RealtyShares have democratized and amortized the costs of investing in real estate with as little as a few grand, services in Singapore – including one or two in the Freeport – allow anyone to store a few bucks' worth of gold behind those steel bars.

But what does gold have to do with living the Nomad Capitalist lifestyle?

A Nomad's Gold Strategy

Admittedly, having anything stored in a super-spy vault like the ones at Le Freeport is pretty cool. You should do it just to tell someone at a cocktail party that you have hard assets stored in such a private vault. More significantly, gold is another asset class that you or your business can hold to diversify your risk, protect your downside, and potentially increase your upside. Just as you should not hold all your assets in one currency, you should avoid holding all of your assets in currency alone.

For many offshore companies, owning gold is just another investment. In a few countries, it can even be a tax deduction, although those are typically the countries that do not tax you to begin with. (No tax means no deductions.) For some entrepreneurs, this can be an excellent way to diversify.

Take the story of Chance, a young Australian entrepreneur I worked with recently. Chance downright hated the idea of having to do any accounting, which effectively ruled out any of the more trustworthy places to set up his company. While Hong Kong is willing to exempt certain businesses from paying taxes there, they are not willing to exempt them from filing audited statements every year.

Chance was petrified of the idea of being responsible for such accounting, saying his anxiety would cause him to freak out any time a form came requesting information or he had to work with an accountant. I helped Chance form a company in the Caribbean where no books or records would be audited. However, that limited his potential to open good bank accounts, as most of Europe, Hong Kong, and other high-profile banking centers are now all but done with zero-tax countries in the Caribbean.

After advising Chance of two of the only banks that would accept his company structure, I suggested that he diversify into gold as a way to protect his cash. Since Chance ran a high-margin business, he frequently had a lot of cash just parked in the bank, with no need to use it. Rather than rely on the emerging world banks that I recommended to hold every penny of his business cash, I suggested he siphon money off into a private precious metals account each month.

Sure, gold prices could drop (although they could also rise), but over time his money would be relatively safe. Additionally, it was one less bank account for his anxiety to have to deal with. While I do not expect his banks to have any problems, knowing that every bank on earth could go under and his gold will still be sitting there, ready to be converted back into cash, is a good feeling for him.

I like to approach business with a German sense of calculation to determine what the downsides are, rather than a traditional American sense of optimistic exuberance. That philosophy applies to my banking, as well. No matter what currency you and your business deal in – and especially if you deal in shaky markets like South Africa where currencies rise and fall – owning a little gold and silver is a good insurance policy to make sure you are always treated best. It is also a great way to plant another flag outside of where you bank so that your funds are distributed across more countries in case anything ever happens.

Nomad Capitalists are all about protecting their wealth. Sadly, the term 'asset protection' conjures up images of some septuagenarian wearing a smoking jacket and puffing away at a cigar while the sugar baby de l'année drapes her svelte arms over his bald dome. The industry does little to combat that notion.

Protecting both your personal and business assets – be it cash, shares in your company, property, or whatever else – is extremely important, but the concept has become so convoluted to the point that everyone thinks 'asset protection' means setting up a $50,000 Cook Islands trust when that is not necessary for most entrepreneurs. Gold, on the other hand, is an easy, cheap, and low-barrier-to-entry way to protect a part of your money.

If you think gold is a little bit of a kooky investment for an entrepreneur, allow me to suggest otherwise. Your offshore company can easily invest in precious metals titled in the company's name. If you run a cash cow business that leaves money sitting in bank accounts, consider moving part of that money into precious metals that are not correlated to the same risk factors as currency. While gold is not as liquid for making payroll or investing in inventory as cash in the bank, it can be liquidated quickly and comes with the added benefit of diversification.

As a cautionary tale, about a year ago, I got a call from a frantic father-son business team. Their company was based in Hong Kong and HSBC was shutting down their business account. They had amassed nearly $3 million in an HSBC current account but were about to have nowhere to put that money because HSBC Hong Kong no longer wanted US citizens to hold accounts there.

Opening an offshore bank account is just the beginning of the diversification process. It is one step, and certainly not the be all and end all. In fact, this family's story is why I recommend that your company have at least two foreign bank accounts, not just one. And, eventually, you need to diversify out of just bank accounts.

Having $3,000 in one bank account is forgivable because, if your account gets closed, you figure it out and move on. Having $3,000,000 in a one bank account, on the other hand, is irresponsible and reckless. You should not rely on only one place to handle all your money. You should never, ever trust everything you have to any one entity.

So, while you may never have considered owning gold, or have been turned off it because its most vocal promoters wear tinfoil chapeaus, realize that it can be an excellent alternative asset to hold in your business – if not personally, as well. If you have spent a lifetime paying a good chunk of your profits away in taxes, you might not realize how quickly a tax-free or lightly taxed income can add up and, before you know it, you will need more buckets to hold your wealth.

While offshore companies can often own assets such as real estate or shares in other people's companies, such assets may not be as useful if your business decides to expand. With privately vaulted gold or silver, you simply sell the asset, wire the cash back to your bank account, and you are liquid again. For that reason, the best precious metals to buy are those with a low spread, or a low ratio between the buy and sell prices.

Gold and silver are the most widely traded and, as such, usually come with the lowest spread if purchased correctly. This makes them better than metals like platinum and palladium if your goal is preserving liquid wealth that you can use if need be. While Le Freeport might not get you the lowest spread, others in Singapore can. As for what to buy, I recommend buying gold bars that are small enough that you can sell only part of your lot if you need to. Hundred-gram bars are good because their current sales price of around $4,000 each allows you to own a number of them.

If you need even more portability and you plan to physically withdraw your gold or silver to carry in your backpack, then one ounce gold coins issued by major mints may also be advisable, but you will pay an extra percentage point or so for the convenience. Coins issued by mints like the US Mint, Royal Canadian Mint, Austrian Mint, or Perth Mint are easy to sell, not only because the people you bought them from will take them back but also because they are widely recognized by everyone else.

There are any number of places to buy and store gold, from services with an e-commerce interface to large vault operators themselves to Hang Seng Bank's central branch in Hong Kong. At the latter, you can pay cash in Hong Kong dollars to buy up to about ten one-ounce gold coins per day and walk around town like a Dark Ages monarch who kept coins to toss at peasants.

There are also services that will offer you the chance to buy just a piece of a huge gold bar, or a fractional interest in what is in their vault. While this might be better than a stock because it is backed by actual gold and silver, these services are not the same as actually owning a coin or bar of gold in your own name. Your goal is to obtain segregated, allocated storage of the metals you own, not just a piece of someone else's pie. Likewise, avoid bank safe deposit boxes, as these require form filling by the taxman and have little protection if your bank has a problem.

Golden Insurance

Even if you do not have a bucket of extra cash, moving a small part of your wealth into gold and silver as you accumulate cash is an excellent way to be prepared, even if gold is not perfect and subject to its own market fluctuations. Unlike paper currency, gold has held its value for thousands of years. Name one paper currency that can do that, or that will do that long after we are all dead. Gold and silver offer protection against the political and geopolitical events that affect paper currencies, all while remaining liquid, divisible, and universally recognizable.

The United States is no place for a young entrepreneur to learn about currency collapse because no one has ever seen one. Indeed, for most of our lives, the US dollar has been relatively strong, propped up by the fact that the rest of the world does not trust their own currencies, even when perhaps they should.

As a student of the world wanting to better understand the impact of currency collapse, I decided to go to a place where people had more recent experience with a tanked economy: the Balkans. While the Balkans now include some of the most business-friendly countries on earth, things were a lot different not so long ago. I knew a trip to present-day Serbia could give me some insights into the region's past currency crisis.

After spending my first week in Belgrade, I had an idea of how the place worked, but I still lacked a clear understanding of the country's history. I was not leaving until I found out. One June night (long before I met Mrs. H.), a girl in a white button-down shirt tucked into trendy but sensible jeans caught my eye as I walked back to my hotel from dinner. Her refined demeanor made her stand out on a street full of Serbians and expats just out looking for a good time. I approached with whatever seemingly high-brow conversation starter I could muster.

"It's refreshing to see someone that seems so sophisticated," I bumbled.

The woman laughed in the pleasant way a nice girl from a wealthy family would acknowledge such an attempt and extended her hand, "I'm Jovana," she said, shaking my hand.

After introductions were made, she agreed to join me on my walk home seeing as she was going in the same direction. As we strolled down the streets of Belgrade, I learned that she was indeed from a wealthy and somewhat prominent family. She had become a successful dentist in town and busted on me for occasionally covering my mouth. "Are you ashamed of your teeth?" Jovana teased. "You shouldn't be hiding them!" She had mastered the art of charming European banter, the kind that leaves you feeling like a million bucks.

Pulling my hand away from my teeth, I flashed her a hesitant smile before summoning my courage, "I have to admit why I decided to approach you," I began. "I came to Serbia not just to learn about how the country works and the investment opportunities here but also to understand the country's past. When I saw you, I had a feeling you were the kind of person who could give me some insights on the topic."

"It's your lucky day," Jovana said. "My family learned some important lessons from the war. Lessons I'm sure would give you the perspective you are looking for."

"I knew my instincts were right!" I said. We had arrived at my hotel, but before we parted ways, I suggested we talk over dinner upon my return from neighboring Macedonia.

"It's a date," Jovana beamed.

Over our dinner the next week, Jovana told me about her family's personal experience and how they had failed to diversify. Despite being a successful family, their political influence meant that they kept a lot of their money in what was then Yugoslavia.

When war broke out, the national currency – the dinar – became a mess. Her family lost practically everything they held in local currency. Their cash became worthless, and their real estate got whacked. However, her family had two things that saved them from total ruin: a stack of US dollars and, as she recalls, about fifty gold coins. Unlike the dinar, gold was something the government could not print more of, and it was not subjected to the shocks of what happened in one place on the map.

Yugoslavia may have been in the middle of a conflict, but gold was global. It could resist the fluctuations of a crumbling economy in the far reaches of Eastern Europe. Because of that, Jovana's family was able to maintain their financial stability and eventually recover from the war's devastation.

My assistant from Montenegro, shared a similar experience when, at an early age, her father would come home from work with a bag full of paper money, greeted with cries of "Daddy, you're rich!" Then her father would just toss the money at her and her brother and encourage them to play with his now worthless hours-old paycheck.

I prefer to be optimistic and hope that none of us will have to deal with the vulnerabilities of fiat currency like hyperinflation, but that does not keep me from insuring myself against such a possibility. Just as you would insure your home against disasters that you hope will never hit, your wealth needs insurance from financial disasters that could wipe out what you have worked so hard to build up. Gold is that insurance.

Storing Gold

Once you have begun to accumulate gold, finding the proper place to store it is your next layer of insurance. The best place to store gold is in an offshore private vault. The reason is simple: like anything else, the country you live in is probably not the best place to store gold. Nor is the country you want to spend time in; while Thailand might be a fun place to live, the periodic bombings and coups do not make it an inspiring choice to store lots of shiny metals.

Seeing that gold and silver are as good as where you store them, the saner solution is to store them in a safe place far away. That could mean buying gold directly from the vault you want to use, or shipping gold you already own to a vault of your choice. The key is that your assets are stored in a place where the people in power there are different than the those in power where you bank or run your business.

There are even services now in Singapore that will allow you to borrow against your stored bullion. That means that you can buy gold or silver, put it in a non-reportable private vault account, and then borrow back a good chunk of the value either for personal investments or business expenses, depending on who owns the gold.

In the recent past, if you wanted to diversify out of paper currency by buying hard assets like gold and real estate, you would have to do each separately. For example, $100,000 in gold and $100,000 in real estate would require $200,000 in capital. However, thanks to innovation in Singapore's gold vault market, you can now purchase as little as $125,000 in gold, store it in a private vault knowing your exposure to paper currency is reduced, and then borrow the $100,000 you need for property at an extremely low interest rate.

It also just so happens that Singapore is among the best places to store gold. There is almost zero crime, so the idea of anyone breaking into a super secure facility is rather remote. While you cannot drink water on the subway without being fined, people do carry cash and flash expensive electronics around all the time without issue. Singapore also has just about zero corruption.

Part of what makes Asia a great place to store assets is that they are making a big push to do so. Where a pro-business culture and desire to serve comes first, the Asians are well positioned thanks to their eagerness to dominate this market. The fact that Hong Kong has literally no restrictions on bringing in or taking out cash helps, too.

Storing Gold in the Old World

Singapore is not perfect, though, and it is not for everyone. There are other countries in Europe that will be equally happy to store your gold under similar terms. And while Singapore's role as a new country means that facilities like Le Freeport are newer and have more robust security, Europe has been successfully storing gold for centuries.

While you might imagine that Switzerland's heritage as a wealth haven makes it the best choice in Europe, you would be mistaken. In fact, just like Swiss banks, some Swiss vaults also refuse to deal directly with US citizens. That is why perhaps the best place to store gold in Europe is Austria, where a few private vaults take privacy to a whole new level by allowing you to store precious metals anonymously.

After my visit to Le Freeport, arriving at Auerspergstraße 1 in Vienna's Museum Quarter was a bit anticlimactic. The building was surprisingly hard to find using Google Maps, and I was not about to start asking the few random passersby, "Excuse me, do you know where the secret gold vault is?"

My arrival at Das Safe was greeted by an exterior of dull brick walls, a far cry from the Bourne-esque exterior of Le Freeport. I walked inside the building where I was greeted by slightly fraying red carpet and a man sitting at a nondescript desk across a large room, much like I imagine Bond must have felt when walking in on Karl Stromberg eating dinner.

"Hallo," the older man greeted me from across the room as I came nearer.

"I'm here to inquire about storing some gold in your vault."

"Of course," the man replied, hobbling up from behind the desk. He had a slight paunch under his dark pinstriped suit vest, just how I would imagine the overseer of a cryptic European vault to look. "I'd offer you a business card, but we don't have them," he advised, excusing himself per Austrian social protocol. "Our business card isn't the kind of thing most people want their dry cleaner to find left in a jacket pocket."

The man began to show me the facility and, without going into excruciating detail, explained that Das Safe was a privately owned facility that used to be part of a bank. As such, the building was well secured, despite its gloomy exterior. "The police would be here in sixty seconds in the event of any trouble," he insisted.

He showed me how to enter a PIN to gain entrance to the facility, promising that I, too, would be able to choose my own combination of numbers. Upon being granted access behind two sets of reinforced glass doors, we walked down a ramp into the vault area.

My first impression was that the bland eggshell-colored boxes appeared like the kind of place where a German trucking company would store logistics records. Inside box #7241 could be Kiefer Müller's route maps of the Frankfurt to Warsaw route from 1999 to 2003. However, it was far more likely that the facility housed any number of precious metals, as well as business and personal documents. Nevertheless, without much to see or any silver in a cage to point at, I summoned my tour guide to return me to the lobby.

There, he shared the details of the real reason people come to Das Safe: anonymity. For an extra annual fee, you can rent a box at Das Safe with complete privacy. You are not required to provide your name or any identification, something the Austrian government is apparently totally cool with as one of the last bastions of privacy in the European Union. While I suppose some use this as a way to protect themselves from drop-ins by the tax authorities, there are a number of other legitimate reasons to want to be left alone.

My host explained that the smallest boxes at Das Safe had long been sold out, meaning the only boxes available for rent were the large ones that looked like they housed old shipping manifests.

Of course, anonymity and well-secured space in central Vienna do not come cheap, which means that Das Safe is an option for someone with quite a lot of metal or other stuff to store.

At a cost of about $600 to start and upwards of $1,000 per year, there are probably better options for someone getting started with gold. It is also not much of a solution for businesses because someone has to go down to the vault, carry the loot out in a bag, and sell it to a dealer on likely worse terms than in a managed vault.

The amazing part is that, while $1,200 or so sounds a bit steep to those storing minimal amounts of gold (a reasonable storage rate for gold is under 1% annually), it is insanely inexpensive when you consider that private vault storage is actually available to the masses. It is yet another democratized service formerly available only to the rich, but now available to those of us in the know. If you do not believe me, tell a girl on your first date that you have locked away a box of gold coins in an anonymous Austrian vault. She might think you are boring for telling her, but she will no doubt leave thinking that you are also very rich.

Whether you choose to stack gold and silver coins in a secret vault that you wear a trench coat to visit, or you choose to establish a more straightforward private vault account at one of the growing number of facilities operating online, owning at least some precious metals is an important part of living the Nomad Capitalist lifestyle. In fact, it is ownership of assets like gold that differentiate Nomad Capitalists from the more garden-variety digital nomads who are only focused on lifestyle and not on securing and growing their money as well.

Your How-To Action Plan

Immediate Action Steps: Your gold should be stored outside of your home country. If you cannot leave home yet, you can buy gold online and have it stored in vaults in places like Singapore.

Travel Action Steps: Taking your gold offshore with you can pose some challenges. Be aware of the rules and attitudes towards gold in the countries you are flying through. Some will treat gold as a cash equivalent. If you are carrying gold valued over a country's declarable amount, you will face a lot of questions, at the very least. In some cases, it may be easier to liquidate your gold holdings in your home country and then repurchase gold overseas. If you have over $100,000 in gold that you want to move overseas, you may be able to tap into higher-level solutions.

Holistic Planning: I highly recommend incorporating precious metals like gold into your international asset allocation strategy. If you have not invested in physical gold yet, consider adding it to your investment portfolio.

G

GROW YOUR MONEY

Chapter Eleven: Investing Overseas

A Home on Every Continent... and a Cattle Ranch Too

Dateline: Phoenix, Arizona

A number of years ago, before I totally detached from the United States, I was traveling almost as vigorously as I do now. While I did not call any one place 'home,' I did rent a formal condo in the US that I would come and go from when needed.

Despite my many travels, I had not found the desire to establish a base in any foreign locale quite yet. Besides, the real estate market in the United States (and particularly in Arizona where I lived) had taken such a beating that there came a time when prices were so ridiculous that it seemed silly for me to keep renting a condo for 'flexibility.' So, with prices in the gutter, I went house shopping.

I called a real estate agent named William, verified that he had the credentials I wanted, and hired him on the spot. We discussed two properties that seemed great on paper: newly renovated four-bedroom homes that were boring enough for me to decorate to my liking but would still be easy to sell when I wanted to. William and I promptly set a time to see both properties.

The first property was ideal. It had plenty of room, nice finishes, a livable floor plan for a single guy, but still marketable to families. The second place was a total dump.

"Well, I think this is a good start," William said while standing inside his open car door. "I'll pull some more properties like the first one and call you to set an appointment."

"No need," I told him. "Let's make an offer on the first one. We'll need to be aggressive." William was stunned. As I have since learned, apparently many people in the western world feel a compulsive need to peruse dozens of properties before finally deciding. I, however, have come to appreciate being able to take prudent action quickly.

In this case, I figured that not only did the first property meet my needs well enough to preclude further shopping, but even if I changed my mind in a few years, I could always sell and buy something else. Surely, getting things done quickly now would be a bigger boon to my business than spending my days in search of some magically better option.

I went on to buy that house for $170,000, barely half its peak value a year or two earlier. (If you are not from the United States, you may be surprised to hear that four-bedroom houses with pools near civilization can sell for that price.) A little more than two years later, I sold the property for $262,000, a 54% profit and about 19% annualized. Not bad for a snap decision.

In reality, my purchase of the home was not a snap decision. I had done enough research on each of my desired areas before even looking at homes. My mindset was that research was just that, research — not merely dreaming and blowing off steam as it can quickly become. Then, I created a game plan for the type of property I wanted and executed the plan.

The same principles can be applied to foreign real estate investments. The only difference is that travel is the tool that helps you determine your ideal area.

Today, I utilize a similar approach when making most decisions: know what I want, research and find it, and then attempt to make a decision the same day. For example, I once bought an apartment near Georgia's free trade zone for all of $5,200. We needed an apartment for several clients to use and the price could not get much lower. The decision to buy was simple, so I went for it.

It was that deal that gave birth to a philosophy that I now live by: know why you are buying. The reason this philosophy is so vital is that not all investments are made equal. Consequently, the decision-making process behind each type of investment will change according to the purpose of your purchase.

For instance, I often look at investment decisions in the context of what else I can buy for that money. The idea that you could buy a home – ratty as it may be – in Georgia or Serbia or any number of other places for the same amount some folks blow in one weekend in Las Vegas is astonishing. Heck, you could buy land and build a small home outside of the big city for that price. Being able to buy a home for $5,000 in any number of cities reveals the potential of investing overseas. It also demonstrates the benefits of globalization and how the world is now an investing playground for all of us.

If buying a home in a small village is not your speed, there have been any number of turnkey investments with minimums of $5,000 or less. The United States and Europe lead the race with crowd equity and crowd debt sites like RealtyShares, Peerstreet, and France's Wiseed that allow anyone to invest in a share of everything from residential rentals and fix-and-flips to sprawling commercial properties, and all with as little as $1,000.

No longer do investors have to rely on real estate investment trusts ("REITs") to invest in high-yielding property. Now, you can invest in a far more intimate way where you actually see where and to whom your money is going.

With such low barriers to entry, investing overseas could become your form of recreational gambling. The benefit that foreign real estate investments have over actual gambling, however, is that you have a much better chance of making your money back. In fact, while you can easily adopt a solely recreational approach to foreign investment, there are numerous benefits to investing overseas as a serious investor.

Indeed, you may find it surprising that there is an entire chapter on foreign investments in a book largely for entrepreneurs. However, investing is an excellent way for entrepreneurs to diversify, create long-term wealth, and achieve their desired lifestyle. Let's look at each advantage.

The Advantage of Diversification

Foreign investments are an ideal method entrepreneurs can use to spread the risks involved with running one principal business. Even as many entrepreneurs extol the virtues of letting go of "solopreneurship" and working on your business rather than in it, entrepreneurship still comes with certain risks.

For example, I have worked with a lot of Amazon FBA sellers – guys who source products from China, send them to

Amazon's warehouses, then let Amazon do the selling – and many of them are confident that it will not be a lifelong business. As investor Robert Herjavec says, there is nothing wrong with entering a business to make a 'whack of cash' and getting out when the market changes. However, it is important to have some idea whether yours is a short-term 'whack-of-cash' business, or something you want to keep for the long-haul.

In the case of Amazon FBA, sellers are at the mercy of Amazon, which can change the rules or even shutter their business at any time. Investing offers a way to offset this risk by creating passive cash flow to fund your Nomad Capitalist lifestyle above and beyond what you earn from your business.

For instance, comedian Jay Leno hosted The Tonight Show for more than twenty years, yet famously claimed that he never touched the money he earned from the gig. Instead, he chose to bank all of it while living off money he earned as a stand-up comedian. In the same way, I like to use investments to support my current lifestyle, while leaving my business profits in the company.

This is a particularly profitable strategy for folks doing business offshore. If you are a US citizen and your business is pulling down millions, you cannot take that money out of your offshore company without paying a lot of tax… but you can reinvest it. The idea of sucking every penny out of your company is not always the best idea anyway, even if you do not have to pay tax. To that end, finding the right investments is a critical step to funding your day-to-day life.

Personally, I prefer to let my main business be a 'cash cow' that generates money for other investments that then produce the passive income that I can live off once I begin reinvesting my business profits. Not every business has to reinvest its profits, though. While the e-commerce guys I have helped are constantly plowing every dime back into new products and expansion, plenty of consulting, coaching, and other 'expert businesses' bleed cash with few expenses.

I will never forget the day when my CFO told me that Nomad Capitalist had just had its best month ever, spurred by marketing spending of $337. We basically did – and still do – zero advertising, relying on word of mouth and content marketing to bring customers. The kind of client I seek makes online advertising of limited interest because my business grows when I share more of my life, not by barking at people more.

Just because my company is a 'cash cow' does not mean that your company must be one in order to invest and diversify. Whatever type of business you run, the point is to diversify. Personally, I never understood the idea of the perennial start-up machine where an entrepreneur puts all his eggs in one basket, betting the farm that his or her latest venture will work out. Do not get me wrong, the courage is admirable, but the risk is high.

A while back, I read an interview with Elon Musk in which he said that he reinvested his PayPal fortunes into Tesla and Solar City so promptly that he had to borrow money for rent. While perhaps a bit hyperbolic, Musk is definitely a guy who goes all in with his business ventures; heck, he basically resuscitated the idea of a conglomerate in an era when even General Electric had sold off a lot of non-core businesses.

However, from my perch overlooking the fjords in Montenegro, I ask myself if businesses that employ Musk's strategy are constantly in 'chasing' mode, going after the next big thing but never really getting there. No doubt Musk has become incredibly successful. However, not only is there one Elon Musk for every 1,000 who fail but even the successes of Elon Musk have been called into question by some investors who consider him more of a social entrepreneur than one actually achieving the profits he appears to be chasing.

Ask yourself: do you want the appearance of success, or its results?

If living the Nomad Capitalist lifestyle is your goal, you do not have to push as hard as Elon Musk. When I see investors that are no doubt better at reading technical charts than I am tossing $50 billion at Uber, I have to ask, "What happens if it all fails?" Are they pursuing the life that they want or are they just investing in the latest trends to look like they have got it all together? Rather than chasing after big investments, why not let the life you want come to you? Why go all-in at dramatically higher risk when you can enjoy the same lifestyle benefits without the Silicon Valley mindset?

In that way, the Nomad Capitalist lifestyle is the anti-Silicon Valley. I take minimal risks yet enjoy many of the perks. I hire affordable, yet highly skilled and teachable employees at a tiny fraction of the price of Bay Area help. I pay almost zero tax without hiring an army of accountants. And I am free to deploy the profits from my business either back into the business or into the vast number of investments we will talk about in this chapter.

As Tim Ferriss explained in *The Four-Hour Workweek*, many of the trappings of wealth that we expect to enjoy once we reach our own version of Elon Musk's success are available now, without waiting or killing yourself to get there. Imagine any perk that the average successful start-up has, and chances are that you can enjoy it now, or realize that you do not really need it.

For example, even though I enjoyed driving a Mercedes in the United States, I much prefer not having the hassles of a car now. However, if you want to drive an amazing car, you can lease the most exotic cars on earth for a few thousand dollars a month. You are likely paying that in taxes already, and one simple business tweak could essentially make your dream car free.

You want multiple homes? You can have them, as I will explain in this chapter. While my beach house is not in the Hamptons, traveling around the world has made me loathe that 'scene.' Nevertheless, you can easily rent a halfway decent place in the Hamptons for a month for $50,000 or find a better version of it overseas in Ibiza, Monaco, Rio, or Dusa Nua.

But how do you get to that point? How can you diversify correctly so that you do not have to worry about your one business going under and leaving you to beg your friends for rent money?

Creating a Perpetual Runway

This is where your perpetual runway comes into play. A 'runway' is the amount of cash an entrepreneur has available to burn before their next business needs to take off. You might think that an entrepreneur who already had a successful business would not need a runway, but the fact that Elon Musk claimed to be one step from homelessness shows that everyone's resources are limited.

However, rather than worrying that your runway is running out, focus on creating what I call a 'perpetual runway.' This is done by focusing on the process I described in the section above: reinvest business profits into 'cash cow' investments that generate monthly income that you can live on and use to enjoy a dream lifestyle, all while focusing on growing your current business or businesses.

But how do you begin this process? Start small and work your way up. Look at your first project in any area as a test, whether it is a business running niche websites or real estate in a new country. While the goal is to have a profitable exit, the real benefit comes from what you learn in the process.

For example, the first property I bought in Tbilisi, Georgia cost $49,000 to buy and another $12,000 to fix up. While I eventually decided to make the property my home in order to scout out more investments, I was able to receive an offer for $70,000 before I took it off the market. While a $9,000 profit would not have been amazing, the benefit of getting paid while you learn is powerful.

Along the path to that small profit, I got to see my chosen contractor in action, learn about the city's building rules, figure out where to buy furniture, and generally have an inside look at the process. As I like to say, the best way to learn how to do something is to do it. Once you figure out where and in what to invest, it is best to dive in and learn along the way. In real estate and any other investment, you make money when you buy, so figure out how to buy and you will learn while making a profit.

For cash flow, I prefer to purchase a lot of apartments, commercial real estate, and other cash-flowing assets. I focus less on properties with potential appreciation and more on those that I am happy to have be linear (that is, assets that do not go up in value in a big way in the long term) but that throw off lots of cash.

As long as the market outlook is generally positive and the government is friendly to investors, I worry less about capital appreciation, so long as the cash flow is good. In some cases, I am getting a 10%, 11%, or even 22% cash yield. By following this system, I can double or even triple my percentage return on subsequent deals.

Most people go a different direction and swing for the fences on their first deal. Sometimes it works and sometimes it does not. I have seen people get out of markets with a lot of potential because they got burned on one bad deal by going too big. On the other hand, going small on the first deal and focusing on minimum viable success will help you learn more lessons and scale.

I know of a British couple that bought one of the beautiful old stone houses along Kotor Bay, Montenegro after vacationing there for years. They invested almost their entire life savings to pay €240,000 for the place and another €80,000 repairing it to its former glory. Last I heard, they had finished the renovation and had it listed for €500,000, which I am told is a fair price. They will make a great profit.

However, imagine what would happen if something bad were to transpire. Their entire life savings would be locked up in a stone house they never intended to live in. Even if the investment itself was not bad, they might have needed that liquidity due to a job loss or a drop in business at home. Not smart.

As Nomad Capitalists, we invest not to hit that home run but to generate sustainable income flows from passive sources like rental income or side businesses with scalable processes. Most investors fixing and flipping real estate, for example, do not create procedures on how to handle what they do. They have to reinvent the wheel every time they take on a new project, rather than automating the process and the income it generates.

The first step, then, is to assess how you can automate the processes involved in whatever investments you are making and then carry out the automation. If you cannot find a plausible form of automation, the next step is to determine whether that particular investment serves a different purpose beyond diversification. Take, for example, land…

Foreign Land Investments

Unlike investing in rental properties or automated systems for fixing and flipping, investing in land will not help you build your perpetual runway. "But wait a second, Andrew. Doesn't real estate go up in value?" Sure. It also goes down in value. There are, no doubt, places in the world where real estate has defied the odds and gone up year after year. There are parts of Istanbul that have not seen a downturn in twenty-five years. And, up until recently, there have been fundamentals to explain why – namely, investment from rich Arabs buying an escape hatch from the Gulf.

However, you cannot live off appreciation and keep the investment. The Nomad Capitalist lifestyle is fueled by cash flows from investments that work now, rather than ones that you might be able to sell for such-and-such a price later. However, foreign land investments do serve other goals of the Nomad Capitalist lifestyle.

For instance, owning raw land is another way to diversify your wealth as it accumulates. While land is not exactly liquid (buy the wrong land and it could take years to sell), it can be an excellent alternative to keeping money in the bank. It is more like buying gold or silver bullion – it is a hard asset, but it generates no cash until it is sold.

If you are a US citizen, foreign real estate is the second of the only two types of non-reportable assets available to you. That means that you can legally choose to not disclose to the IRS your ownership of property in another country, adding an element of privacy to your finances that no bank account can offer. In addition to privacy, owning land can either serve as the beginning of your next great business opportunity – such as my hotel friend's interest in building an $8 million hotel that could net $3 million a year – or as a long-term hold to increase your wealth over time.

In that regard, agricultural land is one of my favorite raw land investments for long-term growth. There are several reasons to consider including agricultural land in your foreign investment portfolio. One of my favorite reasons is that you can often get crazy deals on this particular type of land since there are times when people really need quick cash in exchange for their land.

This means that you can pay less than its current worth because what it is worth now is usually a less-than-tangible number. Unlike on a residential property (the price of which can more accurately be pinpointed), the price of agricultural land is more of a range rather than a specific value. The only judge of the worth of agricultural land is what someone is willing to pay for it.

You can get some very attractive entry points on agricultural land. Compare that to similar long-term assets like gold and silver, which have highly defined entry points. Everyone knows exactly what the price is, and you know what an ounce of gold is worth to the penny. Because of that, no one is going to sell you gold for $200 under spot just because they need quick cash. They do not have to. Precious metals are a well-defined liquid market.

Agricultural land is not like that; you can get some very attractive entry points on foreclosed land or quick sales. You can also get very cheap land in emerging markets by buying in bulk and cutting it up and reselling it in the future. Agricultural land also has some solid long-term fundamentals behind it. As the world population rises and economies develop, emerging countries will demand more high-quality proteins. If this plays out, the value of agricultural land will surely increase.

Because of that, whether it is agricultural land or some other piece of raw land, these type of real estate investments are a great way to build up your long-term wealth over time. You may make more money starting a business, but you should not want all your money in businesses. Nomad Capitalists want diversification and not just total return.

Land allows you to put some of your money into assets that cannot be taken from you and in locations that subject your money to a different set of rules. Depending on where you go, foreign real estate could be adding currency diversification to your portfolio too. If you accrue key land investments along the way, you can diversify to serve your long-term goals. In fact, I recommend investing overseas over traditional retirement planning.

Investing for Long-Term Wealth

For years, I have been telling people to avoid putting money into retirement accounts such as IRAs, RESPs, and other plans in their home countries, even if they are tax-deferred. For one, no matter where you live, your retirement account is always at risk of the government helping themselves to it. Bankrupt countries from Ireland to Hungary to Argentina, among others, have a history of taking their citizens' private wealth by dipping into retirement funds when they need to plug a gap somewhere else.

Politicians prefer to merely kick whatever fiscal problems exist down the road. Then, one day, when the problem explodes, they will reach in and take what they can. It is hard to ignore the over-$20 trillion in debt the United States has racked up over the years and the high debt-to-GDP ratio other western countries have managed to produce. With over $25 trillion in retirement accounts in the US alone, it is not that far-fetched to assume that your broke government will succumb to the temptation to dip into those retirement funds. Eleven countries and counting have already done so in the not-so-distant past, so it is not without precedent.

In the United States, even Republicans who have long argued against means-tested Social Security have begun to argue that the government needs to cut benefits. I could easily see these same politicians argue that while you have $200,000 in your government IRA, since you have $2 million in another account, they are just going to borrow some of your money – as already happened in Poland in 2014.

As a Nomad Capitalist, I am not ready to hand over the control of my retirement funds to a government that can change the rules at any moment and make it legal to 'borrow' my money. And even if they do not change the rules, I still want the flexibility of doing with my money what I want. I cannot get that with an IRA that tells me where I can and cannot invest, and when I can and cannot touch my money.

While tax-deferred retirement accounts may make sense for someone planning to sit at a desk for forty years and retire with a gold watch, they make far less sense for entrepreneurs and investors. And they make absolutely no sense for entrepreneurs and investors living the Nomad Capitalist lifestyle.

For example, politicians have discussed forcing private retirement accounts into buying government bonds or treasuries. Those things throw off pretty paltry returns, potentially preventing any funds in your retirement account from keeping pace with inflation. This is confiscation by stealth.

Entrepreneurs should not be squirrelling their money away for low-single-digit returns when they could easily take that money and turn it into a profitable business. If you are smart, you can double, triple, or even 10x your money. If you can do that, why would you tie that money up in an IRA just to get a tax deduction?

To the average citizen, the idea of a 'guaranteed return' on their retirement account sounds halfway decent. For entrepreneurs, the idea of locking money up in an account that they cannot touch for decades should come as an absurd idea, especially when all you get in exchange is a piddly tax reduction. You get a tax deduction on the money you put into certain retirement accounts the same way Wile E. Coyote lays down birdseed for the Road Runner on the exact spot where the boulder is supposed to drop. It is just a distraction to keep you from realizing the true cost of remaining in the system.

For example, when Roger came to me wanting to save on taxes but reluctant to leave the US for the full tax benefits, I asked him how much he had paid in taxes the previous year and what he would have done with that same amount of money if he had gotten it all back. He answered that he had paid $200,000 to the taxman and indicated that he would have invested that same amount of money in property.

"Alright," I persisted. "And what would that property make you in a year?"

"It could have easily earned 10% a year," came the reply. "So, $20,000."

"Okay, so not only are you missing out on the $200,000, but you're also missing out on the $20,000 that you could have earned by investing it?"

"Yes," Roger admitted.

I continued, "And if you put the $200,000 into a property today and you made $20,000 in the next year, you wouldn't just stop making money, right?"

"No."

"In fact, unless the property burns to the ground, it will make $20,000 every year, correct?"

"Yes."

"Okay," I said. "So, if you buy a house for $200,000 – free and clear, no mortgage – and you can net 10% every year for a $20,000 annual return, after ten years you'll have made $200,000 back. Could you get that kind of return by putting your money in a retirement account in exchange for a small tax deduction?"

"Not a chance," Roger conceded.

"Unfortunately, Roger," I told him, "That's the real cost of paying taxes. That's the cost of living in the United States." And that is the cost to you as well, whichever tax-happy western country you currently reside in.

One of the most powerful ways to build long term wealth is to be in control of your own money. Do not put it in low-yield retirement accounts that subject you to a list of dos and don'ts when you can put it into businesses and investments that you control and that will give you a much higher return. And do not count on tax reductions when you could just take measures to exit the system and completely eliminate your tax burden.

If you already have an IRA in the United States, it may be possible to roll it into an offshore company that can make a far wider range of investments on your behalf. However, this is often counterproductive for younger people, since I advise having at least $75,000 in an IRA to offset the expenses involved. If you are young and just getting started, the best approach is to get out of the system now.

You do not want to end up like Mark, who had both US and Canadian citizenship and wanted to renounce his US citizenship to reduce his taxes. However, because he had more than $2 million in assets, he would have to pay the exit tax to renounce. Despite his high asset value, Mark was in the tricky situation of having very little cash on hand. His assets included a house and a bunch of pensions in Canada. He had bought his home for next to nothing but, like everything in Toronto and Vancouver with all the Chinese coming in, the home's value had shot through the roof in recent years. So, between his house and his pensions, he had more than $2 million in assets.

Consequently, after applying the exit tax, the cost to renounce his citizenship was roughly $300,000. And, because his money was tied up in his home and his pensions, he could not afford to renounce his citizenship. He either had to sell his home or take out a loan.

The moral of the story? First, there is a benefit to having cash on hand, not just to renounce your citizenship but to pursue all the other opportunities that are available to sharp businesspeople and investors. Investing in retirement accounts and pensions is counterproductive to this goal. You want 'cash cow' investments that give your assets flexibility. Second, get out before you are too big. The 'safety nets' many western governments have put in place for retirement are not tailored to someone like you. You will fare much better on your own.

Making Lifestyle Investments

We have already seen how pursuing opportunities overseas can help you find better investments in order to diversify business risk and create long-term wealth, but what about the kinds of investments that allow you to build your desired lifestyle? As I mentioned earlier, many of us erroneously imagine that our desired lifestyle is unattainable in the here and now. On the contrary, achieving the life you want is usually a matter of making a few tweaks and doing the right investment deals.

The first step is to determine what kind of lifestyle you actually want. While you can probably list off several lifelong dreams right off the bat, it could take you some time to figure out your exact dream lifestyle. As we discussed earlier, there are many ways to live abroad, from the perpetual traveler who never stays in one place too long to the expat who picks a spot and settles down. The kind of lifestyle investments that each individual will make will vary depending on those preferences.

For example, I once worked with someone who wanted to own a condo on every continent, both to live in and to invest. This is an incredible example of how you can live a dream lifestyle by detaching from your current reality. I am working on a somewhat whimsical list of dream residences of my own, as well. Instead of a home on every continent, however, I prefer a home for every kind of mood or activity: the ski chalet in the Alps, the beach home in Montenegro, the cattle ranch where I can build my 'Summer Palace' and get away from civilization, the list goes on. Owning land gives you the flexibility to customize each location to your liking.

As a profit-minded investment strategy, the idea of managing a single piece of real estate in Mexico City, Medellin, Amsterdam, Sydney, Bangkok, and Dakar is daunting. (And this coming from a guy who has about 23 plates spinning at any given time.) As a lifestyle investment, on the other hand, it may make perfect sense. While I love staying at five-star hotels on a regular basis, it is nice to have a place to call home. If you choose to make a similar investment, just recognize that it is a lifestyle investment, which is very different from the other investments mentioned in this chapter.

The most basic rule when it comes to lifestyle investments is to avoid making stupid ones. For me, the best way to prevent stupid investments offshore is to evaluate opportunity cost. When I first set up a base in Kuala Lumpur, I evaluated apartments in my desired area near the Petronas Towers. Why live in a city of skyscrapers without a view of one of the most iconic skyscrapers on earth?

I quickly found that while the apartments themselves seemed overpriced, considering the never-ending building boom going on in town, rental prices were quite cheap – no doubt a result of that same overbuilding. Back then, the Malaysian ringgit was stronger and a nice two-bedroom with a view was running $650,000. However, one of those same apartments was available for rent for a mere $1,700 a month.

Faced with buying a property that earns a tiny 3% gross yield – what I would expect in Switzerland or some other boring, super-secure country – or being the guy to run the property into the ground while someone else assumed the currency risk and the low yield, I chose the latter. Fortunately for me, the ringgit ended up falling apart during my tenure there and my rent dipped as low as $1,200 a month for a brand new, gorgeous penthouse in the hottest part of town.

The lesson I relearned from this experience is that home ownership is dramatically overrated. In the West, real estate agents tell you that, "Your home is your best investment." Nonsense. If you averaged out the people like me who make large profits selling property in the US with everyone who has broken even or taken a beating, the results would not be pretty. When I rented my home in Malaysia, I not only avoided a terrible investment property but I got to keep $644,900 in my pocket because I was renting and not buying.

The reason to buy your own home is so you can control what you do there. It is not an investment, it is emotion. Emotion is worth something because being happy and comfortable in your home has value. In fact, I rarely stay in Airbnbs or other vacation rentals because most people are not as OCD about home organization and that makes me less productive than in a sparkling clean hotel room or my own home. Productivity from comfort equals money, but labeling an emotional real estate purchase as a pure 'investment' is not accurate. You are investing for a certain lifestyle, not necessarily for profit. That is fine, so long as you know what you are doing. Problems emerge when you are consuming when you think you are investing.

If you are pursuing the full Nomad Capitalist lifestyle and intend to plant flags wherever you go, lifestyle investments can also include those made to obtain a second residency or passport. I am currently working on a residency in Eastern Europe for which I am required to purchase a home in the country. Fortunately, there is no price threshold; you can buy any house for any price. And the cost of land in this particular country is dirt cheap. While I found one 600 square meter home for €4,300, I plan to purchase a 2,000 square meter parcel of land for €6,000 that will allow me to build a second structure, or whatever else suits my fancy.

In this case, with one minimal real estate investment, I will be able to qualify for a second residency, purchase a home, and have extra land available that grants me the flexibility to do whatever I want with it. For me, I could not ask for a better situation. It may not be a profit play, but the purchase fits perfectly into my lifestyle.

How to Invest Overseas

Once you know why you want to invest overseas, the next step is to determine exactly how to do it. The first issue you must address is how much money you have available to invest. After factoring in monthly expenses, I prefer to save a set percentage of my earnings as part of an emergency fund for the cost of living overseas. You want this to be a one-to-two-year emergency cash reserve that is easily accessible, regardless of what the situation may be or where you are located.

After that, I calculate the amount of money I want or need to reinvest in my business in the next six months. From there, I consider all remaining money part of my immediately investable assets, which I then divide between cash-flow properties, long-term land investments, gold, businesses, and other overseas investments.

I recommend putting 10-15% of your investable portfolio in something like agricultural commodities that have a long-term upside. Personally, I choose to invest roughly the same percentage in long-term agricultural investments as I do in precious metals. If you were to allocate around a third or a quarter of your investable portfolio in tangible, long-term assets – part in precious metals, part in land – you could then have somewhere between 10-25% in cash, while the rest you would invest in income-generating assets that are much more liquid.

In my case, I want a much greater percentage of my portfolio in real estate that I can sell relatively quickly at a comparatively reasonable price. For instance, residential property that I know people are buying and for which there is an active market. I want a lot more of my money in those kinds of properties that bring in income and that I know are relatively liquid compared to other lands. But I still want that smaller, yet significant part of my portfolio in land investments that I can sell in the long-term.

Having addressed your asset allocation strategy, the next issue to resolve is how you will find the properties you want to purchase. There are several ways to find land for sale overseas. However, none are immediately obvious if you do not have any knowledge of the country in which you are looking to invest.

One option is to use a broker. This may work for apartments and commercial properties, but most real estate brokers do not deal in land. In fact, many brokers do not see the long-term value of owning a non-reportable hard asset with improvement potential, meaning you will be hard-pressed to find someone able to help you with such long-term land investments. Another option is to search for foreclosed real estate. I have purchased bank-owned lands before, but most banks only have a limited selection of development land. Micro-finance institutions sometimes have parcels of land as well.

The best strategy is to conduct personal on-the-ground research in your chosen location. I have been able to apply basic investing and negotiation principles in each market and have never overpaid for my first property in any country, but you will not get the truly great deals on your first go. And you most certainly will not get them if you are not willing to put in a little time where you are looking to buy.

I like to search out real estate deals in every country I visit. In some cases, I choose to visit a country precisely because I want to research their real estate market. In general, all the advice that you will receive from folks about this market or that country has some kind of bias. That is why nothing beats going to a place yourself and checking out the deals in person.

For that reason, after many years of hearing conflicting opinions about the real estate options in Albania, I decided I needed to go there myself...

"Mr. Henderson, as a valued Starwood guest, we've upgraded you to our best suite," Natasha, the front desk girl at the Sheraton in Albania's capital of Tirana announced as I sat slumped in a chair in front of her.

I cannot say that I was surprised. Tourism to Albania is not exactly big business, and especially not in December. Natasha – whose above average height, blonde hair, and soft features made her seem a rarity in the Southern Balkans – handed me my room key and advised me to enjoy my stay.

Upon arriving in my room, I realized exactly why I was there. While the Sheraton's staff was quite generous, the hotel itself – even the proclaimed best suites – were in need of an upgrade. Well-maintained but dated furniture reminded me of days spent in my father's Cleveland, Ohio office in 1997.

I had just arrived in Tirana from my summer home in Kotor Bay, Montenegro. The four-hour drive along winding coastal roads was aided by the Mercedes my assistant sent to chauffeur me along my southward path. Truth is, had I wanted luxury, I could have just stayed put. Instead, I was in search the of the next great European beach city; a yet-to-be-known hamlet with potential, but few investors.

In that regard, the Egyptian-style table lamps that adorned my suite were just perfect. As opposed to Montenegro (which at least had the Hotel Splendid that was featured in Casino Royale and the overly ballyhooed Regent Porto Montenegro), Albania had no real trophy hotels that would attract a high caliber tourist.

While Albania was the first of the non-European Union Balkan states to defect from the former Yugoslavia, it has found itself far behind the likes of Serbia and Montenegro in terms of development. In my world, that spells potential opportunity. Earlier in the year, I had befriended the executive vice-president of a mid-size hotel chain based in Greece. He had helped the company grow from a couple of hotels in Greece to two dozen around Southeastern Europe, and now he was looking for new places to expand. Over dinner in Bulgaria several months earlier, he suggested that Albania was the last slice of undeveloped coast in all of Europe.

He was right. Western Europe has long been well-developed, Greece is Greece, and the former Yugoslav states of Croatia and Montenegro are already a growing playground for affluent beachgoers. Albania is the odd man out. It is funny how the idea of lines on a map dictates which beaches we go to and which ones we do not.

As an example, Sarande, Albania is basically just across the border from Corfu, Greece. Corfu is so well-known in some circles that no one actually calls it 'Corfu, Greece,' it is just 'Corfu' – like Cancun. Meanwhile, Sarande has a smattering of low-priced waterfront condos, but no huge draw. As an investor, I would far rather invest in Albania with its flat 15% tax rate and openness to investors than Greece, which hiked property taxes by some 700% a few years ago. There is much more potential in Albania.

Similarly, on my frequent drives from Phoenix to Los Angeles in the mid-2000s, I always wondered who would live in Blythe, California when Quartzsite, Arizona was just a few miles away. On one side of the invisible stripe in the sand, residents paid high California taxes and dealt with crazy California regulations. Just down the road, residents paid moderate Arizona taxes and were left well enough alone. Same ugly desert, much different costs of doing business. It was not as if Blythians were lapping in the fake boobs and air-conditioned parking lot lifestyle of Orange County, so why would they want to bear the brunt of California's anti-business policies? Why stay on the wrong side of the imaginary line?

In the same way, there is not much differentiating the beaches in Corfu to the beaches of Sarande. I believe that countries like Albania will eventually develop as more and more tourists are born each day. Not only do many middle-income countries like Malaysia and Serbia want affordable places where they can travel, but an entire swath of wealthy travelers is growing up in places like China and the Gulf. That means we will need, among other things, more beach resorts. And better ones.

My hotel friend had told me that oceanfront land in parts of Albania started at prices as low as €25 per meter, or about 150 times less expensive than prime land in Beverly Hills. I remembered a friend of mine who had spent much of the early 2000s buying up oceanfront land outside of San Juan del Sur, Nicaragua, which – in terms of my Arizona-California example – is about as close to the far more developed Costa Rica as you can get in Nicaragua. Within a decade, his land was worth ten times that, and now probably even more. The takeaway? If you find the next big place, you can make a fortune.

Hence, my trip to Albania. The morning after checking into the Sheraton, I woke up early to the Egyptian-style lamps and a wake-up call on an old-school hotel phone. I quickly went down to the lobby where Natasha was sitting, acting as if she was waiting only for me. I explained that I wanted to visit several beach towns with potential. On the list were Durres a mere thirty minutes away, Vlore two hours away, and Sarande five hours away. As one of my mentors often says, "Go as far as you can see, then see further," so I figured I would start with the closest one and go from there. Why overexert myself?

"I'd like to go to Durres," I told Natasha.

"Shall I call you a Mercedes?" she replied, alluding to my comfortable journey into town the day before.

"No," I told her. "I'd like to take the bus." I realized that if I wanted to see how everything in Albania worked, I should forego the Mercedes.

Natasha, in typical Balkan fashion, was unfazed. She explained that Tirana did not have a formal bus station, but rather an ad hoc departure point for buses heading all over the country.

Upon my arrival at the bus station, I was met with the typical chaos you would associate with a bus terminal in an emerging country; guys selling bootlegged cigarettes and any number of buses itching to run you over if you linger in one spot for too long. I spotted a bus headed to Durres and, as it appeared to be taking off at that very moment, ran to the door.

There, the employee on the bus welcomed me in and shepherded me to what seemed to be the last seat at the back of the bus. Of course, a welcoming bus attendant in a country like Albania can be a double-edged sword, and just as we hit the street, he welcomed a rather rotund lady to fill in the half-seat next to mine. Then, the kid sitting next to me started making the kind of noises you would expect from a horny lion. I suppose you cannot expect much for $1.

Other than my portly seatmate digging her elbow into me from time to time, the ride was quite pleasant. At one point, I even thought, Why don't I slum it on the bus more often? Then, just as the amalgamated body odors of the bus passengers began to cut through the uncirculated air like a knife, we arrived in Durres.

There I was, a mere forty-minute drive from the capital city at some of the last remaining undeveloped coast in Europe. As I walked from the grim bus terminal into the city center, I stopped at a mini market to buy a Coca-Cola where the owner determined I was American and proceeded to point at me and shout 'American' to other customers and passersby. It was as clear an indication as any that the hordes had not yet found this place. Imagine if every American in Barcelona received such a reception.

Shortly after arriving, I received a phone call from a guy selling an apartment near the beach in Durres. My assistant had contacted a lot of potential sellers, but few had the investments I was looking for. While I was in Albania specifically to investigate cheap oceanfront land, I decided to see what the apartment market looked like as well. My assistant informed me that few people respond to emails in the Balkans; you have to email them, then call them to tell them that you emailed them.

I managed to visit a 1,000 square foot apartment two blocks away from the sea. While the price was good on a global scale – about $600 per meter – there was nothing about this place that screamed 'beach holiday. Plus, the elevator in the lobby was plastered with random advertisements and did not seem to be in good working order.

Upon climbing the four flights of stairs, I discovered that the apartment was in poor working order, too. There was no way to fix it up and remain within any confines of reality, especially considering my goal here was to find the 'next great beach city,' not to buy a dump that might rent out in ten years.

The problem with beach apartments in many cities is that you can build so many of them. In cities like Budva, Durres, Hua Hin, Antalya, and countless others, anyone can simply buy land and build another building. There is no scarcity. That is exactly what seemed to be the case in Durres. If anyone can just build another apartment building next door, your beach condo is a dime a dozen.

I called my assistant and told her to pass on the apartment. Having a clear vision of what you are after is important, and I had allowed myself to get distracted. Fortunately, my assistant informed me that she found a seller with something much closer to my goal: five acres of land in the untouched Cape of Rodon, not far from Durres. I quickly hailed a taxi to leave Durres, realizing it was not for me.

In the end, I did not purchase any land in Albania. As much as I wanted to find the perfect deal, for the time being, Albania did not make the cut. I never would have been able to make a proper judgment, though, if I had not taken the trip. That, in itself, is valuable information, as it meant I could confidently strike it off the list for the time being and move on to the next place.

Buying land can be a pain no matter where you go. It is doable, but difficult. For some, the difficulty of finding the real deals either keeps them from entering the foreign real estate market or leads them to seek easy options that never lead to the best deal. If you look online, you will find properties that are not real, were sold several years ago, have the wrong number listed, or are reported in hectares when they should be in acres or vice versa. It is not as sophisticated or as organized as in the United States and other more developed markets. But that is precisely why the opportunity is so golden for those willing to put their boots on the ground and seek out the great deals.

The foreign real estate market also works quite differently when it comes to purchasing. You may be used to the idea of getting a mortgage when you buy a home, but not only do the 3% down mortgages often seen in the West not exist in most countries, but most foreigners will have difficulty getting a mortgage when buying property overseas.

Bankers are boring and not particularly progressive. They do not want you to live the Nomad Capitalist lifestyle, which is precisely why finding the best offshore banks is important. If bankers were interested in working remotely and traveling the world, they would not be stodgy bankers. As a result, their perfect candidate to loan money to is someone like them: an employee who clocks in at 9:00 am, drives the same car to work every day, and plans to live in their home for the next thirty years as they pay back their home loan with automatic withdrawals from their interest-free checking account. You do not want to be that person.

You will not have much luck convincing a Spanish bank to loan you money for an investment property in Barcelona. You do not have a Spanish credit record, nor does the bank have any recourse against you other than taking the property. Still, I never quite understood why a bank would not be willing to put up half of the money, figuring that rarely does property drop 50% in value. After all, they are in the business of lending money, right? Alas, it does not work that way.

In your home country, if you default on a loan, the bank knows where to find both you and the property. That is not true overseas. One of a few exceptions to this policy is the United States, where both US citizens living abroad and foreigners can theoretically borrow money. However, as difficult as it was for me to borrow money as a self-employed business owner when I lived in the United States, you can imagine how hard it can be if you live overseas. Even US citizens who use the tax strategies in this book will have challenges.

If you want an easy loan, go to Belize. A few of the banks there will loan money on almost any property in the Central American countries down to Panama. While they prefer to loan on the overpriced bubble properties built for and marketed exclusively to gringos, you might be able to convince them to loan you money on something you could actually resell for what you paid for it. In exchange for the privilege, they will give you 50% of the money and charge interest rates in the low double-digits. Basically, higher than the 'hard money' rates developers pay in the United States.

The situation is the same in my beloved Georgia where, once in a blue moon, a bank will lend money to a foreigner who has obtained residency in the country. The caveat is that interest rates are the same rates your parents paid during the Carter administration, hovering somewhere in the low- to mid-teens. One developer friend of mine offered me as much as 23% a year to lend him money on a project because even he could not fully fund his projects with the banks.

To me, though, there is a silver lining to the lack of financing overseas: it forces you to find good deals. When you are buying an asset entirely with your own money, or your company's money, you find better investments because you can use leverage (i.e., a loan) to cover it up.

This, of course, brings us to the final question: where can you find the best foreign real estate investments?

Where to Find the Best Foreign Investments

We have looked at the fundamentals, you know why you are investing, you are willing to put in the effort and do on-the-ground research, and you have the money to invest in a property. Now, where do you go?

If you want exceptional gains, you either need to know the market and do a lot of work (i.e., fix and flip), or find a place that is growing. Finding a growing market means understanding how that market operates. In Europe, for instance, the city center is still the central business district and the most valuable real estate. This can be a shock to those of us from the United States or Australia who are used to companies moving into the suburbs in exchange for well-manicured lawns and free, easy parking.

While you can play the gentrification game in already expensive cities like London where you can invest where the growth is moving, finding the best opportunities in those situations can be challenging. What I find much easier is studying a country. Unlike London, where you need to live there to know what move to make, you do not even have to leave home to create a list of candidate countries with growing real estate markets. If you want to earn passive income while growing your principal over time, investing in up-and-coming markets is an excellent way to do so.

It is important to note that these markets should be 'up-and-coming' and not already 'on top.' The goal of investing as a Nomad Capitalist is not to chase what is already obvious. Your first instinct upon hearing that Hong Kong is capitalism run amok, has low taxes, and is filled with neurotically hard-working people might be to rush there and buy any real estate you can get your hands on. The only problem is that you are about thirty years too late.

Investors like Jim Rogers and speculators like Doug Casey often use the term 'crisis investing' to describe investments where the knife has no lower to fall. These are investments where a place has gotten beaten up so badly that the deals are now excellent. It can be tough to know when a country has taken its final blow and is on the way up, so new investors might want to avoid crisis investing for the same reason they would be well-advised to avoid catching falling knives.

Hong Kong in the late 1980s, however, had some of the markings of a crisis investment situation. For some time, the British had been negotiating with China over the return of leased territories in Hong Kong, with the Chinese suggesting to Margaret Thatcher that their military could take over the whole place by lunch. Eventually, the negotiations resulted in the British handover of Hong Kong to China.

Hong Kongers panicked. Despite the idea of 'one country, two systems' that would grant Hong Kong special rights to retain its über capitalist leanings for at least fifty years, tens if not hundreds of thousands rushed to apply for residence permits in the United Kingdom, not wishing to live under Chinese rule. Property prices plummeted, a true sign of desperation among Chinese investors who typically view real estate as an infallible investment.

In short, the place was a mess. However, as time went on and the transition moved along, things went back to normal. Some people made 1000% returns on property. Today, Hong Kong is back and more expensive than ever, with $100 million properties dotting the hills near Victoria Peak, and us commoners forced to live in $15,000-a-month one-bedroom closets along the MTR line.

Hong Kong is viewed by many foreign investors, and even more so by mainland Chinese investors, as a bastion of security. As such, prices have become insane, and yields have become quite low. To many Chinese, real estate prices always go up, and that has proven true for many years in Hong Kong. However, the territory does not exactly offer the best conditions for a Nomad Capitalist seeking to invest.

Hong Kong is now at the top of the hypothetical bell curve of a country's success, which is exactly when it is too late to invest in a country's real estate market. Instead, as we discussed earlier, the key is to find the 'next Singapore' – a place that is moving up the bell curve but has not made it past the peak quite yet. These are places where growth and friendly policies will lift the country into a future success story.

In contrast to the falling knife scenario, Singapore started out at the bottom of the curve and had to work its way up. After becoming an independent nation in 1965 following its exit from the Federation of Malaya (now Malaysia), the country was a mere speck on the map. Singapore was nowhere near western levels of development and some cruelly joked that it was not much farther along than it was in its days as a muddy swamp some century and a half earlier.

But the country was willing to do whatever they could to not only survive but also thrive. They wanted to be big and that meant they needed to attract the right investors and businessmen to jumpstart their microscopic economy. The late President Yusof bin Ishak is now a legend in Singapore for his vision and leadership as he implemented policies for racial harmony and economic openness that ushered in unprecedented progress.

Today, it costs between $50,000 and $100,000 just to get permission to drive a car in Singapore. And the apartment buildings they park those cars in are far more expensive. Like Hong Kong, such properties offer relatively poor investment metrics other than the promise of bank-like stability. And like Hong Kong, Singapore is now at the top of the bell curve.

Once a country makes it to the top of the bell curve, not only do investments no longer make sense but other opportunities begin to vanish as well. All those favorable policies once put in place to attract investors are cancelled as politicians move their focus away from attracting powerful investors and toward ensuring that the streets are clean and their citizens get the entitlements they tend to vote for.

In 2013, Singapore closed its immigration program down and it is now very difficult to get citizenship or even an EntrePass residency there. Likewise, Hong Kong recently shut down its Capital

Entrance and Investment Scheme in which you could put $1.2 million anywhere (even the bank!) and get residency. At this point, why would Singapore or Hong Kong need another guy with a million dollars to come in?

If you have $100,000 to invest in a country, that is great. That is better than what most people can do. But Hong Kong and Singapore are not looking for that level of investment anymore. The good news is that there are still countries out there that are looking for the kind of investment you can offer. These are the 'next Singapores' of the world, the up-and-coming markets that not only need your investment but make it clear that they want it with favorable policies and attractive offers.

Now, up-and-coming markets may be up-and-coming for any number of reasons. Real estate in some parts of Italy doubled in the two or three years following adoption of the euro. Estonia's real estate saw gains of about 60% in its first three years in the eurozone. On average, that kind of gain is excellent and is due, in large part, to the political and economic impacts associated with joining the eurozone.

The most common cause of up-and-coming markets, however, is purely organic growth. Quite simply, the population of the world is growing, particularly in emerging countries where populations tend to be younger. You do not need to be a rocket scientist to discover these countries.

Other indicators of a country going in the right direction on the bell curve include pro-business and pro-wealth policies, improvements after a war or conflict, urbanization, climate change, and countries with a growing middle class or with low per capita GDP where both institutions and the workforce are undergoing a transformation.

What you want to find are not the countries like Nigeria – which are at the very, very beginning of the bell curve – but the countries that are moving up the bell curve and will continue to move up. These are places like Georgia and Montenegro and, to a certain extent, even Serbia and Nicaragua – maybe even Mexico, too, for openness, investment and residency.

You want to go where you're treated best. So, where do they make it easy? Go there. Where do they have a good attitude toward business? Go there. There are countries out there that will jump at you like someone desperate to get into a relationship. If they have good fundamentals, go there.

Once you find a place that is headed in the right direction, do not wait too long to get in. The European investment programs that allowed you to get an affordable EU residence have largely come and gone. Hungary's €300,00 investment for residency? Gone. Ireland's business and investment program for residency? Gone. Now they only want you if you are the next Merck or Facebook. They went up and over the bell curve and the opportunity was gone before you knew it.

While some countries will welcome you with open arms, do not adopt the arrogant attitude of many in the West who simply assume that because they are from the US or the UK or some other western country that everyone else in the world is going to cater to their every need. These countries want to know how you are going to help them advance. If you are in a position to do that, you have a great opportunity to invest, but do not assume that they will always want your money.

The world is advancing at an incredible pace and inaction will become costlier as time goes by. This is what happens with globalization. No longer do we have the haves and have nots of the first world versus the third world. There are still places that have their challenges, but in less than sixty years, the percentage of the world's population living in abject poverty has gone from 45% in 1960 to 10% in 2015. Think of that, in your parent's' lifetime, nearly half of the world lived in extreme poverty! Now it is below 10%.

With growing economies around the world and new governments opening their doors to international investors every day, if you are not one of those investors, your investment strategy is probably stuck in the 80s. There are infinitely more opportunities and benefits in foreign markets now versus ten, twenty, thirty years ago. As countries continue to rise and develop, you can catch them on the way up. Do not be the person who looks back and says, "I should have done that." Just do it.

Whatever way you prefer to invest, it can be done overseas with higher yields, better diversification, more opportunities to plant flags and create your desired lifestyle, lower entry points, higher probabilities of success, and more options and benefits. But you cannot afford to wait. The countries that are making their way up the bell curve today will be at the top sooner than you know it. If you invest now, you will take part in their growth and grow with them. If you wait too long, you will miss the boat.

Your How-To Action Plan

Immediate Action Steps: Determine why you want to invest overseas. Do you want higher returns? Are you looking for investment immigration programs? Are you working to build your personal Trifecta Strategy and find a new home base? Why you want to invest will impact how and where you invest and what will constitute a good deal.

Travel Action Steps: Foreign real estate investments are best made on the ground. If you want the best deals, be ready to travel.

Holistic Planning: You can strategically plan your investments to help you plant other offshore flags, from residencies to citizenships and from lifestyle design to currency diversification foreign investments can play an integral part of each one.

Chapter Twelve:
Cryptocurrency

The Most Profitable Investment of the Decade

Dateline: Bogota, Colombia

The cameras were set. The audio was in place. The beautiful background of my home in Bogota reflected my wife's personal touch and my own design tastes. And then the call came in. I accepted. My screen filled with the view of a lavish study. Bookcases sparkled with the gilded covers of a well-curated book collection, and a large, ornate boat model sat behind the businessman I had been looking forward to interviewing for some time.

His illustrious business career had included everything from computer simulation modeling at DuPont to the creation of data mining software, and from $10-million-contracts with McDonald's to running a publicly traded company that would sky-rocket his personal net worth into the billions by the early 2000s. Over the years, he had been named the KPMG Washington High-Tech Entrepreneur of the Year, the Ernst & Young Software Entrepreneur of the Year, a Top Ten Entrepreneur, and an Innovator Under 35.

But my reason for setting up an interview with Michael Saylor had nothing to do with his 30-plus years of business experience; it had everything to do with the bold moves he had made within the last year. Beginning in July 2020, through his company MicroStrategy, Saylor began purchasing Bitcoin. By February 2021, his company had acquired over $2 billion in Bitcoin investments.

"This is the biggest thing that has happened in our lifetime," Saylor confidently declared in our interview. "Bigger than Google, Facebook, Apple, Amazon, Microsoft – bigger than the internet – and you are in the early days. Everybody needs it. Only 1% of the people understand it. Nobody can stop it. It's the single most useful thing you can do to make your life better."

Saylor is not alone in his opinion of Bitcoin. Crypto enthusiasts the world over have gone all in on the digital currency, and many have been rewarded substantially for their confidence. Even so, I am not a crypto maxi, let alone a Bitcoin maximalist. I do not advocate one cryptocurrency above all the rest, nor cryptocurrencies in general as the only investment of choice. If the rest of the chapters in this book are not evidence enough, my personal philosophy is in diversification. I do not put my every dime into cryptocurrencies. I am not opposed to including them in my portfolio, though, and have dabbled in the crypto world since the early days.

More importantly, I have had numerous clients come to me over the years who have made millions and tens of millions from their crypto investments and have needed help to create an offshore plan that could legally protect their new-found wealth. The borderless nature of cryptocurrency goes hand in hand with the principles I have been promoting through Nomad Capitalist for over a decade, which has led to many crypto-centered plans for clients and a plethora of content covering the topic on my blog and YouTube channel.

While I am not a cryptocurrency expert, I have become an expert at creating offshore strategies for crypto investors. And with this new addition to my book, I am giving you an inside look at my thoughts regarding the new digital monetary network and how the Nomad Capitalist philosophy can inform your crypto investment strategy to protect the wealth you create through what Saylor described as "pure monetary energy."

What is Cryptocurrency?

Even those who have amassed fortunes investing in cryptocurrencies may not fully understand them. I will let the crypto experts tell you exactly how it all works, but for those who are new to words like Bitcoin, cryptocurrency, and blockchain, let me give you a few definitions that will make the rest of this chapter go down smoothly.

We spent the last chapter discussing foreign investment opportunities that can only be found on the ground in other countries. And many of you already have substantial investments in your home countries, whether they are stocks, bonds, REITs, real estate, or something else tied to where you live. But cryptocurrency is neither foreign nor domestic. It is a borderless digital currency that is international in every sense of the word.

While fiat currencies and assets are represented by physical quantities – be they paper printed by a government or precious metals mined from the earth – cryptocurrency is completely virtual. It exists only electronically. It is mined through a process of algorithms that adds each transaction to a digital distributed ledger called the blockchain. This blockchain is secured and validated through cryptographic principles; hence, the name cryptocurrency.

And instead of being created or managed by a centralized authority, cryptocurrency is completely decentralized. No one person controls the process. Currently, there are two ways in which new coins can be produced - Proof of Work (PoW) and Proof of Stake (PoS) - and both systems lend themselves towards decentralization.

In a Proof of Work system, crypto miners must dig through mountains of data to extract a solution to process and validate the transaction history. This cryptographic work is rewarded with a token, a single digital coin. Under this system, the only way that one miner could act as a centralized authority is if they controlled a majority of the computers processing the information. But this is unlikely to occur as the mining process requires a massive network of computers.

Under a Proof of Stake system, miners can only validate block transactions according to how many coins they already hold. If they hold 2% of the existing coins, then they can only mine 2% of the blocks. This both encourages decentralization and reduces the threat of attack from miners and mining pools.

If that all sounds too technical, the main point is that cryptocurrency is made to foster decentralization. In fact, the first Bitcoin emerged in 2008 in the wake of the financial crisis and Occupy Wall Street protests to eliminate the corrupt middleman, stamp out interest fees and other charges, and make transactions transparent at a time when faith in big banks was at its lowest. With no need for anyone to be in charge, theoretically, anyone can mine, buy, and sell crypto.

Another unique characteristic of cryptocurrency is that it is a deflationary currency system. Most cryptocurrencies have a hard limit of how many tokens or coins can be produced. Bitcoin has a limit of 21 million producible tokens. Unlike fiat currency that can be printed into existence at the whim of governments with no regard for inflation, once a given cryptocurrency has hit its limit, that is it. Other types of cryptocurrencies can be produced, but once Bitcoin hits the 21 million mark, no more Bitcoin can be produced. Many see this as one of the main benefits of cryptocurrency.

Technical systems, mining methods, decentralization, and deflationary virtues aside, there is no denying that cryptocurrencies have been the most profitable investment of the past decade. Despite Bitcoin's extreme volatility, no other investment asset has matched its overall return (or even come close).

It is no surprise that the many positive characteristics of cryptocurrency have created unprecedented opportunity for investors around the world. It may be a lot to wrap your mind around, but it is the kind of investment worth adding to your portfolio – if anything, as a hedge against the current world system that always seems to be teetering on the edge. Buying your first cryptocurrency is kind of like getting your first second passport or residence permit. It may seem foreign at first, but once you get your first one, it instantly makes you feel more comfortable.

Up ahead, I will walk you through the ins and outs of investing in cryptocurrencies and address the various risks and challenges you are up against as a crypto investor. Then, I will show you how the offshore strategies we have discussed so far in this book can be applied to these challenges to not only shield your crypto investments but also protect and enable you to live a life of greater freedom and prosperity.

Investing in Cryptocurrency

Had you invested in cryptocurrency on the first available Bitcoin exchange in March 2010, you would have paid a mere $0.003 for one Bitcoin. Over a decade later, at the time of this writing, your investment would have earned an unbelievable return of roughly 1,317,900,000%. Yes, you read that correctly – over a trillion percent increase. While Bitcoin prices change by the minute and often drastically, this snapshot in time is extremely telling. The S&P-500 has averaged a 9.8% annualized return over the last 90 years, a rate most investors and mutual funds struggle to equal, let alone exceed. And even gold has seen returns of only 18% in comparison. Clearly, Bitcoin and cryptocurrencies in general are in a league of their own.

But what exactly is it that continues to draw more and more people to invest in cryptocurrency? As we have already discussed, one of its main appeals is its borderless nature. Cryptos are a true international currency, which means that there are no exchange rates and there are minimal fees or other charges involved when using them. While governments are now trying to find a way to jump into the crypto space with Central Bank Digital Currencies (CBDCs) and other methods, most existing cryptocurrencies are untethered to any specific country. Some governments are attempting to regulate their disclosure and use, but they cannot control them as they do fiat currencies, for now.

Many in the crypto space see this as the greatest benefit of Bitcoin and other digital currencies. Holding crypto protects against the whims of political forces like the inflationary policies of quantitative easing that have become so popular in the West over the past decade. The returns on crypto investments can more than keep pace with the rampant inflation now taking over many parts of the world.

Regardless of current circumstances, cryptocurrencies can always serve as a backup to whatever is happening in your own country. As Saylor pointed out as our interview progressed, the international nature of cryptocurrencies means that you can tap into the most intelligent capital anywhere in the world, irrespective of your location. You could buy Bitcoin in Cleveland, Ohio and store it in a cold storage wallet and forget about it. Meanwhile, someone in Hong Kong could come up with a derivatives exchange that will enable new trade and finance and attract hundreds of billions of dollars in capital, driving up the price of Bitcoin. You will wake up richer because of something that happened in a different country, language, and jurisdiction all while you were sleeping.

In Saylor's words, "The beauty of Bitcoin is that it is global, it is open, it is nationless, and anybody can do something to help it. It will always be improved by the highest common denominator."

While I do not plan to go all in on Bitcoin like Saylor and prefer to diversify into other stores of value to protect against the volatility of this new digital currency, it is hard to deny the fact that Bitcoin has been the most profitable investment of the past decade, and perhaps even in world history. And it is just getting started. It will only develop and mature from here.

But it does have its drawbacks. I would rather diversify than turn my entire investment strategy into a philosophical statement about government control and the future of the financial world. Cryptocurrency is so new that there is still a large divide between the utopia of what crypto could be and the reality of the world we live in. This is one reason the asset remains so speculative. Many in the crypto space are there for ideological reasons, and while I agree with their skepticism of government authority, I also believe that these individuals are preventing cryptocurrencies from becoming mainstream.

In the past several years, more than half of all existing Bitcoins have not been used in a single transaction. This is clear evidence that current Bitcoin investors see it as a store of value rather than a functioning currency. It does serve as a solid store of value, but until cryptocurrencies are used as actual currency, they will never become mainstream enough to supplant cash.

This can all be explained by an economic principle known as "Gresham's Law", which assumes that bad money will drive out good money. For example, if you had two coins of equal value but one is made of gold and one of iron, you would use the iron coin first because it has a lower perceived value. You are more confident that the gold will retain its value, so you choose to hold onto it and spend the iron instead. The same phenomenon is occurring with Bitcoin. All things equal, the deflationary pressure of cryptocurrency encourages people to not spend it because it will be worth more tomorrow. If you have equal amounts of fiat currency and crypto, you will use the traditional funds first, just as you would use the iron coins before the gold.

Until this can be resolved, crypto will remain a highly speculative environment because it will not have a practical use within the financial system besides acting as a store of value. This is one reason why Roger Ver spoke so highly of Bitcoin Cash at Nomad Capitalist Live and preferred to forego his speaker fees and instead surprise everyone in attendance with their own Bitcoin Cash investment. Not only is Bitcoin Cash easier to use as an actual currency but sharing it with more people also means that we are one step closer to using cryptocurrency as an actual currency.

For now, even setting "Gresham's Law" aside, blockchain-based currency is so new to the world that it will take time for it to develop its proper footing and build the necessary infrastructure to facilitate its wider adoption. The current market is too dispersed, and regulation is still in its infancy. It will likely become a more permanent fixture of the economic landscape – whether through CBDCs or otherwise – but for the time being, it will chiefly be used as a store of value, a means to facilitate trade, and a way to sidestep the nanny-state currently waging its war on cash in its attempt to control how and where you spend your money.

I am cautiously optimistic about cryptocurrency. It has been declared dead hundreds of times but has continually managed to recover and come back stronger than before. There will always be naysayers, but that has never stopped me from following through on any other Nomad strategy. Everything we do at Nomad Capitalist is about creating options and giving yourself an escape hatch for any circumstance. Cryptocurrency fits that bill, which is why I recommend it as part of a diversified strategy to anyone who can stomach its volatility.

How to Invest in Cryptocurrencies

If I have piqued your interest and you want to start investing in cryptocurrencies, the next question for those who are completely new to the crypto world is always, "How do I invest?" The crypto industry is a bit of a Wild West. With little regulatory oversight and plenty of controversy over the years, it can be difficult to know which cryptocurrency is worth your investment and how to jump on the bandwagon in the first place.

The most straightforward way to invest is through a Centralized Exchange, which essentially acts as a broker that can both execute and store your coins on your behalf. While easy, this can also create some complications. Many Centralized Exchanges now apply KYC regulations, especially for Americans. In many cases, they will want to know your address, net worth, your reasons for investing, and even your Social Security number. The privacy many people are seeking through crypto investments can often be thrown out the door with these measures, especially when the information you hand over is processed by a third party with subpar safety standards.

A more private alternative is a decentralized exchange. While these exchanges are a bit more technical, they often do not even need an email address to get started. Everything is peer-to-peer, so there are no intermediaries, and the only record of your transaction is what appears on the blockchain itself. Decentralized platforms can be illiquid, though, so it could be challenging to find someone selling the amount of crypto you want to buy or sell at any given time.

No matter how you obtain your cryptocurrency, you are responsible for its storage and safety. While you could use an online wallet, the safer route is to store your crypto offline. This does not mean that you are taking your coins off the blockchain, just the key that grants you access to those coins. You could store this key (a long string of alphanumeric symbols – i.e., a password that is often simplified into a seed phrase) in a "paper wallet" which is literally just a piece of paper. Or you could invest in a "hardware wallet", a custom-built machine with built-in security features and ciphers that will sign for you and give you an extra layer of protection. Once stored in your hardware wallet, you can remove your key from the internet and even your computer, protecting it from potential hackers. Just be sure to buy your hardware wallet from the manufacturers directly to avoid scams.

When you have decided where to store your new coins, the next question is which coins to buy. As I write this, there are over 6,000 different cryptocurrencies available in the world. Bitcoin was the first successful cryptocurrency and remains the most important one to date, but every new cryptocurrency introduced to the world has unique characteristics, functions, challenges, and benefits. You could easily start by looking up the top five cryptocurrencies, but how do you differentiate between them and the other 6000-plus coins?

In general, there are two types of coins: stablecoins and free-float coins. Stablecoins are pegged to the value of a good, service, or asset in the same way the US dollar used to be pegged to gold before the gold standard was abandoned. The advantage is that the coin is stabilized by assets that are uncorrelated to the cryptocurrency industry itself, reducing risk. However, it does not always reduce volatility. The free-float coin, on the other hand, derives its value primarily from its scarcity and market demand – Bitcoin being the most prominent example.

Whatever way you choose to invest, you need to have a strong stomach to dive into crypto. More importantly, you need to go in with a plan and then carry it out. I suggest investing for the long run. Many people opt for a dollar-cost-averaging strategy and invest a set amount on a weekly or monthly basis without respect to market conditions. It can be difficult if not impossible to time the market with something as volatile as cryptocurrencies, so keeping a long-term perspective will save you the psychological turmoil of every up and down.

Others have made considerable amounts of money by becoming crypto traders. With a market as volatile, dispersed, and active as cryptocurrency, there are plenty of opportunities to make money via arbitrage. This is one area, though, where living in the wrong country could become very costly. In some places, you may be taxed per transaction. And even within each trading platform, you may be subjected to additional fees. This particular strategy is worth thinking through before you attempt to make money and end up with an unprofitable trade.

There are also ways to make money from crypto by mining it yourself. Previously, it was possible to use your laptop to solve the cryptographic problems needed to update the blockchain, but today, mining has been taken over by server farms in countries where electricity and hardware are cheap. While mining remains a great way to create your own crypto without going through KYC regulations, it is much harder to do today and will require a considerable amount of capital to compete with those already in the space. A more accessible option now available is to invest in crypto mining companies in the stock exchange.

The Tax Challenges of Crypto Investment

"I've made more money in the last ten months of the pandemic than I ever thought possible!" The enthusiasm coming from my young client on the other end of the call was almost palpable. "Who knew I just needed to be locked up in my apartment with nothing to do except work from home to inspire me to start a side hustle business that would generate $800,000 in less than a year? I mean, I made $250,000 of that in this last month alone!"

"It's amazing what you can do when you get out of the rat race, isn't it?" I replied.

"Yeah," Matthew agreed. And then his face fell, "But now I have a new problem."

"Taxes?" I asked.

"Taxes," Matthew concurred. "I was riding high after such an incredible year, and then my tax bill came due – $375,000! Andrew, that's almost half!" he looked like he was going to be sick. "Half!" he repeated in shock.

"That's rough," I said in total empathy. "But can I rub the pain in just a little more?" Matthew cocked his head to one side with a quizzical expression, then nodded and I continued. "What would you have done with that $375,000 if the government hadn't demanded that you hand it over?"

"Well, I've always been bullish on crypto. Before the pandemic, I was investing my savings from my job into cryptocurrency. Now that I have my business, I had planned to put a good chunk of that $375 into my crypto savings," Matthew explained.

"Let's run the numbers, then," I said. "What would that investment in crypto have become by now if you had been able to invest it?"

Matthew and I worked through the numbers, considering when he would have invested certain amounts and how those assets would have increased over time. When we finished our calculations, Matthew breathed out a long sigh and then looked up at me in disbelief. "$784,000," he said.

"$784,000," I confirmed. "That, Matthew, is the cost of staying where you are. That is the opportunity cost of tax."

Beyond taxes, crypto investors like my young client face even greater opportunity costs simply by being US citizens. Just as FATCA regulations have discouraged foreign banks from taking on US clients, increasing crypto regulations in the United States have prompted many ICOs (Initial Coin Offerings – the crypto equivalent of Initial Public Offerings) to shut out anyone with US indicia from even participating. Americans are denied some of the best opportunities to get in on promising new currencies just because of their citizenship.

And even if you can participate in crypto deals, you will have to pay tax. Or if you have an active business that runs on crypto, you will have to pay tax on that too. At some point, folks like Matthew end up asking themselves, How much am I going to lose by staying in my country? As with so many things, the longer you wait, the more you lose in opportunity cost. These are the typical challenges any investor faces living in a high-tax country, but if you are a crypto investor, high taxes and lost opportunities are only the beginning of your troubles.

The biggest challenge I see is the uncertainty about what is to come as governments step into the crypto space and attempt to regulate the industry. Many western countries are enforcing more taxes and more regulations specifically targeting crypto. In October of 2020, the IRS officially released the infamous virtual currency question now found on Form 1040: "At any time during 2020, did you receive, sell, send, exchange, or otherwise acquire any financial interest in virtual currency?" Companies must also report their crypto holdings. Like the FBAR and FATCA for offshore bank accounts, whether you have gains or not, your crypto investments are now reportable.

The age of transparency makes it impossible to hide your assets. Too many crypto ideologists arrogantly argue that you can just hide your crypto holdings and not report them to your government, but that stinks of the same 80s' mentality of anonymous, numbered offshore bank accounts. I do not wish to be a criminal or a liar or spend all my time looking over my shoulder. I understand that the government does not always do things ethically, but I do not want to lie to people, even if they lie to me.

And do not assume that the government will never find out that you have crypto if you simply do not report it. It is not as private as people want to believe. Plus, the IRS is getting better at figuring out who has cryptocurrency. If you are claiming that you do not have crypto, but you have a low paying job and then buy something expensive (like a Ferrari or a mansion) the IRS is going to figure out that you have been trying to hide your crypto investments from them. And even if you do not spend it, they can still trace it back to you in many cases. Bottom line? Never hide your money from the government.

Staying in the US and not reporting your crypto is like when people buy US real estate and put it in a Cooke Islands trust. It gives you some protection, but I know someone who had his US real estate in an Isle of Man trust and the US judge ordered it seized and sold. The trust did not really matter. They knew where it was. They can ask you where it is. And what happens if you do not answer them? They can freeze your passport. They could put you on trial. If you are overseas and feel like you are untouchable, it might be harder for them to get to you, but they can still freeze your passport.

As with anything offshore, investing in cryptocurrency is a high-risk move – not because it is inherently illegal, but because people do not understand it. Investing in crypto is not a criminal act, but if you are not following the tax rules, it is illicit. As the goody-two-shoes of the offshore industry, I must tell you that. Under no circumstance do I encourage tax dodging, especially when there are perfectly legal ways that your crypto-related profits could be tax-free. I will show you those strategies in just a moment, but the bottom line is that if you are holding assets outside of the United States – be it crypto or other foreign assets – if you are still living in the US or remain a US person, you are liable for tax and will always be required to report your assets.

But reporting your crypto assets to the government is only the beginning. What comes next is the true wild card. There have been discussions about an income tax or capital gains tax on crypto, and there are already rising capital gains in general. There is even the possibility of a tax on unrealized gains, not to mention the possibility of a more demanding exit tax and additional regulations on crypto loans and other laws making it harder to cash out on your crypto.

As I write this, there is new legislation on the table in the US Congress that could require brokers to disclose crypto trades. Why? So that the government can "raise" $28 billion in tax revenue from crypto investors to pay for an infrastructure package. As a US person, you can confidently assume that whenever the US government needs money for something, they are going to come to you. I do not want to paint a bleak picture, but I do want to be realistic about the situation.

You do not know what taxes and laws will be passed in the future. What we do know is that increasing crypto values means that more governments are trying to regulate virtual currencies. The OECD (which is basically a lobbying group that goes around shaming low-tax countries) is already trying to put together a standard for how they are going to deal with crypto. As with the internet, the wider the adoption of the new digital monetary network, the more the masses will dictate its future. You cannot control that.

What you can control are your options – your backup plan – so that you can duck out of the system before it forces you to lose too much.

Offshore Solutions for Crypto Investors

While die-hard cryptocurrency fanatics will promote the technology as a way to evade government scrutiny and taxes, I am not interested in perpetually living in fear of the consequences of illegal actions. I do not want to live at odds with the government, especially when I can go where I am treated best and legally avoid crypto taxes and regulations altogether. Start by doing everything legally within your home country, but then work to create an offshore strategy that will give you an out.

Throughout this book, we have already discussed many of the major strategies that you can implement in any offshore plan. Now that we have built the foundation, we can apply those strategies to the specific circumstances of a crypto investor. The first strategy is to simply understand that you can go where you're treated best. While many countries are waging war against cryptocurrency because they view it as a tool for criminals and tax evaders (or as a direct competitor to their national currency), other countries have embraced virtual currencies. They want crypto investors and have created incentives for them to make that point clear.

Portugal, for example, will not tax crypto profits if you are an individual instead of a corporate entity. Germany will not tax profits below €600 for coins held for over a year. Singapore will not tax individual or long-term holdings. And Belarus will not tax profits from mining, trading, ICOs, or capital gains until January 1, 2023. Other countries have simply refrained from regulating the industry at all, making them technically tax-free for the time being.

And then there are the countries that will let you set up crypto operations within their jurisdictions, pay for immigration services with Bitcoin, or access certain banking benefits for crypto. Some, like the government of Georgia, have even adopted blockchain technology. Countries like these are often less commonly known and less powerful and they are looking for an edge to attract capital and innovation. In pursuit of that edge, they have enacted crypto-friendly policies that you can use to your advantage.

It is these countries that have become the crypto havens that are facilitating the growth of the industry through crypto-friendly legislation. Why stay and face the crypto challenges in your home country when you can go to one of these places and have the red carpet rolled out for you? If you are a crypto investor, you can find banking jurisdictions that are better for you and corporate laws that are designed specifically for you. Better yet, you can implement Nomad strategies to exit your high-tax system as well as diversify out of your crypto holdings to achieve greater diversification and the security that comes with it. Let's look at each piece of the puzzle in more detail.

1. Offshore Banking with Cryptocurrency

Offshore banking with cryptocurrency is a two-fold equation. One half of the equation is to find countries that have crypto-friendly banking systems. The other half of the equation is to use cryptocurrencies to facilitate your offshore banking. Because these virtual currencies are so new to the world financial system, you will need to know the places and the strategies that will allow you to marry the existing financial system with the new digital monetary network.

If your current bank is not pro-crypto, it will be difficult to convince them to get involved. For instance, I have not found banks in the UAE or Singapore to be very crypto friendly. The better option is to go to banks that are already involved in the crypto space. As far as countries are concerned, the banking systems in Liechtenstein, Bermuda, the British Virgin Islands, Hong Kong, and Switzerland have all shown promise for crypto investors. The BVI, for example, is the second largest crypto jurisdiction in the world.

For good or bad, banks and governments are not always on the same page when it comes to cryptocurrencies. While the Georgian government has adopted blockchain technology, the banks there are not crypto-friendly. Conversely, though Hong Kong banks were some of the first in the world to offer cryptocurrency ATMs and other crypto innovations, the government is currently looking for ways to regulate the industry.

And then there is Liechtenstein, where the government does not offer any financial incentives or disincentives for crypto but is generally open to cryptocurrencies and other blockchain technology. Even the Crown Prince is personally involved in crypto. In a situation like this where there are pro-crypto sentiments but no legislation, the most important factor in Liechtenstein is that the banks there regularly deal in cryptocurrencies and have even advised several ICOs.

In contrast, Bermuda's government has been very proactive in approving crypto-friendly legislation and the banks there are open to crypto dealings. Since 2018, Bermuda has offered a separate class of banking licenses that favor FinTech and encourage crypto technologies. They have also passed a law that allows for the quick approval of ICOs. The country has been unabashed in its efforts to become a crypto incubator, and they have been awarded for those efforts with numerous crypto companies flocking to their shores and banks.

The ideal is to find a jurisdiction like this where both the government and the banks are on the same page. Switzerland is another example of this ideal situation where the government was an early adopter of pro-crypto legislation. The low-tax canton of Zug – now home to hundreds of blockchain startups – is already known as "Crypto Valley" and the country as a whole is vying for the title of "Crypto Nation." With a well-established banking industry in the country that is open to crypto, Switzerland is not only a good place for crypto companies but for banking with cryptocurrency as well.

Now, for the other half of the equation. How can you use cryptocurrency to facilitate your offshore life? There are both opportunities and challenges that come with using digital currencies offshore. The opportunities come from their inherently borderless nature, which we have previously discussed. Because it is virtual, you can literally take it anywhere with you and use it to directly pay for goods or services (there are over 100,000 merchants worldwide that allow you to buy with Bitcoin).

But chances are you will still need to make some purchases in regular fiat money. To do this, you can access your funds in your destination country with a platform like LocalBitcoins that allows you to buy or sell cryptos for a specific currency. There are also multiple-currency accounts and cards like Revolut that allow you to transfer your cryptocurrencies into various fiat currency accounts. You can also use platforms that connect you directly to a bank account.

In fact, cryptocurrencies are a great way to fund an offshore bank account. While traditional options for funding an offshore account include wire transfers, ATMs, and Wise, crypto adds options like LocalBitcoins, as well as Coinapult, which allows you to freeze your Bitcoins to the value of a foreign currency, gold, or silver until you are ready to move them to your offshore bank.

While Coinapult and other services allow you to transfer money to a connected bank account, remember that not all banks are open to crypto transfers and liquidation. Some banks will even freeze or close your account if you attempt this, so know what your bank's policies are before making a transfer. One way around this issue is to liquidate your crypto holdings elsewhere before transferring the money to your bank. Many of our clients have purchased gold with their Bitcoin and then, after liquidating their gold holdings, use that cash to fund an offshore account.

Again, there are both opportunities and challenges when it comes to using a new technology in a world where banks and governments are still deciding whether to shut them out, embrace them, or find other ways to simply keep up. But if you are flexible and know where to look, you will almost always find a solution to whatever need you have.

2. Offshore Crypto Companies

Compared to finding a crypto-friendly bank, setting up a crypto company offshore is easy. Jurisdictions such as Hong Kong, the Cayman Islands, Bulgaria, Estonia, the British Virgin Islands, and Malta all make it particularly simple to set up shop there. For example, Malta has created a regulatory body specifically tailored to crypto startups. They offer low net corporate tax rates, EU banking options, and pro-Bitcoin legislation. Malta's prime minister has called crypto "the inevitable future of money" so it is no wonder that Malta has come to be known as "Blockchain Island." Malta wants crypto business.

But setting up an offshore company that deals in crypto is not a quick solution to the high-tax challenges you face from your home country. Remember the tax-friendly quadrant that we discussed in Chapter Nine. You must address both the personal and corporate to effectively and legally lower your taxes. You cannot move your crypto funds into an offshore company and assume that you will never have to pay tax on them, especially if you are a US citizen.

There are laws governing Controlled Foreign Corporations (CFCs) that dictate that a foreign company owned by a US person must pay US corporate taxes and report to the US. If you live in a country where your company already pays tax, you may get a tax credit or a tax treaty and laws like GILTI will come into play, but you are not going to save on taxes by offshoring your crypto holdings to a foreign company if you are personally living in a high-tax country or remain a tax resident there.

You may, however, still want an offshore company for your crypto business to access other non-tax-related benefits. For instance, an offshore company could give you better access to trading opportunities. Or there may be crypto deals that you cannot access through your home country's legal structures that are available to your offshore company. Or maybe you are looking for certain asset protection benefits.

There are plenty of legitimate reasons to use a company overseas for your crypto dealings that are not tax related. But the idea that you can just migrate an asset like crypto and it can sit in your offshore company tax-free while you sit in your high-tax country and never pay anything or tell anyone is wrong. You must address the personal part of the equation and leave your high-tax country yourself to access the full tax-saving benefits of a crypto-friendly offshore company.

3. Exit the High-Tax System

With the tax-friendly quadrant in mind, we can address the crypto-specific opportunities for those looking to get a second residence or passport that will enable them to personally exit their high-tax system and realize the full potential of their crypto investments. The bottom line is that you need to get out. Too many crypto people are winging it. You need to have a solid tax plan in place, and you need to get a second residence or passport. If you have not done so already, now is the time to act. You do not want to be the guy whose Bitcoin is going through the roof and has no plan to deal with the tax fallout.

In all honesty, you could apply many of the general strategies that we have already discussed in this book and be set. For everyone who is not a US citizen, you want to have tax residence in a tax-friendly country and a new place to call home. If you are a US citizen, getting a second passport from a country that will not bother you should be your top priority. You could move yourself and your company to the UAE or the Cayman Islands or buy a house in the

Bahamas and get residence there. You may need to compartmentalize where you live versus where you bank versus where you have citizenship to make it all work from a crypto standpoint, but there are plenty of options.

Your first consideration when deciding between all these options should be your specific needs. For instance, how fast do you need your passport? If you are not a US citizen, you could take the naturalization route toward a second passport to save on money because time is not as big of an issue. But if you are a US citizen and you calculate the opportunity cost of remaining in the US, you may find that it is worth paying more upfront to get a quick second passport. Paying $100,000 now for a Caribbean citizenship by investment that you can get in a matter of months could have a substantial impact on your tax bill if your crypto investments are close to pushing you over the threshold to become a covered expatriate when you renounce.

Other personal considerations include deciding if you want to live where you have citizenship or get a residence somewhere else. You could also explore investing in bonds or real estate to get your second passport if you are worried about the opportunity cost of divesting from crypto to pay for your new residence or citizenship. The returns on bonds and real estate will likely not match your crypto investments but it may be better than simply donating your money for citizenship. That said, from a tax perspective, taking part of your crypto wealth and investing or even donating it for a second passport or residence will pay dividends well into the future.

The next question to ask is whether you can get a second passport using cryptocurrencies. I would never recommend getting a citizenship just because there is an option to pay for it using Bitcoin, but if the available options meet other criteria that you may have, it is worth your consideration. Vanuatu was the first country to accept Bitcoin as payment for their citizenship by investment program. The cost was higher than if you paid in cash, but it was an option.

Antigua and Barbuda now accepts Bitcoin for its citizenship by investment program as well, which is just one testament to the crypto-friendliness of this island country. Roger Ver acquired his second citizenship in Antigua before renouncing his US citizenship and has also chosen to live there for much of the year due to the country's open attitude toward crypto, especially Bitcoin Cash. The digital currency is widely accepted throughout the country and can be used to buy gas, pay a taxi, order at restaurants, or even book a villa.

There are ways that you could create your own crypto immigration opportunities as well. For instance, if you acquire residence or citizenship by investing in real estate and the seller accepts crypto as payment, you could complete the entire transaction in crypto and walk away with a new place to call home and an exit strategy to leave your high-tax home country.

Once you have your residence or passport in hand, you can then use it as a Plan A to take immediate action or save it as a Plan B if things get bad enough at home. Whatever you do, do not wait to get that Plan B in place. Some people want to wait until the price of crypto drops to go after that second passport and renounce, but I believe in the power of insurance. You cannot buy insurance after your house burns down. If your country proposes a new tax law and passes it a month later, you will not have time to even do the paperwork for an instant second citizenship before the new laws come into effect. But if you already have your second passport, you can leave and renounce within a month.

You can always find a reason to wait. Maybe the St. Lucia passport costs two Bitcoin today and you want to wait until it costs one. But you cannot control when Bitcoin will go up or down. You cannot control what anti-crypto laws your government is going to introduce next. But you can control whether you have an insurance policy. So, if you are in crypto, just do it. Just get the second passport. You will feel the relief the moment the control returns to your hands alongside your shiny new passport.

Once you have your second passport, you can choose to time when you renounce or leave the system. If you live in a high-tax Western country, you will have to pay a one-time capital gains tax on your cryptocurrency when you leave. Outside of the US, this may be part of the process to become tax non-resident. In the US, you may have to pay the exit tax when you renounce. In both cases, you can reduce or even eliminate the amount you owe by leaving when your assets are worthless. Because crypto values fluctuate, you can choose your net worth when you leave the country by exiting the system when crypto prices drop.

If you are an American, another great option is to move to Puerto Rico first to freeze your capital gains. There is no way to avoid taxation on passive income as an American, even if you are overseas. Puerto Rico is the one exception. I have had clients move to Puerto Rico to lock in the 0% rate on capital gains available there while they figure out the rest of their plans. Once they have their plan in place, they can then sell while they are locked in at 0% and then expatriate. You can make this plan work by staying in Puerto Rico for as little as five months a year and then spending the rest of your time traveling abroad and even visiting the United States while enjoying the immediate benefits that come with Puerto Rico's program before renouncing.

Whatever you do, you need to skate to where the puck is going, not to where the puck is. You have to figure out where the puck is headed, or you will fall behind before you even arrive at your target. If your crypto investments are growing, have a plan for what will happen a year from now, two years, even five years down the road. As a crypto investor, you are at a higher risk that your government is going to regulate the market to your disadvantage. Having a plan in place to be able to leave that kind of environment when the time comes is more essential for you than many other investors, high-net-worth individuals, and entrepreneurs. Plan accordingly.

4. Diversify Out of Crypto

No Nomad plan would be complete without proper diversification. Cryptocurrency, for all its many virtues, should never be your one and only option. There are risks involved with cryptocurrency that we have yet to even address. For instance, it is one of the few asset classes with the potential to be worthless. The value of crypto is partially dependent on the capital-intensive nature of crypto mining. If quantum computing becomes a reality, it could shatter the very foundation of crypto, potentially rendering the virtual currency null and void. That is the risk of betting everything on technology. It is always changing.

There are also some digital currencies that will simply fail to survive. Perhaps they will never achieve enough interest to become profitable. Or maybe hostile regulatory bodies will destroy the currency before it can even take off, as occurred with Facebook's Libra before it began its comeback as Diem. And then there are the countries like Algeria, Bolivia, China, Colombia, Ecuador, India, Morocco, Nepal, Pakistan, Russia, Turkey, and Vietnam that have strongly warned against or even prohibited its use or outlawed cryptocurrency altogether.

Putting all your eggs into a basket that is so polarizing in so many ways is a level of risk I would never want to take on. No investment is beyond risk, but cryptocurrency is particularly speculative. Because you can never fully insure against every risk affecting a given asset, it is best to diversify so that you do not depend on a single geographic location or investment.

I am not a financial advisor so I will not tell you how much of your portfolio should be in crypto. I have clients who do not own any at all. I have had others who have built fortunes as large as $100 million from crypto alone. My personal belief is that Bitcoin and other cryptocurrencies are tools to create a life of greater freedom and prosperity, but they are not the only ones. If you want to experience true freedom, you need to use all the tools in your toolbox to create a holistic and diversified plan.

I have also found that it is worth diversifying out of cryptocurrency for practical reasons, especially if you want to implement the other Nomad Capitalist strategies that we have discussed. Institutions like banks and embassies want to see that you have a normal bank account and steady cash flow. If you are working toward a second passport or need to get a visa to your next destination, you will want to start making regular monthly payments to your bank long before an embassy requests your bank statements. And if you run a company, you will likely need fiat currency to pay your employees.

In the end, I am a pragmatist. Ideology can only get you so far. I want to do what works. And the reality is that the world does not yet revolve around cryptocurrencies. I want to be able to live and operate in the systems that exist today, even while pushing the boundaries of what is. I want to invest in cryptocurrencies for all their benefits – from keeping money out of the banking system to acquiring its store of value – but I also want to give myself other options. At the end of the day, diversification in all its forms is the name of the game for a Nomad Capitalist.

The Future of Cryptocurrency for Nomads

Cryptocurrency is one of the most exciting developments in the financial world in years – possibly centuries. It has the potential to change how economies and markets work, but that potential remains largely unrealized for now. The cryptocurrency market is maturing and developing its own decentralized financial institutions, but we are only at the beginning of what could be. The cryptocurrency industry still has room to grow and develop, but the world is also deciding how to adapt, adopt, and regulate it, which will undoubtedly impact its future as well.

Given its current volatile and speculative nature, I would advise against making cryptocurrencies your primary holding, but seeing as they have proven to be the most profitable investment in human history, it makes sense to consider them as part of a healthy and well-diversified portfolio. Not everyone is going to agree that crypto is a good investment and that is fine. It is not necessary to the Nomad Capitalist life, but it is compatible with the principles and practices we promote.

If you are new to the crypto world, know that it is still not too late to get started. Crypto, like anything else, is a matter of getting comfortable. There is a psychology to it that applies across the many strategies involved in a holistic offshore plan. Whenever you discover crypto, the best time to invest will always be now. Just understand why you are investing. Whether you have lost faith in fiat currency or the banking system, you want to trade or get in on the good returns, or you prefer the borderless nature of a digital currency and how it can facilitate an international lifestyle, there is value in cryptocurrencies.

My main encouragement is that you approach crypto investing as a financial decision, not a philosophical one. Have an early adopter mindset, but do not get attached to a movement. See it as the tool that it is and base your assumption of its value on those factors. Do not choose your investments because of their ability to communicate your beliefs about government power and the future of world financial systems.

And once you do invest, recognize that crypto investors in the high-tax West face the most demanding and unpredictable future when it comes to taxation and other regulations. If it becomes a significant part of your life, know that there are places where you and your crypto investments will be treated best. Many countries offer crypto-friendly policies and institutions. You can incorporate these places into a holistic offshore plan that will address your unique needs as a crypto investor to increase your freedom and prosperity offshore.

Your How-To Action Plan

Immediate Action Steps: If you have not invested in cryptocurrencies already, go buy some right now.

Travel Action Steps: If you are in another country and need fiat currency, you can use platforms like LocalBitcoins to liquidate your crypto in the local currency and save yourself from bad exchange rates and high fees. If you are in a country like Antigua and Barbuda that is open to cryptocurrencies, you can make your purchases directly in Bitcoin Cash and other virtual currencies.

Holistic Planning: You can use cryptocurrencies to facilitate your offshore activities like funding an offshore bank account, but you may also need to do more planning to fit your crypto holdings into your offshore strategy. You will need to consider specific crypto-friendly jurisdictions for both banking and business and ensure that your tax-friendly quadrant addresses the unique challenges you face as a crypto investor. If you deal almost exclusively in cryptocurrencies, find ways to diversify into other assets to reduce risk and meet the practical needs of the Nomad Capitalist lifestyle.

Chapter Thirteen: The Final Frontier

If It's Not Risky, It's Too Late

Dateline: Siem Reap, Cambodia

The rhythmic beat of my feet hitting the pavement created a familiar cadence as I walked along the bustling streets of Siem Reap, Cambodia. The cozy tourist destination is famous for the Angkor Wat ruins, an ancient temple complex that forms the largest religious monument in the world.

But my feet were not taking me toward Angkor Wat that morning. I had heard rumors of a modern-day Cambodian legend born in the same city just over a decade before and I was marking a path to the reputed location of its legendary birthplace. I soon arrived at the Sofitel Hotel of Siem Reap and stepped out of the heat.

My contact, Jacob, was waiting for me in the lobby and escorted me to the hotel restaurant overlooking the beautiful Sala Lake. As we savored the expansive breakfast buffet, Jacob began to tell me the story of The Blue Pumpkin and how one French expat and his Thai wife became millionaires by starting a simple fruit and cake stand in Cambodia.

It all began with Arnaud Curtat, a French expat who worked his way up to become one of the top pastry chefs in Bangkok's competitive hotel scene. Then, sensing opportunity further east, he and his Thai wife packed their bags and moved to Siem Reap where he took a chef job at the very Sofitel in Siem Reap where I sat enjoying my breakfast that morning.

With no job, his wife started a small business in a tiny storefront that cost about $250 a month. She first sold carved fruits to locals, then she took a leaf out of her husband's playbook and sold small cakes. The fruits and cakes were a hit, and she expanded into other baked goods.

Within a year, Arnaud Curtat quit his job at the Sofitel and joined his wife to expand the product line of the business that they would soon name The Blue Pumpkin. Fresh baked breads were made and quickly sold out – they could not keep them in stock. Arnaud used his connections in the Siem Reap hotel scene to sell large orders to seemingly every hotel in town and the business grew.

As time went on, the Blue Pumpkin empire expanded. Fruits and cakes turned into bread turned into ice cream. The original small storefront on a dusty road was replaced with a much larger facility and, eventually, nine company-owned locations throughout town. More and more places around Siem Reap wanted to sell Blue Pumpkin products, which are now available in practically every supermarket and tourist area of the city.

In well under ten years, Blue Pumpkin went from a tiny fruit and cake stand like countless others in Cambodia to a food empire. Blue Pumpkin locations are now ubiquitous throughout Phnom Penh, as well, with a non-stop flow of tourists buying ice cream cones and cheesecakes in the company's western-styled stores. Local Cambodians have taken notice and appreciate the more international theme of Blue Pumpkin's stores. Arnaud never wanted his stores to be in the traditional Khmer style; he realized that tourists and locals alike want a taste of another part of the world every once in a while.

After ten years in the business, Arnaud sold a little over half of his stake in Blue Pumpkin to some serious investors for around $1 million – quite an accomplishment for a couple who came to Cambodia with just a dream to work for someone else and a desire to make a second income for their family. Now, after more than 15 years in business, they plan to franchise the concept to Thailand and Malaysia, hoping to become the first Cambodian brand to expand outside the country.

Just like immigrants who traveled to The Land of the Free long ago, countries today like Cambodia offer immigrants 'fresh off the boat' the opportunity to do whatever they think can make a buck, without a lot of government interference or the need to know and adhere to a lot of regulations. That leaves people like Arnaud the ability to focus on creating great products rather than being hassled by bureaucrats.

Compare that to opening a bakery in California: you would have to jump through hoops with numerous three-letter state and local agencies, take hours of bakery classes to get certified, buy special equipment that has passed standards, and hope you did not violate any of the innumerable ordinances, laws, and regulations governing everything from food serving to hiring to advertising. In a frontier market, you rent a space, hang your shingle, and start baking. It is a lot easier to start making money quickly.

If you live in a western country, a bakery is probably not at the top of your list of businesses to start, anyway. The return on your time invested is just not that great, and the barrier to entry is so low that supply exceeds demand, leading many businesses to fail. In rapidly developing markets, however, demand often outpaces supply, creating an enviable position for business owners on the ground.

But how do you find the right frontier market for you and the business ideas you have been itching to give a try? Cambodia is just one of many frontier markets where conditions are right for an adventurous entrepreneur to come in and create a successful business on the ground. You literally have the entire world to work with.

Unlike the strategies we discussed in Chapter Nine about offshore companies and tax savings, where you simply take the business you have now and incorporate it in an offshore jurisdiction, frontier market entrepreneurship entails doing actual business in the local market. You can still choose where to incorporate your business, which country's rules you will play by, and what your tax level will be, but you can also choose a specific market where conditions are perfect for your particular product.

Whereas the first option follows more of the *Four-Hour Workweek* model of running a business that markets to western consumers while living on the beach in some exotic foreign locale, becoming a frontier market entrepreneur involves doing business in those exotic foreign locales.

But before we get too far ahead of ourselves, let's examine these various locales to understand their different markets and why frontier markets in particular are where you want to establish your next successful business. For the most part, investors tend to break the world up into three different markets: developed, emerging, and frontier.

Developed markets are usually those that seem like they have everything figured out: high per capita income and gross domestic product (GDP), ease of capital movement (developed capital markets with high levels of liquidity), efficient market institutions, decent economic growth and security, high levels of industrialization, a generally high standard of living, and widespread infrastructure. They also tend to have higher levels of education and literacy and relatively good health indicators.

Just think of the most economically advanced countries in the world and you have got yourself a list of the world's developed markets. This list includes countries in most of Western Europe, as well as Canada, the United States, Australia, Singapore, Hong Kong, Israel, Japan, New Zealand, and South Korea (at least on some lists).

There is a good chance that you are in one of these countries right now. And for all the great things about these places on paper, you have probably begun to realize that there are downsides to developed markets as well, especially for entrepreneurs. The most obvious downside is that the taxes are high. It is not that hard to start a US LLC or UK Limited Company, but it can be incredibly expensive to maintain one thanks to the taxes. Developed countries are often run by imperious governments that do not want or need you yet make it hard to leave.

They can also make it difficult to get anything done. Some emerging markets can make things difficult as well, but if you find the right one it can be worth it. But it is usually the developed markets that have become more bureaucratic. If you want to build a store, for example, they will probably ask to do a soil sample on this and a study on that and will require numerous proposals and endless presentations. In a developing country, if you let the government know that you want to start a business, more likely than not, they will clear out and let you have the area.

But it is not just about the government or the taxes they charge and the hoops they make you jump through. Developed countries are slowing down. They have some of the slowest growth rates in the world, many with well under 2% growth in GDP a year. Birth rates in developed countries are also so low that they are now below replacement levels. Where is your market going to be with birthrates like that? Who is going to buy your stuff?

There is also a growing malaise in these countries that begs the same question. If you go to the United States, it seems to get poorer every year. Where is the middle class that is ready to spend money? Compare that to a place like China where they are currently growing middle-class consumers like weeds. From my perspective, the lifestyle is just not there. I find so much more excitement in a place like Mexico where things are developing and growing instead of a place where they are developed and stagnant.

Mexico is one of many emerging markets around the world that offer a more interesting prospect. By definition, emerging markets have a little more work to do before they 'emerge' into a developed market. This usually means that they are in the process of rapid growth and development. While they share certain characteristics with developed markets, they have lower per capita income and less mature capital markets than their more 'advanced' counterparts.

Emerging market countries include places like Brazil, Russia, India, China, Chile, Malaysia, Eastern Europe, Turkey, South Africa, Mexico, Indonesia, Egypt, Colombia, and others.

For the investor or entrepreneur, there are other characteristics that make emerging markets attractive. For instance, while they certainly present some risk, they have an expanding middle class, improving standards of living, increasing social stability, as well as encouraging institutional transformations, more economic openness, and greater fiscal responsibility.

I recommend including emerging markets in your international investment portfolio, but when it comes to entrepreneurship, emerging markets are often already saturated, and the competition can be high. If you want a wide-open playing field as a global entrepreneur, I suggest you look to frontier markets.

Frontier markets are a rung lower on the development ladder; they have begun to develop but have not become completely stable. They also have smaller market capitalization, higher volatility, fewer financial regulatory institutions, yet are still open and accessible to foreign investors and entrepreneurs.

The risk involved in pursuing these final frontiers is what keeps a lot of investors and businesses from entering the market within these countries. However, for the risk-tolerant, this means that you will have open access to countries with great fundamentals for high returns and incredible business success.

The Benefits of Frontier Market Entrepreneurship

There are numerous benefits to doing business in a frontier market, let's examine just a few of them.

Contributing to Positive Development

From a less profit-minded perspective, the first benefit of frontier market entrepreneurship is the knowledge that you are contributing to the growth and development of other countries. The reasons these countries are open and accessible to foreign entrepreneurs is because they would love to have your contribution. That is why they have policies that encourage you to come there.

When you go where you're treated best, you are helping people. The people living in Poland under communism, for example, were not going to Egypt and spending money on five-star resorts like they do now. As a result of Poland's development, Egypt's growth went up. The same thing can be said regarding Cambodians eating hamburgers, the Chinese driving more cars, and Latin Americans fueling the fastest growing smartphone market on the planet.

This is why, whenever folks choose to paint successful entrepreneurs who want to do business overseas as tax cheats or unpatriotic, greedy thieves, I have to respectfully disagree. I see frontier market entrepreneurship like the concierge medicine trend that is growing in the West. People often question how the wealthy could ever dare to have concierge medicine that costs them $40,000 to $160,000 out of pocket every year while the masses could never afford such service. I have to shake my head at such questioning. Some of the most important advancements in medicine that are now available to the masses at much lower costs have become available precisely because the wealthy were willing to pay much more for them first.

While the objectors concern themselves with the tiered healthcare system at home, we already have a tiered system throughout the world. Folks in the US may be wondering how these wealthy individuals dare to get better medical care than the rest of their fellow Americans, but the real question is how dare Americans get better care than someone in Guatemala. We are all human. Borders do not change our shared humanity.

But I am never going to improve the wellbeing of the folks in Guatemala or the United States or anywhere else by living in a hut so that we can all be equal. We cannot poverty ourselves into equality. Just as the wealthy individual who pays for concierge medicine pushes for medical advancements that will one day be available to the masses, the frontier market investor pursues the profits in growing markets, contributing to the development of the countries that are most in need.

If I go where I am treated best – where there are sound investment fundamentals and positive government support for entrepreneurs like me – I am going to do so knowing that my money and my businesses are contributing to the growth and development of these countries. This is how the world advances.

Long-Term Growth

But going where you're treated best does not mean going to frontier markets simply because they need the help. You are obviously looking for something in return. The good news is that the rewards are high for those adventurous enough to explore the world's final frontiers.

The biggest reason why you should look at frontier markets is the potential for long-term growth. Imagine being able to get in on the ground floor in an emerging market like Thailand forty years ago. Between 1970 and 1990, Thailand's GNP quadrupled, per capita income tripled between 1965 and 1995, and the country topped the charts of the fastest growing economies for almost a decade with a peak growth rate of 13.6% in 1988.

While Thailand's economy has slowed down considerably since then, the city of Phnom Penh, Cambodia today is the Bangkok of thirty years ago. Look at Bangkok and compare the markets from the eighties to the more developed markets now. Imagine how many times people have made their money back. Those same opportunities are still available today, but you are more likely to find them in Cambodia than the more developed Thailand.

This all goes back to what we talked about in Chapter Four when we discussed second passports and how they factor into having a 40-year plan. When you start a business in a frontier market, you are investing in the country and its potential long-term growth just as much as you are investing in your company.

Higher Returns

By placing capital where growth is just taking off, you are putting yourself in the perfect position for monumental gains in the future. Even small increases in the standard of living in frontier markets can create serious returns on your investment.

The same thing that makes frontier markets an excellent investment opportunity is the very reason fewer people actually invest: namely, the risk. Because of the risk, there are fewer foreigners on the ground doing research and investing in less developed but rapidly growing economies. This gives those of us with the appetite for a little risk another good reason to invest – less competition and a greater potential for yield.

For example, my friend runs a property fund in Cambodia and can conservatively buy properties in blue-chip areas and get 10-15% rental yields unleveraged. Compare that to somewhere like the UK, the United States, Australia, or God forbid, Switzerland, where you might be looking at low single-digit returns. In a frontier market like Cambodia, you can expect to reap a good double-digit yield while you are waiting for that long-term growth to materialize.

Diversification

Another great benefit of frontier markets is that they are often isolated from the rest of the world, making them less dependent on the global monetary system. Because of this, they are generally immune to global recession and depression.

Cambodia has not had a recession in more than 20 years. In fact, there has not been a single year in the last decade when growth in Cambodia has been less than 7-8%. It has even enjoyed double digit growth. It has been one big growth chart. Skipping the Asian Financial Crisis of the 1990s, the tech bubble of the early 2000s and the Global Financial Crisis of 2008, Cambodia's economy has shrugged off the rest of the world's problems. It even largely avoided the worldwide pandemic of 2020, both in terms of health and economic impact.

So, while frontier markets may be risky by one account, they can also be an important part of a diversified portfolio. An entrepreneur who spreads their risk by placing some capital in overlooked markets that are in their infancy will be better off than those who place all their capital in 'developed' markets that are all susceptible to global financial crises.

Obviously, there are challenges, but if you know what you are doing or have someone who can do it for you, you can enjoy uncorrelated growth even while the rest of the world suffers. In this way, investing in a frontier market may protect some of your investments in a way that a developed market cannot.

Low Competition and High Probabilities of Success

In the West, smart businesses have become all about niche. With so much supply in the market, it can be a death sentence to compete with huge, established players in a large market. In frontier markets, if you can offer affordable products for a market with increasing buying power, opportunity is everywhere.

There is huge potential in these markets precisely because they have very few of the services common to the western world. In some developing countries, the types of businesses that you might take for granted in your home country often do not even exist yet. If there is no pharmacy chain or high-end furniture store, it offers the perfect setting to create your own.

Investing overseas is not just about the real estate investments we discussed in the Chapter Eleven. E-commerce and simple service industries all have a greater chance of succeeding in a market where competition is almost nonexistent. Not only that but without the risk of an economic downturn every seven or eight years, as happens in the West, more businesses can ride out periods of global financial crisis.

When you realize that the frontier and developing markets' penchant for western style affluent living is largely untapped, your list of potential opportunities will grow exponentially. Combine that realization with the simpler processes to many business practices and it is easy to ignite your passion for finding new products and services to market by answering the call of these rapidly increasing economies.

Lower Costs

Another factor adding to your chances of success is the low entry costs for businesses in frontier markets. Rather than developing some complex business plan that may or may not work after investing tons of money (and if it does work, will subject you to huge taxes), you could go to Laos and open a parking lot. Or you could set up a delivery service for products like cosmetics, which cost as much as 70% less in Thailand and are subject to low import duties. You could engage in any number of businesses which you could easily sketch out after observing things for just a few weeks.

Every business I have started began with a small amount of money and a basic concept of improving an existing market. I have never dumped a million bucks into a company because I was 'just sure' it would work. My small investments have brought almost immediate cash-flow and future appreciation. At the end of the day, solving simple, everyday problems in simple ways is what entrepreneurship is all about. I just so happen to believe that it is a lot easier to not only get started and to do business but also to be successful in emerging and frontier economies.

It is easy to start a website these days no matter where you are in the world, but if you are the brick-and-mortar business type, you can set up shop for a heck of lot less in somewhere like Vientiane, Laos than you could in any city in a developed market. Renting office space is also much cheaper in frontier markets compared to western prices. Average prime office space rents per square meter are as low as $21 in the Philippines. Plus, if you want to save on the cost of renting an office, the region is home to some of the best cafés and co-working spaces around.

The lower costs of doing business hold true when it comes to hiring labor, as well. Average manufacturing wages in Vietnam are still just $107 a month; and in countries like Laos, they can be as low as $45 a month. Southeast Asia has a large and growing labor pool, high birth rates and a relatively young population. Countries like Malaysia and the Philippines have highly literate, English-speaking workforces, which is useful not only for someone launching a service-sector company, but also leads to opportunities in complementary industries.

In *The End of Jobs*, Taylor Pearson points out that by 2020, "there will be 40% more 25-34-year-olds with higher education degrees from Argentina, Brazil, China, India, Indonesia, Russia, Saudi Arabia, and South Africa than in all OECD countries." This is just one sign that there are better places to be hiring than in the West. And the fact that you can get better labor for lower prices while also paying those individuals a good wage for the cost of living in the country where they live makes it a win-win situation for everyone involved.

Lifestyle Benefits

As we discussed earlier, there are great lifestyle benefits that come with living overseas. These benefits will not disappear if you decide to set up a location dependent business in a frontier market. The model that many expat entrepreneurs and digital nomads have followed has been to move to Southeast Asia, enjoy the low costs of living and freedom from US income taxes, and make money selling a productized service or other offering to Americans back home over the internet.

This strategy has often included following the *Four-Hour Workweek* model of outsourcing your technical work to people in India, the Philippines or another less developed country. While this model is still an option, those looking for something more ambitious – say, those that might have been attracted to Silicon Valley ten years ago – should consider a business that is not only based in Southeast Asia but markets to its people as well.

You get all the same coconuts and low costs of living, but you are also tapping into one of the highest-potential markets on the planet. More importantly, you do not have to reinvent the wheel to find success in this region of the world. Several of the world's newest and most successful unicorns (companies valued at over $1 billion) are Asian startups that simply copied existing concepts from the West. With a little bit of thought and local knowledge, bringing an American concept to Asia can lead to huge returns. And you can enjoy all the lifestyle perks while you are at it, too.

How to Find the Right Market

There are many different frontier markets and each one has a unique profile. From Ghana, the Ivory Coast, and Namibia in Africa, to Bulgaria, Lithuania, and Latvia in Europe, to Asia and the Middle East, there is no shortage of frontier markets to choose from. One of my favorite frontier markets is Cambodia. I visited Serendipity Beach in Sihanoukville, Cambodia a few years back and spent much of my time talking to expats who came to Cambodia from places like the

United States, Australia, and Canada with a small amount of money and a dream to start their own simple business.

And when I say small amounts of money and simple businesses, that is exactly what I mean. Many started out with as little as $5,000, $10,000 or $15,000 and began businesses like restaurants, guest houses, and bars. And just as Arnaud Curtat and his wife did with The Blue Pumpkin, these expat entrepreneurs also achieved great success. The best news of all, however, is that their success is just the tip of the iceberg of what they can experience down the road. Tourism is going to be a big driver of the Cambodian economy as more people from the western world realize that Cambodia is a great place to visit, and as more people in Asia have disposable income and want to use it to explore.

Cambodia offers a great opportunity to start a simple business now. It is not as prominently on the tourism map yet, but you can enjoy a low cost of living and make good money without a lot of overhead and very few regulations. By getting in now, you can set yourself up to reap bigger rewards down the road.

The country is a great place for an entrepreneur with a sense of adventure to come with a small amount of capital, do something low key, and potentially be very successful. But not all frontier markets are at the threshold of growth and development like Cambodia. Some certainly are, but the right indicators are not always obvious to the everyday businessperson. That said, here are some of the most important trends to look for that indicate the greatest potential for growth and business success.

1. The Fundamentals

Finding the right frontier market largely depends on knowing the fundamentals. If a country has solid fundamentals, it is worth stopping in to look around and get the creative juices flowing to whip up your next business idea. Some of the most important fundamentals to look for include:

- Low Per Capita GDP: Countries with low per capita GDP have room to grow, but the best combination to look for is a country with low per capita GDP where both institutions and the workforce are undergoing a transformation.

- **High Population Growth**: This leads to an ample working-age population, which can give a powerful boost to GDP under the right conditions. One look at a world age chart will tell you everything you need to know. The West is getting older while emerging and frontier markets have population projections that almost perfectly mirror their varying degrees of emerging status.

- **Health**: Good health is essential for growth and productivity. Data on life expectancy can give you a general idea of the overall health of a population. Still, do not completely write off countries with lower life expectancy. Improvements to health and sanitation facilities can greatly improve living conditions and lead to the kind of economic growth that is good for business.

- **Urbanization**: Larger cities can increase productivity in frontier economies because they encourage economies of scale in production and distribution. Companies also benefit from knowledge transfers and a larger, more diverse labor pool.

- **Widespread Tech Usage**: Knowing basic statistics like the number of mobile phone subscribers in a country is vital to future success. The same goes for any type of e-commerce businesses. While in its infancy in many frontier markets, e-commerce has the potential for explosive growth in many areas of the world.

- **Ease of Doing Business**: This is a crucial factor to take into consideration when determining which markets will not only be open to your business but also make life easier when it comes to setting up and running your business. The World Bank's Ease of Doing Business Index is a great place to find information on the business atmosphere in each country, as well as the Heritage Foundation's Index of Economic Freedom.

It is important to take these and other factors into account when choosing where to invest or do business. Setting up shop in a country simply because it is a frontier market can be a very foolish move. South Africa, for example, has great beaches (tourism potential) in Cape Town, but the fundamentals – especially on the government's end – were never in place and the economy has subsequently come crashing down.

Find a combination of a young and growing population, some progress towards development, and governmental understanding of economic freedom and the need to attract talented people. If you can find these fundamentals in one location, you will put yourself in a great position to take advantage of the new economy that is unfolding.

Culture Matters

Many people never consider one essential fundamental: culture. Culture matters. The culture in the West is simply not business friendly. Do you feel that people respect successful businesspeople where you are from? Do you feel that they are accepted as valuable members of your community? If the answer is no, then it might be time for a change.

In many places in the West, businesspeople are disdained as the greedy one percent. But the cultural issues do not stop there. Western culture makes for unattractive hiring conditions too. When I do any freelance hiring and an American and a Venezuelan both apply for the position, asking for the same pay, I am going to hire the Venezuelan because I know that they will take the job more seriously. For one, you are actually paying them a good wage per their cost of living. And because of the rising educational levels around the globe, the quality of work is likely to be very similar.

Americans get upset that Mexicans work for much lower wages but ignore the fact that they live ten to a house in order to live on that wage. It is as if they assume that Americans are entitled to a white picket fence forever... because America. I do not say all of this just to bash on the United States – it has its perks – but it is hard to deny the cultural flaws that make it less attractive to do business and hire workers there. The entitlement culture is largely a phenomenon of the West. You can still find people throughout the rest of the world who are hungry to do great quality work, and without demanding holiday pay, maternity leave, contributions to their retirement, overtime, or unionizing.

And there are plenty of countries where entrepreneurship dominates the culture. Instead of looking down on businesspeople, they welcome them with open arms. Countries like Uganda, 'communist' China and Vietnam, and others like them rank at the top of the entrepreneurship reports. In the meantime, only 12% of folks in the United States plan to open their own business in the next three years. The culture is simply more conducive to success in frontier and emerging markets.

Countries to Watch

So, which countries fit all these parameters? There are quite a few. On a regional level, I personally lean toward both Southeast Asia and Eastern Europe. While the typical raison d'être of digital nomads in Southeast Asia is the cheap cost of living, it is also one of the easiest places in the world to start a business. Though Eastern Europe is also a good place to live, hire, and run a business, Southeast Asia's competitive edge is that it has larger domestic markets.

Companies from Rocket Internet to Lazada have poured into Singapore, Malaysia, Thailand, and even more developing markets like Cambodia. Today, some of these countries represent the hottest commodities in the tech space, from regional e-commerce to SaaS to FinTech and more. In Malaysia, Penang is the hotspot for start-ups. It offers a diverse workforce and a culture far more open to foreign business than Thailand.

Vietnam has a huge domestic market of 92 million people, among the largest in Asia, and its role in the region will likely only increase. Major investment is driving the startup scene there, as is a small incubator and an innovation fair that aims to make Da Nang the 'Innovation Hub by the Sea.' Foreign investment in Vietnam has always seemed to be a long game, so I would not expect overnight success, but Da Nang is on a lot of people's radar.

One of the most interesting trends in recent years has been the lifestyle business scene. Idyllic places like Bali – Ubud and Canggu in particular – have become digital nomad hubs, leading some to call the island 'Silicon Bali.' While much of the growth in Bali has been driven by digital nomads, the impact on Bali's entrepreneur community is now well-formed and it is possible that Ubud could rise from a cheap lifestyle haven for bootstrappers into a startup hub in Indonesia.

If the likes of Vietnam and Indonesia are not adventurous enough for you, Laos is the final frontier market I would recommend considering in Southeast Asia. Just like in Cambodia, the middle class is growing. The mountainous terrain of Laos makes it seem a world apart, as if it were a country that has never been exposed to the outside world, but almost every house in central Vientiane has a motorbike these days. Average wages have gone from paying $100 a month or less to several hundred dollars in just a few years and domestic consumers are spending more money.

The entrepreneur in me sees a lot of opportunity in Laos, in the same way I do in Cambodia. Considering that there are already numerous cafes in Vientiane, along with a few western brands, Laos is not exactly a blank slate, but it is close. Any large-scale business requires good connections. You cannot expect to open a franchise store in Laos without knowing a few people and paying your respects to the government. However, you could start a small business with the intention of growing it throughout the country or throughout the region.

Laos is still a one-party socialist government but, unlike neighboring Myanmar, Laos is much more open to foreigners coming in with small businesses. Whereas being small works in your favor in Laos, you would need to be the size of Coca Cola to enter Myanmar. That means the fundamentals in Myanmar are not quite there yet, while Laos shows potential.

In Eastern Europe, I favor both the Balkans and the Baltics. While Western Europe favors complicated revenue systems with high rates and multiple tax brackets, many Eastern European countries prefer to stick with one low flat tax. The market in some countries in Eastern Europe may be too small to reach a critical mass, but there are some true gems throughout Eastern Europe that I can recommend without hesitation.

Following the collapse of the Soviet Union, many former Soviet states began to embrace pro-business economic policies in an effort to turn things around. Like neighboring Latvia and Lithuania, Estonia is one of the great Baltic success stories. All three Baltic countries offer something different, but Estonia in particular is working hard to cater to businesspeople and was the first country in the region to introduce a flat tax in 1994. Estonia continues to be the clear economic leader in the Balkans and was ranked as the most entrepreneurial country in the European Union according to the World Economic Forum.

In addition to business-friendly laws, Estonia is finding innovative ways to attract capital and preserve freedom, including their e-residency program and zero corporate tax model. It has some of the best offshore banks in the world and its capital, Tallinn, is fast becoming a hub for entrepreneurship. As any Estonian will proudly tell you, Tallinn is where Skype was founded.

The Balkans present an even greater opportunity. It is a very interesting, emerging region. If you want to invest somewhere that is absent the EU but close to European markets, the Balkans will provide you with more area to grow.

Montenegro is very open to business and foreign investors. For entrepreneurs looking to do business on the ground, options are somewhat limited to tourism due to the country's size and small population of only half a million people. But they are very open and eager to do business. Literally, I met with the prime minister's right-hand man to discuss investment promotion. That does not happen in every country I travel to, but you will find that there are a lot of small countries like this with open-door policies.

Macedonia is another good country that is trying very hard to stand out. Geopolitics are making things a little difficult for them, but the country is becoming more and more transparent and attractive for business. Macedonia is very well-located close to other markets where you could expand your business. More importantly, nobody knows that they copied Estonia's deferred tax model that we discussed in Chapter Nine with a corporate tax rate just half of Estonia's at only 10%. Macedonia is a very interesting place, but it is not for every kind of business. It is a small market and it will take some time to see how conflict in the region plays out.

Another great country in the Balkans is Serbia; however, I enjoy living there much more than the idea of running a business in the country. The tax rate is a decent 15%, but I do not see as much potential in Serbia for someone starting a business on the ground. If you are looking to hire, though, Serbia has some of the best talent out there for great prices.

If you want to be in the EU, Romania and Bulgaria are easy to work with. They do not have all the benefits of the countries I just mentioned, but if you want a base in the EU, it is better than doing business in high-tax France. Romania is very pleasant when it comes to doing business, and Bulgaria is very stable and quite progressive with a flat tax rate of 10%.

My favorite frontier market in the region, by far, is one that is often considered to be a part of the Middle East instead of Eastern Europe. The country of Georgia is the kind of place where everything is easy. If you have a big enough idea, they are open to hearing it, there is very little bureaucracy, everyone you deal with in the government and elsewhere is young, and it is easy to get land. Everything is easy. The fees are low, taxes are just 15%, and the government is open and eager to make things happen.

2. Residency Options

Another approach to selecting the country where you will establish a business is to not only consider the fundamentals of the country itself but what the country offers you in return for merely setting up shop and staying in business. Specifically, you can obtain residency in a country in exchange for planting your business on their soil.

Most countries have some type of program by which they grant residency in exchange for your business, especially in Europe. For example, residency in Belgium can be obtained by anyone willing to start a small business there. There are no official requirements, but the most important factor in getting approved is to provide a good business plan, which should usually include hiring at least one part-time employee.

There are more specifics about what they do and do not want. For one, your business should not be set up as an EU company because they want you to specifically be in Belgium. You could also qualify by simply demonstrating significant means to support yourself (usually around €1 million). The cost of setting up a business as an entrepreneur in Belgium is still cheap: €12,400 in paid-up capital, or potentially even less if you have a business partner to go in with you. And while income tax in Belgium is high, capital gains taxes are zero.

Many other countries in Europe have similar programs. I have helped clients obtain a residence permit in Bulgaria by hiring ten people, which enables them to live in the EU and pay 10% tax. Lithuania will grant you residence if you hire just three people and make a small initial contribution to your company in the low-five-figure range.

Portugal's Golden Visa program is, in some ways, even more attractive than Bulgaria's program if you compare the requirement to hire ten people at face value. Portugal has higher taxes, so I would probably just run a staffing agency through the country rather than live there. However, if you prefer to live in Portugal, you can get a visa and pay the higher tax rates.

Other countries are not as explicit about what they want you to do, but they will take you if you can show you have a good business. Ireland is like this and generally all you must do is hire one person. Turkey will give you a passport if you hire 50 people, which I think is a little overpriced, but it is an option. And Macedonia will give you a passport if you hire ten people.

There are several countries outside of Europe that will also give you residency in exchange for starting a business there. Malaysia has a program through which they will give you a residence permit if you have a business that pays enough tax.

Singapore and Hong Kong both have programs, but they are very strict and high-end. You do not have to have as much money to get a permit in Hong Kong as you do in Singapore. Still, Hong Kong may not be the best place to pay taxes (although it is getting better), but if you hire someone you can get a residence permit there.

One place you may have never considered is Colombia. Anyone looking to start a business there can get the added benefit of a second residency in Colombia with as little as $20,000 in capital that you can spend immediately on your company. You can get the residency without hiring locals, but you must demonstrate that something is going on to qualify, and the easiest way to do that is to hire someone. If you have been planning on starting a company or were already planning on investing $20k in your current company, you can deposit that money into a Colombian bank account and then use it to build your business there and qualify for residency.

The interesting thing about considering residency as a factor for where you will set up your business is that many folks often only think along the lines of going to a place with low or even zero tax. However, there may be a place you have not heard of that has an even more attractive option than zero tax like residency or even citizenship in exchange for your business.

3. Fund Someone Else's Business

The final option for someone interested in investing in frontier markets is to invest in someone else's business. If you can provide venture capital, you do not have to start a business on the ground to benefit from the incredible growth in frontier markets. There is plenty of room for improvement in these countries, starting with basic infrastructure such as transportation, banking, and telecommunications.

Many companies have already established themselves in these markets and there is always a need for investment. If you are looking for something less hands-on, there are investment funds that will allow you to invest in these businesses without much hassle. However, if you want more control over the kinds of investments you make and the potential return they will give, here is my fail-proof strategy:

When I go to a new country, I start by hiring a great lawyer. I overpay them. They then introduce me to other people that I need to connect with – real estate agents, developers, government officials, the 'who's who' of the local entrepreneurship scene. My lawyer then helps me figure out how to place job ads and does stuff that even a lawyer usually would not do. He or she becomes my point man.

From there, my lawyer might hire an assistant and together they go out and bring in people with properties and companies. They ferret out the bad ideas and then I talk to the best of the best.

It is as simple as that.

There are even opportunities to purchase great companies at steep discounts in many frontier economies during times of general market weakness.

Another option is to invest in crowd equity funds. In Europe, for example, crowd equity into start-ups has become quite a hot trend, with investment minimums as low as five euros. Companisto, for example, allows you to invest as little as 500 euros into start-ups and growth companies throughout Europe. Originally, the entry point was just five euros! For less than the price of a cheap sandwich, you could invest in companies ranging from craft breweries to beach review websites to security companies.

Some of Companisto's companies have real revenues and a proven track record of making sales, as opposed to much of the fare we see on shows like Shark Tank that have brought on more and more 'pre-revenue' companies as they cleaved toward Hollywood and away from real business.

The Challenges & Risks of Frontier Markets

There are reasons why the entire world has not flooded into frontier market investments yet. They can be very difficult to gain access to and often require being on the ground and figuring things out yourself in an unfamiliar environment.

If you want to trade stocks in Mongolia, you will need to personally visit the country and set up a brokerage account. It is the same deal with real estate. Doing market research in a foreign language, finding contractors in a place where services do not usually meet international standards, or simply finding a grocer to buy the food you want while you are there are all challenges that most people do not want to deal with. That is why there is an opportunity for people like us who are willing to go through with it.

Just looking at the data will not paint a full picture of a place, nor will it prepare you for the various challenges of investing in frontier markets. It takes time to learn the economy's unique commercial environments, estimate the demand for products, and navigate the country's financial and legal infrastructure. There are challenges. There are risks. No great opportunity comes without them.

After years of doing this, I prefer the risks of frontier markets and all things offshore in comparison to the risk of becoming entrenched in systems that no longer work. I would rather be at the forefront of the new economy than following the herd.

Just ask yourself: What else used to be considered risky? In the twentieth century, college was not only considered risky but also something few could obtain. For many, even today, starting a business is considered a risky endeavor. If you are reading this book, chances are you have already reaped many of the rewards for being one of the few to take that risk.

But are you really on the edge of the new economy? Perhaps you feel you have pushed so hard and come so far that you have made your way into an entirely different world of opportunity. And you have because everything that you have done up to this point is risky. But why stop now? Why content yourself with being an entrepreneur in the West when there is more opportunity in the rest of the world?

If you are willing to take on the challenges and risks of frontier market entrepreneurship, there are several tips you can follow to not just reduce the risk of failure but multiply your chances for success:

Tip #1: Be on the Ground

There is nothing as crucial as being on the ground when it comes to doing business in a frontier market. The best and often only way to learn about the opportunities in any given country is not from reading blogs or calling lawyers but from boots-on-the-ground intelligence. You cannot effectively scout out a great business idea without being there in person.

While books like this can serve as a tool to provide guidance, suggest ideas, and point you in the best direction for your interests and risk tolerance, they will not replace seeing an opportunity with your own eyes. Setting foot in a new place gives you the chance to observe trends that are going on there. You can read about these places all you want, but things only really come into focus once you can personally see for yourself what you have been reading about.

A few years back, I helped a friend of mine start a property fund to invest in Cambodian real estate. Though it is very open to foreigners, Cambodia presents some of the typical challenges you will find in frontier markets. My friend started his business riding around on his motorbike looking for deals that were not available publicly. He learned the Khmer language for 'for sale' and would write down the phone numbers from the signs he would find. Then, he hired a local assistant to call the phone numbers. It was not glamorous at all. It was not the sort of work you learned about in the ivory tower of a business school, but it was exactly what needed to be done.

Once he found a property, payment was made in cash and fingerprints were taken at the local town hall (which is like a hut) to seal the deal. More often than not, frontier markets will require this level of hands-on work.

Tip #2: Network & Have a Foreign Business Partner

One step you can take to both improve your chance of success and reduce the amount of work you must do on the ground is to network and find a foreign business partner. I have always focused on creating a strong network of locals who know the ins-and-outs of deal making in their specific market.

Local associates substantially decrease your risk of being 'ripped off' and increase your chances of finding the best deals. If you want to hire someone for help, plan on overpaying a little bit. It will make a world of difference, especially if you are employing the help of an English language person working on the ground.

It also helps to have a foreign business partner. You can have the best business idea in the world, but if you cannot execute on it, it will not matter. You will still need to do your own work scouting out the country, especially since it is hard to find a local business partner sitting at home on the couch. Many countries make it plenty easy to start a business on your own. However, dealing with government interference and adapting to the culture can be done with greater ease by finding the right partners for your business.

Tip #3: Adapt Your Culture and Improve on Local Culture

When it comes to doing anything offshore, there is a delicate balance between the culture and ideas you bring with you and the culture, practices, and ideas that you will find along the way.

The importance of finding this balance applies to frontier market entrepreneurship as much as it does to investing, living, banking, and everything else offshore. In fact, it is so key that the following chapter is entirely dedicated to dissecting the key components of this balancing act.

Tip #4: Understand the Government's Hot Buttons

Finally, if you are going to do business in foreign countries, it is important to understand the government's hot buttons. I have lost track of how many different countries I have gotten the tip to stay under the radar. Running a quiet business that grows over time is fine. Running a crazy, in-your-face business... not so good.

Just because there are far fewer rules in frontier markets than in your home country does not mean that there are no rules at all. To navigate your way through those rules, it helps to follow all the tips we have already covered here. You have to do your research, put in time on the ground, and preferably involve a local in your business. Even frontier market governments have their limits.

When It Is No Longer Risky, It Is Too Late

To me, the most exciting thing about frontier markets is that things are happening all the time. After years of running offshore businesses and making overseas investments, the air is still as fresh as ever. Frontier markets are exciting. As unemployment and underemployment become a fact of life in the developed world, it may not be long before entrepreneurship becomes a means of survival worldwide. The lesson to be taken here is that you should take steps now to start growing a business and to protect your wealth while you are still ahead of the impending pack.

Frontier market investing is not for everyone. There are two types of people who are suited to this type of high-risk investing: someone with a large amount of risk capital or a young person who has nothing to lose. For the average person looking to invest in a frontier market – someone who is not really that adventurous and who is a bit freaked out about the risks and the chances of getting ripped off – you should probably just have someone handle it for you, to be honest. My recommendation: consider investment funds.

If you are anything like me, though, just do it. Figure out what level of risk (and adventure) you are willing to take on before deciding to invest in frontier markets and then go for it. Just know that by the time this stuff is no longer considered risky by the rest of the world, it will be too late to invest.

Five years ago, I was in Singapore looking into the EntrePass residency program offered there for folks planning to start a business in the country. One person I spoke to let me in on a little secret and said that one of the things the Singapore officials really loved to see were restaurants. Inspired by the story of The Blue Pumpkin, I asked out of curiosity if opening an ice cream shop would be the right fit.

The answer? They would love it.

I was not really looking to start an ice cream business in Singapore, so I let the opportunity go. About a year later, the Singapore government changed the laws of the EntrePass program; they no longer accept folks with business plans for low-end, small business ideas. All they want now is big businesses, making it extremely difficult to get into Singapore. The moment was there, and then it was gone.

Singapore was not necessarily a frontier market five years ago, but the opportunity illustrates the principles of successful frontier market entrepreneurship: it is frontier because the time is limited. There are business opportunities and flags out there, but you have to hurry to fully take advantage of them.

Maybe you do not want to start an ice cream parlor or sell cosmetics in Laos, but there is always an opportunity for you to do something, somewhere. The world is advancing, and markets are growing and developing across the globe. This is great news for the folks who want to be a part of that development and help bring it about. It can present some challenges and risks, but when the risk is gone, so are the rewards.

Your How-To Action Plan

Immediate Action Steps: If you are not already overseas, you can start by looking at your existing business (or business ideas) and finding where the demand for what you offer is high but supply is lacking. You can also research countries that offer entrepreneur visas where you could move your existing business in exchange for residence or even citizenship.

Travel Action Steps: Once you are on the ground, it will be much easier to identify and carry out business ideas in local markets. You can start your own business or follow my instructions in this chapter to create a network within the country to fund someone else's business. Feel free to start with the countries I have mentioned that sound the most interesting and promising to you and go from there.

Holistic Planning: Always remember to balance opportunities to do business and plant flags with the tax implications of every jurisdiction. If you can get residence in a country for starting a business there but you will have to pay high corporate taxes or will be roped into paying personal income tax as well, you will likely want to forego the opportunity in search of something that better fits your holistic goals.

Chapter Fourteen: Conquering Dogma

The Pigeons Don't Speak English

Dateline: Wroclaw, Poland

My first visit to the charming city of Wroclaw was very ill-timed. In a deeply Catholic country that values family as Poland does, visiting in the shoulder month of April when temperatures are still chilly and the students empty out of town for Holy Week meant that I spent the Friday before Easter finishing work in my apartment before going into the town's almost abandoned Rynek, the central market square.

Owing to the mass exodus of students who made up a large part of the city's population returning home to their villages, many of the restaurants in touristy Rynek had shuttered. My best choice for my first meal of the day was a small kebab shop with no room to sit inside. Taking a seat at the wooden table amidst the cool gusts outside, I retrieved my shawarma and began to indulge in my meal. Before I knew it, two pigeons descended on my food with a vengeance. On any other day, they would have had a wide selection of diners to disturb in hopes of a meal to peck away at, but today, I was their only hope.

As I began to shoo the pigeons away with my hands, an older man in a fedora walked through Rynek heading in the direction of the kebab shop.

"Go away, pigeons!" I bellowed as he slowly sauntered by. Then, the elderly man stopped. "The pigeons here don't speak

English," he said calmly before continuing into the shop and placing an order.

His comment stopped me long enough to end my frenzied battle with the pigeons and consider what he had meant. It was a needed reminder that I was not immune to one of the great mistakes that nomads of every kind commit while abroad: cultural isolation. All too often, despite being physically present in the world, we create a bubble around ourselves based on our own experiences and comforts, essentially isolating ourselves within the culture we left behind and preventing ourselves from learning anything valuable from the people and places in our immediate surroundings.

As a result, we tend to dismiss the experiences of others and the way things are done by people and cultures that are different from our own. We do not do it because we intend to be mean but because it is easy and comfortable to live in a state of what we know. But as with most things, living inside our comfort zone leaves us little room to grow.

My dismissing of Wroclaw's pigeons in English is a simple example of how we operate in that bubble. After all, if the pigeons spoke any language, it should have been Polish. If I were to banish them from the proximity of my meal, I should have howled "idź stąd!" or, in the event they were older pigeons from Wroclaw's days as part of Germany, "geh weg!" Why would I think pigeons in Poland would speak English? While Wroclaw is home to as many as ten universities with students of varying English proficiency levels, few sexagenarians in Poland (or pigeons, for that matter) speak any English at all.

All too many of us assume that the rest of the world operates in the same way we do, whether we expect everyone to speak English, be on time to everything, or have great customer service. But giving in to the temptation to do or demand what is culturally comfortable for us will only hinder our results when seeking better opportunities in unfamiliar territory. So, how do we overcome the temptation? Start by getting out the door.

One of the chief benefits I have gained through the Nomad Capitalist lifestyle is a sense of reflection that is hard to get anywhere else. Living far away from the cultural surroundings of home can be the beginning of beneficial reflection and help to shatter limiting beliefs.

One example of this is how my western belief concerning car ownership changed after living overseas. If you live in a western country, you no doubt own a car. Who doesn't, right? The US, Canada, and Australia are all car-happy to the point that it takes a lot to stand up and say that you do not need one. It is even worse when you consider that these countries have limited public transportation options, with taxis and Ubers costing a small fortune.

I enjoyed driving a Mercedes around before I left the US, but I never owned a car during the time that I spent traveling from hotel to hotel, giant Tumi suitcase in tow. When I set up a base in Kuala Lumpur, my local friends asked me if I was going to buy a car. I had not even thought about it until they asked. When I left the United States and stepped into 'Nomad mode,' I never felt the need. Cars are depreciating assets, they require upkeep, and occasionally you bang your side mirror on the garage door. Who wants to own a car?

If you live in one place, you may imagine that life without a car would make you as lowly as the maligned maid taking the bus. However, something magical happens when you break free from the dogma of living where you come from. You abandon what does not serve you and begin to focus on what does. For someone living the Nomad Capitalist lifestyle, living without a car can be a simple way of not only going where you're treated best, but also doing what treats you best.

Doing what treats you best does not mean that you are forbidden from living inside your own little bubble from time to time when you travel. I would be lying if I told you that I have become fluent in Malaysian culture while living in Kuala Lumpur. KL has served as a place to live as a base, not somewhere to invest in real estate, start my next company, or hire the best and brightest talent at reasonable prices. Because of my specific needs, and because most people in Kuala Lumpur's center speak very passable English, I have never fully acclimated to the local culture.

I understand that your move to Montenegro may be more a vote in favor of beautiful beaches and low taxes than it is a desire to learn the Crmnički Oro. You do not necessarily have to assimilate into a new culture everywhere you go. Perpetual travelers would face quite the challenge if they tried to learn the language and culture of every different country that they spent time in.

However, some of the best advice I was ever given very early on in my travels was to avoid being dogmatic – in other words, to avoid the assumption that the way things are done in another country are inferior to what you are used to. In many cases, sticking to what you think is the right way of doing things will not get you the results you want or expect. You will not be doing what treats you best.

Adapting Your Approach and Expectations

I see this principle manifested in business on a regular basis. Recently, I was helping a guy named Jack negotiate the purchase of some rental properties in Tbilisi, Georgia. Jack arrived from London ready to wheel and deal. At our first visit with a seller, he was ready to make an offer. "$39,000," he told my assistant who was translating. The seller, who was asking $50,000 for the newly renovated property, was taken aback. In Georgia, like many other countries, making quick lowball offers is not the way to get deals done. And Jack's more aggressive style was not helping anything, either. Acting like Kevin O'Leary batting down a startup's valuation may work in the West, but it does not work in countries used to a more personal touch.

That does not mean that you cannot make lowball offers in these countries. I have shaved off quite a bit from many asking prices, but it requires a certain finesse. Admittedly, finesse is not my forte – I am just as inclined as Jack to bark out a number and beat the seller down until a deal is done. That is why I employ translators and lawyers to help me operate within the system that they understand.

Despite my early efforts to tell my lawyers and assistants to 'be more aggressive' on certain deals, they knew better than I did and worked within the local culture. They knew how the deals could be made successfully. And they always came through for me. For example, I once saved nearly 30% on a property in Georgia by not only having one of my assistants call to negotiate the deal in Georgian but also by having my lawyer call and make a much more serious presentation. The deal was seamless, and I saved a five-figure sum as a result of entrusting the process to professionals who understood the local culture.

We all have our way to negotiate, but sometimes it is better to admit that we do not fit the local culture and accept that we either need to change our style or let someone else handle things for us.

Adapting your approach and expectations can also help you find deals, not just make them. For example, while it is the main method used in the West, turning to the internet to research real estate for sale in foreign countries is usually a terrible way to find potential properties in many emerging and frontier markets. While helping a friend find land for sale in rural Ecuador a few years ago, we came across a website with a wide variety of appealing listings. Upon calling the firm, we discovered several setbacks.

The first was that no one at the firm spoke English. My friend was somewhat surprised that in Ecuador – official language: Spanish – nobody spoke English. The assumption that we would find eager professionals waiting to serve us in our native tongue did not hold up. Since Spanish is a widely spoken language, I have found that many Latin Americans rely on doing business within the world of their fellow Spanish speakers; no need to learn English when there are enough native speakers of your own language to keep food on the table. You probably do the same with English – are you busy learning Russian, or are you happy to keep your interactions to your native tongue?

The second and more difficult issue was that the listings of interest had been sold four years earlier. Yes, my employee and I were speaking in our patchwork Spanish to a real estate agent who had not updated their website in four years. If this were anywhere in the West, agents would be freaking out if their Zillow, Trulia, and Hotpads were not updated in the last four hours.

You could get upset with a situation like this and walk away, or you could let go of your dogma and adapt to the situation as it is. In our case, we realized that the very fact that no one at the company spoke English and that the site had not been updated meant that the prices for the properties that were available would be lower than on websites targeted to an English audience expecting a pretty website and perfect English.

Ecuador may not have been the easiest country to navigate for real estate, but it made for a great place to invest in a developing real estate market at entry-level prices. If you are willing to deal with issues like this that you will not likely run into at home, you will open yourself up to possibilities that are not even available where you are from.

Becoming a Global Citizen

If you think your country does everything perfectly, you will never leave. Why would you? Just as we are conditioned to go where we are comfortable and not where we are treated best, we are indoctrinated into believing that everything we need is at home. The danger of this belief is that it keeps us from growing and attaining greater freedom, both personally and financially.

I recently met with a couple in Mexico that had come from Colorado in the United States to check out Merida as a potential new international base. Kathy and Nate loved the area, they were enchanted by the city, and they felt that the whole region was a truly hidden gem of Mexico. Merida has free Wi-Fi on its main streets, everything is being renovated, and the beauty of the city is unparalleled.

Nate was ready to move there that instant, but Kathy was unsure. She loved the area just as much as her husband, but she had several concerns that she did not hesitate to voice.

"What about the kids with school?" She began. "And how are we going to make friends?"

I was about to answer when she continued to list her concerns, "And what if I can't find someone to replace my hairdresser? I'm sure no one here is as good as Kim. And where am I going to get my organic kale? I'm not going to go to Walmart, and I doubt I can really find good quality kale at the street markets."

I wasn't sure how to respond anymore. Kathy's concerns reflected the mindset of many of the people who come to me for help who are focusing on all the wrong issues. The answer to her quandaries was not to point her in the direction of a good hairdresser.

"I understand that you have concerns, Kathy," I began. "But I have to be honest with you, you are not going to be able to walk into everything being perfectly figured out. You may have to test out a few new hairdressers. Nothing is going to be solved overnight, but that shouldn't hold you two back from making a change for the better."

I do not know if I adequately assuaged Kathy's concerns or just managed to step on her toes, but perhaps I can help resolve some of your concerns. It is easy for many of us to recognize that our lives are not exactly perfect at the moment, but it is much harder for us to make a change if we cannot see that the future will be perfect. We tie ourselves to a mindset in which it is better to accept where we are, as unhappy as we may be, than to take a chance on a future that is uncertain, even if it is certainly much better.

But the future does not have to be perfect to be better. And you cannot expect to be perfect at living abroad when you begin an international life, anyway. You cannot expect to just step into an entirely new way of life without a few hiccups. You can start out like Kathy and Nate with all your worries and cultural preferences and little by little you will become more of a global citizen.

For instance, every British guy I know seems to speak English wherever they go. They could be in Brazil where people clearly speak Portuguese and rarely speak English, and yet they will insist on speaking in English and expect that everyone else will understand. As annoying as that is, it is okay for you to be that person when you start out. Do not let that keep you from going. The point is to change as you go. You are going to find your sea legs and you will figure out where you want to be, learn the language, get accustomed to the culture, and take on whatever challenge comes next.

There is no need to think in black and white as if your only options are to be a homebody or an expat. You do not have to fully be one or the other. And you certainly do not have to be a full-blown global citizen to understand that not everyone is going to speak English or do things the way that you expect them to be done. It is easy to paint life abroad as a walk in the park and to see things in black and white, expecting high costs of living and high taxes in your home country, and total and complete freedom elsewhere. The truth is, there are costs to living overseas.

There are always costs.

When my friend first visited me in Malaysia, she made the startling discovery that strawberries at Kuala Lumpur's western-friendly grocery stores cost at least 1,000% more than they did in her native Europe. When her friends came to visit, it became a source of amusement to send them to go buy strawberries at the market just to see their sticker shock.

For some Nomad Capitalist hopefuls, the high price of strawberries could be a terrible disappointment. But there are other ways to view the situation. While they do not grow strawberries in Malaysia, they do have papaya, melons, coconuts, dragon fruit, jackfruit, and more. Is it a bad thing that you now have the opportunity to try papaya and beautiful limes and dragon fruit and pineapple and coconuts, but have to sacrifice strawberries?

More importantly, are you going to sacrifice half a million dollars in taxes more than you would like to pay just so you can eat cheap strawberries? With all the money that you will save on taxes, you will be more than able to afford the strawberries at twelve times the price you are used to... if they are really that important to you. But you could also just adapt to the dragon fruit. Why spend your time fretting over expensive strawberries when you could be enjoying the great variety and abundance in the world?

For me, these differences are part of what makes global citizenship so enjoyable. When Europe is frozen over, it feels great to be in Southeast Asia eating tropical fruits and shopping at modern malls. By the time summer rolls around, the urge for something different kicks in. You can use the need to adapt to your advantage and get your fill of different local foods, experiences, and places. You can explore new and exciting things and save thousands of dollars in taxes.

Not every experience or place will be exactly what you expect, but that is part of the adventure. And if you are going to successfully adapt to the Nomad life and embrace your new global citizenship, you will eventually have to face the reality that it will be a bit of an adventure from time to time. You will be living somewhere that is different from what you are used to. I do believe that the quality of life in most places will rise over time, but for now, you will need to learn to adapt if you want to thrive overseas.

Are You Coming Out Ahead?

If you are really worried about the language or the amenities, you can always move to Dubai or any English-speaking country. Many older people move to Belize for the beaches and the fact that they speak English there and they will not need to learn a new language. You could also move to countries like Malaysia, Singapore, or Hong Kong where English is common and modern infrastructure and amenities are above and beyond much of what you will find back home. You can wade into the Nomad Capitalist lifestyle in any of these locations and start by going where you feel comfortable.

This then begs the question: What makes you feel comfortable? What do you value? Do you want the language or the strawberries, warm weather, or a big city? I have joked for years when people ask me if I miss the United States by telling them that occasionally I like clean tap water or free refills on soft drinks. Sure, there are some places that I travel to where it is annoying to pay five euros for a bottle of water or the service is lacking or the people are too rigid or too slow, but I value other things more for me to give up on the entire lifestyle just to get free refills.

I have also found that many places outperform the US on every single one of those amenities and services. The best service I have ever received was in a boutique in Mexico City. The staff spoke perfect English and they were helpful, knowledgeable, and altogether on the ball. Dogma would have dictated a different expectation. So, while you may not find things exactly the way they are where you are from, there is a good chance that you can find something similar or even better by traveling to new destinations.

An even more important question to ask is, are you coming out ahead? So many people get stuck in a rut because they fail to see the potential that lies beyond the horizon. Whether they stick with a job they hate or stay in a country that they believe has taken away their freedoms, it is easy for them to justify inaction by assuming that it cannot get any better – even if they really know that it can.

I know from experience that it can get better. Between visiting dozens of countries to get the scoop on investment, business, and expat opportunities, my travels allow me to spend time relaxing in some of the most beautiful places on earth. I can sip on guava juice for all of $0.25 and spend the afternoon strolling through one of the world's best shopping districts. My work allows me flexibility, fulfillment, and freedom. From my perspective, I am coming out way ahead.

You will have to ask yourself the same question, but in most cases, the answer will be yes. It just takes having the right mindset to see it.

Adjusting Your Mindset

If you are sitting in your home country thinking that it is the best country in the world but have only ever traveled to a handful of other countries, you are probably not qualified to become the authority on what makes a country the best. And if you stick to that mindset, you will never discover the place that really is the best for you.

It is the same paradox that occurs in countries like the United States that are so busy believing that they are the greatest country in the world that they fail to realize that other countries are doing things ten times better than they are. Why follow the example of other countries and improve things if you are already the best? It is no wonder that 'pride comes before the fall' because it keeps you from seeing what you need to fix.

Several years ago, the comedian and political commentator Bill Maher argued that the US had to stop bragging that it was the greatest country on earth and start acting like it. He recognized that the US had done many great things, but then asked what America had done for itself lately. When the US is number fifty-five in one category and ninety-two in another, it looks a little silly to keep waving the big foam 'number one' finger and pretending that it is 1955 when the US was number one in everything.

He then pointed to an ad campaign at the time that promoted decreasing US dependence on oil by using alternative fuels. At the end of the add, Bill Clinton made an appearance to say, "If Brazil can do it, America can, too!" In response, Maher asks, "Since when did America have to buck itself up by saying we could catch up to Brazil? We invented the airplane and the lightbulb, they invented the bikini wax, and now they're ahead?... As long as we believe being 'the greatest country in the world' is a birthright, we'll keep coasting on the achievements of earlier generations, and we'll keep losing the moral high ground."

If you insist on maintaining the dogma that the US or the UK or Australia or wherever you are from is the greatest in the world, you will lose more than the moral high ground. You will miss the opportunities that are all around you, whether you stay at home or decide to travel the world. You could travel to every country on the planet, but if your mindset stays at home, you will miss the boat toward greater progress and freedom.

It is the countries (and people) that recognize that they have room for improvement that achieve some of the greatest advancements. The country of Georgia, for example, is the first country in the world to be putting its real estate on the blockchain. They innovate because they know that they have to do something interesting and different to stand out and make a name for themselves. You want to find countries that are a bit self-conscious like that because they are more responsive to opportunities to change and improve. In a sense, you need to be the same way when it comes to your personal mindset toward growth.

Business Dogma

If you can combine an open personal mindset with a country that has an open mindset as well, you are well on your way to going where you're treated best. Take, for example, doing business in Vietnam. Unlike other more insular Asian cultures, Vietnam is aware of its smaller size and has a willingness to work with foreigners. Compared to China or even Japan, where tightly connected family networks run highly insulated business networks that no blond guy with blue eyes could ever penetrate, many Vietnamese prefer to work with foreigners over locals.

But just because Vietnam is open to foreigners does not mean that you can expect to do business exactly how you think it should be done. You have to be open to change as well. Like any other foreign culture, leaving your notions of how things 'should be' at home is essential. You can run an online or location independent business with no hassle, but if you open a cupcake shop, you will likely have to pay homage to a few local authorities. It will not necessarily be expensive, but it will be a part of doing business. Vietnam is open to foreigners, but you still need to be open to doing things the way they are done in Vietnam.

Even if you do not start a business on the ground somewhere, it has become increasingly important to learn how to work with individuals from other cultures as online businesses turn toward hiring virtual assistants overseas. The lower costs are just one reason many entrepreneurs look to places like the Philippines to hire VAs, but I have also heard plenty of people complain about the quality of work completed by the foreign VAs they have hired.

While there is always a chance that you just hired someone who is incredibly incompetent and lazy, my first suspicion when someone complains about an individual who they hired is that misunderstood cultural differences are at the root of the problem. My friend who lambasted Filipino workers may not understand the Filipino culture of micro-management. For the most part, there is no such thing as autonomy when tasks are handed out to workers in the Philippines. Bosses sit on employees at every turn. And that means employees have been trained to wait for assignments every step of the way.

If you are not interested in micro-managing people, then the Philippines may not the best place for you to hire, but that does not mean that it is not the right fit for another business or that Filipinos are lazy and incompetent – just different. And that kind of different may even be perfect for you if you can learn to adapt to the work culture. Wherever you go, learn to respect the culture and make an effort to understand how it works outside of the normal business culture you are used to. You may learn a thing or two.

More Reasons to Stay

Whether you are doing business in Vietnam, hiring VAs in the Philippines, buying real estate in Ecuador, or adapting to the local culture, the counsel to avoid being dogmatic affects everything in the Nomad Capitalist lifestyle. Adapting is essential as trends, laws, and attitudes change every day. I once advised against obtaining citizenship by investment in a country where I am now a citizen. As circumstances changed and I was presented with more facts, the bad economic citizenship turned into my perfect solution.

Narrow-minded views of the world are everywhere, even in today's globalized era. The western media is littered with stereotypes about 'third-world countries' and how bad it would be to live there. We have all seen images of children begging in the streets on dusty roads in Central America or Africa. I even saw a TV drama on a flight once where the main character threatened to send his rival's daughter from the US back to Bucharest, Romania to get what he wanted. Oh, the horror of being sent to a charming city in a country that is part of the European Union!

However ignorant the West may be about the rest of the world, you can still use such ignorance to your advantage. While all your friends and colleagues are crawling over each other to get VC funding for their 'pre-revenue' app that is likely to fail, you can go another direction. Instead of fighting for a small piece of the cake, take advantage of the largely untapped emerging and frontier markets to stake your claim and build a legacy.

The world's emerging markets are crying out for more options, better service, faster fulfillment, and greater product selection. Consider starting and basing a business overseas. It will give you the flexibility to live cheaply, hire affordable labor, potentially save on taxes, and tap into fast-growing markets. True, you will need to learn about your new local culture and there will be a period of adjustment, but if I can handle it, so can you.

Do not assume that another country is 'worse' than where you come from just because they do things differently. Learn to adapt and let the inessentials go. I understand that living overseas may not be what you think or expect it to be, but if you make the leap, I promise that you will find more and more reasons to continue the Nomad Capitalist lifestyle as you go.

You are likely to find that the reasons you have for leaving today will change with time as well. When I first began traveling and exploring with greater intensity, I watched the movie, Up in the Air and it sparked something in me. George Clooney's character flew 350,000 miles each year around the United States to fire people. The 322 days that he spent in seat 2C were only offset by '43 miserable days at home.' I told my friends that I wanted more travel like that in my life.

And that is exactly what I did as I moved my life completely out of the United States and pursued a life of perpetual travel for many years. However, I recently watched Up in the Air again and I found myself with an entirely new perspective of the movie all these years later. The movie's screenplay took four years to write and reflected the writer's changing attitudes toward life and love, and the same thing had happened to me. Watching this move again after so many life changes made me realize that no amount of glamour or wealth or adventure is worth a life whose chief accomplishment is the collection of hotel statuses, airline miles, or meaningless countries on a list.

But as I have flown across the world and accumulated hotel statuses and airline miles, I have also developed friendships with people I have met along the way and relationships with the people I work with and help. I have found places that feel like home to me more than anywhere I have ever been. I have learned from other cultures, grown as an individual, and been inspired by the people in my life to continue fighting for a truer sense of home and the relationships that count.

And just as I have found more reasons to continue the Nomad Capitalist life, I have also found ways to adapt to those new needs and desires. You are going to find reasons to continue doing what you are doing as well. And, even if you do speak to the pigeons in English when you start out, you will get better at it as you go. But you will only become more of a global citizen and less dogmatic once you get yourself out the door and begin to travel and realize all that the world has to offer.

Your How-To Action Plan

Immediate Action Steps: Not everything is going to be perfect, and you may need to adapt to certain aspects of life overseas. Do not let that keep you from starting. You will figure things out along the way and come out ahead in the end.

Travel Action Steps: Learn from the people and places you visit throughout your travels. If something is done differently than what you are used to, do not be dogmatic and assume that your way is the only right way of doing things. You can contribute to and improve the places where you go but they can also inspire and help you grow.

Holistic Planning: You could create the perfect offshore plan, but if you are not willing to adjust your mindset, you may never bring that plan to life. If you find yourself struggling with the culture or frustrated with the way things are done somewhere, remind yourself why you chose this life in the first place. If you are coming out ahead, a few discomforts that push you to grow and adapt should be worth the reward.

TAKING ACTION

Chapter Fifteen: The Nomad Mindset

8 Ways to Activate the Life of Your Dreams

Dateline: Cancun, Mexico

For three years, Nomad Capitalist hosted an annual conference called Passport to Freedom, with keynote speakers like Peter Schiff and Jim Rickards and a host of offshore experts. But in January 2016, I stood on the stage in Cancun and announced that I was done.

Our theme for the conference, I told the audience, was 'abundance,' the idea that taking action alone was not enough. Coming to conferences every year, only to do nothing and then return for the next party was certainly not enough. We had to act abundantly and with purpose, willing to invest what was required to accomplish our goals. I had decided that I was no longer going to enable what I called 'faux action taking' by hosting conferences.

I had a lot of fun getting together with a big group each year to discuss the stuff you have read about. However, too many people would pay for their ticket every year, fly down to Mexico for a few days, hear some speeches, commiserate with other freedom seekers, and then go home... to do nothing. One lady attended all three conferences before she asked me where to get the paperwork to open her offshore bank account, a process that would have taken her a matter of days... had it been done two years earlier. Knowledge without action is meaningless.

That is why I was only willing to revive the conference years later as Nomad Capitalist Live when I was confident that we could help those who were ready to act as part of the conference experience. When my team members were inundated with a steady stream of people ready to take action at the end of the conference, I knew we had found the solution. I do not share my experiences and understanding of the offshore world for mere entertainment. I want you to be able to use that information to make meaningful change in your life.

So, how do you start implementing these strategies? It all starts with the right mindset. Mindset comprises the vast majority of what it takes to successfully execute your own Nomad Capitalist lifestyle. It is possible to achieve success in the offshore world with the wrong mindset, just as it is possible to find a life partner while being bitter or become a successful salesman while being dishonest. However, you will have a lot harder time getting there and may be dissatisfied with the result.

I started out like most people in the offshore world, chasing shiny objects and doing things that made me feel like I was taking action, yet never yielded any real results. Throughout the years, I went from making phone calls, reading articles, and doing excessive research – all while clinging to my pennies – to opening up and getting stuff done in a positive way. From experience, the satisfaction of getting things done feels great and not only inspires more action but answers many of the questions that cannot be answered fully until you stop thinking and start doing. Here is what worked for me.

1. Have a Growth Mindset

In the excellent book, Mindset: Changing a Fixed Mindset into a Growth Mindset, N. Louis Easton explains why brains and talent do not necessarily bring success, and how keeping a 'growth mindset' can help you greatly enhance your results in whatever you do.

The idea is this: in a fixed mindset, we believe our intelligence or talent are fixed traits unable to be changed. We are happy to have them but may have a tendency to use them to delude ourselves. We spend our time keeping tabs on our talent and intelligence rather than developing them, believing that merely possessing these traits makes us better equipped to achieve success and the life we want.

Easton suggests that this mindset is the wrong way to look at things, suggesting that focusing on 'how smart we are' is a trap that holds us back. In the context of Nomad Capitalists, this often manifests itself in people talking about all the suckers still paying taxes, or still banking in their home country, or still investing in real estate at home.

"They don't even know that there's a huge bubble about to break. They're sheep! They're drinking the Kool-aid!" These are the retorts I have overheard at offshore conferences by perfectly pleasant, well-meaning people excited that they are at least several steps ahead of the rest of society that has yet to catch up to the realizations they have made.

Those other people who have yet to 'figure it out' do not matter. Only you matter. What they think and how they live is a reflection of exactly where they want to be. Ask them why the Federal Reserve has not raised interest rates and they may reply with a blank stare because they have made the decision not to worry about it. And that decision is none of our business.

One of the hardest but most rewarding things I have done is to let others and their opinions be. You are not likely to change hearts and minds, nor is it your job to. As compelling as it may be to try to convince our friends to stop investing in that 'bubble' real estate market, or get your parents to move overseas with you, they have to make the decision on their own.

When we apply a fixed mindset, it appears that we need others to agree with us to prove that we are right. For instance, my parents extolled the virtue of going where you're treated best throughout my life, but they never moved out of the United States. They ultimately did what was best for them, and that is just fine. Nothing about their decision makes my beliefs any less valid or any less real.

In other words, before making the Nomad Capitalist lifestyle a cause you promote, it must be a cause you live. Once you apply it in your life, you will find the peace to allow others to live theirs. Not everyone will share your vision or even agree with what you do; that is for them to decide.

There is something about those of us who want to buck the system that makes us different. We refuse to live by others' rules, preferring instead to live on our own terms. We tend to stay ahead of the curve on everything from location independent businesses to frequent flyer miles. In our world, life is one big thing to be 'hacked.' However, this can sometimes come to a point where the idea of 'this-or-that hacking' seems to have gone too far.

What is wrong with the idea of beating to our own drum? Nothing... until it impacts our ego. It is so easy to get wrapped up in the idea that we have cracked the code on life that we spend our time defending our beliefs to others when there is no need to. Feeling superior to others who have not reached your level will only hold you back.

That is why I argue for a carefully curated network of friends while living this unique lifestyle; it is important to have people who understand your lifestyle but also to ensure that you do not fall into the trap of only hanging out with expats who insult the local culture in a dogmatic way, or angry grudge-bearing libertarians who only complain about the system instead of constantly improving themselves.

2. Have an Abundance Mindset

The Four-Hour Workweek and the countless digital nomad blogs inspired by it have popularized the idea that traveling the world can be done on the cheap. Travel hacking, geoarbitrage, and a host of other strategies have been designed to help you live a life of travel. I love those strategies and have used many of them.

As much as I appreciate the finer things, I still shudder when I think back to the $800-a-night hotel room in Vancouver or the $37 hamburger in Monaco. We all get a thrill out of a room upgrade at a hotel, or free airport lounge access from our credit card. However, it has become difficult to know when you need to hire a professional to handle your offshore needs. It has become easier than ever to live the multi-millionaire lifestyle without being a multi-millionaire, but you still need to be thinking like a multi-millionaire, and that means not cheaping out where it counts.

That is why I like to call the Nomad Capitalist lifestyle Four Hour Workweek 2.0. If Tim Ferriss' sage advice on how to start and scale a muse business was the first step, then going where you're treated best is the second step. You do not get an offshore company for your first muse; you get an offshore company once your muse is established and you cannot stand paying that $47,000 in taxes any longer.

As a Nomad Capitalist, nothing you do should be average. That does not mean everything has to be expensive. As my friend and marketing guru Matt Dubiel says, "Avoid the middle." If you own a car, get the beat-up truck or the purring new BMW. Do not get stuck in the middle. When you live the Nomad Capitalist lifestyle, you can choose from tasty pad thai in Hua Hin, Thailand for $1, or Sichuan lobster medallion at Hutong in Hong Kong for $250.

I have found a nice blend of my taste for luxury and generic cheapness by setting my average hotel price at a goal of $250 per night. That is enough to get me into the nicest hotels in most cities whose name is not 'London' or 'Vancouver,' while allowing wiggle room in other cities. The Ritz-Carlton, The Majestic, or The Shangri-La in Kuala Lumpur will run you as little as $100, which leaves you room to splurge on other nights at the London Edition, or the Gresham Palace in Budapest, or the penthouse suite at Wynn Macau.

While there are some perfectly comfortable three-star hotel chains (Ibis comes to mind), my suggestion is to stay at nicer hotels or Airbnbs that you will not want to leave. Working from cafes and other digital nomad hangouts has a tendency to make you feel rushed in many situations, and bouncing from one Starbucks to another is not exactly productive. Test it out and see if you can notice the difference. Being a Nomad Capitalist is all about high performance – the old 'work hard, play hard' – and if you are earning the kind of money where the tax savings can add up to real money, you can afford to stay at a place with a few extra thread count.

One area where you cannot afford to be cheap is with your actual Nomad Capitalist strategy. Sure, you can Google 'cheap offshore company' and get several decent articles on the topic (heck, you will probably find one of mine telling you that they are not a good idea), but you will also find a lot of inaccurate and uneducated information. In the offshore world, you get what you pay for. The 'lawyer' in the Seychelles hawking offshore setups for under $1,000 is likely not too familiar with his own country's laws – few as they may be – let alone your country's laws (which are the ones that matter even more). Those types will tell you that your offshore company is tax-free, which is true in their country, but may not be in yours.

Worse yet, low prices are the hallmark of most offshore scams. Note the lack of deductive reasoning there; not all low-priced offers are scams, but most scams use price as a lure. In one case, a couple of guys tried to use an 'inside connection' to offer passports in an Eastern European country until their rogue hook-up flew the coop on them. Panicked, they had to find another country where they could move their clients' business and ended up having a local agent dummy up papers to get clients passports under the table.

We are trained to look for a bargain. That is especially true considering the likelihood that these clients' motivation was citizenship as an insurance policy. Who wants to pay for insurance? However, some of these clients eventually landed in hot water – or at least got quite a scare – when they realized what had happened behind the scenes and saw just what a 'cheap' second passport looked like. If it is worth your effort to get a second passport or save on taxes, it is worth doing right. That means paying for quality.

I get it: you are a smart person. You would not be reading this book if you were not smart. When it comes to going where you're treated best, most of the bad information, gringo pricing, and outright dishonesty can be avoided by paying for a little help. One of my favorite tactics comes from the motivational speaker Joel Weldon who suggests that you shout out "I won't pay it!" when a service provider gives you a price. Bewildered, the provider might offer to take 10% off the price, but Joel will suggest going the other direction. His philosophy is to never negotiate on price and, instead, even offer to pay more to make sure that your case is treated with the best care possible. In the offshore world, this is great advice.

3. Be Decisive

Derek Sivers, who sold his business CD Baby to a charitable trust for some $17 million, lives by a simple principle: "Don't say 'yes'… either 'hell yeah!' or 'no'." The idea is that we are all busy and need to be decisive to avoid overload. An excellent motivational technique involves swapping the words 'I might' or 'I'm thinking about' with 'I will' or 'I won't;' similarly, replace 'but' with 'and.' There are so many options and possibilities in this world, but focusing on the ones you really need is critical to getting what is important done.

I have often theorized that most people are not really busy, but still claim to be so to avoid commitment while allocating plenty of time for television viewing and what they actually want to do. When you go where you're treated best, however, you will be faced with more options for what you could do than ever before. The question then becomes, what will you actually do?

That means that decision making is more important than ever. When I need to make a decision, my goal is to decide on the same day that the opportunity is presented to me. For example, if I am visiting a country to scope out a new second residency opportunity with me as the 'guinea pig,' I will do my research on the opportunity as best I can and then make an appointment with a top attorney there. During my meeting, I will listen to the opportunity, ask questions based on my research and past experience, and then try to come to a decision right then and there, before I leave the office. When it comes to real estate or other investments, I will often ask for 'until sundown' or '24 hours,' and promise to do any further calculations and advise them of my decision in that time.

This means that I have real engagement in the process before even setting foot in the real estate agent or lawyer's office. The opportunity has to be a potential 'hell yes' before I even take any action. I resist doing pointless research when deep down I know it will not be worth my time. There is great power in not making excuses and telling people 'Yes' or 'No' promptly. So much so that it has helped me get the greatest results when I put myself on a clock.

This offshore stuff is sexy. Beach bungalows and James Bond-like second passports are just the tip of the iceberg when it comes to all the cool things you can do as a Nomad Capitalist. That said, I do not recommend dedicating your valuable time into researching them unless you are fully committed to executing on them. Having an offshore company is exciting. Researching them and knowing a lot about them is not.

That is why I suggest that potential Nomad Capitalists should sit and plan what they are willing to commit to, then jump in. Once you are out of the research and due diligence phase, commit to being in the decision phase. If you think you want a second passport, ask yourself why you want one. If you cannot think of a good reason (even if that good reason is "I'm rich and it will be fun!"), that might mean you should not do it. If you can think of a good reason, go forward and find the best way to get it done.

Getting it done means just that. If you are committed, do not make excuses. I have learned firsthand that wishy washy delay eliminates the ability to get the results you want. There are lawyers who I told I would "get back to soon" six years ago, before I devised my system of action.

And even taking action is not enough. You have to take the right action. Living the Nomad Capitalist lifestyle will present you with more opportunities than ever before and you will need to get good at screening out the ones that do not serve your specific end goals.

Because few people ever venture out of their home city, most people deal with very few choices. When it comes to real estate investment opportunities, most folks are taught to go to university, get a good job, and settle down in a house financed by a thirty-year mortgage that will keep them in debt and tether them to one place for the best years of their life. This tethering is convenient for government, too, as it means thirty years of living in one city and paying whatever taxes are decreed by the politicians.

Adopting the Nomad Capitalist mindset means that not only can you invest all over your home country, but you can also choose to invest outside of the country to get a better return. When you go from one city in one country to thousands of potential cities all over the world, you have to be clear about your goals and in your ability to say 'No.' That is why the key to being decisive is all about knowing exactly what you need.

4. Avoid Complaining

As we discussed in the last chapter, "Don't be dogmatic," was some of the best advice I ever received about living and doing business internationally. The logic was simple: the rest of the world operates in a different way than you are used to and if you want to survive, thrive, and be happy, you need to be able to adapt.

Some aspects of internationalizing will be difficult, and it is possible to become confused or even irritated. If you are used to setting up a limited liability company in the United States, you might be surprised to discover that an offshore company requires a few more procedures than just filling out a one-page form and paying $50. Those procedures can often be handled by a professional in a day or two, but the work is still there.

If you gripe about every minor hassle, your Nomad Capitalist lifestyle will not be nearly as enjoyable as it will be if you go with the flow. Put your trust in professionals and use the expertise that they have spent a lifetime acquiring. Whenever you feel the urge to complain about your circumstances, realize that by living the Nomad Capitalist lifestyle you are among the freest people in the history of the world. You are leaving behind the things that do not serve you, and that is something to be happy about.

5. Do Not Follow the Herd

Going where you're treated best is all about living on your own terms. You do what you want without reservation or judgment. You accept that others may not agree with you, but you do it anyway. The last thing you want to do is copy what everyone else is doing as you build the life that you want.

At times, it seems that some of the digital nomad flock stick together as if they have replaced the cubicle at an insurance company with a cheap apartment and a motorbike in Thailand. There is nothing wrong with living life on the cheap in Southeast Asia if that is what you want, but avoid being sucked into the latest trends of the work-and-travel crowd. Make your own trends. If you want to live in a $200-a-month apartment and eat street food, do it. If you want to live in a $5,000-a-month penthouse and dine at fancy restaurants, do it. Socializing with other people on the same journey is important, but I have found that too much of it can result in groupthink – the very groupthink that you avoided to go where you're treated best.

Being a Nomad Capitalist is all about choosing your culture, not being a product of it. This way of living and doing business is growing, but it still has a lot of growth left in it. When I started visiting China for business in 2009, I remember learning that cell phone numbers started with a different area code than landline numbers. Any home-based freelancer or consultant was effectively 'outed' as not having a 'real office.' Fast forward just a few years and nobody in the western world really cares that your office is mobile; other parts of the world are not quite there yet. We can expect many more changes like this in the years to come as the number of people like us increases.

The best part about living as a Nomad Capitalist is the lack of cultural norms to follow. My life as a perpetual tourist in Malaysia has meant that I have never been tied deep enough into local Malaysian culture to be mocked for not owning a car. No matter how many locals have insisted that a car is necessary for getting around (which is not true if you live in the city center), they have never slighted me for hailing Ubers. After all, I am just a guy visiting. Not having to conform is liberating.

Compare that to the social pressure on high earners in big cities in the West. A Danish friend of mine once told me about all the law and accounting firm partners he knows who earn $300,000 a year yet are totally broke because their entire salary goes toward keeping up with the Joneses; a nice house on the right street, a highly tariffed Range Rover in the driveway, and perfectly groomed Danish kids sent to the right schools. Just hearing him tell me about it was exhausting as we kicked back €3 glasses of wine on the cobblestone streets of Croatia, far from the showmanship we both escaped.

Being a Nomad Capitalist means choosing what you want, whether that is a $15,000 month-long stay at the George V hotel in Paris or a cheap co-living space in Bucharest. No longer do you have to rent 'the right apartment' in midtown to impress your boss and colleagues, but feel free to rent that apartment if that is what you want.

6. Have Thick Skin

In 2011, the television show 60 Minutes ran a long form hit piece on companies moving their operations to Switzerland. Calling the moderate-tax country 'the new tax haven,' the show used extreme examples and sensational language to gin up anger against companies that were not paying their 'fair share' of taxes in the United States.

Let's face it: most people do not like the sound of the words 'tax haven.' That is why politicians and the media use them. They are playing to their base. Watch any television show that involves offshore banking in the plotline and you will no doubt hear terms like 'money hole,' 'tax cheat,' or 'money laundering' used. Even though numbered bank accounts have long gone the way of the dodo bird, the news and entertainment media speak of them like every crook and his dog still have one.

The bottom line is that you cannot trust the mainstream media to accurately report on the realities of doing business overseas. And, since the average Joe thinks banking in Singapore must make you a crook, you will have to develop thick skin when dealing with people not in the know. Sadly, humans are hardwired to try to diminish anyone climbing farther up the ladder, out of spite. When a few of us decide to put aside cultural norms and do what is right for us and our families, those who have not yet discovered how to do so will complain.

Rather than lower taxes for everyone, politicians blame those that exploit the loopholes they themselves created through their backroom dealings and attempt to make them pay more to make things 'fair.' Somehow, a whole host of countries make do with personal income tax rates of 10-15% — or even 0% — but high-tax western governments will not rest until the guy paying 20% pays 30% because some other poor sap already does. Rather than let everyone keep more of their own money, they argue that those not paying enough should pay more.

The scary part is that people on the street eat this stuff up. They pay no mind to the idea that their tax rate could be lower, except for general talking points like 'more childcare deductions.' For the most part, citizens of high tax countries have been so indoctrinated that when I joked with a conductor in Sweden that a train delay should be impossible for all the taxes they pay there, he responded that things were running poorly since taxes had been cut to 55%.

Do not waste your time trying to convince the indoctrinated that there is a different way to do things. You are not going to change the world. You have a big enough job to change yourself. The Nomad Capitalist lifestyle is emerging, but as it does, so are calls from tax-hungry politicians to demonize it. Some might call you a 'traitor' or a 'tax evader,' but these statements are not legally true because doing business offshore is legal if done properly. Many people do not let the facts get in the way of their opinion. You will have to learn to deal with it, or better yet, keep your affairs to yourself. Ultimately, the most important thing is that you know that you have made the right choice for you.

7. Be Trusting

When I was merely running from one threat or annoyance after another, the magic never seemed to happen in as big a way as I would have liked. Now, I run toward my desired results and everything works much better. I have found it to be much easier and better when I place my confidence in the right people and trust that it will work out.

If you are going to go offshore, you will be in situations where you are not sure who you can trust. The first time you do anything, it is hard to know who to trust, or whether to trust the process itself. In Georgia, many properties are purchased for cash. When I say 'cash,' I do not mean just purchasing without a mortgage, but by slinging a stack of Benjamins across the table like a spy making an offer that you cannot refuse.

My first property in Tbilisi was a bit more expensive, but I bought it through a developer who allowed me to pay in installments and via wire transfer. The next property I bought was a retail store for the grand total of $22,000 and, being that it was in an emerging part of the city, the seller was old school and wanted US dollars. All two hundred and twenty banknotes worth.

I remember going to the bank with my lawyer and withdrawing $22,000. Before doing so, I thought about what could happen to the money, like if I were attacked by a Georgian ninja on the way to the closing, or I stuck the money in one of my needlessly shallow pockets and it fell out without my knowledge. And so, I withdrew the money, jammed it into an envelope, and put the envelope in my jacket's breast pocket as I began a five-minute walk with what I imagined looked like an elephant on my chest. But no one noticed and I made it to the closing table where the seller was also surprisingly ninja-free.

To this day, I take extra precautions to make sure things are setup properly. Each time I purchase property in a new country, I ask my local representative to make sure that there is no funny business. To date, there has been all of none. However, that first time I bought property in cold, hard cash reminds me that the fear we have is mostly of our own making.

One other principle that has served me well in trusting is having an abundant lifestyle. For most traditional digital nomads, the key identifying point of their lifestyle choice can be summed up in one word: 'cheap.' An entire cottage industry has been built up around people who prefer living on $1,000 a month in Chiang Mai to working in the City of London for $100,000 a year. There is nothing wrong with that lifestyle, but it does condition you to think, "How can I get this done for cheap?"

If you search on digital nomad forums or social media groups, you will quickly find people asking total strangers the most sensitive and complicated of questions, including many in the field of tax, all in the interest of avoiding a $500 phone call to an accountant. This can be a false economy; as I say, sometimes the cheap offshore company you set up on your own can end up costing you a lot more down the line when you realize it was set up incorrectly.

Living the Nomad Capitalist lifestyle is not 'cheap.' Nickeling and diming will not lead you to have more money to splurge at five-star resorts or take care of those you love. This will only come from investing in yourself in a big way. Remember that you are choosing this life so that you can enjoy yourself and live in abundance. Distrust is not part of the formula for an abundant life. It keeps you from getting things done and it keeps you in old patterns that are better left in the past. Abandon the distrust. Trust the people you are paying. And enjoy the life that you want.

8. Feel the Pain

Being in pain is a powerful transformational tool. You are reading this book because, somewhere, you have a pain that you would like to solve. Something is not working quite the way you feel it should. But few of us crave a 'second passport' the same way we crave Oreos.

I remember talking to an American guy who came to me seeking help shortly after I started working with people to create their own Nomad Strategy. After he told me of his frustrations with the US government, the high taxes there, and everything else, I asked him, "So are you ready to feel more pain to make the pain go away?"

"Absolutely not," he said. "Why would I want more pain?" For him, the idea of digging in and doing the hard work was too painful. And when I looked back at his initial 'pain,' it was not really pain at all. It was the anger and frustration that, for so many people, is the emotional high sought out to feel cathartic.

Getting a second passport takes some work. If you choose to do it yourself, you are going to have to figure out what to do, who to get to help you, and then fill out a bunch of forms and make all the payments. The same goes for getting your company set up overseas, or for buying property. There is a period of pain that is required before getting to the pleasure.

As a guy who works at my laptop a lot, I frequently find myself with sore shoulders from hunching over the keyboard. Of course, because I go where I am treated best, I am often in places where a good Thai massage costs a mere $10 or $20. During the hour I receive the massage, the active pain of a fist digging into my shoulder is often far worse than the passive pain of simply having a knot in that shoulder. A massage is not necessarily meant to feel good during the experience but to make you feel good afterwards.

Humans are so focused on instant gratification that we push the pain away as soon as we encounter it. That is a mistake. The dull shoulder pain that makes it uncomfortable to lay down is the same as the ongoing pain of paying taxes. At a certain point, it does not seem right, but you have become used to it. The idea of encountering more pain to make the pain you already have feel better seems silly. But that is what is required if you want to fix the problem.

Just like the guy who yelled at me for wanting him to feel more pain before things got better, I frequently encourage people to sit in the pain. Merely dulling the pain may feel good, but it is not a recipe for success. Instead, use that pain to transform your life and get more of what you want and less of what you do not. Acknowledge and use the pain you are experiencing to transform and create a long-term positive change.

This approach is common in business, but not one we take in our personal lives. Whenever I hire a new team member, that person needs to be trained. Investing my time to train them, and in many cases my money to have someone else train them, may seem like money better spent elsewhere. If you have ever had to fire someone, you may have thought – as I have at times – that it would be easier and less expensive to keep the underperforming employee rather than fire them, find someone better, and train them.

But the underperforming employee is likely costing you more than you realize. For example, I once hired an expat girl who was working for me for $1,500 a month. (The benefits of globalization). After about two months, I found myself repeating things too much for my liking but figured that the girl was fundamentally a good person and smart, and that she would learn. It was not until I asked my team leader to investigate her emails that we realized the big pain: $60,000 in lost business due to the underperforming employee not following the original training.

Boom! I went from passive pain to active pain and frustration. And now I had to take action. Taking over some of the work myself while my team leader and I trained an existing employee to handle the most important tasks was not an option, but a necessity. Before the discovery, rather than having the pain of the employee who just blew $60,000, I had the pain of the guy with a sinking suspicion something was wrong, but no great urge to investigate.

We tend to look at taxes the same way. The tax lawyer I screamed at for wanting to charge me $15,000 to help me slash my tax bill by moving overseas was on the wrong end of a guy who found the idea of paying $15,000 more painful than continuing to do what I had already done. Not long after that, I paid three months of taxes that surpassed what I could have paid the lawyer to help me solve my problem long-term.

If you feel more comfortable sending a large check to your government than stepping out into a brave new world that can legally eliminate that tax bill, you never will. That is why I ask people who want to save on taxes what they would do with the money they save. If their answer is too vague, I can safely assume that the person is unlikely to do anything to effectively lower their taxes. When you realize the $100,000 you paid last year could have been re-invested in Facebook ads and generated $300,000 in additional sales, you start to realize what is at stake, just as I did when I discovered my employee had chased $60,000 in business out the door.

Studies show that the feeling of experiencing pain is a powerful motivator to change, and even Proverbs warns that "pride cometh before the fall" for those who do not acknowledge their pain. Saying you would like to pay less in taxes 'just because' is a much less powerful motivator than connecting with the reasons behind that desire, whether they are slumming it in four-star hotels rather than the Four Seasons, or not being able to reinvest in new products to grow your revenue. Find the pain and lean into it; that is where the solution lies. Be the person who fights the pain in the face of a challenge.

— — — — —

The strategies I have listed above form the kind of mindset that is important when going offshore. I have learned (often the hard way) that how you think is more important than what you do when deciding to implement the Nomad Capitalist lifestyle.

For some reason, we are often hardwired to believe that we cannot go where we are treated best. This leads us to find excuses and put roadblocks up to stop us from achieving what we want. Considering how many people have told me that they want to live this lifestyle, versus how many take the necessary steps to do it, mindset and the willingness to take action is far more critical than knowing the specific steps to take. If you are motivated enough, you will do what it takes to find out.

Your How-To Action Plan

Immediate Action Steps: You do not need to travel to start working on your mindset. Wherever you are, you can begin working on the principles we have discussed in this chapter.

Travel Action Steps: Travel! Go! Just get started. There is great power in action. If you are struggling to get started, it is likely that you are struggling with one of the Nomad Mindsets that we have discussed here. Pinpoint what that is and work through it until you are ready to act.

Holistic Planning: One of the reasons I addressed the Nomad Mindset in this book is because it is the one thing that I see my clients struggle with more than anything else. It is easy to tell someone where to incorporate their company to save on taxes. It is much harder to change the way they think. If you want a holistic offshore plan to work for you, start with your mindset.

Chapter Sixteen: How to Get Started

A Summary

Dateline: Prcanj, Montenegro

It was a gloomy autumn day along Montenegro's coast. The hordes of Russian tourists in too-tiny bikinis had long vacated town and had since been replaced by a constant drizzle of cold precipitation. Anka, the general contractor I had hired to handle the renovation of my new summer beach home in Kotor Bay, piloted a muddy wagon along the waterfront as we departed the worksite to search for the best sofa and furnishings to complete my new home.

As she skillfully batted away a barrage of incoming calls like some kind of real estate ninja, Anka and I discussed the plans for the apartment furnishings as we debated whether I should rent it out while not there.

"Since we are going with a Santorini theme for the décor, what do you think of white furniture?" I asked.

Anka raised a skeptical eyebrow, "I would not allow children stay there with white furniture."

"Horny couples might pose an even greater risk," I chuckled.

Anka smiled and reached into the center console to offer me a mint. "Mentos?" she asked, her voice a unique cross between a sultry cocktail waitress and a steely Russian spy.

Here I was with a woman I had just hired on the advice of a woman I barely knew, going furniture shopping and being offered a mint. Perhaps, I thought, Anka was making a move. As it turns out, Anka was merely competent at her job. Extremely competent. As we got to know each other on the drive, I asked her if she would prepare the documents proving my ownership of the flat so that I could apply for residency.

In Montenegro, owning a property automatically qualifies you for residency, even though obtaining citizenship is not possible without greater effort. The trouble is that my Montenegrin lawyer, Vesna, had not only proved to possess poor communication skills but was also unable to tell me what was required so that we could complete the process. Anka told me that she could retrieve the documents and handle the residency process for me herself, and likely with far more competence than the lawyer who made a living shuffling paperwork.

While attorneys are often a great source of contacts (and I have made a lot of money from connections acquired through good ones), I have also often found myself helping my non-western-world attorneys organize their business processes to complete my case. One of the biggest services I offer the people I help is making it easy for them to complete simple processes that local lawyers (and governments) make complicated for no good reason. Over the years, I have developed great relationships with attorneys that started with me organizing their workflow to streamline the process for my clients and me.

Part of what I do traveling around the world is to test new opportunities and also new people. Sometimes, I go to a new country with high hopes, only to realize that the place is unworkable. Likewise, I also make a point of going to a new place to test out different service providers and find out who can really help me. This can involve a lot of trial and error.

Many people think that hiring a lawyer in a shiny office tower is the best move. In some cases, they are right. However, it is often better to work with someone who has done the work on the ground if you want real results. Lawyers are great for connections, but they often do not understand why you are doing what you are doing. Vesna certainly did not understand or care why I wanted Montenegrin residency. She definitely did not know enough to point out what I already knew: if my 'why' was Montenegrin citizenship, residency through property ownership was not the way to do it.

Like many lawyers, Vesna dealt in the art of robotic paper pushing. As an entrepreneurially minded person, you may well have no patience for robotic people. I would much rather deal with someone who understands my needs than just have my papers put through and be forced to figure out the actual strategy on my own. After all, the best way to do something is to do it.

The reason I pay experts thousands of dollars to do research for me in everything from Thai real estate to remote African residency programs is partially so that I can sit at home and eat Bon-Bons while their experience does the heavy lifting. Even if you could create an entire offshore strategy all by yourself that is 100% legal and perfectly crafted to address every single aspect of your life and business, you will need the help of professionals to turn that plan into a living, working reality.

Paying someone is a commitment. You have to determine what it is that motivates you to make that commitment and put it in place so that you can get started and not end up like one of those folks who is always promising that action is just... around... the corner. Every day that you do nothing, there is a cost. It is up to you to determine what that cost is. And do not tell yourself that 'doing nothing is not an option.' Doing nothing is always an option, and it is the option that most people choose.

Most people claim that they are taking action and that they want help and want to do something, but then they continue the cycle of information consumption that they have grown accustomed to (reading articles, calling random lawyers, scouring the internet, etc.) and they rarely make the progress that they deserve.

Often times, the people who come to me for help tell me that they are different – they are an action-taker – but then they proceed to waste more time, make more excuses, and ask more of the wrong questions. I should know, I used to be one of them. But after several years of trying to master the offshore world on my own, I realized that I could accomplish my goals with greater speed if I learned to trust the experts.

Since then, I have capitalized on the strengths of the professionals I seek out in each field and each country wherever I go. Because of this, I have achieved incredible results. I have become the expert, a general contractor of sorts able to master the entire construction process of an international life for myself and other people.

You can do the same, but you must do it, not just talk about and research an endless array of topics about going offshore. You need to be decisive and act – you will figure the rest out as you go along.

I have people come to me for help who ask me questions like, "Andrew, can we buy a van in Tbilisi if we move there?" I am sure that you can, but that is the wrong question to be asking. If you focus on what you need to do to get there, the van will figure itself out. So many people hold themselves back with little excuses when they just need to make a decision and go for it.

So, it is decision-making time. If you have been completing the How-To Action Plans found at the end of every chapter, pull out the list that you started in Chapter One and add a list for first steps. I am going to walk you through every part of the EKG formula that we have discussed throughout this book, and you are going to walk away with a plan to start your Nomad Capitalist life. It may not be the full plan. It is highly likely that you will need the help of professionals to create and execute a completed holistic offshore plan. But if you will put in the work right now, you will finish this book headed in the right direction.

E - Enhance Your Personal Freedom

We began this book with a discussion of my five magic words: go where you're treated best. This principle can be applied to every part of the EKG formula, but when it comes to enhancing your personal freedom, these five magic words are best applied to how and where you choose to live. That involves everything from the way you travel to the kind of passports and residencies you acquire to the relationships you develop and how you take care of yourself.

The first step is to decide what enhancing your personal freedom looks like for you. How are you going to approach life overseas? Are you going to dip your toe in with a few trips here and there while remaining in your home country? Are you going to plan a six-month piecemeal strategy to test out different locations? Do you already have a location in mind where you want to set up a base or create a permanent home? Do not keep reading until you have decided what you will do. Making a decision means you are done asking questions and you are ready to act. So, what is it going to be? How are you going to adopt the principles of the location independent lifestyle?

Decision made? Good. Now, what immigration procedures do you need to complete to make that happen? Do you need a residence permit? Can you get citizenship by investing in one of your desired locations? What other benefits do you want from getting a second residence or passport? What countries will give you those benefits? What programs do you need to pursue? What methods for obtaining citizenship will you use?

If you are considering renunciation, determine how quickly you will need a second passport to enable this step. If you only want a second passport as a Plan B to give yourself the option of renouncing if things ever get bad enough at home, maybe you can afford to take a slower route toward your second citizenship. If time is of the essence, decide now what citizenship by investment program you want to pursue. Then, do not delay getting that process started.

If you have a significant other, remember to communicate, compromise, cultivate and choose to work together to make these decisions, in addition to the choices concerning where to give birth and how to educate your children as you travel (if a family is a part of your plan). If you have not found 'the one' quite yet, decide if a serious relationship is something that you want to pursue right now and how that will affect where you go and what you do. Enhancing your life includes making your most important relationships (and relationship goals) a priority.

Finally, consider your personal health and wellness objectives. For some, just knowing that you can get world-class healthcare outside of your home country is all you need to know to have the confidence to get out the door and start exploring the world. Global citizenship seems a little less daunting when you realize that you will not have to compromise your health for all the other benefits that come from offshore living. For others, Nomad healthcare could be the main motivation to travel. If it is, plan that trip to Prince Court Medical Center and go. That is an easy way to begin enhancing your life overseas.

K - Keep More of Your Money

Going where you're treated best applies to your money just as much as it applies to you personally. And taking your money where it is treated best is often much easier to do than the process of moving yourself offshore. That is one reason why I recommend that everyone start their Nomad journey by opening an offshore bank account. While opening your first offshore account is a bit more difficult now than it used to be, it is still relatively easy to do, especially if you are willing to get on a plane.

Once you do move your money offshore, your confidence in the strategies we have discussed will grow and you will begin to feel more connected to the places where you have planted new flags. You do not have to make elaborate plans about lifestyle design and passport portfolios to simply get on a plane, open a foreign bank account, deposit some money, and fly home. That is why it is the perfect first step. You could start with somewhere as close to home as TD Bank in Canada or go for more exotic destinations with easy banking solutions like Ecuador or Georgia. Or if you have the money, just go straight to Singapore.

With at least one offshore bank account under your belt, you will be ready for more complex offshore planning – namely, the tax-friendly quadrant. If you did the work above and started making decisions about how to enhance your personal freedom, you should have already tackled Quadrants One and Three – where you are personally leaving and arriving. But before you move on to the other quadrants, be sure to look at these personal quadrants from a tax perspective. How are you going to exit the tax system in your home country? Do you need to establish a new tax residence? How will your lifestyle design impact your taxes?

Once you have addressed the personal quadrants, you can then answer the questions about where your company is leaving and where it is arriving. Figuring out the details of how to move your company offshore could be simple or complex depending on the inner workings of your business. This is one area where I would not skip on professional advice. Work with someone who knows offshore and what is required to move your company out of its current jurisdiction.

With a plan in place to address Quadrant Two, you can then focus on Quadrant Four to choose your corporate tax rate. Review the four corporate tax systems in the world and determine which one is the best fit for your business. Which jurisdictions offer the best balance between low or zero taxes, favorable legislation, and functional business operations? Will offshore banks want to work with a company incorporated in your jurisdiction of choice?

Finally, keeping more of your money is about smart diversification. You can easily diversify out of the banking system by not only investing in assets like gold but choosing to store them in safe offshore vaults located in places like Singapore and Austria. Like offshore banking, it is easy to get started with an agnostic strategy like offshore gold storage. You could literally jump online right now and order gold that will be stored in a high-security vault in Singapore.

G - Grow Your Money

Getting started with the last part of the EKG formula may require more planning and hands-on work than you can do while sitting, reading a book. After all, the best foreign investments are found on the ground. The greatest opportunities for frontier market entrepreneurship can only be discovered in the final frontier. And you may never be forced to conquer dogma if you do not adventure out into a world that challenges everything you think, feel, and do.

One easy way to diversify is to invest in cryptocurrency. From an offshore perspective cryptocurrency does not live in any particular jurisdiction and is therefore easier to plan for. If crypto is part of your plans this may make for an easier offshore planning experience, and if you decided not to invest in a cryptocurrency then simply cross this off your list.

Once you have done that, book your ticket to the investment market of your choice. If you really want to get started growing your money offshore, go offshore. Explore the opportunities that are out there. All the other questions you have buzzing around in your head will change once you go beyond the imaginary lines of your home country and step out into the world. Instead of asking yourself if you can buy a van in your new home or whether or not you will be able to get kale at the local market, you will begin asking these questions instead:

How much will I pay in taxes tomorrow, this month, and this year if I decide to stay in my home country?

What opportunities and lifestyle choices will I miss out on if I do not make a change?

How will my retirement plans be affected by continuing to do what I am doing now?

What will happen in five years if I keep only one passport? Or what might happen that I am not willing to risk?

There will always be a level of uncertainty when it comes to living an international life. The only thing that you can really be certain of is that you are going to pay 46% tax next year on your entire income. That is for certain if you keep doing what you are doing. The uncertainty comes when you make a change for the better.

As one of my coaches likes to say, "Uncertainty is where the magic happens." If everything were certain in life, you would never progress. Most things are uncertain, so just allow them to be so and throw yourself into taking bold and decisive action. That is where beautiful things happen. If you are like many of the people that I help who are paying $100, $500, $1,000 a day or even more in taxes, feel insecure about being tied to one country, and want to make more money to retire early and enjoy life, then you need an action plan.

The principles in this book and the first steps we have discussed in this chapter should give you somewhere to start. Where you go from there depends on your goals. I have always viewed your personal Nomad Strategy like a puzzle; each piece on its own is useless, but when fitted together, the completed puzzle works beautifully. Which pieces you need are up to you and what you want to achieve. Determine which strategies will help you reach your goals, and then hold yourself accountable to achieving those results.

The world is an incredible place full of so many opportunities. Not everyone has the eyes to see it for what it is. They are too trapped behind imaginary lines to realize that there is greater freedom and prosperity beyond those borders – more freedom and prosperity than has ever been available in the history of the world. All you have to do to begin your life as a Nomad Capitalist is to get out there and see it for yourself.

I hope this book has given you a vision of what is possible. I hope you have been empowered to take the kind of action that accomplishes your desired results. And most of all, I hope that you, too, can follow my five magic words and go where you're treated best.

Yours,

Andrew Henderson

The Nomad Capitalist